ON WAR AND MORALITY

STUDIES IN MORAL, POLITICAL,
AND LEGAL PHILOSOPHY

General Editor: Marshall Cohen

ON WAR AND MORALITY

Robert L. Holmes

PRINCETON UNIVERSITY PRESS
PRINCETON, NEW JERSEY

Library of Congress Cataloging-in-Publication Data
Holmes, Robert L.
On war and morality / Robert L. Holmes.
p. cm.—(Studies in moral, political, and legal philosophy)
Bibliography: p.
Includes index.
ISBN 0-691-07794-0 ISBN 0-691-2300-X (pbk.)
1. War—Moral and ethical aspects. I. Title. II. Series.
U22.H65 1989   88-19479
172'.42—dc 19   CIP

For
Becky and Tim

. . . all I ask is that, in the midst of a murderous world, we agree to reflect on murder and to make a choice.
—Albert Camus

CONTENTS

PREFACE

The conviction underlying this work is that no consideration of the problem of war, whether by just war theorists applying traditional standards to war's assessment, or by strategists examining how best to incorporate power most effectively into policy, or by government leaders responsible for the actual making and implementation of war policy can hope to speak to the issues of central concern to humankind if it does not face squarely the question of whether war in the modern world can be morally justified. I answer that question by arguing that it cannot. This is the principal aim of what follows.

A secondary aim is to present enough of the moral and intellectual thinking about war over the years to provide a perspective on this issue that will help enable people to make their own assessment or at least encourage them to think further about the issue. Had my concern been merely to present an argument, the book would be somewhat shorter; had it been to do a thorough review of historical and contemporary literature, it would have been considerably longer. As it is, I have sought to strike a balance between the demands of a sustained line of reasoning, on the one hand, and those of a presentation of what I consider some of the most important thinking on war and morality, on the other (hence the attention to the views of St. Augustine, Reinhold Niebuhr and Herman Kahn, for example, central figures respectively in the just war theory, political realism, and the theory of nuclear deterrence).

I have not written primarily for academics and have accordingly tried to keep to a minimum the specialized vocabulary and methods of argumentation characteristic of such approaches, particularly among philosophers. Not that such approaches do not have their place; they are as legitimate as any other, and for certain purposes better than most. It is just that there is no particular virtue to them, either, if with greater effort they could be made accessible to a wider audience of nonacademics. In particular, I believe that much, if not most, of philosophy could be done in such a way (whether or not I have succeeded in doing so here) as to be profitably shared with nonphilosophers as well.

There is an American perspective to at least some of what follows partly because certain of the views under examination, as in the case of twentieth-century political realism, have their principal expositors among American writers, and partly because some of what I say is directed specifically to Americans, who as citizens of one of the superpowers in the nuclear age share greater responsibility than most for many of the greatest risks facing humankind today. Nothing in this orientation is meant to imply any superiority of American culture or values over those of any other country or that the issues, sufficiently abstracted, could not be detached from the author's sociocultural background (though I consider some views in the final chapter that would deny this) and dealt with purely theoretically. Nor, I should add, is the fact that I have followed standard grammar in using so-called "masculine" pronouns for contexts that are unspecific with regard to gender meant to imply any favoritism toward one sex over the other.

During the writing of this volume, I profited from the comments, criticisms, or suggestions of many persons. I would particularly like to thank Richard Feldman, Gerald Gates, Ernest Keene, Douglas MacLean, Margery Bedford Naylor, Liane Norman, Christine Park, Andrew Rehfeld, Ferdinand Schoeman, and Veronica Slivinski, all of whom have either read portions of the work in progress (Douglas MacLean and Margery Bedford Naylor provided detailed and thoughtful comments on the entirety of an earlier draft) or made valuable suggestions in discussions pertaining to it. I also want to thank Richard Werner for many discussions over the years that have helped to clarify and shape my thinking on the problems of war, as well as Sanford G. Thatcher, Editor in Chief of Princeton University Press, for the efficiency and consideration he has shown from the outset in the process leading to the book's publication. While perhaps only a few of the preceding share my basic conclusions, and none, of course, is responsible for any of the shortcomings of the book, their contributions of time, effort, and in some cases primarily support, are warmly appreciated.

Some material from the first and last chapters has been published previously, although it appears here in significantly rewritten form. My thanks to the original publishers for use of material from "Violence and Nonviolence," in *Violence*, edited by Jerome Shaffer, © Longman Inc., 1971; "The Concept of Physical Violence in Moral and Political Affairs," © *Social Theory and Practice*, 1973; and the "The Sleep of Reason Brings Forth Monsters," © *Harvard Magazine*, 1983.

Finally, for invaluable assistance in preparing the manuscript I would like to thank Anna Harrison, Lynne McCoy, and Charlene Witkowicz.

ON WAR AND MORALITY

INTRODUCTION

The first thing to realize is that, if there are not to be nuclear wars, there must not be wars.   —Bertrand Russell

The paradox of contemporary civilization is that beyond a certain
point the individual's security begins to vary inversely with the
power embodied in the systems meant to ensure that security. Not
only can the increasingly powerful domestic security apparatus of
the state at any time be turned against him—a potentiality kept
from fruition chiefly by chance, circumstance, and, where they exist, by the fragile safeguards of democracy—but, even more importantly, the capacity for destruction which states have acquired
through their efforts to outdo one another in the pursuit of security through armaments effectively deprives all of the security they
seek. In consequence, as civilization moves farther from its primal
state, it becomes increasingly like that state in the insecurity it
holds for the individual person. Its claims to progress ring hollow
when its achievements contain the seeds of its own destruction.

War epitomizes the gravity of this paradox. For if war is no more
capable of undoing civilization than is, say, overpopulation or the
depletion of natural resources, it is nonetheless capable of doing
so with greater dispatch and by means that are all the more tragic
because they are designed and implemented for the express purpose of killing people. We have to deplete natural resources in order to live. But we do not have to kill other human beings. We
have to cope with conflict in order to live socially. But we do not
have to wage war. However much we wrap our rationalization in
the language of necessity, we *choose* to do these things. And as
with all our choices, these are subject to moral assessment.

This is the aspect of the problem that concerns me in the present
study. For I believe it is the most urgent of the problems we face
today. If we do not in the near future resolve the problem of the
proper relationship of the individual to the state, the world will
continue on, characterized, to be sure, by injustice and oppression
but at least with hope of eventual amelioration of the situation.
The same with poverty or overpopulation. But in the case of war

we face a threat to the very conditions under which progress toward the resolution of these and other problems can even be made. It is a threat to the very conditions under which human rationality and moral sensibility can continue to exist. As such it dwarfs in importance the controversies between Jews and Palestinians in the Middle East, Protestants and Catholics in Northern Ireland, or communists and capitalists in the ideological struggle of the cold war; not because the issue of war per se is necessarily more important that these others but because of the form the problem takes in the modern world. Alfred Nobel, founder of the peace prize, believed the key to peace lay with the development of war technology and that once the nations of the world acquired the capacity to annihilate one another—and he expressly included civilian populations here—war would disappear from the face of the earth. This was the technologist's dream. But we can no longer stake our future on such a dream. It is precisely the failure of technology and militarism to slow the acceleration of civilization toward castastrophe that must be confronted. And to do so requires trying to understand the problem of war in its moral dimension.

There has, it is true, been increased awareness of the problem, but it has taken the form of an almost exclusive concern with the threat of nuclear war. As commendable as this is, it has had one untoward consequence. The preoccupation with nuclear war has fostered the idea that the problem of war in general can wait; that as desirable as it would be to rid the world of war, to do so is a project for the future, after the nuclear threat has been defused and we can be confident there will be a future. Accordingly the growing opposition to nuclear war has been accompanied by a growing acceptance of conventional war. This is true even among many so-called "nuclear pacifists," who feel that national security demands that nuclear disarmament, or even a significant reduction in nuclear armaments, be accompanied by a buildup of conventional forces. Conventional war thus acquires a kind of respectability. It seems an acceptable compromise between the magnitude of the violence of nuclear war, on the one hand, and the abhorrent quality of the violence of terrorism, on the other.

This attitude is understandable, but I believe it is misconceived. What is wrong with war is as wrong with conventional as with nuclear war. In that sense there is no moral difference between the two. But more importantly, I believe there is no realistic hope of counteracting the nuclear threat without dealing with the general problem of war as well. The acceptance of conventional war, with all that implies in the way of attitudes towards killing and destruction and the institutionalization of violence in society, makes nuclear war virtually inevitable.

Let me make clearer why I think this is so. Assume for the moment the legitimacy of war. If a nation may justifiably go to war, what may it justifiably do in the course of waging it. Should it restrain itself, or is restraint in such an undertaking an absurdity?

The answer is yes or no, depending upon what we take the question to mean. As I shall argue in Chapter Three, moderation is not an absurdity if we suppose it to require only that we refrain from inflicting gratuitous death and destruction beyond what is necessary for the attainment of the ends of war. But the answer is arguably yes if one means that nations should exercise restraint in the sense of knowingly doing less than is minimally necessary to achieve their objectives. One resorts to such bloody and destructive measures as war because the objectives are thought to warrant them. If, then, once these measures are undertaken one deliberately does less than is necessary to achieve them, it would indeed seem absurd, a violation of the tenet of rationality, that to will an end is to will the indispensable means to its attainment. This tenet, as we shall see later, underlies the principle of military necessity. And it is probably accepted by every nation that goes to war.

This means, I suggest, that given the rationale behind resorting to war in the first place, in any circumstances in which attainment of the objectives of war requires the use of nuclear weapons, they are likely to be used; and when they are not possessed but the need for them is foreseen, they are likely to be acquired. The logic of war demands it. The fact that the weapons are nuclear *in and of itself* makes no difference. Moreover, in circumstances in which they are possessed and national survival is believed to be at stake, it is virtually certain they will be used. Few world leaders would preside over the destruction of their country if they thought that by using nuclear weapons they could prevent it.

The evidence for the truth of these two claims is substantial. The one wartime use of atomic weapons occurred when the United States thought it could further its objectives by dropping them on Japan. And those were not even basic objectives; the war was already won. They were the subsidiary goals of minimizing the loss of American and perhaps Japanese lives. As for acquisition, the superpowers today multiply the numbers of nuclear weapons they possess, and nonnuclear nations strive to acquire them.

But might not the resort to nuclear war risk crossing a threshold

5

beyond which one's objectives *cannot* be achieved, because it would threaten a level of destruction that would jeopardize the attainment of *any* objectives at all? And would not the logic of war, with or without a principle of military necessity, preclude such resort?

While nuclear war does indeed risk crossing such a threshold, it does not necessarily involve crossing it. The atomic bombings of Hiroshima and Nagasaki did not, and they *did* serve American ends. And many scenarios for nuclear war do not involve crossing the threshold. In fact, many projected limited nuclear wars involve fewer casualties than the major conventional wars of the twentieth century: the more than 50 million dead left by World War II would equal those of a fairly large nuclear war. Resort to war of any sort risks an outcome in which one's objectives become unattainable, if only because going to war risks losing; and inasmuch as no war has more than one winner, and some have none, history is replete with examples of conventional war taking one or the other or both sides over that threshold.

Still, it is true that conventional war rarely takes a nation over the threshold beyond which no objectives can be attained *ever again* in the way in which all-out nuclear war would. But it has happened. The Romans annihilated the Carthaginians in the third Punic War as effectively as if they had dropped a nuclear bomb on them. And it could happen today. A third world war fought without nuclear weapons, but with large-scale use of chemical and biological weapons, could rival a nuclear war in its effects. And if not the third, then the fourth or the fifth or the nth world war could do so. The sophistication, accuracy, and destructive power of conventional weapons is rapidly closing the gap between conventional and nuclear war. Nuclear weapons will always have greater *destructive* potential. And they are quicker. But once war of either sort can destroy civilization, those differences become relatively unimportant so far as the threshold in question is concerned.

Even if this were not so, the preceding consideration argues only against *crossing that threshold*, not against using nuclear weapons. True, using nuclear weapons at all increases the probability of crossing the threshold; and it is doubtful that nations could be expected to exercise sufficient restraint to avoid that outcome. But if it is unrealistic to expect nations to deploy nuclear weapons and yet to restrain themselves from using them in time of conflict, it is equally unrealistic to expect them to make full use of conventional weapons and yet to restrain themselves from *producing* nuclear weapons if they are able. Why suppose that the restraint necessary to refrain from using nuclear weapons in an otherwise conventional war, or to limit their use if they are resorted to, is greater than that necessary to refrain from producing them if rising tensions or the exigencies of a long war argue for it? And is that not what is supposed when it is proposed to ban nuclear weapons but to allow conventional armaments; or to allow nuclear weapons but to limit their numbers and kinds? Except for the fact that they can more *readily* be used if possessed than produced and used if not possessed, it is hard to see a difference here. If people want to minimize the prospects of annihilation, they will not go to war at all, conventional or nuclear.

Thus, while we can assuredly discern a moral difference between *all-out* nuclear war and most conventional wars, we can also see a moral difference between all-out conventional war and most nuclear wars. My point is that nuclear war is not *in itself* any worse morally than conventional war, even if (which may not even be the case) the worst possible nuclear war might be worse that the worst possible conventional war. Death and destruction are central to both. So is the inevitability of killing innocent persons. And the magnitudes of death and destruction can vary on either side.

I

What I have said thus far, of course, is more or less theoretical, in the sense that the situation we actually confront in the world today is one in which both superpowers are heavily armed with nuclear weapons and prepared to use them if necessary. And there is little likelihood of that changing in the near future.

This situation underscores the difficulty, perhaps the near-impossibility, of both preserving conventional war and eliminating nuclear weapons, even if it should be conceded there is a significant moral difference between the two. On the one hand, as I have said, the increasing destructiveness of conventional weapons and the refinement and sophistication of both conventional and nuclear weapons is blurring the distinction between the two. When B-52 bombers can in a matter of minutes drop explosives equivalent in power to the atomic bomb that leveled Hiroshima, and when nuclear weapons can be made so small as to be fired on the battlefield from conventional "dual capacity" weapons, there is a merging of nuclear and conventional weapons into a single warfighting capability. If military necessity calls for a job to be done that can be done more efficiently by tactical nuclear weapons than with conventional ones, we can have little confidence that the use of such weapons will long be foregone. Nor, if one accepts the premises underlying the resort to war, is it easy to see why it should be.

On the other hand, the use of nuclear weapons has been so integrated into policy planning as to make their elimination virtually impossible short of dramatic change in such planning. When I say the "use" of such weapons I do so advisedly. Nuclear weapons are being used today and can be expected to be used in the future.[1] Not that they are being detonated; that has not happened in wartime since Hiroshima and Nagasaki. But that is not a requirement of their being used. A man uses a gun when he sticks it in your ribs and demands your money. He does not need to fire the gun. And a country uses nuclear weapons when it makes it known that it may launch them unless certain conditions are met, as the United States did against the Soviets in the Cuban Missile Crisis, against China during the Korean War, and against North Vietnam during the Vietnam War. And the very threat of retaliation that is at the heart of nuclear deterrence is a *use* of nuclear weapons, even if it is not the actual exploding of them.

Moreover, nuclear weapons are used when they are relied upon as an express or implied threat in escalation. And that threat is an integral part of current strategic thinking. Secretary of Defense Casper W. Weinberger made this clear when he said that an adversary "must know that even if his aggression should succeed in achieving its immediate objectives, he faces the threat of escalation to hostilities that would exact a higher cost than he is willing to pay."[2] He then added, "Thus the United States must maintain a credible threat *both of escalation and of retaliation* to secure deterrence across the spectrum of potential conflict" (italics mine).

When the United States refuses to renounce a first use of nuclear weapons in Europe, it is to convey to the Soviets that we might initiate a nuclear war in response to a conventional attack against NATO forces. Indeed, the positioning of U.S. troops so they will

[1] As has been pointed out by Daniel Ellsberg in his "Call to Mutiny," in *The Deadly Connection: Nuclear War and U.S. Intervention*, ed. Joseph Gerson (Cambridge: American Friends Service Committee, 1983), pp. 17-32 (reprinted from *Protest and Survive*, Monthly Review Press). See also Douglas P. Lackey, *Moral Principles and Nuclear Weapons* (Totowa, N.J.: Rowman & Allanheld, 1984), p. 1.

[2] "U.S. Defense Strategy," *Foreign Affairs* (Spring 1986): 679.

unavoidably become engaged with Warsaw Pact forces at the outset of hostilities constitutes a trip wire, involving us and providing a rationale for resorting to nuclear weapons if that should be deemed necessary. The Rapid Deployment Force, or Central Command, serves a similar function in the Middle East. It has in fact been called a "portable Dienbienphu," in reference to the decisive battle of the French Indochina War during which the United States offered the use of nuclear bombs to break the Vietnamese siege. British unwillingness to support such a use dissuaded Eisenhower from proceeding with the plan. Moreover, the threat of escalation to nuclear war provides a protective covering for U.S. operations in the Third World, as it did in Cuba, and later in Granada and Nicaragua. It is virtually inconceivable that the Soviets would commit troops to combat in those areas under threat of U.S. escalation. This gives the United States a free hand to wield the conventional sword under a nuclear shield and makes it highly improbable—assuming a continuation of current thinking—that it would ever agree to eliminate all nuclear weapons. It is simply too dependent upon them.

II

For all of this, there is symbolic significance to the distinction between conventional and nuclear war. Once that line is crossed it will be easier to cross it again or, having crossed it, to escalate to all-out nuclear war. To the extent that keeping the line clearly in view lessens the likelihood of a nuclear holocaust, it is important to do so.

But there should be no illusions about the chances of success so long as the assumptions and values underlying the readiness to wage war of any sort are left unchallenged. Any line *can* be crossed, whether in the use of weaponry or in their production when the capability is possessed. What makes the difference is the attitudes toward war itself. The risk of nuclear war is a function of more than the mere possession of nuclear weapons; it is a function of attitudes concerning ideology, national interest, self-defense, conflict resolution, and, perhaps most importantly, toward the use of violence and the taking of human life. Leave these unchanged and there is little chance of eliminating the risk of nuclear war. The war system has a momentum and logic of its own. When a country's economy is permanently war-oriented, when nearly half its scientists and engineers work on military-related projects, and when force and the threat of force are accepted features of its foreign policy one can hardly expect to reverse a movement that is a product of these forces. *We minimize the magnitude of the problem of nuclear war if we suppose that anything short of a radical change in our thinking has the remotest prospect of success in dealing with it.*

John Dewey recognized the futility of trying to deal with the problem of war in piecemeal fashion. In thoughts that have relevance to our present concern, he said:

> The proposition . . . is not the moral proposition to abolish wars. It is the much more fundamental proposition to abolish the war system as an authorized and legally sanctioned institution.
>
> How long have we been taking steps to do away with war, and why have they accomplished nothing? Because *the steps have all been taken under the war system.* It is not a step that we need, it is a right-about face; a facing in another direction.
>
> If there be somewhere some grinning devil that watches the blundering activities of man, I can imagine nothing that gives him more malicious satisfaction than to see earnest and devoted men and women taking steps, by improving a legal and political system that is committed to war, to do away with war.[3]

This, regrettably, is what one sees in so much of the antinuclear movement. In leaving the war system intact, we in effect are saying that we want to continue playing the game without having to accept the consequences. We want to keep the war system but eliminate the risk of nuclear war.

If the likeliest way a nuclear war will start is by escalation of a conventional war, then we must deal with the threat of conventional war. And if readiness to wage conventional war is a function of the institutionalization of violence on a massive scale, we must find ways to deinstitutionalize violence. It is not nuclear violence alone that is the threat to mankind. It is the willingness to kill and destroy our fellow human beings—the innocent as well as the noninnocent—for political ends. Unless we are willing to redirect our time, energy, and resources away from perfecting the means of mass destruction of whatever sort and into exploring nonviolent

[3] Joseph Ratner, ed., *Intelligence in the Modern World: John Dewey's Philosophy* (New York: The Modern Library, 1939), pp. 515, 523.

alternatives to war itself, our efforts to combat the threat of nuclear war are likely to be of no avail.

But is this not asking too much? Whereas people might conceivably be prepared to dismantle nuclear weapons, is it not too much to expect that they come to grips with the whole problem of the war system itself?

Perhaps. But this is only to say that we may be incapable of saving ourselves. A man overeats, smokes heavily, drinks too much, and gets no exercise. He learns he has high blood pressure and a weak heart. He decides to switch to filters, drink a little less, skip seconds on desserts, and walk a few blocks now and then. Is that not a step in the right direction? Certainly. But it probably will not save him. What he needs is a change in his whole way of life. We, too, can go on fueling the furnace of war and take our chances on being able to control the heat. But let us not deceive ourselves that this is likely to save us either. The whole history of civilization shows that we have never been able to resist heaping more fuel onto the fire. Or to avoid burning ourselves periodically with increasing severity. Less of what we have been doing wrong is not good enough. We must stop doing it.

What the people of today's world need first and foremost is ruthless honesty about themselves. And about their condition. For it is more serious than they want to believe. If we detach ourselves for a moment from our customary outlook in which the acceptance of war is deeply engrained, we can better appreciate the predicament we have created.

If a visitor from outer space were to come to know individual beings on this earth, but to know them only in their personal lives, at work and play, and without knowledge of human history or international affairs, what would he conclude?

Undoubtedly that virtually everyone values peace, happiness, and friendship; that most people love their families, desire basic creature comforts, and seek neither to suffer nor to cause pain to others; that they rarely harm one another, and then do so mainly under duress or in fits of anger directed against friends or loved ones and regretted soon after; that while they can all be insensitive, and a few of them cruel, they for the most part treat those they know with friendly feeling and others with civility; and that most of them wish nothing more than to be left alone to work out their life plans according to their lights, which they do with varying degrees of success when given the chance. If having observed all of this the visitor were then told that a scheme had been proposed by which to improve the world—not in the foreseeable future or in any future the proposer could identify—but which for the present would require that people pour their wealth into the production of weapons of destruction, organize vast authoritarian bureaucracies called armies, train their youth to kill and periodically send them off to slaughter and be slaughtered by other youths similarly organized by their governments; a scheme that above all would require risking for everyone the horror of thermonuclear annihilation; if the visitor were told that humans could improve their lot provided only that they do all of these things, he would ridicule the scheme as not having the slightest chance of success, and even less of being accepted by rational beings.

Yet this is precisely what humankind has been led to accept in the case of war. It has proven willing to abandon virtually everything worth living for and to do things all agree are abhorrent for reasons few understand and for ends like peace, which history shows cannot be secured by these means.

How have we let it come to this?

Perhaps because at no time did any one generation have to confront the choice of the whole of this state of affairs. Had it done so, it might have seen its full absurdity. Successive generations simply responded to the perceived threats of their day without regard for the cumulative effect of such responses over the course of history. In the process most societies gradually became transformed into war systems, geared socially, politically, and economically to the maintenance and often the glorification of their capacity for organized violence.

As a result, we today have inherited a world deeply committed to war as the ultimate means of settling disputes.

Since originating an estimated forty thousand years ago, war has consumed more wealth, demanded greater sacrifice, and caused more suffering than any other human activity. In shaping history it has eclipsed even religion, in whose service it has so often been enlisted. But although war has brought out the worst in man, it has also brought out some of the best. While it cannot be said to have done much for music, it has inspired literature and poetry and brought advances in science, medicine, and technology that otherwise might have been long in coming. Ruskin claims that it has been essential to art as well. It has sometimes been the cohesive force that has brought together divided peoples to form strong and durable societies. Not least of all, it has given the virtues of courage, loyalty, and self-sacrifice unexcelled opportunities to flourish—so much so, in fact, that some have been led to deny that war is even bad. They are convinced that in its absence mankind becomes flabby and decadent and that periodic trials by fire are necessary for the moral health of persons and states.

This was the outlook of various nineteenth-century German writers and is reflected in twentieth-century Fascism. "Mankind has grown great in eternal struggle," Hilter wrote, "and only in eternal peace does it perish."[4] And in an 1895 address to the Harvard graduating class, Oliver Wendell Holmes, Jr., said that "war, when you are at it, is horrible and dull. It is only when time has passed that you see that its message was divine." While expressing hope that we would not soon be at war again, he said that we need a teacher like war in order that

> we may realize that our comfortable routine is no eternal necessity of things, but merely a little space of calm in the midst of the tempestuous untamed streaming of the world, and in order that we may be ready for danger. We need it in this time of individualist negations . . . revolting at discipline, loving flesh-pots, and denying that anything is worthy of reverence.[5]

To be sure, Holmes here speaks only of the need for a teacher like war, but the admiration for what war instills in man, and the sense of its ennobling functions, is clear. It was in deference to this conception, in fact, that William James argued that the only way to do away with war is to replace it with the same kind of commitment and sacrifice. He considered martial virtues absolute and permanent goods but thought their development could proceed by alternative means—a "moral equivalent" of war, as he put it—particularly in the form of national service.

Most people, however, do not think that war is a good thing. They would agree with George Kennan that "major international violence is, in terms of the values of our civilization, a form of bankruptcy for us all . . . that all of us, victors and vanquished alike, must emerge from it poorer than we began it and farther from the goals we had in mind."[6] But they see no alternative. They view war as a problem so large and complex as to be incapable of solution by the efforts of the individual and that therefore can only be accepted as though it were part of the nature of things. And

[4] *Mein Kampf* (Cambridge: The Riverside Press, 1962), p. 135.

[5] Julius J. Marks, ed., *The Holmes Reader* (Dobbs Ferry, N.Y.: Oceana Publications, Inc., 1964), p. 104.

[6] *Memoirs: 1950-1963* (Boston: Little, Brown & Company, 1972) 2: 102-103.

thus, portending the defeat of the human imagination and spirit, they resign themselves to being swept along by the currents of history to whatever end chance or fate decrees.

But war is a problem of our own creation, and it can be solved by our own effort. To do so requires courage, determination, and a resolve to effect a revolution in our moral and conceptual thinking—which have been left behind with the acceleration of civilization down the path of technological development—comparable to the Copernican Revolution in astronomy. A part of that effort must, in the first instance, go into trying to understand the moral problem of war. For if war is *not* wrong morally, then nowhere will be found the resources with which to rid ourselves of it. To do so, in fact, may not even be desirable.

III

My contention is that war in the modern world is not morally justified. I say "in the modern world" because my aim is not to try to assess wars that have been fought throughout past history, much less those that might be conceived in the imaginations of philosophers or writers of science fiction. The consideration of some of those is useful for purposes of illustration or the clarification of the finer points of theoretical analysis. But they are not the wars of vital concern to people. The wars that engage our moral sensibilities are those which nations are prepared to wage today, for whose preparation they gear their economies, and into whose waging they pour their wealth, their hopes, and their youth.

The argument is not that wars under all conceivable conditions are morally impermissible, an absolutist position that properly understood, is neither particularly interesting nor defensible. My position differs little in principle from that of the ordinary person. He does not believe that all wars under all conceivable circumstances are justified, but only that war under certain conditions is justified. The difference between his position and mine concerns what the conditions are. He believes that war is justified in circumstances calling for national defense, or to assist in the defense of other nations, and the like, whereas I maintain that the conditions that might theoretically justify war simply are not met in the actual world, hence that war is impermissible in the world as we know it.

This is a moral position, and many people are uncomfortable discussing morality in a serious and sustained way, as though to do so were a giveaway that one has succumbed to emotionalism and subjectivity. But objectivity does not consist of having no opinions; it is not neutrality. One can fail to have opinions on issues of great importance only by not thinking at all. Nor is objectivity to be found in concealing one's opinions. One either has opinions or not, and if he does, to conceal them—even when that is done successfully—merely deprives others of the opportunity to weigh them when assessing what is presented. Such sham neutrality is no particular virtue. Objectivity consists rather of treating one's subject matter in as fair, open, and accurate a way as possible, whatever one's own views, and of minimizing so far as possible the risk—which exists whether one professes neutrality or not—of distortion and misrepresentation.

When people talk about the morality of war, it is usually to proclaim that we all "know" that war is wrong. However, they usually continue with a "But . . ." and proceed to say that although we all hate war, nonetheless some wars are necessary to avoid greater evils. And in any event, there have always been wars and always will be, and you cannot change that unless you change human nature.

This combination of views—that war is immoral but nonetheless necessary—effectively removes the need to question the morality of war. Its wrongness has already been conceded in a way that allows for the continuation of war and even for a belief in its inevitability.

Those who take this line do not mean that war is wrong in the sense I mean it, however. What they mean is that war is bad, or unfortunate, or tragic, not that it is morally impermissible. And these are different modes of assessment. Plagues, pestilence, floods, and droughts are bad, but they are not immoral. The reason they are not is because they are not the acts of rational beings. Certain of them can be caused by the actions of such beings. But even then it is the act of bringing them about that is immoral, not the phenomenon itself. Everyone but the most fervent glorifier of war agrees that war is bad. That is not the issue. What is at issue is whether it is wrong. What I mean by saying that war is wrong is not only that it is bad but that it ought not to be waged, that governments ought not to declare and fight wars, societies ought not to provide them with the means by which to do so, and individuals ought not to sanction, support, and participate in wars.

My concern throughout will be with actions that are fully authorized and carried out in execution of governmental policies;

15

that is, with actions which are in all nonmoral respects fully legitimate. My intention is to distinguish such actions from those many cases of acts in wartime that are universally condemned even by those who believe that wars are necessary and sometimes justified—acts, for example, like the massacre at My Lai during the Vietnam War. Important as they are to the question of morality in the conduct of warfare and to understanding the psychology of men in combat, such acts are of minor interest so far as the question of the morality *of* war is concerned. It goes little toward showing that war is unjustified to argue against actual or hypothetical wars that fail to meet even the standards to which the war advocate holds.

It is not, in other words, such recognized acts of atrocity that we shall be concerned with, or the carrying out of illegitimate orders, or the incidental acts of gratuitous barbarism that have always been a part of warfare; but rather the fully sanctioned acts that are part of the ongoing process of fighting a modern war, and for whose performance, if it demands unusual bravery, people are honored and deemed heroes by their countrymen. These acts, unlike those at My Lai, are not aberrations. They do not arise from the occasional failure to abide by the rules of war. They are rather the norm. It is their assessment that must be at the heart of any critique of war.

In the first chapter I point out that war is organized and typically institutionalized violence, and therefore to understand the nature of war one must understand the nature of violence. Because the concept of violence by its nature is partly evaluative, implying the intent to harm those against whom it is used, war by its very nature cannot be assessed independently of moral considerations. I try to show why the doing of violence to innocent persons is presumptively wrong, meaning that one may not justifiably do such violence unless he can produce reasons why that presumption is defeated in the circumstances in which he proposes to do violence.

Some may be prepared to grant this for the usual case, but they deny that it has any bearing upon warfare. In warfare, they hold, as in international affairs generally, morality is either irrelevant or of limited relevance. That is, two main approaches are open to those who want to defend war. They can simply deny that morality has any significant bearing upon international relations at all, and hence that judgments such as that war is morally wrong are misconceived. This may be part of a more sweeping rejection of morality itself, as in the case of moral nihilism, or part of a narrower outlook, called political realism, that typically acknowledges morality among individuals but denies that it has central relevance to the conduct of nations. Or, they can accept the relevance of morality to international affairs but argue that war can be justified on moral grounds. This, in effect, is the course of reasoning represented by the just war tradition.

Any thorough assessment of the morality of war must take account of both approaches. Accordingly, I examine political realism in chapters two and three and argue that in the forms it has taken in American thought, it provides no compelling reason to discount the role of morality in international relations, much less in war in particular. Moreover, I argue that the doctrine of reason of state, which one finds embedded in much of political realist thought in the notions of national interest and national survival, opens the way in principle to a government's use of force against its own citizens with the same severity usually reserved for foreign enemies.

In chapters four and five I examine the just war theory, beginning with its foundations in Augustine's thought, highlighting some of the most important features in its historical evolution, and looking at the forms it takes among contemporary writers. I argue that by failing to confront squarely the question of the justifiability of what one must do in the waging of any war, the tradition fails to provide a moral justification of war in the modern world. For modern war, I maintain in the sixth chapter, inevitably kills innocent people, not only because of its weaponry but also because of the implicit or explicit principles bound up in its conduct. Of particular relevance here are the well-known principle of military necessity and what I call the principle of just necessity, both of which can readily conflict with any principle prohibiting the killing of innocent persons. My contention is that the strong presumption against the moral justifiability of killing innocents in wartime is not defeated by the usual arguments thought to warrant such killing. In short, my contention is that if modern war inevitably involves killing innocent persons, then one cannot justify modern war.

The theory of nuclear deterrence, however, holds promise in the eyes of many of providing a paradoxical guarantee of peace in the world, a peace in which the very threat to annihilate millions of innocent persons serves to guarantee that such annihilation will never come about. Even if actually waging such war should be immoral, credibly threatening to wage it is not immoral if it prevents such a war from taking place. In the seventh chapter I examine the reasoning underlying such thinking. I argue, first, that the threat to retaliate massively in the event of a nuclear attack is not rational; and, second, that contrary to the usual wisdom, we have no good reason to believe that nuclear deterrence has worked in the past or that, if it has, it will continue to do so in the future. More than that, I point out that even if nuclear deterrence should be one hundred percent effective, it still increases the probability of nuclear war.

Finally, I propose in the last chapter that there is available to people, if they choose to develop it, an alternative mode of conflict resolution in the form of nonviolence, which can be adapted to national defense. It provides, I contend, not only a moral response to conflict and conflicts of interest but also very likely a more effective practical means than violence of creating the conditions for a lasting peace.

O N E

VIOLENCE AND THE PERSPECTIVE OF MORALITY

I object to violence because, when it appears to do good,
the good is only temporary; the evil it does is permanent.
—M. K. Gandhi

"The characteristic feature of all ethics," Simone de Beauvoir once wrote, "is to consider human life as a game that can be won or lost and to teach man the means of winning."[1] The point, we may suppose, is that without ethics there is no purpose to life, no winning or losing, no reason to live one way rather than another. This, we may suppose further, is true even for those with a religious commitment, for even religion bears upon conduct only to the extent that it at least implies an ethics.

De Beauvoir was speaking here of individual human life, of course. But much the same might be said of the collective life of humankind. And one need be no more than a casual observer of the course of events in the nuclear age to appreciate the fact that humankind may not win the game of life. Without a change in the direction of civilization it may not even have a future.

Can ethics "teach" us a way of winning this game? Not in any ordinary sense. It imparts no simple prescriptions that will miraculously achieve that end, and such prescriptions as are offered in philosophical and religious thought often contain divergent counsel. The means must be worked out by people themselves, drawing upon their own resources and wisdom. But without ethics it is unlikely they will succeed.

There are many possible ethics, among them the ethics of power, love, freedom, profit, work, and honor, each comprising a system of rules and principles for the guidance of conduct or, alternatively, presenting models—religious, historical, political, or

[1] *The Ethics of Ambiguity* (New York: Citadel Press, 1962), p. 23.

19

even literary—of how to live and what sorts of considerations to regard as final in giving direction to one's life. Each, to extend de Beauvoir's metaphor a bit, represents a different way of playing the game of life. And each counts different things as winning. Ethics becomes embodied in various ways of life when people so shape their lives by its values as to give a certain bent to the very character and design of their convictions, which in turn gives a unique quality to their engagement with the world and those around them. This can come about in different ways: sometimes from unexpected, momentous events, as with Paul on the road to Damascus; sometimes from deliberate choice. For most people it comes about through the gradual and almost imperceptible assimilation of a life pattern from family, friends, and society.

The fundamental question of ethics, therefore—indeed of human existence, if we may dramatize it a bit—is how should I live? or what sort of person should I be? And it is a question to which we all give an answer, if only tacitly, in the decisions and commitments we make in the course of living. This is as true of the scientist as of the theologian, of the militarist as of the pacifist. Short of rejecting life itself, all that is open to us is whether to bring reflection to bear upon the answering of the question or simply to allow ourselves to be swept along by whatever currents come our way.

I

The ethical question in this sense is not, however, the fundamental moral question. Indeed, one way of answering the ethical question is by opting for the moral life. Morality is a perspective or way of viewing life—a game of life, if you like—that one may adopt or reject along with the others. And it too comprises values and standards that one may or may not choose to honor. But while it may embrace the values implicit in many of the above ethics, it cannot be reduced to any of them. It involves a commitment to assess when relevant any other point of view from its perspective and to override the other's claims if they conflict with its own. And its claims, unlike those of most of the others, are binding irrespective of whether one adopts its point of view. As Kant saw, one cannot release himself from moral obligations merely by disavowing an interest in the ends that actions discharging those obligations promote. Being amoral does not preclude one's also being immoral.

20

Is there anything that compels us to view the world in a moral light? Or, more specifically for our purposes, to approach the problem of war from a moral perspective? There is not. This should be acknowledged at the outset. One *can* view the world in amoral terms if he chooses. One can so intellectualize behavior that, in those terms, it is no longer susceptible of moral assessment. And one can compartmentalize moral concerns in such a way that whole domains of behavior are exempt from that assessment. Socrates made this clear as he awaited the hemlock in Plato's *Phaedo*. Why was he sitting there when he had been given a chance to escape? One could have answered this by describing his bodily movements, the contraction of his muscles, the changing positions of his bones and tendons, and so on. But to do so would have left out the fact that it was a *moral decision* that was central to his being there, a rational act. No description of bodily movements alone adds up to the performance of an action. It must include the notions of intention, deliberateness, and self-directedness, as well as at least implied reference to the values that are part of the makeup of the character of the person in question. And no purely scientific explanation does this, either, however microscopic in detail. We could describe Lincoln's assassination quite correctly as the rearrangement of one set of molecules (those making up Lincoln's brain) by another set (those making up the bullet fired by Booth). But the event becomes invested with moral significance only when it is seen as the killing of a person as the result of a deliberate action by another person. Human beings, by some scientific accounts are just byproducts of chance combinations of chemicals millions of years ago and can be described painstakingly in those terms exclusively. But to do so is not to describe persons as moral agents and as fitting subjects for moral praise or blame.

Only if we choose to do so can we view the world as a moral world, suffused with value and raising questions of good and bad. And only then do the doings of human beings constitute conduct subject to standards of right and wrong. To view the world in this light does not commit us to any particular values or standards. It does not tell us precisely of what morality consists. It does not provide us with a moral theory. But it provides the perspective in which moral questions can arise and in which moral theory can make sense.

I stress this because it is from a moral perspective that we shall approach the problem of war. I shall not take seriously moral nihilism or even skepticism; not because there are not interesting

21

and challenging arguments to be confronted from each of those directions but because to deal with them adequately would take me afield from my main concerns. I shall take seriously, however, attempts to show that morality does not extend to the sphere of international relations, and to war in particular. For this represents one way of trying to compartmentalize moral concerns and to suspend them in one major area of human activity. Not that one *cannot* do this. It is done all the time. One finds it in academic studies of war and international relations. And one suspects it is the accepted mode of treatment of these matters by governments. Just as there are ways of describing individual behavior that render it impervious to moral assessment, so there are ways of describing the behavior of nations that do the same. Political realism, as we shall see in the next two chapters, does precisely this. But one need not do this. And I shall argue that if one allows the relevance of morality to individual human conduct, it cannot consistently be denied to the conduct of states. For the moment, however, I want to say more about the moral perspective from which I shall be proceeding.

Morality's concern, I say, is with conduct, specifically with its rightness or wrongness. But rightness and wrongness have no meaning in the abstract. They are significant only in the context of purposive human activities. And these activities vary greatly. There are right and wrong ways to swing a golf club, bake a cake, fly an airplane, or launch a military attack, determined by the aims, goals, or purposes of these undertakings or of those of which they are a part. But there are not only right and wrong ways of performing specific operations like these (in which right and wrong have very nearly the force of "effective" or "ineffective"), there are also right and wrong ways of treating persons, whatever the activities in which one is engaged. These are determined by the moral point of view, whose function, at the minimum, is to minimize suffering and unhappiness.

Sometimes what is required of us from one point of view, or from the standpoint of some ethical system of the sort enumerated above, conflicts with what is required from another. This happens, for example, when self-interest or prudence conflicts with a legal obligation, as may happen when one receives a draft call during wartime or when that same legal obligation conflicts with a felt moral obligation to oppose an immoral war. All of us feel the pull of varied and sometimes conflicting obligations as we shift from one role to another in our daily lives. But it is only the moral obligations among these that can properly claim highest priority for

22

anyone purporting to lead the moral life. That life involves recognizing that the demands of morality not only supercede personal desires and interests, including self-interest, when and if they conflict, but also override other obligations as well. Thus, violence that is militarily justified (say, by the principles of sound strategy) may or may not be legally justified from the standpoint of international law; and what is militarily and legally justified may or may not be morally justified. There is no reason to believe that correct assessments from these and other points of view will always coincide, and when they do not, precedence must be given to one over the others if one is to act rationally at all.

If right and wrong presuppose criteria from some perspective or point of view, what criteria distinguish morality? Western moral philosophy answers this in different ways. But the answers center about different ways of assessing the relevance of *consequences* and *value*. Those who affirm the paramountcy of consequences in the making of moral judgments usually stress that what is important is the value produced by those consequences, either in itself or relative to the disvalue that is realized. They typically assert that acts are right if and only if they realize as great a balance of value over disvalue as any alternative action, and obligatory if they realize a greater balance. Those who deny the paramountcy of consequences hold either that the value actually produced by actions is irrelevant, as Kant believed, or, more often, that it is relevant but not decisive, and that other kinds of considerations, such as whether one is violating a moral rule, acting unjustly, or infringing moral rights, must also be considered.

When dealing with substantive moral problems, philosophers typically stake out a position among those described above and then try to show how, within it, one or another stand on the issue in question (whether it be abortion, capital punishment, euthanasia, or whatever) is justified. I shall not do this. In the absence of some a priori apparatus by which to certify some moral standards over others, I believe we must start at the other end, so to speak, and decide first where we stand on particular issues and only then look to see to what that commits us in the way of a more general theory. That is, I believe that one cannot convincingly do moral philosophy of a normative sort by first stating the whole array of theories, selecting one, and then proceeding to defend it against every objection of which one can think. One must first try to understand what is right in particular cases, or at least particular types of cases, and only then look to see to what sort of theory this commits one. It is this that I propose to do with the question of the morality of war.

I shall, however, proceed from a minimal basis of what may be called moral personalism, by which I mean the conviction that any plausible moral theory must have at its center a concern for the lives and well-being of persons. If we do not value persons, including ourselves, there can be no point to valuing other things—not property, possessions, national boundaries, the flag, or anything else. I shall take this to mean at the least, so far as conduct is concerned, that we should minimize avoidable harm to ourselves and others (including, I should add, animals, who, though they are not moral agents, are capable of experiencing pleasure and pain and hence deserve moral consideration).

This gives the barest rudiments of a moral position. But it suffices to establish the importance of violence to the moral assessment of human affairs. For violence is the paradigmatic way of mistreating persons. It involves harming or killing them and destroying things they value. As H.L.A. Hart has said, it is rules that "restrict the use of violence in killing or inflicting bodily harm" that are the most important. "If there were not these rules," he asks, "what point could there be for beings such as ourselves in having rules of *any* other kind?"[2]

II

There has always been violence, of course, and it might seem that there is little reason to give it anymore than usual attention today. But with modern technology it has metamorphosed into new and frightening forms, some of which we scarcely comprehend and most of which we are incapable of controlling with any justifiable confidence. Nuclear weapons, radiation, and biological agents cannot render a man anymore dead than the broadsword or the crossbow, but they have added a new dimension of horror to warfare. And they have done so at just the time that mechanization and bureaucracy have desensitized us to that horror. As Konrad Lorenz put it:

> The man who presses the releasing button [of modern remote control weapons] is so completely screened against seeing, hearing, or otherwise emotionally realizing the consequences of his action, that he can commit it with impunity. . . . Only

[2] H.L.A. Hart, *The Concept of Law* (Oxford: Oxford University Press, 1963), p. 190.

thus can it be explained that perfectly good-natured men, who would not even smack a naughty child, proved to be perfectly able to release rockets or to lay carpets of incendiary bombs on sleeping cities, thereby committing hundreds and thousands of children to a horrible death in the flames. The fact that it is good, normal men who did this, is as eerie as any fiendish atrocity of war.[3]

The heroic spectacle of brave men contending on a darkling plain has given way to the prosaic impersonality of modern industrial society, in which the efforts of millions of ordinary persons—from taxpayers and defense workers to comfortably isolated functionaries in air-conditioned missile silos—conspire to promote and sustain a system for which everyone, and yet no one, is directly responsible. A multitude of loyalties are so arrayed as to generate a potential evil far greater than the goods they severally constitute.

Moreover, the problem of violence once seemed of manageable size. Wars could be waged full tilt, so to speak, with all of the zest and enthusiasm that dangerous adventures inspire; but when they were over the world went on pretty much as before—scarred and shaken sometimes, but always with hope of a better future, or at least of some kind of future. Now all of that has changed. The nuclear age has done more than just enlarge our capacity for violence; it has transformed the whole context in which our thinking about it must take place. Whereas previously violence could be used rationally in the service of human aims, at least in the sense of providing a means to certain clearly attainable ends (whether or not these in turn were rational), its character today threatens the very conditions essential to the attainment of *any* ends, good or bad.

This is a problem of our own making. Whereas our greatest struggles were once against the forces of nature, today they are against forces of our own creation. These include not only the brilliant means devised specifically for the purpose of destroying our fellow men but also the complex socioeconomic and political systems designed to better human life but whose operation redounds in countless ways to the advantage of a few, the despair of many, and the ultimate impoverishment of all. However else we characterize them, they represent ways of doing violence to the world and its inhabitants.

Contributing to the problem is the root assumption of most so-

---

[3] *On Aggression* (Harcourt, Brace & World, 1963), pp. 242-243.

cial and political thinking, which is that without the constraint of coercive institutions our fellowmen (always others, never ourselves) would immediately fall upon one another, plundering, murdering, and raping at will; that only the threat of force restrains them, and hence that the agencies and institutions making good that threat must be maintained at all costs. This assumption provides the basis for our fear of anarchy and the belief that anything less than a firm response to disorder will be interpreted as weakness. And weakness, it is thought in turn, can only whet men's appetites to push the limits of restraint ever farther back, until the very fabric of civilization disintegrates and we are all cast into that cauldron of unrestrained violence that Hobbes calls the state of nature, in which life is "nasty, brutish, and short."

Such thinking places a premium upon the use of violence. To the extent the Hobbesian state of nature is feared, its avoidance is sought by reliance upon the very behavior deemed most dreadful in it. If harm is what each most wants to avoid, then what better way to avoid it than to threaten it in return—if not personally, as in the state of nature, then collectively, through the state? It is thus that there grow up laws, police, and prisons by which to carry out that threat domestically and armies by which to do it internationally. Violence has in fact become a fixture of contemporary civilization. The production and maintenance of means for its use have become a major commitment of most societies, sustained by the economy, government, and educational system. Beneath the overlay of courtesies and formalities that ease our daily interaction lies a readiness to use it not only against other peoples but, through the agencies of police and government, against one another as well. If only a few of us ever wield the nightsticks or carry the rifles, we are the mainstay of those who do.

This fact of the pervasiveness of violence has been noted by Sergio Cotta, who contends that violence has come to dominate our times. Modern communication has brought about what he calls a perception of the "spatial diffusion" of violence; it is perceived as omnipresent. It dominates the news (and, we might add, film and television) to such an extent that "violence appears as the norm rather that the exception. Only excessively brutal violence becomes exceptional."[4] Relatedly, he contends, the rush and immediacy of news, pervaded by reports of violence, gives a perception

[4] *Why Violence? A Philosophical Interpretation* (Gainesville: University of Florida Press, 1985), p. 9.

of a concentration of violence in time as well. And there has, he says, also been an extension of the field of violence. Whereas previously not all harmful or unjust acts were characterized as violence, today violence is perceived to pervade activities and institutions to the point where "[s]cience, instruction, and knowledge in general are considered subtle and hidden forms of violence against the one who must learn, regardless of the use that may be made of them."[5]

Cotta sees two attitudes predominating here. One views today's violence as differing little from that of the past; the other sees it as entirely new in meaning and historical significance. Politically the *Realpolitiker* represents the first point of view, the revolutionary the second. But neither of these, he thinks, adequately reflects the nature of the current dominating influence of violence. What is genuinely new, he contends, is our perception of violence and our *exaltation* of it.

> In fact, if we have violence in *everything* and *everywhere*, we have one, and only one choice: either to suffer it with resignation (in which case violence appears to be the supreme law of life, man's destiny) or to try to eliminate it. But if we choose the second, we become prisoners of an all-encompassing premise: in order to eliminate violence it is necessary to make use of it, since there is no other means for antiviolent action. Such action, therefore, will not renounce the *materiality* of violence, but will reverse its direction: something destructive will be rendered constructive in the hope that through this reversal it will be neutralized and will disappear.[6]

Cotta here puts his finger on the most persuasive of the justifications for the use of violence: that it is necessary to prevent violence. The worse one considers violence to be, the readier one is to use it in return, to the point where, if the violence threatened is unlimited, one's response will be unlimited. Carried to its logical conclusion, this provides the rationale for the balance of terror in the nuclear age.

If I am correct about the assumption underlying most social and political thinking, and if Cotta is even approximately correct about the contemporary exhaltation of violence, we can see the power of the forces impelling us to rely upon it. There is no simple way to

[5] Ibid., p. 13.
[6] Ibid., p. 16.

defuse them and for that reason no simple solution to the problem of war. The overriding moral issue is to confront that "all-encompassing premise," as Cotta calls it, to the effect that the only way to eliminate violence is to use it; and confront it, for our purposes, by asking whether the violence of war can be morally justified. This requires looking more closely at the precise nature of violence and the moral issues its use raises.

III

It has been argued that the very concept of violence, as well as that of nonviolence, is inherently confused. For this reason it has also been said that "a number of familiar questions are also confusions to which no coherent answers could ever be given, such as: when it is permissible to resort to violence in politics; whether the black movement . . . should be nonviolent; and whether anything good in politics is ever accomplished by violence."[7] If this should be correct, then the central questions that concern us in connection with warfare, and that have occupied just war theorists over the centuries, are likewise unanswerable, for they can be formulated only by presupposing that violence has some coherent meaning.

The advocate of this view, Robert Paul Wolff, takes violence to be *"the illegitimate or unauthorized use of force to effect decisions against the will or desire of others;"*[8] or again, "the political use of force in ways proscribed by a legitimate government."[9] This he claims to be a normative account, distinguished from a parallel descriptive

---

[7] Robert Paul Wolff, "On Violence, " *Journal of Philosophy* 66 (Oct. 1969): 602; reprinted as "Violence and the Law" in R. P. Wolff, *The Rule of Law* (New York: Simon and Schuster, 1971), pp. 54-72. Page references are to the former.

[8] Ibid., p. 606.

[9] Ibid., p. 610. He also recognizes other interpretations. One is of violence as "uses of force that involve bodily interference or the direct infliction of physical injury"(p. 606). But he thinks that this definition "usually serves the ideological purpose of ruling out, as immoral or politically illegitimate, the only instrument of power that is available to certain social classes." He also acknowledges a possible definition of violence as the unjustified use of force (p. 608). Wolff's account should be distinguished from claims *about* legitimate violence, such as those put forth by E. Friedenberg. Friedenberg says that "our belief that *legitimated* violence is morally acceptable is very deeply rooted, and stems, I believe, from our opportunism—for this is ever the land of opportunity where failure, not murder, is the unforgiveable sin." See "Legitimate Violence," *The Nation*, June 24, 1968, p. 822. Friedenberg also holds that "if by violence one means injurious attacks on persons or destruction of valuable inanimate objects . . . then nearly all the violence in the world is done by legitimate authority . . . yet their actions are not deemed to be violence." See "The Side Effects of the Legal Process," in Wolff, *The Rule of Law*, p. 43. By this account there are legitimate authorities, and what they do is not deemed violence but is so in fact.

account in which it is understood simply as "the use of force in ways that are proscribed or unauthorized by those who are generally accepted as the legitimate authorities."[10] He then claims that the notion of legitimate authority is incoherent and, that being the case, that the concepts of violence and nonviolence, and the host of questions about their use, are also incoherent. This means that the issue turns upon the analysis of the concept of violence: specifically upon whether it is normative and, if so, whether it yields the alleged conclusion.[11]

People do sometimes speak as though violence were wrong by definition, which would make violence a normative concept, in the sense that to characterize something as an act of violence would suffice to settle what its moral evaluation should be. To establish that an action or policy is violent would suffice to condemn it. For this reason we sometimes hear slums, poverty, and ignorance characterized as violence, while acts of war—the paradigms of violent acts—are often referred to merely as the use of force.

But this view does not hold up well under scrutiny. To see why it does not, let us begin by distinguishing broadly the different sorts of things we mean by violence.

[10] Wolff, "On Violence," p. 606.

[11] Both sides on the issue of whether "violence" is a normative term are found in the literature. Bernard Gert gives an expressly normative analysis of an act of violence in terms of the intentional violation of certain moral rules in "Justifying Violence," *Journal of Philosophy* 66 (Oct. 1969): 616-628. Charner Perry builds both evaluative and normative elements into his account, characterizing violence as "in its nature, evil, a violation of rights, an offense against society." See "Violence—Visible and Invisible," *Ethics* 81 (Oct. 1970): 9. Francis C. Wade distinguishes between descriptive and normative senses and similarly takes the notion of a violation of rights to be central to the latter in "On Violence," *Journal of Philosophy* 68 (June 1971): 369-377. Newton Garver introduces a normative element in terms of the violation of personality in "What Violence Is," *The Nation,* June 24, 1968, pp. 819-822, reprinted in expanded form in A. K. Bierman and James A. Gould, eds., *Philosophy for a New Generation,* 2d ed. (New York: MacMillan Company, 1973), pp. 256-266. Gandhi likewise tacitly defines violence normatively when he says that "there is no violence when there is no infraction of duty." See M. K. Gandhi, *Non-Violent Resistance* (New York: Schocken Books, 1961), pp. 167-168. A normative account similar to Wolff's is given by R. Hartogs and E. Artzt, eds., *Violence: Causes and Solutions* (New York: Dell, 1970), p. 14, who say that "violence may be defined as an extreme form of aggression making illegitimate or unjustified use of force." And in his *On Understanding Violence Philosophically* (New York: Harper and Row, 1970), p. 19, Glen Gray interprets force in terms of legitimate authority and violence in terms of the absence of such authority. On the other hand, R. B. Miller and R. Audi both characterize violence in such a way that it is not wrong by definition. See their "Violence, Force, and Coercion" and "On the Meaning and Justification of Violence" in J. Shaffer, ed., *Violence* (New York: David McKay, 1971). For a good critique of Wolff's argument, see P. Flanagan, "Wolff on Violence," *Australasian Journal of Philosophy* 50, no. 3 (Dec. 1972): 271-278.

On the one hand, there is the violence of nature represented by hurricanes, earthquakes, windstorms, and the like. On the other hand, there is the violence done by humans, including violence against other living things (persons and animals) and that against property and inanimate things. As environmental issues become of increasing concern, there is growing awareness of what might be called violence against nature as well. As it is the effect of violence upon living things—whether or not directed specifically against them—that is of ultimate moral concern, and inasmuch as only such of that violence as is done by humans is subject to moral assessment, I shall call violence by persons against living things primary. Violence against property or inanimate things is of interest only insofar as it has some bearing upon the lives and well-being of living things.[12] For that reason I shall call it secondary.

We can better understand this by considering that there are *central, extended,*and *peripheral* uses of the concept. Consider the following statements:

A

Historically speaking, violence and assassination have marked almost every society created by man.[13]

Our own era is marked by the collective self-concept of a country in which violence is prevalent and in which there is a growing fear of falling prey to a violent criminal in the streets.[14]

The emergence of the U.S. as a great power has been accompanied by a growing commitment to violence as a technique for implementing policy.[15]

B

[The Liberal Church] is furthermore usually oblivious to the fact that nonviolence may be covert violence. Children do

[12] Not that it may not sometimes be as, or more, important than primary violence. One can, as Gandhi noted, sometimes do a person more harm by destroying his property than by physical violence against his person (*Non-Violent Resistance*, p. 371). But when this is the case, it is still the effect of violence upon persons that invests it with moral significance.

[13] Harrison E. Salisbury, "Introduction" to *Assassination and Political Violence, A Report to the National Commission on the Causes and Prevention of Violence*, J. F. Kirkham, S. G. Levy, W. J. Crotty (New York: Bantam Books, 1970), p. xxi.

[14] S. Endleman, ed., *Violence in the Streets* (Chicago: Quadrangle Books, 1968), p. 9.

[15] Ibid., p. 20.

starve and old people freeze to death in the poverty of our cities.[16]

What the school determines to accomplish it does so in a constant and total atmosphere of violence. We do not mean physical violence; we mean violence in the sense of any assault upon, or violation of the personality. An examination or test is a form of violence. . . . Compelled attendance in the classroom, compulsory studying in study hall, is violence.[17]

The injustices within Brazilian society constitute Violence Number One, and terrorism is Violence Number Two.[18]

C

Destruction and violence! How is the ordinary man to know that the most violent element in society is ignorance.[19]

We need only think of the cacophony of sound that does violence to our traditional image of concert music. . . . Not only is the resulting composition violent in character; its method of execution is violence also.[20]

An interviewer can do violence to a reputation simply by quoting verbatim.[21]

The references to violence in group A call to mind the phenomena most often associated with violence in our common-sense thinking, and for that reason I call them central uses. Here the idea of destructive physical force is prominent. Those in group B are extended uses in that, although they refer to primary violence, it is not of an exclusively or even prominently physical sort (though the third quotation in B juxtaposes a central use, the second occurrence, with an extended use, the first occurrence). Most uses that relate closely to the concept of violation fall into this second category, as do those relating to what has come to be called psycho-

[16] Reinhold Niebuhr, *Love and Justice: Selections from the Shorter Writings of Reinhold Niebuhr*, ed. D. B. Robertson (Cleveland: World Publishing Company, 1967), p. 257.
[17] C. A. Reich, *The Greening of America* (New York: Bantam Books, 1971), p. 148.
[18] Brazilian priest, Dom Helder, quoted by J. A. Page in "The Little Priest Who stood Up to Brazil's Generals," *New York Times Magazine*, May 23, 1971.
[19] Emma Goldman, "Anarchism: What It Really Stands For," in *Nonviolence in America: A Documentary History*, ed. S. Lynd (Indianapolis: Bobbs-Merrill, 1966), p. 121.
[20] R. G. Francis, "Kapow ! !: An Argument and a Forecast," in Endleman, ed., *Violence in the Streets*, p. 152.
[21] W. J. Weatherby, "Talking of Violence," in Endleman, ed., *Violence in the Streets*, p. 85.

logical violence. The second quotation illustrates both. Those in category C I call peripheral uses because they are either metaphorical or highly attenuated (though the first passage contrasts a peripheral use with a central one).

In some of the passages, notably those in group B and C, violence is tacitly defined in such a way as to convey disapproval of the phenomena characterized. In fact it is probably the strong disapproval most people feel toward violence that explains why the notion is so readily extended to other modes of conduct of which they disapprove. Thus when paint was splattered on a Soviet violinist during a New York concert, a reviewer wrote that "[t]his work [Bach's Chaconne in D Minor] is so demanding and musically profound, that when it is well performed . . . such an act of violence is akin to taking a knife to the Mona Lisa."[22] Such statements conceal a condemnatory moral judgment. Given the strong negative emotive force of the word "violence," to apply it in this way serves to focus upon the act the full force of one's disapproval. Splattering paint upon a performer during a concert is a symbolic act and (presumably) causes no injury. But however wrong it might be, it is not an act of violence in any strict sense. Any word that has strong emotive meaning in the way in which "violence" does (and words like "terrorist" do) is subject to such use.

The lines dividing these categories are not sharp, of course, but they do not need to be for our purposes. I want to focus upon the central uses, specifically those that relate, as do most or perhaps all of them, to physical violence. In its strictest sense physical violence is the use of force with the intent to harm, kill or cause destruction; or at the least, the use of force that has harm, death, or destruction as a foreseeable outcome (a terrorist's bombing is an act of violence even if the intention is only to publicize a cause). This leaves it open whether a given act succeeds, since success in execution is not necessary to an act's being an act of violence (the shot may miss or the bomb fail to explode). By "force" in this characterization I mean pronounced physical force. We can use force (such as to lift heavy objects), do things forcefully (like arguing a point of logic), or force others to do certain things (like moving their king in a game of chess), without resorting to violence. This is because the use of force in its broadest sense is the effecting of change, and this may be done violently or nonviolently. Indeed,

22 Peter G. Davis, *New York Times*, Nov. 9, 1976.

Gandhi in his concept of Satyagraha, or Truth Force, and Martin Luther King, Jr., in his philosophy of Soul Force, expressly utilized the concept of force to designate nonviolent ways of effecting change. But physical violence cannot occur in the absence of such force, even if it does not need to be exercised directly by dint of one's own effort (sometimes it is enough to pull the trigger of a gun or depress the plunger of a detonator). So while we often use "force" and "violence" interchangeably, the two cannot be equated.

There is, of course, some violence in which there is neither a specific intention of the required sort nor expectable consequences of harm, destruction, or death. A deranged person flailing about in a padded cell or someone who is drugged or whose brain has been electrically stimulated may be violent but have no intention at all, much less be able to foresee any consequences of what he does. Almost anything from waging an argument to conducting an orchestra can be done violently without any intention to harm. This observation relates to the use of "violent" to characterize the *way* something is done rather than what is done. Not all things done violently are acts of violence, nor are all acts of violence done violently.

Put another way, imagine a scale of human behavior, one end of which represents calm, controlled, self-directed behavior, the other of which represents strenuous, agitated, and sometimes uncontrolled behavior. As one ascends from the former to the latter there will be a threshold at which it begins to be appropriate to characterize what is done as done violently, whatever it is that is being done. Between that point and the extreme of agitated behavior there is a further threshold at which it begins to be appropriate to speak of the *person* in question as becoming violent—in each case without reference to purposes, intentions, or expectations. In neither case will it be appropriate, without expansion of the descriptions, to characterize the behavior as involving the commission of *acts* of violence. These uses of "violent," unlike those in expressions like "act of violence," will sometimes be central and sometimes not, depending upon whether the conduct so characterized is purposive and, if so, to what ends. Thus we can distinguish a vertical scale of degrees of turbulence in behavior and a horizontal scale of projected and expectable consequences considered with respect to whether they cause harm, destruction, or death. Both are relevant to determining the appropriateness of various uses of the concept of violence. Normally it is only those

33

cases on the vertical scale that also have a place on the horizontal scale that fall within the range of central uses because only those are directed against persons and things.[23]

There are, however, some uses of force to cause destruction that are not acts of violence in any usual sense: the demolition of a building, the sinking of an obsolete ship by gunfire, or the use of explosives in mining operations. Destructive uses of force *as such*, in other words, do not constitute violence. The reason why they do not is because they may or may not be legitimate and which they are makes a difference to the appropriateness of calling them violence.[24] To this extent Wolff's analysis is on the track of an important feature of the concept of secondary violence. It is hard to think of any uses of physical force against objects or property that can unequivocally be called acts of violence (excluding acts so-called by virtue of being violently done) if they are not unauthorized or illegitimate.[25] But the distinction between authorized and unauthorized force does not do the same service in the case of force directed against persons. Hangings, executions by firing squad, and shootings by police are acts of violence however legal they may be.

For this reason it is important to mark off two separate dimensions, or, if you like, two different concepts of physical violence, the one relating to force used against persons or animals, the other relating to force used against objects only. Thus primary physical violence is the use of force with the intention to harm or kill (or where that will be a foreseeable consequence). Secondary physical violence is the unauthorized use of force to cause destruction. This gives conceptual acknowledgement within the range of central

[23] Although the behavior of deranged persons is often properly characterized as physical violence, I am confining my attention to purposive conduct of the sort usually signified by expressions like "act of violence."

[24] On this issue see R. Audi, "On the Meaning and Justification of Violence," pp. 57-58, and R. B. Miller, "Violence, Force, and Coercion," pp. 17-20, in Shaffer, ed., *Violence.*

[25] Speaking here of domestic violence. International violence is a more difficult case, partly because so much of it is primary violence, partly because even straightforward property destruction resulting from acts of war is always unauthorized by the nation suffering the destruction and authorized by the nation inflicting it. Thus there is no mutually acceptable frame of reference from which the question of authorization can be settled. There is, of course, the overarching point of view of international law; but it conspicuously fails to duplicate effectively the function of domestic law. Even where war has been duly declared and the targets are "legitimate" military targets, the fact that authorization from the nation suffering destruction is absent seems to suffice to render these acts of violence.

uses to the distinction marked earlier between primary and secondary violence.

Harm is the key notion in the concept of primary violence. Sometimes it suffices to warrant saying that when someone has been harmed he has been caused pain, suffering, anguish, and so forth. But in a stricter sense, going back as far as Plato, people have been harmed only if they have been made worse off as a result of what was done to them. This might or might not be as a result of having been caused pain. Even in the most expert and successful of treatment doctors and dentist often unavoidably cause pain and suffering; probably more so in fact than do many who use violence against others (the average mugger, for example, probably causes less pain in the world than the average surgeon). Though it is appropriate to say in these cases that my doctor or dentist *hurt* me in the course of treatment, it is not appropriate on the strength of that alone to say that he *harmed* me. Nor of course is it correct to say that doctors and dentists do their yankings, cuttings, and sawings *in order* to harm, even in the weaker sense. This suggests that the causing of pain in order to benefit (and, we might add, where it can reasonably be expected that benefit will result) is not usually thought of as the causing of harm. Even less is it thought of as violence. But *unless* deliberate infliction of pain against a person's will, or the doing of things that can reasonably be expected to cause pain, are done with a view to benefiting him, they can be said to constitute harm at least in the weaker sense. It is not enough to have had no intention to worsen a person's overall state when causing pain in order to be said not to have harmed him (forcibly abducting a person at gunpoint for terrorist purposes without actually intending to harm him in the stronger sense might meet that condition). One must have intended to better it, or at least have had a warrantable expectation that betterment would result.

Nor, it should be said, does the fact that acts of primary violence are usually performed against the will of the person affected mean that they would cease to be acts of violence if consent were involved. In this respect Cotta misleadingly characterizes both force and violence as forms of what he calls "activity contra," meaning that they are exercised "without the consent of those affected."[26]

[26] Cotta, *Why Violence?* p. 60.

Typical cases of violence, to be sure, are nonconsensual; but contravention of the will of the person affected is not a necessary condition of violence. Shooting someone is no less an act of violence for the fact the person asked to be shot. Nor is it always an act of violence deliberately to kill another person, even where such killing clearly constitutes murder. An injection that brings about a peaceful death is not an act of physical violence (whatever the morality of such killing) because it does not involve the appropriate use of force.

Neither primary nor secondary physical violence, it should be noted, can be understood in purely behavioral terms. Acts of secondary violence require an institutional setting in which the notions of legitimacy or authorization acquire meaning.[27] They cannot be understood simply by reference to physical behavior or to the destructiveness of the force used. Acts of primary violence do not similarly presuppose an institutional setting and for that reason cannot be understood in terms of the legitimate/illegitimate distinction. But they do presuppose certain purposes or expectations pertaining to the causing of harm. It is these that distinguish them from accidental uses of destructive or deadly force. We do speak of "observing" acts of violence of both sorts, of course, but this is because the context normally warrants assumptions about intentions, expectations, or authorizations not warranted by the observation of physical behavior alone. As we saw earlier in our discussion of the concept of morality, human behavior alone, however closely described, does not by itself add up to the performance of actions. Acts of violence of the sorts I have characterized are therefore not among the more primitive facts about the world. On a scale from primitive to complex facts (including at the latter end what have come to be called institutional facts), violence of the two sorts I have been describing would fall between the two, with secondary violence higher on the scale than primary violence.

If this is correct, and if Wolff's account aims to clarify the central uses of the concept of violence, that analysis is inadequate. For the notion of morally legitimate government plays no role in those uses. If, on the other hand, his argument is intended to elucidate only what might be called a political concept of violence, then even granting that there is such a concept, and that it is analyzable as

[27] For a discussion of some theories of violence that expressly relate it to social settings, see H. Bienen, *Violence and Social Change* (Chicago: University of Chicago Press, 1968), pp. 68-69.

he proposes, one could accept his argument insofar as it applies to uses of that concept and still maintain that all of the social and moral questions about justification can be asked with regard to the central (and other) uses. Either way there is no reason to believe that questions about the use and justifiability of violence and nonviolence are incoherent and cannot in principle be answered. And that is all that is necessary to justify the central place of violence in the assessment of war.

IV

We can now say that primary violence is an evaluative notion by virtue of the centrality to its analysis of the notion of harm. In its stronger sense, as we have seen, harm is what makes a person worse off. To determine that someone has been harmed requires making an evaluative judgment. But this does not make primary violence wrong by definition, if by that we mean actually or absolutely wrong. If to establish that someone has knowingly harmed someone does not suffice to show that he has acted wrongly, then showing that someone has performed an act of violence against someone does not suffice to show that either. It is important to distinguish between evaluative concepts in our judgments of the goodness or badness of things and normative concepts used to judge that conduct as right, wrong, or obligatory. Violence in its central uses is of the first type. Acts of violence, as we have seen, involve the intention to harm or the expectation that it will result. Absent a theory about the nature of moral obligation and the relationship between obligation and value, there is no warrant for saying that the fact that an act is harmful by itself renders it impermissible, anymore than the fact that the act is good by itself renders it obligatory. For either of these further judgments one needs a premise connecting the notions of value and obligation or some reason to believe that there is a conceptual link between the two. No final moral assessment of acts that result in harm to oneself or others can be assumed to be dictated by the mere characterization of such acts as causing harm, and accordingly no such assessment is dictated by the notion of an act of violence. Otherwise, we should be able to show that war is wrong simply by noting that it involves performing acts of violence.

But if violence is not wrong by definition, it is nonetheless prima facie wrong, or wrong all other things being equal, just by virtue of the fact that it is prima facie wrong to harm people. Whether

37

this connection between harm and prima facie wrongness is a necessary one, written into the very meanings of the concepts themselves (which *would* give violence a normative as well as an evaluative character by entailing that acts of violence are by definition prima facie wrong), or a contingent one requiring an additional substantive premise, we need not determine; though *if* rightness and wrongness are definable by reference to value terms, then the concept of harm is a plausible candidate for inclusion in their analysis. Either way, if what I am maintaining is correct, then while acts of violence are not wrong by definition, they are all of them prima facie wrong and in need of justification. Secondary violence, on the other hand, has a clearly normative character by virtue of its incorporation of the notion of authority or legitimacy. But it is not evaluative in the manner of primary violence. One can speak of an object's being destroyed without being committed to a value assessment of the object or its resultant state in a way that he cannot when he says of someone that he has been harmed. Moreover the notion of authorization as we have employed it does not say anything about the moral legitimacy of the form of government under which it is gained. It does not even entail the legality of all authorized uses of force within the broader context, say, of a country's constitution (local governments might authorize actions that higher courts later rule unconstitutional; but this would not alter the fact that the initial actions were genuinely authorized). Much less does it imply any actual or possible form of government under which such authorization is given is morally justified.

V

What I have been saying should not be taken to mean that all wrongdoing consists of violence. Critics of pacifism correctly point out that there are ways of harming people other than by violence. In the quotation cited earlier, Niebuhr speaks of nonviolence as sometimes being "covert violence," where he has in mind by violence the results of poverty, freezing, and starvation. And he pointed out elsewhere that boycotts of British cotton by Gandhi's followers in India could have deleterious effects upon the textile workers in Lancashire, England.[28]

Gandhi himself acknowledged the problem and attempted to meet it head on. A critic had written:

[28] Reinhold Niebuhr, *Moral Man and Immoral Society* (New York: Charles Scribner's Sons, 1932), p. 241.

38

Gandhi, as I understand him, proclaims the Way of Love. And yet he does not see that 'Non-co-operation is a way of violence.' Suppose the milk drivers of New York had a real and just and even terrible grievance. Suppose that they should strike and cut off the milk supply from the babies of New York. They might never raise a hand in violent attack on any one and yet their way would be the way of violence. Over the dead bodies of little children they would by 'non-cooper-ation' win their victory. As Bertrand Russell said of the Bol-sheviki, 'such suffering makes us question the means used to arrive at a desired end.' Non-cooperation means suffering in Lancashire and is an appeal in the end to violence rather than reason.[29]

In his reply Gandhi distinguished between a strike simply to protest, say, against the municipality for mismanagement of its trust and one in which the drivers were starving as a result of un-derpayment and had exhausted all other means of redress. In the first case, he said, their action would be a "crime against human-ity," but in the second it would be justified. In elaborating, he said of the second case: "Their refusal will certainly not be an act of violence though it will not be an act of love. They were not philan-thropists. They were driving milk carts for the sake of their main-tenance. It was no part of their duty as employees under every circumstance to supply milk to babies. There is no violence when there is no infraction of duty."[30]

Of conceptual interest here is the fact that Gandhi implicitly de-fines violence in a normative way, so that an act qualifies as vio-lence only if it constitutes a violation of duty. We have seen grounds for rejecting this as an adequate account of physical vio-lence, but as we shall see, there is more to be said for it in connec-tion with the notion of psychological violence. Of moral interest is the fact that Gandhi apparently does not regard consequences as decisive in appraising the moral quality of acts. The conse-quences—that is, the deaths of the babies—might be identical in the two hypothetical cases. Yet on this view the one act is justified and the other is not. What makes the difference for Gandhi is the circumstances of the performance of the acts. What precisely it is about the circumstances that makes the difference he does not specify. Some of what he says suggests it is the fact that in the one

[29] Gandhi, *Non Violent Resistance*, p. 166.
[30] Ibid., pp. 167-168.

case, but not in the other, it is a matter of either not acting and letting one group of persons starve (namely, the milk drivers) or acting and allowing another group to starve (namely the babies), and that the drivers qua drivers have no duty to supply milk to the babies. Even so, their act, he says, would not in that case be an act of love; it is just that it would not be an act of violence either. Implied in all of this, though he does not develop the point, is the judgment that we have at least a qualified duty to regard the well-being of those who may need our help but to whom we have no fixed commitment to provide help. The more general question is whether we are principally obligated to do good for people, or simply to refrain from harming them, issues that we shall encounter in Chapter Six.

My concern for the moment is to acknowledge that there are literally non-violent ways of harming people (by which I mean merely ways that involve no physical violence) that are as bad as violent ways. This means that there is no particular virtue in non-violent or pacifistic action per se. Intentions to cause harm, destruction, or death commonly associated with acts of violence may be equally present in nonviolent actions. It may be an awareness of this that prompts Cotta to remark:

> Its correlation with the idea of revolution and of "new beginning" explains why violence was able to prevail so widely during these last years over the opposite ideal of nonviolence, which seemed destined to worldwide success in the wake of Gandhi. But violence succeeded even in making nonviolence its own instrument. In fact, the nonviolent techniques are now reversed from their proper sense and utilized for the tactics of a more crafty and effective struggle.[31]

The absence of physical force in nonviolence is not, then, in and of itself particularly relevant. There is, of course, the difference noted earlier between violence and nonviolence that acts of violence are by their nature prima facie wrong whereas acts of nonviolence are not. But both must be appraised in the contexts in which they are contemplated, with due regard for the character of the acts and their consequences. The mere absence of war, as Augustine perceived, does not make peace in any meaningful sense; there must be justice and tranquility as well. Likewise the mere absence of violence does not make nonviolence in any significant sense. There must be some positive features of conduct, minimally

[31] Cotta, *Why Violence?* pp. 17-18.

in the way of a concern or respect for others, in order for it to exemplify nonviolence as a moral position. This has been true of the philosophies of nonviolence advocated by Tolstoy, Gandhi, and King.

The harmful consequences of "nonviolent" actions (as I shall denote acts that are nonviolent only in the sense of not involving violence) may be either purely physical, as in the case of the hypothetical milk drivers, where it is the starvation that is at issue, or mental. That is, we need to distinguish physical and mental harms and to recognize that one can be as bad as the other and that either can be caused by violent or "nonviolent" actions.

Consider the following account by Jonathan Kozol in *Death at An Early Age*:

> Although Stephen did poorly in his school work, there was one thing he could do well. He was a fine artist. He made delightful drawings. The thing about them that was good, however, was also the thing that got him into trouble. For they were not neat and orderly and organized but entirely random and casual, messy, somewhat unpredictable, seldom according to the instructions he had been given, and—in short—real drawings. For these drawings, Stephen received considerable embarrassment at the hands of the Art Teacher. . . . If Stephen began to fiddle around during a lesson, the Art Teacher generally would not notice him at first. When she did, both he and I and the children around him would prepare for trouble. For she would go at his desk with something truly like a vengeance and would shriek at him in a way that carried terror. "Give me that. Your paints are all muddy. You've made it a mess. . . . I don't know why we waste good paper on this child." Then: "Garbage. Junk. He gives me garbage and junk. And garbage is one thing I will not have." . . . [S]he did not know or care anything at all about the way in which you can destroy a human being.[32]

The teacher used no physical violence. She had not even caused physical harm or injury of the sort represented by the poverty or starvation alluded to in the earlier examples. Yet she was causing harm. But it was of an emotional or psychological sort. So great may such harms be—extending in extreme cases to the devastation

[32] Jonathan Kozol, *Death At An Early Age* (New York: Bantam Books, 1968), pp. 2-4.

41

of a personality—that the term "psychological violence" has come increasingly to characterize their infliction. Mental harms can be inflicted by means of physical violence, with torture probably being the best example. But they may also result from "nonviolent" actions. And with regard to "nonviolent" acts we may distinguish between those whose express aim is to effect harm and those in which such an outcome is merely a byproduct, perhaps unforeseen, of acts directed toward other ends. Brainwashing illustrates the former; in it a person's mental processes can be so altered that he is no longer certain of what he has done in the past and can eventually become convinced that he has done things he in fact has not done. Given enough time, almost any normal person can be broken down in this way. On the other hand, effects that, though not comparable to these, are nonetheless severely damaging, can be brought about in the course of child raising, sometimes by parents who have no intention to harm their children but who nonetheless treat them in ways that cause irreparable harm by destroying their confidence and self-esteem.

Language has a convenient resource for enabling us to distinguish these different modes of violence. It is in the idea of "doing violence." This notion is not as close to the surface of our commonsense thinking as is that of physical violence. But it is important to assessing the ethical questions in the use of violence. Consider the debilitating effects of prolonged and intensive brainwashing, or of ghetto schools upon young children, or of the continual humiliation and debasement of a child by parents. In none of these cases need physical violence be used. But in each case violence is done, and of a sort that may be far more injurious that most physical violence.[33]

---

[33] Violence was seen in the Old Testament to be bound up in pride (Psalms 73:6), wealth (Micah 6:12), and in leading others astray (Proverbs 16:29). And the Stoic Marcus Aurelius catalogued a variety of ways in which a man might "do violence" to himself, from becoming vexed to being insincere and threatening harm to others. See *Meditations*, (Pleasant Valley, Pa.: Gateway, 1956), p. 18. Eastern philosophies often expressly distinguish mental from physical harms and associate violence with both. The second Yama, or restraint, of Yoga ethics requires that "if we adhere to the principle of nonviolence we shall have to give up falsehood, because if we are not truthful and thus deceive others we shall cause them mental injury." See I. C. Sharma, *Ethical Philosophies of India* (Lincoln, Neb.: Johnsen Publishing Company, 1965), p. 209. Gandhi clearly intends the same when he says that "under violence I include corruption, falsehood, hypocrisy, deceit and the like" (*Non-Violent Resistance*, p. 294). Tolstoy makes much of this aspect of violence, even though he does not always distinguish it carefully from physical violence. See, for example, his *A Confession: The Gospel in Brief and What I Believe* (New York: Oxford University Press, 1961), pp. 321 and 351.

Violence in this sense, as Newton Garver has pointed out,[34] has a closer kinship with the notion of violation than with physical force. We may violate laws, rules, orders, good manners or the spirit of an agreement; and we speak of the violation of persons in at least one type of physical violence, namely, rape. Similarly one can *do violence* to a wide range of things: language, facts, the truth, an author's intentions, the memory of a deceased, and to persons, including oneself. In each case something having value, integrity, dignity, sacredness, or generally some claim to respect is treated in a manner that is contemptuous of this claim. According to what I have called moral personalism, persons are preeminently worthy of respect and have claims upon those whose conduct may affect them to be treated in ways that do not diminish them. To deprive them of their freedom, degrade them, or destroy their confidence are all ways of doing the latter. And all are accomplishable without resort to physical violence. Indeed, most of them can be effected through the subtlest forms of personal and social interaction, inasmuch as it is in these areas that people are often the most vulnerable. The preceding example of the teacher simply illustrates the doing of violence in a relatively heavy-handed way. The insidiousness of racism, for example, consists in the fact that some of its most damaging effects are essentially unquantifiable ones, wrought upon the psyche of a whole people through prolonged oppression. The same with sexism.

This highlights the importance I have stressed of distinguishing between physical and mental (or psychological) harms. The former tend to be conspicuous and come most readily to mind when one thinks of harm. The latter are often inconspicuous and for that reason discounted or insufficiently attended to in the assessment of ways of treating people.

Philosophers have, however, at various times showed an awareness of such harms and occasionally even provided the rudiments of a theory for understanding them. Plato, for example, holds that

[34] Garver, "What Violence Is," pp. 819-822. Garver's is one of the more influential analyses of violence, and his essay contains a good discussion of the notion of psychological violence. For a critique of his discussion and an argument against analyzing violence other than by reference to physical force, see Joseph Betz, "Violence: Garver's Definition and a Deweyan Correction," *Ethics* 87, no. 4 (July 1977): 339-351. See also Robert Audi, "On the Meaning and Justification of Violence," in Shaffer, ed., *Violence*, and William Robert Miller, *Nonviolence: A Christian Interpretation* (New York: Association Press, 1964), chap 1. Gandhi is interpreted by Erik H. Erikson as grounding his opposition to nonphysical harms in the injunction never to violate another person's essence in his *Gandhi's Truth: On the Orgins of Militant Nonviolence* (New York: Norton & Company, 1969), p. 412.

to harm a person is to make him less perfect, where this means disrupting the inner harmony of the soul that enables one to function effectively as a rational being. He may even have thought, as his mentor Socrates did, that this is the only way to harm a person and that what we are calling physical harms cannot really harm a virtuous person and might (in the form of punishment) even benefit one who is not virtuous. We shall see in Chapter Four how rather similar thinking is developed by Augustine in the context of Christianity. Other philosophers like Kant, Dewey, and the existentialists, by stressing freedom and the value of the person, explicitly or implicitly direct attention to the fact that one can be harmed in other than physical ways. Marx does the same in characterizing the forms of alienation under capitalism that he believes dehumanize and ultimately reduce men to the level of animals. While it is not possible to sum up this mode of violence in anything like a neat formula or definition, we may say that to do violence to persons in any of these ways is to diminish them as persons.

I shall speak of the use of physical or psychological violence against persons as the doing of violence to them. And the doing of violence in these ways I take to be prima facie wrong—that is, wrong all other things being equal or in the absence of countervailing moral considerations. Many things are wrong other things being equal, of course, but nonetheless right in practice. There is not even invariably a presumption that what is prima facie wrong is also wrong on balance because often acts that in some respects are prima facie wrong are in other respects prima facie right.[35] But there is, I believe, a presumption of wrongness about the doing of violence to people. In fact, the infliction of the sorts of harms it represents is a paradigm of how not to treat people.

This, however, is not the central claim I want to advance. I want to defend only the weaker claim that it is presumptively wrong to do violence to *innocent* persons. One must start somewhere in morals as well as science, mathematics, or any other mode of inquiry with something for which further justification is not asked, at least for purposes of that inquiry. I propose to do that with this claim. For there is probably no stronger presumption is morals. It is not one that tips the scales in the assessment of war one way or the other. Both militarists and pacifists can equally accept it; in fact, as we shall see in Chapter Five, something approximating it

[35] Following W. D. Ross's explication in *The Right and the Good* (Oxford: Oxford University Press, 1930), chap. 2.

is the mainstay of most conceptions of what constitutes justice in the conduct of war. It does not even tip the scales within morality between advocates of one type of moral theory as opposed to another. Those who view morality as purely a matter of consequences can accept it as well as those who think morality is mainly a matter of rights or of largely nonconsequentialist considerations. It tips the scales only, as I have indicated, between those who are willing to view the world in a moral light and those who are not. Morality as experienced, and not necessarily as treated in the abstract, presents some things to us as right and others as wrong, some as right or wrong all other things being equal, and some as carrying presumptions of varying strengths as to their rightness or wrongness. The doing of violence to innocent persons—the use of violence against them, physical or psychological, killing or harming them, or inflicting mental or physical injury—is, I propose, in this sense presumptively wrong. This does not mean that doing these things is never justified; whether that is so must be determined by examining the various kinds of circumstances in which one might propose to do them. It is just that the burden rests upon anyone who proposes to do these things to innocent persons to produce the justification. I take this to be the starting point for dealing with the moral problems of violence and war.

If what I have been saying is correct, it means that we cannot adequately understand violence apart from at least tacit reference to moral and evaluative questions. This does not mean, I stress, that violence is wrong by definition; that would be too easy a way with many complex moral problems. But it does mean that one omits relevant considerations if he tries to assess violence apart from any considerations of moral factors.

VI

Because war by its nature is institutionalized violence, it, too, cannot be fully assessed independently of moral considerations. And these considerations extend to the consequences of both physical and psychological violence. For war inflicts both.

While it is the physical violence that is usually stressed, war's consequences also include the incalculable grief and anguish of those who lose loved ones, and whose lives are sometimes permanently diminished as a result of those losses, as well as harms done those combatants who survive only to go through the rest of their lives emotionally and psychologically impaired. These never appear in statistics about war. Yet they are among its highest costs. Lives shattered by alcoholism, drug abuse, or suicide as a result of wartime experiences—as, notably, have been those of many veterans of the Vietnam War—are casualties of war as surely as those shattered on the battlefield. Those who suffer such harms have been done violence whether or not they have suffered physical wounds.

Their sufferings are the same, of course, whether they voluntarily offered themselves up for the business of war or not. But, morally, they are particularly tragic when they are the result of their having been compelled to fight. And more often than not they have been compelled. For most nations rely upon conscription to supply their war machines—almost universally, once a war is underway, and often in peacetime as well. And conscription represents one of the severest infringements of individual liberty the state has devised. To be forced to yield up one's very person to a government, to be told what to do, what to wear, what to eat, and when to come and go is servitude. And to be compelled to do these things is involuntary servitude—about as clear a case, short of slavery, as there is. But, it is not merely the servitude that is significant; it is the use to which conscripts are put. For among the things they are told to do is when to kill other human beings, whether or not they approve of, or even understand, the policies by which they are so ordered and whether or not they have had any say in the determination of those policies (or the choice of those who determine them). Even convicted felons are not made to engage in compulsory killing. Yet the civilized nations of the world demand it of their sons.

The young are impressionable and frequently malleable. For this reason a disproportionate share of the burden of war falls upon them. In the American experience alone, tens of thousands of fifteen- and sixteen-year-olds fought in the Civil War, and the average age of the U.S. combat soldier in Vietnam was nineteen. Many of the Vietnamese fighting with the Vietcong were even younger. And in more recent wars children in their early teens, and sometimes younger, have fought in Afghanistan on the side of the mujahideen, in Nicaragua on the side of the contras, and in the Middle East on the side of Iran. Both boys and girls—between two and three thousand of them—fought in the Ugandan civil war. The Peace Union in Finland estimated in 1983 that children were serving in the military in at least twenty nations.[36]

[36] For further data and a good discussion of the issue of children and warfare,

Many of these are more or less volunteers, often with irregular armies or guerrilla forces. But whether their participation is compelled or not, the psychological effects upon them, as they learn at an early age that the way to resolve conflicts is through killing, must be reckoned among the imperceptible consequences of war, a continuing invisible tax upon societies that exploit their young in these ways.

This does not mean that military training is all bad, by any means. Some youths, and many adults as well, respond to the structure and discipline it provides. Others find that having basic decisions made for them postpones the time when they must assume full responsibility for their lives, something for which they may be unready at the time. And still others, particularly among the poor and disadvantaged, find military life preferable to unemployment. But the fact remains that its primary function is to train them to kill (or to support those who do). And this requires overcoming their natural revulsion to killing and suspending in their minds the connection between some of the highest principles society tries to instill in them, such as respect for persons and the value of human life, and what they are asked to do for the state. They must learn to compartmentalize their moral concerns, to exclude whole populations from the constraints against killing. They must become divided persons.

The techniques for effecting this have been refined, and the armies of the world specialize in them. As a study by the American Friends Service Committee characterized it, "Depreciation of self-esteem, reduction to a state of relatively helpless suggestibility, and then rescue by identification with military superiors, and reliance on early training in the acceptance of arbitrary authority are all parts of a carefully engineered process in basic military training."[37] And these techniques are remarkably effective. Young males the world over—in whom readiness to use violence is easily associated with masculinity—become trained killers by the hundreds of thousands when told to by their governments. And there is not that much difference among them. J. Bronowski reflected upon this in connection with Mussolini's blackshirts and Hilter's storm troopers during World War II. "I did not know the young

---

see Sara Terry, "When Children See Life through a Gun Barrel," *The Christian Science Monitor*, July 7, 1987, part of a series on the exploitation of children entitled "Children in Darkness: The Exploitation of Innocence."

[37] *The Draft?* A Report Prepared for the Peace Education Division of the American Friends Service Committee (New York: Hill and Wang, 1968), p. 13.

men in Italy" he writes, "but I knew them in Germany; I was at school with them there. Nothing in my mind to this day marks them off from the young men with whom I was at school in the same years in England. . . . If you want to recruit for an army of destruction, the material is there, in every classroom."[38]

It was precisely this transformation of human beings into instruments of violence that Simone Weil saw as the deeper function of war itself. In her penetrating study, *The Iliad: A Poem of Force*, she wrote:

> . . . [T]he conquering soldier is like a scourge of nature. Possessed by war, he, like the slave, becomes a thing. . . . Such is the nature of force. Its power of converting a man into a thing is a double one, and in its application double-edged. To the same degree, though in different fashions, those who use it and those who endure it are turned to stone. . . . battles are fought and decided by men . . . who have undergone a transformation, who have dropped either to the level of inert matter, which is pure passivity, or to the level of blind force, which is pure momentum. Herein lies the secret of war, a secret revealed by the *Iliad* in its similes, which liken the warriors either to fire, flood, wind, wild beasts, or God knows what blind causes of disaster, or else to frightened animals, trees, water, sand, to anything in nature that is set into motion by the violence of external forces. . . . The art of war is simply the art of producing such transformations, and its equipment, its processes, even the casualties it inflicts on the enemy, are only means directed toward this end—its true object is the warrior's soul.[39]

Effective armies require virtually unquestioning obedience. And that is secured at the cost of turning rational persons into instruments of violence for use by others. Often it is at the cost of turning young people into instruments of violence for the use of adults. They become, as Weil points out, like things, or forces of nature, precisely the opposite of what is required for considerate and humane social life in community with others. That as many of them as do are able to readjust to civilian life without lasting emotional scars attests to the resilience of human beings, as well as to

[38] J. Bronowski, *The Face of Violence* (New York: The World Publishing Company, 1968), pp. 47-48.

[39] Simone Weil, *The Iliad, or The Poem of Force*, trans. Mary McCarthy (Wallingford, Pa.: Pendle Hill, 1956), pp. 25-26.

the effort of governments to mask the reality of what war is all about. Medals, parades, honors, and speeches are all part of the process. They glorify the enterprise of war and help to focus attention upon patriotism and the willingness to sacrifice for others and away from the true nature of what they are asked to do in fighting, which is to kill and be killed by others who have been transformed by a similar process by their societies.

All of these considerations, I suggest, from those pertaining to the nature of morality, to those showing morality's link with the very concept of violence, establish that, however many other perspectives there may be from which it can be viewed, and for whatever purposes it may be so viewed, war cannot be fully assessed apart from the point of view of morality. And people cannot presume to have given it any but the flimsiest of justifications if they fail to examine it in a moral light. This does not of itself indicate one way or the other what the moral assessment of war should be. Just war theorists who believe that war is sometimes morally permissible can accept this conclusion as readily as pacifists. It means only that one must be prepared to examine war seriously from a moral standpoint if one proposes to engage in it.

For all of this, there are nonetheless those who would challenge this conclusion. They are prepared to accord morality full respect in their personal lives, in the sense of being basically fair, trustworthy, truthful, and nonviolent in their relations to others, but they condone lying, deception, violence, and destruction in international relations, particularly in warfare. They contend that at the international level morality is either irrelevant or at most of limited relevance. Here, they say, duplicity and violence are the norm and one has no choice but to play by the rules. Appeals to morality, on this view, should therefore be foregone in the interests of clear thinking, objectivity, and effective action—qualities precluded by what they allege to be the emotionalism and subjectivism of morality. Such is the counsel of political realism. It is to the examination of this outlook as it has been found in twentieth-century American thought that I want to turn next.

T W O

POLITICAL REALISM: THE CHALLENGE TO MORALITY IN INTERNATIONAL AFFAIRS

> What the devil do you mean, morality?—word of honor?
> Sure, you can talk about word of honor when you promise
> to deliver goods in business.—But when it is the question
> of the *interests of the nation*!? . . . Then morality stops!
> —Herman Goering

> There are only actions by individuals acting as agents for
> the state, for which they are fully responsible; they there-
> fore cannot excuse what they have done by claiming that
> reasons of state made it essential; the state can provide no
> cover for the actions of an individual.
> —Helmuth von Moltke*

Political realism has a certain initial appeal. If, as one analyst
writes, *Realpolitik* is "the only creed appropriate to the conduct of
foreign relations," then power politics "is the only game in town.
The only choice open to the United States is between playing it
effectively or ineffectively."[1] Playing it effectively calls up images

* Goering is quoted by prison psychologist G. M. Gilbert from an interview during his imprisonment and trial at Nuremberg. See *Nuremberg Diary* (New York: The
New American Library, 1947), p. 339. Helmuth von Moltke was a leader of the
German Kreisau Circle that opposed Hitler. He was executed by the Nazis near the
end of the war. The quotation comes from documents published by Ger van Roon
in *German Resistance to Hitler: Count von Moltke and the Kreisau Circle* (New York: Van
Nostrand Reinhold Company, 1971), p. 316.

[1] Colin Gray, "Foreign Policy—There Is No Choice," *Foreign Policy* 24 (Fall 1976):
120. In a similar though less approving vein, Stanley Hoffmann writes that "[t]he
drama of international politics is that there is, as of now, no generally accepted
alternative to Machiavellian statecraft." See *Duties Beyond Borders* (Syracuse: Syracuse University Press, 1981), p. 24. Kenneth W. Thompson represents the Nixon-
Kissinger foreign policy as one of *Realpolitik* in *Morality and Foreign Policy* (Baton
Rouge: Louisiana State University Press, 1980), p. 26. For discussions of the domi-
nance of political realism in American foreign policy, see Robert L. Rothstein, "On
the Costs of Political Realism," *American Political Science Quarterly* 77, no. 3 (Sept.

of decisive, no-nonsense men making hard decisions in the "real world"—men of the sort, we like to think, who won the West and made America great. And it is men like this, the thinking goes, who know how to deal with America's enemies. Unburdened by sentimentality, they know how to wield power, and power, they say, is the only language the Communists understand. They desire peace as much as anyone else, we are assured. But it is the peace that derives from strength, from commanding respect in the world's corridors of power. Morality, according to this view, has reserved for it the "unobtrusive, almost feminine, function of the gentle civilizer of national self-interest."[2]

Though not always held in quite so naive a form as this, political realism has been the most influential outlook on international affairs in twentieth-century American thought, with adherents among leading theologians, historians, diplomats, strategists, and political scientists. These include Reinhold Niebuhr, George Kennan, Hans Morgenthau, Robert Osgood, Arthur Schlesinger, Jr., and Henry Kissinger.[3] Moreover, as I shall point out, much of American foreign policy during the post-World War II period has conformed to realist prescriptions. But if this approach is correct, it vitiates the whole enterprise of trying to give a moral evaluation of war. If there is something wrongheaded about making moral judgments about the conduct of nations, then *a fortiori* there is something wrongheaded about trying to assess the conduct of states in going to war.

1972): 347-362, and Louis Rene Beres, *Reason and Realpolitik: U.S. Foreign Policy and World Order* (Lexington, Mass.: Lexington Books, 1984). George Kennan's views on this matter can be found principally in his *American Diplomacy, 1900-1950* (Chicago: University of Chicago Press, 1951), and "Morality and Foreign Policy," *Foreign Affairs* 64, no. 3 (Winter 1985/86): 205-218. For a philosophical critique of the realist approach, see Marshall Cohen, "Moral Skepticism and International Relations," in *International Ethics*, ed. C. Beitz et al. (Princeton, N.J.: Princeton University Press, 1985), pp. 3-50.

[2] George Kennan, *American Diplomacy*, p. 54. The association of morality with feminine weakness and "realism" with masculine virility runs through much of the writing on international relations, as though there were tacit agreement with Heinrich von Treitschke that "[t]he features of history are virile, unsuited to sentimental or feminine natures." See Hans Kohn, ed., *Politics* (New York: Harcourt, Brace and World, 1963), p. 13. For a good study of this phenomenon, particularly in literature, see Lucy Komisar's "Violence and the Masculine Mystique," *Washington Monthly* 2, no. 5 (July 1970).

[3] While not usually identified with political realism, Schlesinger defends what is in effect a realist position in his "The Necessary Amorality of Foreign Affairs," *Harper's Magazine*, August 1971, and "National Interests and Moral Absolutes," in *Ethics and World Politics: Four Perspectives*, ed. Ernest W. Lefever (Baltimore: The Johns Hopkins University Press, 1972), pp. 21-42.

I

The source of the philosophical problem is not hard to locate. When one compares the conduct of states with that of individuals, the discrepancy between the two stands out. Virtually everything deemed reprehensible in conduct among individuals is widely practiced among states. It was this that led Woodrow Wilson to proclaim hopefully in 1917 that "[w]e are at the beginning of an age in which it will be insisted that the same standards of conduct and responsibility for wrong done shall be observed among nations and their governments that are observed among the individual citizens of civilized states."[4]

Few share such optimism today. But to take morality seriously one must either reject the accepted standards of conduct among nations—with all that implies for the conduct of foreign affairs and the waging of war—or show that they are justifiable. Most have tried to show that they are justifiable.[5] But if they cannot be justified by the standards holding among individuals, then one must either recognize two moralities—one applying to the conduct of individuals, the other to that of states—or try to detach morality altogether from the conduct of states.

Only the second alternative strictly represents political realism. But both are closely bound up with political realist analyses, and both have roots in antiquity.

When Thucydides depicts the Athenians' address to the Lacedaemonian assembly before the Peloponnesian War, he captures an important strand in this thinking. Responding to accusations of imperialism, the Athenians contend that the weak have always been subject to the strong. "Besides," they add, "we believed ourselves to be worthy of our position, and so you thought us till now, when calculations of interest have made you take up the cry of justice—a consideration which no one ever yet brought forward to hinder his ambition when he had a chance of gaining anything by might."[6]

The thought here is that appeals to justice—and by extension, we may suppose, to morality in general—are simply embroidery to the claims of self-interest. Morality and self-interest are as-

---

[4] *The Messages and Papers of Woodrow Wilson* (New York: The Review of Reviews Corporation, 1924), 1: 378.

[5] Machiavelli is often thought to be an exception, but he can be read as maintaining that state policy has a justification by norms other than those bound up in the morality that holds among individuals.

[6] *The History of the Peloponnesian War*, trans. Richard Crawley, rev. R. C. Feetham (Avon, Conn.: The Cardavon Press, 1974), 1: 41.

sumed to be distinct, with the one subservient to the other. When pushed to its limit this way of thinking not only relegates morality to a subsidiary position in international affairs; it eliminates it altogether. As Hobbes later argued, sovereign states have no authority above them, and morality requires such authority. Therefore morality cannot exist at the international level. Nations exist in a state of nature where self-preservation alone is the rule.

There is another closely related line of thought, however, with which this one is sometimes confused. Though suggested by the passage from Thucydides, it receives its clearest classical expression in the person of Callicles in Plato's dialogue the *Gorgias*.

Callicles, like the Athenians, says there that the weak are subject to the strong. But he extends this claim to the whole of nature, the animal kingdom as well as societies. He then makes explicit what is only implicit in the Athenians' speech, which is that this is the way things *ought* to be. It is "natural justice" that the strong rule over the weak. He thus elevates the alleged fact to which the Athenians appeal to the status of a principle of morality.[7] The weak, however, have their own devices, according to Callicles. They create laws and conventions as a means of holding down the strong.[8] They foster the idea that equality should be prized and that it is worse to do evil than to suffer it. Since the weak are in the majority, this has a levelling effect; those who would by nature prevail through superior strength and intelligence become caught up in the net of social values and customs. Being themselves taught from childhood that one should not do evil or seek advantage over others, their natural self-assertiveness is undermined. A distinction thus emerges between what is right by "convention"—that is, according to the norms created by society—and what is right by "nature." A doctrine of two moralities comes into being.[9]

There are, then, two parts to Callicles' position. The first, embodied in the principle that the strong should dominate the weak, implies that might makes right and lays the foundation for *Macht-*

[7] In so doing he makes the first commission of the naturalistic fallacy in Western thought—the inference from the fact that things are a certain way in nature to the conclusion that that is the way they ought to be.

[8] It is this part of Callicles' position that is taken up by Nietzsche in his account of slave morality, except that with the benefit of historical perspective, Nietzsche adds to Callicles' list such virtues as sympathy, compassion, obedience, and self-sacrifice—virtues of historically oppressed peoples like Christians and Jews.

[9] It is possible to read Callicles as arguing not so much for the recognition of two moralities as for the transcendence of morality to something beyond it. In that case the label "natural justice" which he attaches to his basic principle would not actually designate a moral principle, though it would still be normative.

politik.[10] If strength consists of physical power, and it is the strong who should prevail, then the way to be in the right is to acquire power and exercise it over others. This is assumed by Plato's Thrasymachus and comes down to us through Social Darwinism to Hitler and twentieth-century fascism.[11] The second, the distinction between conventional and natural morality, becomes transmuted in subsequent thought into two closely related distinctions that also are easily confused with one another. These are between public and pirvate morality, on the one hand, and individual and collective morality, on the other.

Private morality supposedly governs the conduct of individuals in their personal relations with one another, public morality their conduct in government, business, or public life. Predictably, the two seem often to conflict. Machiavelli noted this when he observed that the prince "cannot possibly exercise all those virtues for which men are called 'good.' To preserve the state, he often has to do things against his word, against charity, against humanity, against religion."[12] Although Machiavelli is often thought to be condoning immorality here, a more charitable reading is that he thinks the prince should simply transcend private morality—comprising the virtues of charity, humanity, and so on that, in defining what is "considered" good, are a form of conventional morality in Callicles' sense—in favor of public morality. Because the standards of private conduct are inadequate to the responsibilities of a leader, one must be guided by other norms, even if that sometimes means performing acts which violate the tenets of private morality.[13]

[10] Callicles' principle of natural justice implies that might makes right if one understands the strong to be those who in fact dominate by nature. It does not necessarily do so otherwise.

[11] As the German General F. von Bernhardi wrote shortly before World War I: "Might is at once the supreme right, and the dispute as to what is right is decided by the arbitrament of war. War gives a biologically just decision, since its decision rests on the very nature of things." See *Germany and the Next War*, trans. Allen H. Powles (New York: Longmans, Green, & Company, 1914), p. 23.

[12] Robert M. Adams, ed. and trans., *The Prince* (New York: W.W. Norton & Company, Inc., 1977), pp. 50-51.

[13] Although in Machiavelli the public morality of the prince is governed by principles very much like Callicles' natural justice, subsequent writers do not all regard public morality in that way. Though they would not subscribe to the doctrine that might makes right, they nonetheless feel that when one serves in public office, or in positions of leadership in the military or the business world, the special relationships in which he stands to others not only permit but sometimes require different conduct from what one would engage in were one acting solely within the scope of private morality. See, for example, Stuart Hampshire, ed., *Public and Private Morality* (Cambridge: At the University Press, 1978), and R. M. Hare, "Reason of

When one ceases to think of morality as governing only the conduct of individuals, the second distinction becomes relevant. For it speaks of individual morality in connection with the conduct of individuals—whether in the form of public or private morality—and of collective morality in connection with the conduct of groups.[14] The conduct of groups is thought to be sufficiently distinctive as to warrant postulating a unique set of norms for its guidance. Thus Heinrich von Treitschke, a nineteenth-century German historian, says that "the State is not to be judged by the standards which apply to individuals, but by those which are set for it by its own nature and ultimate aims."[15] He regarded this "nature" as moral and therefore as providing the framework for a higher morality.

What Machiavelli achieves by giving priority to the public morality of the prince over the private morality of the individual, Treitschke achieves by giving priority to the collective morality of the state over the conduct of individuals. Both give license to the violation of private morality, since both agree that the conduct of states should be judged by different standards than the conduct of individuals.

This Machiavellian thesis, as we may call it—that states should be governed by different standards than individuals—is subscribed to by contemporary political realists. Indeed, it is the denial of this thesis by Woodrow Wilson that provides the point of departure for many contemporary analyses. But unlike Treitschke, and in a grudging concession to Wilsonianism, many realists view the collective morality of states as inferior to the individual morality of persons. The very title of Reinhold Niebuhr's influential book, *Moral Man and Immoral Society*, reflects this. But for various reasons they nonetheless believe that it is unrealistic to try to govern foreign affairs by individual morality.

II

These different strands of thought are woven throughout the analyses of realists and are part of the total fabric of contemporary po-

---

State," in *Applications of Moral Philosophy* (Berkeley and Los Angeles: University of California Press, 1972).

[14] If the conduct of collectivities ultimately reduces to the conduct of individuals, particularly those in positions of leadership, then, of course, the distinction between individual and collective morality collapses back into the distinction between private and public morality. For then what passes for collective morality is simply the public morality of selected individuals.

[15] In Kohn, ed., *Politics*, p. 55.

litical realism. Often, however, the term "political realism" is used simply as a commendatory label, to stand for whatever is effective, clearheaded, and rational in foreign policy thinking—a sense in which no one in his right mind would admit to being anything but a realist.[16] Used in this way the term simply provides a means of trying to elicit favorable attitudes towards policies of which one approves and to foster negative attitudes towards those of which one disapproves. Policies of which one disapproves are called un-realistic or, worse yet, idealistic. The term "idealism" is then re-served for well-intentioned but impractical or fainthearted ap-proaches to world problems—a sense in which no one in his right mind would admit to being an idealist. With one position thus having been defined in such a way as to have no willing defend-ers, the issue between idealism and realism becomes a pseudo-issue—useful perhaps for polemical purposes but performing no service in illuminating the place of morality in international affairs.

It is possible, however, to define these terms in a way that both accords with much of the theoretical work in foreign policy and highlights the underlying substantive issues.

What I shall call positivistic realism holds that morality has no application whatever to international relations. On this view one cannot intelligibly judge, for example, that a nation acted rightly or wrongly in going to war against another nation, anymore than one can judge that nature acted rightly or wrongly in afflicting a people with a hurricane or earthquake. Moral concepts like "right" or "wrong" are simply inapplicable to such phenomena. In each case, as I pointed out in the Introduction, one can judge that what happened was good or bad—value terms are applicable to per-

---

[16] Speaking here of its use by advocates. Thus Robert E. Osgood, in his *Ideals and Self-Interest in America's Foreign Relations* (Chicago: University of Chicago Press, 1953), says that "realism—with a small 'r'—is used in this book to refer to an ac-curate assessment of the ends and motives that determine the conduct of nations; it implies a disposition to perceive and act upon the real conditions under which a nation may achieve its ends in international society" (p. 10). See also J. W. Burton, *International Relations: A General Theory* (Cambridge: At the University Press, 1965), p. 245. Critics, on the other hand, characterize it in equally uncomplimentary terms. Marxists, for example, represent it as functioning "to conceal by more subtle means than hitherto had been the case the threat to peace constituted by imperial-ism" and as "an apology for the use of violence as a means of halting socio-histor-ical progress." See the study by Soviet philosophers, *Problems of War and Peace: A Critical Analysis of Bourgeois Theories*, trans. Bryan Beau (Moscow: Progress Publish-ers, 1972), pp. 191, 198. For a good discussion of realism in connection with the nuclear arms race, see Conrad G. Brunk, "Realism, Deterrence, and the Nuclear Arms Race," in *Nuclear War: Philosophical Perspectives*, ed. M. Fox and L. Groarke (New York: Peter Lang, 1985), pp. 223-239.

sons, objects, or phenomena of nature. But prescriptive terms like "right" and "wrong," which are at the heart of moral assessment, apply only to conduct, and in the view of the positivist they apply only to the conduct of individual persons.[17]

Normative realism, on the other hand, allows that one can intelligibly make moral judgments about international affairs but contends that one ought not to do so in conducting foreign policy. In its stronger form it denies that such notions should ever be appealed to in international relations. It allows that one can make sense of saying that this or that nation acted rightly or wrongly in the performance of a certain action but says we should refrain from making such judgments. In its weaker form, on the other hand, it concedes that morality is applicable to foreign affairs and should have some weight in decision making but denies that moral considerations should be decisive in the determination of policy. Where Machiavelli says that the prince should exhibit virtue when he can (and in any event should always give the appearance of being virtuous), the soft realist of this sort says that states should honor morality when they can. But both believe that when it is expedient to do so, morality should be abandoned.

By contrast, idealism can be defined simply as the view that states ought always to act morally. Now although political realism per se says nothing one way or the other about the nature of the state or about other normative principles that may be associated with it, it is typically bound up with one or the other of two further doctrines, reason of state and national egoism.

It has frequently been argued that the state is necessary for the promotion and maintenance of values, or at least the highest values. Plato held this, as did Augustine, at least so far as earthly goods are concerned; and it has been held by such a mixed group as Treitschke, Hegel, John Jay, and Mussolini. The twentieth-century British philosopher G. E. Moore expressly defends the companion thesis that society (as distinct from the state) is a precondition of the highest goods. It is, in any event, an easy step from this to conclude that the survival of the state comes before all else and that any means to that end are justified. This is the doctrine of reason of state, which finds ready support in the view that public morality should override private morality, since public morality

---

[17] This does not mean, we should note, that the positivist says that such events as wars are morally justified. To say that would imply that moral notions do apply to the conduct of states. He contends, rather, that wars are neither justified nor unjustified. The notion of moral justification is simply irrelevant.

may be thought to require that leaders put the survival of the state above all else. Whatever they might prefer to do in their private lives, national leaders are obligated to preserve the state. A rationale is thus provided not only for those who are willing to sacrifice themselves for the good of the state but also for those who are willing to sacrifice others as well.

One hears little about reason of state anymore. What one hears about is national interest, which, as usually conceived, encompasses national survival but much else besides. It prescribes the whole array of policies deemed essential to the state's prosperity, prestige, and honor in the world. In this sense national egoism—the doctrine that national self-interest should govern the conduct of the state—is a stronger thesis than reason of state. But both entail political realism. If the interest or survival of the state (and I shall use nation and state interchangeably unless otherwise indicated) is put above all else, and if any measures are deemed justified in promoting it, then one is committed to displacing morality either partially or wholly in the conduct of foreign affairs. Even if the interest of the state should always miraculously coincide with what is morally right, the coincidence would merely be a happy one, and it would still, on this view, be national interest that is the governing norm.

There are many forms that political realism may take, however, and it is important to distinguish them. It is said, for example, that nations in fact always act from self-interest. Even some who concede that states ought to do otherwise think that it is pointless to make such judgments in light of this fact.[18] Sometimes, however, this descriptive claim has underlying it the stronger thesis that nations necessarily act from self-interest. One might think, for example, that the very concept of a nation—or, as Hobbes and Clausewitz thought, the idea of a system of international relations—necessitates that states act self-interestedly. Or one might advance theological or metaphysical claims about the nature of man and the human condition, as Niebuhr does and Augustine did before him, that make it virtually impossible for nations to rise above egoistic considerations. Still further, one might try to show that acting upon moral considerations has worse consequences than does acting from self-interest—a line taken by Kennan and

[18] To be plausible this claim must be interpreted to mean that nations always do what they think is in their interest, since it is manifestly false that nations always do what is in fact in their interest. They frequently bring ruin and destruction upon themselves.

Schlesinger and that requires the defense of an array of historical, philosophical, and valuational judgments.

At still other times, however, one finds the different claim that, while nations do not always act from self-interest, they *ought* to do so. This normative thesis rejects both the descriptive and necessitarian theses. But it supports political realism in one or the other of its forms, so long as morality and self-interest do not necessarily coincide and the judgment that nations ought to act from self-interest is not itself a moral judgment.

Now normative realism has been the predominant form political realism has taken in American thought in the twentieth century. There are two strands to it, one primarily theoretical, the other historical. Although the two are often interwoven, it is important to distinguish them. I shall discuss primarily the historical version and comment on only one version of the theoretical approach, namely, the Niebuhrian view that appeals to the theological conception of the nature of man. We shall then look at some of the more recent forms realist thinking has taken.

III

The historical approach focuses upon America's foreign policy during the first half of the twentieth century and alleges that that policy bore near-disastrous fruits between the two world wars.[19]

The problem according to this view has its roots in America's history of isolationism and reached a critical point in America's flirtation with global imperialism during the Spanish-American War. After seizing the Philippines, the United States discovered a distaste for this departure from its traditional stance and backed off from the beckoning role of world power. The belief that America would truly be a world power if only it would act like one has been the lament of realists ever since.

Whereas the older European nations were perceived as war-prone, corrupt, and committed to an immoral balance of power system of international politics, America thought of herself as principled and righteous, according to this view. Equally as important, she thought of herself as secure. The young Lincoln had proclaimed that "all the armies of Europe, Asia, and Africa com-

[19] Robert E. Osgood gives the most sustained analysis of this line of argument, and I shall rely heavily upon his account in what follows. I shall, however, attempt to capture the spirit of this general approach rather than to represent in full the views of any one of its advocates.

bined . . . could not by force take a drink from the Ohio or make a track on the Blue Ridge in a trial of a thousand years."[20] If this was youthful hyperbole, it nonetheless reflected a deeply rooted sense of geographical security. Seeing no reason from such a vantage point why it should become entangled in the petty quarrels of others, America elected to stand alone in majestic isolation— proud, strong, and convinced of her invulnerability.

If Lincoln epitomized the complacency in this outlook, it was Woodrow Wilson who brought its idealistic strain to its highest pitch. It was his conviction that it had fallen to America to play a unique moral role in the community of nations, that of conciliator and peacemaker. Such a role, he believed, could only be performed by a nation that stood apart from the travails of conflict. This conviction and the sense of moral superiority it reflected provided the stuff of America's resolve to stay out of war, a resolve that was soon swept away by the turbulent waters of World War I. But the foundation upon which it was based remained intact, and when America did go to war it did so for reasons every bit as elevated and in keeping with this conception of its high calling in the world as those that previously had dictated neutrality. It went to war—as we have been cynically reminded every since—to save democracy and to end all wars.

How did this moralism allegedly fail, and how was it supposedly responsible for the disastrous drift of U.S. policy between the wars?

The realist's answer is that it distorted our perspective on our proper role in the world and impeded recognition that national interest is at the heart of foreign policy. In Robert Osgood's words:

> If Woodrow Wilson erred, it was not because he led the U.S. into war but because he failed to do everything in his power to prepare the people to see their entrance into a foreign war as an act consistent with imperative principles of national self-interest, as well as with national ideals and sentiments. In fact, by stressing America's disinterestedness as a condition of her mission of bringing peace to the world, Wilson actually directed all the force of his leadership toward concealing what should have been the most compelling reason for American intervention.[21]

[20] Quoted from "Abraham Lincoln on the Challenge of Violence," in *American Violence*, ed. Richard Maxwell Brown (Englewood Cliffs, N.J.: Prentice-Hall, 1970), p. 8.

[21] *Ideals and Self-Interest*, p. 262. He also says that Americans were not wrong in their idealism but rather that they "failed from the first to guide and restrain their

The "compelling reason" for U.S. intervention was national self-interest and the recognition that our security, perhaps even survival, depends upon what takes place outside our own hemisphere. National interest sometimes requires going to war in the absence of direct threats to security. In the modern world, by the time a threat becomes overt one's security may already have been undermined. For that reason one must be prepared to take preventive action even where that means becoming involved in a foreign war. Wilson's mistake, on this view, was not to have led us into a foreign war. It was to have placed too much confidence in the power of "moral suasion" to deter evil in the world, too much confidence in the effectiveness of international organizations patterned after domestic legal models to preserve peace. It neglected the fundamental role of power in the world.[22] In short, we fought the right war under Wilson but for the wrong reasons.

According to realists, Wilsonianism also affected adversely the prosecution of the war and the postwar evolution of American policy.

George Kennan, for example, argues that the war threatened the European balance of power upon which both American and European security depended and for that reason needed to be ended quickly without thought of total victory.[23] But it was precisely, he

---

aspirations and sentiments with a realistic view of national conduct and a prudent recognition for the practical consequences of specific policies" (ibid.). This suggests that from a theoretical standpoint it was peripheral matters that were at fault and not idealism itself. This interpretation, however, conflicts with the main emphasis of his argument, which is that "as long as men owe their supreme loyalty to nation-states, nations ought to act upon idealistic ends only in so far as they are compatible with the most fundamental ends of national self-interest" (p. 21); and it is the latter that I shall stress. Notice, in any event, that the sentiments of the American people have pretty consistently been opposed to war. It is usually only after their leadership has involved them in war that they have—if then—come to support it wholeheartedly. Realists give insufficient attention to the fact that the attitude with which they would have us go to war—namely, a cool, dispassionate willingness to kill for limited objectives—is one that Americans have refused to adopt. Even the military have sometimes been reluctant to accept it. They find it incomprehensible that anyone should wage war without doing so to win. If one is concerned about the "realities" of international affairs, this suggests that the hope of gaining widespread acceptance of a political realist outlook may be unrealistic.

[22] America had long been interventionist within its own hemisphere. Realists tend to ignore the extent to which Wilson was "realistic" in much of his foreign policy, as in the invasion of Haiti and the Dominican Republic.

[23] Wilson did, of course, disagree with this assessment. He said before the Senate on January 22, 1917: "If [the present war] be only a struggle for a new balance of power, who will guarantee, who can guarantee the stable equilibrium of the new arrangement? Only a tranquil Europe can be a stable Europe. There must be, not a balance of power, but a community of power; not organized rivalries, but an organized common peace" (The Messages and Papers of Woodrow Wilson, 1: 351). Here he put his finger upon what has been and is the key problem with balance of power

says, because considerations of power balance argued against total victory that people "rejected them so emphatically and sought more sweeping and grandiose objectives, for the accomplishment of which total victory could plausibly be represented as absolutely essential." When the cause is great and the enemy is perceived as the incarnation of evil, to settle for anything less than unconditional surrender is to compromise with the devil. Thus "a line of thought grew up, under Wilson's leadership, which provided both rationale and objective for our part in fighting the war to a bitter end."[24] Such righteous intransigence, it was thought, prolonged the war to the point where the European balance of power was destroyed and the seeds of World War II were sown.

The critique sketched here is at the heart of those realist analyses which allege that trying to act morally in international relations has bad consequences. It can be seen to be a blend of historical interpretation and normative judgments. Interestingly, it rejects morality on normative grounds.[25]

A crucial question, of course, is whether America's interest, much less her survival, was at stake in World War I. If it was not, then to have persuaded the American public that it was would have been deception. Beyond that, and beyond the question of the accuracy of the representation of Wilsonianism in this account, are the questions of whether Wilsonian idealism in fact had the consequences alleged—that is, whether it led to World War II—and whether, if it did, that shows the inadequacy of morality in international relations. I shall argue later that it does not.

Supposedly contributing further to the longer-range conse-

---

theories, namely, that they presuppose what almost never exists on the international scene, at least for any extended time: a stable system of relations among nations. This conclusion has been persuasively argued by Partha Chatterjee in "The Classical Balance of Power Theory," *Journal of Peace Research* 1 (1972): 51-61.

[24] *American Diplomacy*, p. 67. Kennan does, however, clear Wilson of responsibility for actually holding this view prior to early 1917 (ibid., n. 6). Indeed, Wilson himself in that same Senate speech of 1917 (see n. 23) said prophetically that "[v]ictory would mean peace forced upon the loser, a victor's terms imposed upon the vanquished. It would be accepted in humiliation, under duress, at an intolerable sacrifice, and would leave a sting, a resentment, a bitter memory upon which terms of peace would rest, not permanently, but only as upon quicksand" (*The Messages and Papers of Woodrow Wilson*, 1: 352).

[25] It may, even more paradoxically, be interpreted as rejecting the appeal to morality on moral grounds, an interpretation that would lift the theory out of the realm of political realism altogether. The central claim, that is, may be that morality would be better served if nations ceased trying to guide their conduct by it directly and instead steered their course by the more visible beacons of national self-interest. The assumption is that ultimately national self-interest and morality coincide, a view we shall have occasion to consider later.

quences was postwar disillusionment. Since the lofty ideals in whose name the war was fought were unrealized, the resultant disappointment—nourished as it was by revisionist historical analyses redistributing responsibility for the war—led to an even greater withdrawal of America from world affairs. "Since war could only be justified by exalted goals," Osgood says, "and since this war had failed to achieve exalted goals, it seemed to follow that all war was useless."[26] America's consequent reluctance to become involved in another war allegedly emboldened Nazism and Japanese militarism at a time when greater firmness might have forestalled World War II.

Thus whether American foreign policy during the crucial decades of the twentieth century quite verged on the commission of national suicide, as Osgood maintains,[27] and whether the policies of Christian isolationists were tantamount to "connivance" with tyranny, as Niebuhr contends,[28] these policies were in the view of realists at best seriously wrong-headed, and the moral perspective from which they were believed to have sprung was itself looked upon as a cause of war.

IV

Supplementing and helping to explain accounts like the preceding is the more conspicuously theory-laden account of America's most eminent realist, Reinhold Niebuhr.[29] His analysis keys in upon the very nature of collectivities and the theological and metaphysical foundations of the historical processes at work in their formation.

Niebuhr contends that group relations inevitably express a collective egoism and hence "can never be as ethical as those which characterize individual relations."[30] Their very nature renders

[26] *Limited War: The Challenge to American Strategy* (Chicago: The University of Chicago Press, 1957), p. 99.

[27] *Ideals and Self-Interest*, p. 430.

[28] "To Prevent the Triumph of an Intolerable Tyranny," in *Love and Justice: Selections from the Shorter Writings of Reinhold Niebuhr*, ed. D. B. Robertson (Cleveland: World Publishing Company, 1967), p. 278.

[29] Acknowledging Niebuhr's influence upon American realists, George Kennan has called him "the father of us all." Quoted in Kenneth W. Thompson, *Political Realism and the Crisis of World Politics* (New York: John Wiley & Sons, 1965), p. 23. Niebuhr's analysis does not conform in all of its particulars to the preceding account of political realism. Nor do other realists subscribe to all of Niebuhr's account. But the Niebuhrian analysis sustains the essentials of the analyses of many other realists and yields a similar conclusion about the role of morality in international relations.

[30] *Moral Man and Immoral Society* (New York: Charles Scribner's Sons, 1932), p. 83.

them incapable of responding to moral considerations or of responding in more than a limited way.[31] This gives social and international relations their distinctive character, a fact that must be reckoned with by statesmen as well as by social reformers who encounter the same phenomenon in their dealings with society and intrasocietal groups. Because this phenomenon is built into the very nature of collectivities, it makes Niebuhr's position basically a form of necessitarianism.

The view that nations act without regard for moral considerations conflicts with analyses of realists like Kennan and Osgood, who maintain that the United States was motivated by moral considerations during the period under examination. It is one thing to say that nations do not or cannot act out of regard for moral considerations. It is another to say that they can and do but that doing so has bad consequences. Realists do not always distinguish these claims. Some base their case primarily upon the normative judgment, which conflicts with the explanatory hypothesis presently under consideration; others base it upon metaphysical considerations like Niebuhr's.

Assume for the present that nations do act without regard for moral principles and that individual persons often willingly subordinate their own personal interests to the service of the state. What accounts for this? Neibuhr gives two explanations.

The first lies in the theological-metaphysical orientation of neoorthodox Christianity, specifically in the "stubbornness of sin" in all men. This is an allegedly unalterable fact of the human condition whose ramifications are magnified at the international level. Failure to perceive this, Niebuhr says, is the chief error of those

---

One suspects that Niebuhr regards morality in international affairs in much the same light as he does Christian love, as an "impossible ideal" to be striven for but realistically understood to be unattainable. See his *An Interpretation of Christian Ethics* (New York: Meridian Books, 1956), passim.

[31] Although it sometimes sounds as though Niebuhr believes that nations cannot transcend self-interest at all, he more often speaks as though their ability to do so is simply more restricted than that of individual persons. It should be noted, however, that this claim conflicts with much of the analysis realists give of World War I (and in some cases, World War II and Vietnam as well). It is often contended that the United States *was* acting on moral grounds in those cases, but naively so and to its own detriment. One cannot have it both ways. If nations cannot rise above self-interest and respond to moral considerations, then whatever the proper analysis of America's foreign policy through the first half of the twentieth century, the problem with that policy cannot be that it was guided by morality. It cannot even be, as Niebuhr maintains, that the country was acting hypocritically—which implies that it could have acted morally but sought instead merely to give the appearance of doing so.

"modern moralists"[32] who assume that "with a little more time, a little more adequate moral and social pedagogy and a generally higher development of human intelligence, our social problems will approach solution"[33]—a view, he contends, that goes back to our culture's "romantic overestimate of human virtue and moral capacity."

In this way the problem is tied first to self-interest, then to sin, and finally to the whole traditional Christian outlook upon the world. Augustine convinced Christians that they could serve the state; Luther convinced them that what the state did was not the Christian's business; and Niebuhr would convince them that the evil states do when disconnected from the pacifistic orientation of Christianity must be accepted as part of the tragic nature of things.

When men have lost the fear of God, new life is injected into religion by shifting its focus from individuals to collectivities. The international scene then becomes, in Niebuhr's words, "a perfect picture of human finitude and a tragic revelation of the consequences of sinful dishonesty which accompany every effort to transcend it."[34] He says further:

> Moralists may find this trait of human nature, its grudging concessions, its unwillingness to repent except under chastisement, abhorrent, and they may dream of another kind of history than the actual history of man. But if they examined their own conduct scrupulously, they would find evidences in it of this same reluctance and would learn to appreciate the tragic elements in history as manifestations of divine judgment, without which men would remain in the stupor of sin.[35]

[32] Like John Dewey, whom he is fond of chiding. Dewey did, however, recognize a darker side to human nature, saying that "[t]he old Adam, the unregenerate element in human nature, persists. It shows itself wherever the method obtains of attaining results by use of force instead of by the method of communication and enlightenment. See *The Public and Its Problems* (Denver: Alan Swallow, 1927), p. 154. And Dewey, too, deplored naive optimism in social and international affairs. But he traced it to what he called our "traditional evangelical trust" in morals divorced from intelligence. See Joseph Ratner, ed., *Intelligence in the Modern World: John Dewey's Philosophy* (New York: The Modern Library, 1939), p. 497. For another challenge to optimism in social matters, see Stuart Hampshire, *Morality and Pessimism* (Cambridge: At the University Press, 1972).

[33] "Introduction" to *Moral Man and Immoral Society*, p. xiii. See also *The Nature and Destiny of Man* (New York: Charles Scribner's Sons, 1949), pp. 94-95, 99.

[34] *An Interpretation of Christian Ethics*, p. 119.

[35] "Chastisement unto Repentance or Death," in Robertson, ed., *Love and Justice*, p. 183.

George Kennan charged antiwar activists of the 1960s with much the same failure. He said they failed to perceive "a vitally important truth . . . namely, that the decisive seat of evil in this world is not in social and political institutions, and not even, as a rule, in the will or iniquities of statesmen, but simply in the weakness and imperfection of the human soul itself," by which he added that he meant literally every soul.[36] The upshot is a profound pessimism not only about human goodness but about the power of human resources, even when governed by the best of intentions, to redress the world's evils.[37]

The other explanation of "collective egoism" found in Niebuhr conflicts with the line of reasoning we have just been considering.

It holds that the evil of collectivities is incompatible with the supposition that individual men are good. "No school asks," he says in *The Children of Light and the Children of Darkness*, "how it is that an essentially good man could have produced corrupting and tyrannical political organizations or exploiting economic organizations, or fanatical and superstitious religious organizations;"[38] the intended point being, of course, that there is no answer to this question. But he himself had already answered it in *Moral Man and Immoral Society*, in which he wrote:

> There is an ethical paradox in patriotism which defies every but the most astute and sophisticated analysis. The paradox is that patriotism transmutes individual unselfishness into national egoism. Loyalty to the nation is a high form of altruism when compared with lesser loyalties and more parochial interests. It therefore becomes the vehicle of all the altruistic impulses and expresses itself, on occasion, with such fervor that the critical attitudes of the individual toward the nation and its enterprises is almost completely destroyed. The unqualified character of this devotion is the very basis of the nation's

[36] *Democracy and the Student Left* (New York: Bantam Books, 1968), pp. 8-9.

[37] There are also, it should be noted, secular versions of this approach. They seek to explain war and violence by appeal to innate aggression, will to power, or a territorial instinct. See, for example, Konrad Lorenz, *Human Aggression* (New York: Harcourt, Brace & World, Inc., 1963); Hans Morgenthau, *Politics among Nations* (New York: Knopf, 1966), chap. 8; and Robert Ardrey, *African Genesis: A Personal Investigation into the Animal Origins and Nature of Man* (New York: Delta Publishing Company, 1961), esp. chap. 6. Some of these have a more respectable ring than do sin and corruption to those who aspire to a political or naturalistic science of such matters. But the assessment of human affairs to which they lead is only slightly less gloomy than the one associated with the theological version.

[38] (New York: Charles Scribner's Sons, 1944), p. 17.

power and of the freedom to use the power without moral restraint. Thus the unselfishness of individuals makes for the selfishness of nations.[39]

Here it is the basically good, unselfish, self-sacrificing qualities of individual persons that are held to be the source of the immorality of groups,[40] not egoism or sinfulness. But if man has the traits presupposed in this account, one can no longer credibly maintain a doctrine of the inherent corruption of each and every soul, as presupposed by the preceding account. And though Niebuhr does not regard this as a serious problem, it brings the two accounts into conflict with one another. The very ground of the first account's pessimism is removed by one of the conditions of the paradox in the second account.

Much of what Niebuhr says in this second account rings true psychologically, and there is supporting testimony for it from other sources, including Tolstoy, Dewey, Durkheim, Lorenz, and Koestler.[41] Once such an identification with the larger collectivity is established and people become bonded to it through patriotism, they will sacrifice themselves by the thousands for that collectivity; and they will do so, if unwittingly, in the service of evil as readily as in the service of good. Indeed, this account is in keeping with the insight that the source of the world's greatest evils lies less in the works of evil men than in the works of basically good people whose efforts go awry through ignorance, misunderstanding, misplaced loyalties, and too much rather than too little willingness to sacrifice themselves for others, particularly at the behest of those who govern them.

[39] Page 91. See also *An Interpretation of Christian Ethics*, p. 107.

[40] Carried to one of its possible conclusions, this line of reasoning argues for the perpetuation of war precisely in order to foster these traits. See, for example, Benito Mussolini, "The Doctrine of Fascism," in *Social and Political Philosophy*, ed. J. Somerville and R. E. Santoni (Garden City, N.Y.: Doubleday & Company, 1963), pp. 424-441. Niebuhr is at times intrigued by other beneficial effects of war. Concerning World War II, for example, see his "Chastisement unto Repentance or Death," in Robertson, ed., *Love and Justice*, pp. 180-183.

[41] T. H. Green captured the same thought when he wrote that "the members of the nation in their corporate or associated action are animated by certain passions, arising out of their association, which, though not egoistic relatively to the individual subjects of them (for they are motives to self-sacrifice), may, in their influence on the dealings of one nation with another, have an effect analogous to that which egoistic passions, properly so called, have upon the dealings of individuals with each." *Lectures on the Principles of Political Obligation* (Ann Arbor: University of Michigan Press, 1967), p. 175.

V

What I shall call neorealism emerged as the full import of nuclear weapons was being realized in the mid-1950s. It was then that it was fully recognized that nuclear weapons are not just bigger bombs but rather mark a quantum leap in the evolution of warfare and for that reason call for a rethinking of military strategy.

Although neorealism does not break radically with the earlier realism, it takes a more tough-minded view of international relations. Morality recedes further into the background, the theological metaphysics is sloughed off, and talk of peace diminishes. As a greater frequency of violence is traded off for a supposedly reduced risk of nuclear war, the emphasis shifts from the attainment of peace to the limitation of violence. War comes to be seen as more or less inevitable, if not sometimes desirable. Power continues to be considered the dominant feature of international relations and national self-interest the controlling motive.

When the United States and the Soviet Union became fully fledged nuclear powers, they were likened to a scorpion and a tarantula in a bottle; it was thought that if ever they clashed they would destroy one another. But this was believed to create a special problem for the United States. On the assumption that we would not use nuclear weapons first,[42] and would in any event never use them for blackmail, we seemed to be vulnerable to the ruthless cunning of the Soviets. By manipulating events so as never to confront us with an issue so momentous as to warrant nuclear war, the Soviets could, it was thought, erode our security by repeatedly forcing us to make concessions or risk a needless conflagration. Our horror of nuclear war, as Kissinger argued in *Nuclear Weapons and Foreign Policy*, would paralyze our will. Whereas the fear had previously been that we would be annihilated in a nuclear war, it was now that we would die a death by a thousand concessions. The image of mushroom clouds gave way to that of falling dominoes.

The Berlin crises gave some credence to this theory. They were seen as posing precisely the dilemma of how to counter Soviet actions with regard to the Berlin corridor without risking nuclear war. What was needed, it was felt, was a middle course between doing nothing and igniting a holocaust. "The West," realist Ray-

---

[42] An assumption repudiated frequently by the U.S. government.

mond Aron lamented, "has failed to find a substitute for total war other than peace itself."[43]

The solution was to develop a limited war capability that would give us the flexibility to take the initiative rather than always responding to the Communists and, when responding, would enable us to do so with limited risk of nuclear war. The idea was not to do away with nuclear weapons, or even to stop multiplying them. It was to supplement them so as to be able to deal more effectively with situations for which they were militarily or politically ill-suited. In net effect this opened the door to a policy of interventionism in the hope, as expressed by Herman Kahn, that "the need for intervention may well be decreased if we have the capacity and resolve to do it."[44]

In this way a more dynamic policy was purchased at the cost of a greater willingness to go to war. But it was a willingness that disavowed the crusading, moralistic spirit of the so-called "idealists" and instead pursued limited, "rational" objectives. "To save humanity from thermonuclear war," Aron said again of the world's leaders, "they have saved war."[45]

This strategy bore fruit under the Kennedy administration. But the fruit it bore was the bitter one of Vietnam. Just as Vietnam was the testing ground for new weapons, it came eventually to be the testing ground of a new theory, the limited war doctrine. It also became the testing ground of some of the prescriptions of political realists.

Not that all thinking on international relations during this period fit this pattern. John Foster Dulles, that redoubtable architect of U.S. foreign policy during the middle years of the 1950s, was undeniably moralistic and often dogmatic. Whether this moralism was part of a broader point of view that in fact (and not merely in rhetoric) brought moral considerations to bear upon foreign policy, or was in actuality nothing more than a tougher-than-usual application of the same standards that world leaders normally apply, is unclear. What is clear is that Dulles was strongly motivated by his conception of what constituted the national interest, and even if there stood behind this the conviction that promoting America's national interest was the moral (and Christian and perhaps Presbyterian) thing to do, the practical import was not easily distinguishable from political realism.

[43] *On War* (New York: W.W. Norton & Company, Inc., 1968), p. 37.
[44] *On Thermonuclear War* (New York: The Free Press, 1969), p. 571.
[45] *On War*, p. viii.

In any event, neorealist thinking took shape as the preceding line of thinking fused with anticommunism. The result was a strongly ideological outlook, a view, as one analyst has put it, "championed by military men who felt that the United States had entered a revolutionary new age which rendered traditional diplomatic methods obsolete. . . . Massive mobilization of resources, weapons technology, and a 'battle for men's minds' were keys to the future of world politics."[46] Such realism was as dogmatic, inflexible, and uncompromising as ever the realists thought idealists to be; as much so, in fact, that there came to be a kind of yearning for a return to the good old balance of power approach, which has a greater aura of objectivity and coolheadedness about it.

Insofar as the balance of power approach embodies the implicit normative judgment that the governing principle in the conduct of foreign policy should be to try to maintain a balance of power— and insofar as it takes this to be the basic principle of foreign policy—it entails political realism. The balance of power theory per se has nothing to do with moral considerations. Unqualified adherence to it in fact proscribes such considerations. It calls up images of giant springs, pulleys, and balance wheels, with the only problem being to keep things in equilibrium. This is basically an engineering problem; just as in Keynesian economics, with its dominant metaphor of "fine tuning," the basic problem becomes a mechanical one. In each case, cold, objective calculation is the key, and morality is left aside.

One could reconcile balance of power with morality, of course, if one maintained that maintenance of a balance of power has the best consequences for the international world in general and that the production of such consequences is the dominant concern of morality. In that case the judgment that we should maintain a balance of power would not be a basic principle. It would merely be a secondary principle, requiring constant moral appraisal in light of its consequences. But this is not how its advocates regard it. They consider it as detached from ethics and as having an abstract, scientific quality about it. As Churchill put it, the balance of power "has nothing to do with rulers or nations" but is "a law of public policy . . . and not a mere expedient dictated by accidental circumstances, or likes and dislikes, or any other sentiment."[47]

---

[46] John Franklin Campbell, "What is to be Done?" *Foreign Affairs* 49, no. 1 (Oct. 1970): 84.

[47] Winston S. Churchill, *The Second World War*, vol. 1, *The Gathering Storm* (Boston: Houghton Mifflin Company, 1948), pp. 207-208.

The defects of the balance of power theory have sometimes been pointed up by realists themselves. Niebuhr argued that an "unorganized balance of power" is potential anarchy and cannot preserve peace. "The introduction of a single new factor in the precarious equilibrium," he said, "or the elaboration of a single new force of recalcitrance . . . may destroy the balance."[48] And Schlesinger, in discussing relations among the victors at the end of World War II and the rejection by the United States of a spheres of influence arrangement, observes that the balance of power "had always broken down in the past. It held out to each power the permanent temptation to try to alter the balance in its own favor, and it built this temptation into the international order."[49]

These views merely question the possibility of maintaining a power balance, however, and leave unchallenged—and indeed presuppose—its applicability to international relations. But balance of power theory requires not only that power can be balanced but also that all sides can know when it is balanced. It presupposes furthermore that knowing this will make a difference to their conduct. And all three points are questionable.

Assuming that we can make sense of the notion of a balance of power, the complexity of international affairs is such that it would be virtually impossible to know for certain when it had been achieved. For it would depend in large part on factors like morale, which are not quantifiable. Morale, in fact, as Tolstoy maintained, is a major factor in battles and in warfare generally. Though it is obviously less so in push-botton warfare, it was a major factor—perhaps the decisive one—in Vietnam, in which the morale of the militarily weaker Vietcong and North Vietnamese far outstripped that of the Americans. This helps to explain why American political and military estimates of the power balance—which were invariably and overwhelmingly in American favor when calculated in quantitative terms—were consistently mistaken. It also helps to explain why the almost pathologically optimistic predictions from U.S. officials over the years were so far out of touch with reality.

Even if one could be confident *that* there was a balance of power at any given time, and that all sides could know when it obtains (and this is essential, since a balance of power is of little consequence unless the right people know there is one), it is doubtful that it could guarantee peace. To assume that it could is to impute

---

[48] "Plans for World Reorganization," in Robertson, ed., *Love and Justice*, p. 210.

[49] Arthur M. Schlesinger, Jr., "Origins of the Cold War," *Foreign Affairs* 46 (Oct. 1967): 22-51.

to world leaders a degree of rationality for which history gives little warrant. The temptation of which Schlesinger writes so often grows out of a gambling instinct, a hope that enough daring or bluff will give one the advantage in an otherwise even situation.

That nations do not in any event consistently think of international relations in terms of the balance of power, or at any rate do not consistently believe in acting in terms of that model, is clear. No nation would bolster the armaments of a potential enemy simply to equalize power. What nations desire first and foremost is superiority. They favor a balance of power only when they lag behind or are barely keeping pace.

> Niebuhr sympathized more with the imperialists who, he said
> . . . actually have a more hopeful program than the "balance
> of power" realists. They know that a balance of power must
> be organized and that a dominant power must be the organizing center. They expect either America, or the Anglo-Saxon
> hegemony, or the four great powers, Russia, China, Britain,
> and America, to form the organizing center of the world community.[50]

To this he added, "I think they are right in this thesis and that there is no possibility of organizing the world at all that will not be exposed to the charge of imperialism by the idealists who do not take the problem of power seriously."

This view marks an evolution from earlier forms of realism in recognizing that even self-interest is inadequate to motivate America to realize itself fully in international affairs. Its advocates are refreshingly forthright in presenting their case. As George Liska, one of their more articulate spokesmen, puts it, we must "avoid the necessity for overstating an issue of international order as one of national security. The intellectual indolence and political opportunism underlying the habit of formulating all demanding policy in terms of vital interests affecting national security are self-defeating for any state with more than sporadic external involvement."[51] This conflicts with much of Niebuhr, as well as with the realist position argued by Kennan and Osgood, which keeps national interest at the heart of international relations.

While Liska disavows national interest as the proper goal for

---

[50] "Plans for World Reorganization," in Robertson, ed., *Love and Justice*, p. 210.
[51] George Liska, *War and Order: Reflections on Vietnam and History* (Baltimore: The Johns Hopkins University Press, 1968), pp. 56-57.

America, it is still a kind of national self-interest, broadly conceived, that operates in his own theory.

> National interest so broadly conceived as to coincide with the maintenance of order may be called "imperial interest." . . . Imperial interest is neither the sum of specific national interests nor of group interests. . . . The practical scope of the imperial interest will be in most situations determined by national capability or power rather than by imperatives of immediate national security.[52]

The aim of this conception is world order, but an imperial order that "rests on the fear or respect of lesser powers, secured and held by the judicious alternation of forcefulness, self-restraint, and munificence of the imperial state."[53]

This is the organizing element of which Neibuhr spoke in his characterization of imperial realism. Here there is no longer any condition that a nation can achieve in terms of domestic harmony and prosperity or national security which suffices to establish that its interest has been realized. Its "imperial" interest is expressed in self-assertiveness, and self-assertiveness internationally is restrained only by the limits of a nation's power. A nation aspires to power so as to be able to maintain world order for its advantage. The achievement of national security thus is not an end in itself but only a necessary condition of advancng to more ambitious uses of power. Imperial interest, so conceived, is then an extension of the more usual realist conception of national interest.

Why should America or any other nation commit itself to the quest for imperial power? Certainly not for moral reasons. Nor, basically, for those of national security. Though national security supposedly follows from this policy, it is not its goal. The answer for Liska lies in forces operating within the "system" of international affairs:

> To the extent that the United States is being propelled presently toward an imperial role in the global system, it does so in response to the system's needs rather than its internal strains. . . . Like individuals, so nations worthy of the name will not withdraw into repose in the external dealings and thus, almost inevitably, submit to the momentum of decline,

[52] Ibid., pp. 54, 56.
[53] Ibid., p. 23.

until they have explored in action the outermost limits of possible achievement.[54]

Similar, if less obvious, statements are found in various contemporary writers, as when Kissinger says that "there are no plateaus in international affairs; what is not a stepping stone soon becomes the beginning of a decline."[55] One senses here the ghost of German philosophy and its conception of the state, which either engages in relentless self-assertion or slips into decline. Only here the metaphysics has been stripped away and replaced with metaphors.

The transition from national self-interest, conceived primarily in terms of self-preservation, to this broader conception of imperial interest, marks a departure from earlier realism. According to Liska, "the containment of the more assertive of the communist great powers is still necessary; but it may well be secondary to the containment of disorder caused ultimately by some form of insufficient power."[56] And as "all order, just or unjust, rests in the last resort, if in different degrees, on force,"[57] the pursuit of imperial interest commits America to the use of international violence.

Though there are occasional references to justice in this scheme, if there should be any doubt about the place of morality in it—even to the extent recognized by traditional realists like Osgood, who maintain that there are certain ideals that should not be forsaken no matter what—it is dispelled by Liska's assertion with respect to Vietnam that

> [t]he destruction in South and North Vietnam becomes more bearable [sic] when one regards the war not as a defense of South Vietnam or of the United States, but as an increasingly symbolic contest, with both global and long-range significance for the cause of order and therefore the degree and kind of peace in the world at large. Suffer as they do and must, the peoples of Vietnam are not the first or the last small people to render such a service to the larger commonweal.[58]

Just as traditional realists trace the disastrous consequences of World War I to the alleged fact that America went to war for the

---

[54] Ibid., p. 10.
[55] Henry A. Kissinger, *The Troubled Partnership* (Garden City, N.Y.: Doubleday & Company, Inc., 1966), p. 246.
[56] *War and Order*, p. 27.
[57] Ibid., p. 28.
[58] Ibid., p. 69.

wrong reasons and failed to see the paramountcy of self-interest in its affairs, so the imperialists among the neorealists see a similar failure in the emphasis upon self-interest and would have us move on to the plane of imperial interest.

VI

What has in fact been the motivation of American leaders in the post-World War II period? Has it been essentially realistic in the preceding sense?

The haze of secrecy surrounding so much of high-level decision making makes it almost impossible to answer such a question with confidence. But the drift of U.S. foreign policy in the post-World War II period has been decidedly in the direction urged by political realists. In the case of Vietnam it has been tailor-made to their specifications. In saying this I am going against the views of realists like Schlesinger, who maintain that, for the most part, the problems of the postwar period derive precisely from the fact that U.S. policy has not been realistic.

Schlesinger points out that every American war has been followed in due course by skeptical reassessment of supposedly sacred assumptions.[59] This is understandable, he believes, because war signifies for most people a failure to govern their affairs in a reasonable and humane way. Vietnam was an exception, in that the critical reassessment occurred while the war was still in progress—to a greater extent than occurred during the Korean War, another unpopular war. But Schlesinger is unhappy with much of this reassessment, at least as reflected in the statements and writings of antiwar radicals. He accordingly sets about to detail the mistaken assumptions behind the Vietnam policy.

He sees these mistaken assumptions as growing out of American policy in the postwar era. But their origins extend further back. He argues that World War II concluded under the gathering clouds of the Cold War and that central among the emergent issues was that between "conflicting world orders"—universalism and spheres of influence:

the "universalist" view, by which all nations shared a common interest in all the affairs of the world, and the "sphere-of-influence" view, by which each great power would be assured

[59] Arthur M. Schlesinger, Jr., *The Crisis of Confidence* (New York: Bantam Books, 1969), p. 77.

by the other great powers of an acknowledged predominance of its own area of special interest. The universalist view assumed that national security would be guaranteed by an international organization. The sphere-of-influence view assumed that national security would be guaranteed by the balance of power.[60]

The roots of the Cold War, according to Schlesinger, lay in this conflict. The Soviets were preoccupied with their own security, which they conceived in terms of the maintenance of a sphere of influence. The Americans under FDR were determined (if waveringly) to place stock in international organizations like the United Nations, much as Wilson had done with the League of Nations. Despite occasional leanings, FDR was in principle a Wilsonian, Schlesinger says, one who was checked by the Wilsonian Cordell Hull when he showed a tendency to backslide. He and Hull had widespread support among other members of government for this basic outlook, and opposition to the sphere-of-influence approach "seems clearly to have been the predominant mood of the American people."[61] Thus it was, according to Schlesinger's view, that universalism, "rooted in the American legal and moral tradition, overwhelmingly backed by public opinion, received successive enshrinements in the Atlantic Charter of 1941, in the Declaration of the United Nations in 1942 and in the Moscow Declaration of 1943."[62]

This interpretation is not unchallenged, however, even among realists. Whereas Schlesinger sees this period as a continuation of the tradition identified with Wilson, Osgood heralded it as a turn toward greater realism and viewed it optimistically. For this reason it will be helpful if we can thread our way through the proliferation of "isms" that these analyses generate and try to understand better the nature of this apparent divergence among realists.

To do this requires sorting out the different strands of Wilsonianism—a notion that, like idealism, has become a convenient source of explanation for whatever is wrong with American foreign policy. These strands include the alleged idealism, the moralism, and the universalism. The idealism—the view that foreign policy should be governed by moral considerations—was indeed at the heart of Wilsonianism. It is this that realists reject. The mor-

[60] Ibid., pp. 81-82.
[61] Ibid., p. 83.
[62] Ibid., p. 85.

alism, I will suggest in the next chapter, was not an essential ingredient in Wilsonianism, although it became a conspicuous feature of it after America's entry into World War I. The universalism, in the sense Schlesinger intends, of a shared interest on the part of all of the nations of the world with world events, was an essential part of it but was not entailed by the idealism.

In seeing America's course in World War II as one of realism, Osgood has in mind in large part the rejection of idealism. Certainly this interpretation is supported by statements of FDR to the effect that the United States was in the war not to save democracy but to protect its own interests. And it is supported by his expansion of the notion of self-interest in such a way as to extend our defense perimeter virtually around the world. This has been a recurrent theme in American realism. What realists object to was the attempt, once self-interest and national security are redefined in this way, to place stock in their maintenance by international organizations and legalistic structures patterned after domestic ones. But this means that at least a part of what Osgood calls realism and applauds in FDR Schlesinger calls Wilsonianism and deplores.

This becomes clearer if we note an ambiguity in Schlesinger's characterization of universalism. The first sense, just mentioned, is that in which "all nations shared a common interest in all the affairs of the world," a view which "assumed that national security would be guaranteed by an international organization." This conception is indeed Wilsonian. But Schlesinger also speaks of universalism in a second sense when he says: "By 'universalism' I mean the belief that the United States has an active and vital interest in the destiny of every nation on the planet."[63] While this second sense is probably an overstatement of anything ever seriously held by American foreign policy experts, it is only a slight one and is in keeping with the philosophy of many realists. This is the sense to which Schlesinger shifts when launching his attack upon postwar U.S. policy. Obscured in the process is the fact that what he now calls universalism and identifies with Wilsonianism is precisely what some realists find lacking in Wilsonianism and make the cornerstone of political realism.

Having shifted from one sense of "universalism," the genuinely Wilsonian one, to the other sense, which accords with political realism, Schlesinger proceeds to analyze the policies that eventuated in Vietnam. Here, he argues, universalism led to tragedy.

[63] Ibid., p. 111.

It did so not because the underlying principles were wrong but because they were overextended. There was a convergence of influences here: from the 1930s the notion of "collective security" under Henry Stimson, from the 1940s the "social evangelism" of FDR, from the 1950s the anticommunism of John Foster Dulles. Mix these together and you get Wilsonianism in Vietnam as well.

> The tragedy of Vietnam is the tragedy of the catastrophic overextension and misapplication of valid principles. The original insights of collective security and liberal evangelism were generous and wise. But compulsive Stimsonianism and compulsive New Dealism, stimulated by the illusions of Superpowership, rigidified by an absolutist anticommunism and pressed ever forward by the professional demands of the new warrior class, brought American universalism in time into a messianic phase.[64]

This episode came to a close, he maintains, on March 31, 1968, with Lyndon Johnson's decision not to seek reelection. "What was announced was the collapse of the messianic conception of the American role in the world—indeed, the end of the entire Age of the Superpowers."[65]

This is a replay of the standard realist critique of Wilson following World War I. The same ingredients are there: the implication of self-righteousness, of a lack of realism, of a crusading mentality, of failure to see where the country's interests lay, and of messianism. It is almost as though any period in American foreign affairs that has less than desirable consequences is to be assessed by the same formula. Since any such period will be one in which there will have been mistakes in judgment, policymakers will always be subject to the charge of having failed to be "realistic." Even Schlesinger himself seems to reconsider this analysis when he takes to task both Kissinger and Daniel Moynihan for attributing the defeat in Vietnam chiefly to domestic failures, such as Congress's cutting of aid to General Thieu. Of this, Schlesinger says:

> The reason Americans lost faith in the Indochina war was not at all because their nerve failed but precisely because they came to feel that the geopolitical theory of the war [advocated by Kissinger] made no sense. They simply did not believe it when their leaders told them that the communization of In-

64 Ibid., p. 133.
65 Ibid., p. 135.

dochina would be a deadly threat to the security of the United States. . . . The "misery of it all" in Vietnam was not a failure of nerve on the part of the people, but a failure of intelligence on the part of their leaders. They deceived us, and themselves, when they told us that the future of Indochina would make a serious difference to the future of the United States.[66]

This, of course, does not do full justice to the many dimensions of opposition to the Vietnam War. Many people opposed the war not merely because they did not believe that Vietnam was essential to U.S. security but because they were convinced that what the United States was doing there was wrong. They would have objected to it on those grounds even if a convincing case had been made that keeping South Vietnam under U.S. domination was in our national interest. But that notwithstanding, the depiction of the position of the U.S. leaders in Schlesinger's analysis is precisely in line with political realism: the contention is that the principal justification for the war was national interest. National egoism was the governing norm. That these leaders were wrong in seeing national interest at stake in Vietnam, and were wrong in so many other judgments, in no way affects the fact that if Schlesinger's characterization is correct, the most plausible interpretation of their underlying philosophy is that of political realism. If so, Vietnam was not an overextension of valid principles. It was the fruit of the limited-war strategy born in the late 1950s, conjoined with political realism.

In any event, let us look back a little further to the characterization by a realist of the course on which the United States embarked after World War II and the optimistic prognosis for the future that it contained:

The astounding growth of America's willingness to take an active part in world politics, the amazing speed with which Americans have junked old concepts of neutrality and readily entangled their affairs in political and military arrangements with other nations, deliberately adopting extensive worldwide commitments unthinkable a short while ago; these developments reflect a widespread recognition of the exigencies of survival. They may also signify the emergence of a more stable and effective foreign policy.[67]

[66] "Failure of Nerve—or Intellect?" *The Wall Street Journal*, June 19, 1978.
[67] Osgood, *Ideals and Self-Interest*, p. 432.

79

This is Osgood writing in 1953. These events, he maintains, represent a maturing of the American people in which they "gradually adapted their conduct of foreign relations to the realities of international society." He stresses that in order to achieve the aims of this more effective policy, liberal idealists and international reformers will

> be forced to put the exigencies of power politics ahead of their moral sensibilities. Similarly, if they want to pursue their ideals effectively, they must base American aid to foreign peoples primarily upon the power advantage to the United States and only secondarily upon humanitarian considerations. They must, at times, support reactionary and anti-democratic regimes with arms and money. They must even put themselves in the position of resisting with force the misguided proponents of a social revolution, which arises, in large part, from basic human aspirations which the American mission itself claims to fulfill.[68]

These are the prescriptions of a political realist. And it is hard to see that they were not admirably implemented. The United States supported reactionary governments in Spain, Portugal, and Latin America; based aid upon considerations of power advantage to itself in Greece and South Africa; and fought against "misguided" revolutionaries in Vietnam and the Dominican Republic. It subverted a democratically elected regime in Chile, overthrew the government of Grenada, and sponsored rebels against the government of Nicaragua. And in both Korea and Vietnam it fought the limited wars that realists would have our wars be, in which unconditional surrender was never an objective and in which, despite excesses in Vietnam, restraints in design and execution were continually in effect. Vietnam, at any rate, was a war directed by dispassionate efficiency experts making calculated use of the best of

---

[68] Ibid., p. 438. Notice that Osgood speaks here of what America must do in order to pursue its ideals effectively, as though ideals were to supersede self-interest. This indicates an ambivalence in his thought (characteristic of many realists) between the desire to affirm the paramountcy of national interest and a reluctance to part altogether with morality. The result is sometimes one of trying to have it both ways. More often it results in subordinating morality to national interest. Thus while Osgood contends that "the calculation of national advantage without regard for the interrelation of ideals and self-interest is not only immoral as a national end but unrealistic as a means to an end" (p. 442), he also says that "[if] the United States is to have a stable and effective foreign policy, neither egoism nor altruism must interfere with the rational, objective assessment of the real long-run conditions of American self-interest" (p. 441).

modern technology and military science—precisely the opposite of the moralistic crusade that some realists would represent it as being once it failed.[69] And it was a war rationalized by an entangling alliance (SEATO),[70] waged about as far from our borders as one can get, and justified by appeal to national self-interest. Had that intervention succeeded in 1965 or 1968 one suspects that instead of calling it a moralistic crusade, political realists would today be applauding it as bold, forthright, and hardheadedly pragmatic—and chalking it up to a policy of realism.

This does not mean that political realists themselves are insensitive jingoists. They are forward-looking, intelligent men whose analyses are as thoughtful as they would have our statesmen be. And if Schlesinger overstates things when he says that it was realists who were most skeptical about Vietnam from the beginning, it is certainly true that some of them, like Osgood, thought Vietnam intervention ill-advised as far back as 1957,[71] others, like Morgenthau, were long-standing critics of the war, and still others, like Schlesinger himself, came to be disenchanted with it.[72] But the

[69] See, for example, Schlesinger's statement: "Since it is painful to charge our national leaders with stupidity, one must suppose that this foolish analysis of the relation of Indo-China to the American national interest was only a secondary motive for our involvement in Indo-China. The primary motive, it seems probable in retrospect, had little to do with national interest at all. It was rather a precise consequence of the belief that moral principles should govern decisions of foreign policy. It was the insistence on seeing the civil war in Vietnam as above all a moral issue that led us to construe political questions in ethical terms, local questions in global terms, and relative questions in absolute terms" ("National Interests and Moral Absolutes," in Lefever, ed., *Ethics and World Politics*, p. 37). See also Schlesinger's *The Crisis of Confidence*. This way of viewing matters has come to constitute almost a formula for instant and superficial analyses of American foreign policy over the years. Major failures are automatically explained as owing to "not enough realism," to the holding sway of visionary idealism, to the unrealistic attempt to implement moral judgments in foreign policy. And thus the cry is raised anew, as after World War I and World War II and again after Vietnam, for a return to a hardheaded understanding of the realities of international affairs—in short, for a return to realism.

[70] At least much of the time. Almost every remotely marketable "justification" was given a try at one time or another.

[71] See *Limited War*, pp. 214-226.

[72] See *The Crisis of Confidence*, chap. 4. Kennan wrote in 1954 of our involvement in Indochina that "[o]ur government is obviously making a concentrated and determined effort to come to grips with the problem. We can only wish them well and give them our confidence and support." See *Realities of American Foreign Policy* (Princeton, N.J.: Princeton University Press, 1954), pp. 95-96. In 1967, acknowledging that "the Vietnam involvement . . . marches under the same semantic banner"—namely, that of "containment"—that had become closely associated with him in the early 1950s (though see his comments on the allegation that he authored a "containment policy" in his *Memoirs: 1925-1950*, vol. 1 [Boston: Little, Brown and Company, 1967], chap. 15), he said that it should be apparent to anyone who re-

fact remains that to assign paramountcy to national interest commits one to the rationalization of *any* magnitude of evil that circumstances might render necessary to protect that interest. What this philosophy cannot allow, or allow to be decisive, is that a war like Vietnam could be successful beyond the wildest dreams of its executors and yet be totally and unqualifiedly wrong from a moral standpoint.

That Vietnam was an American tragedy militarily, politically, and morally some will dispute. That it was never in the national interest to intervene there some will dispute. But that it was a product of the *kind* of foreign policy advocated by political realists is indisputable.

---

flects upon the "official rationale and methodology" of Vietnam policy that it does not accord with the concept that he advocates (from an abbreviated version of an address delivered at Harvard in Spring 1967 under the auspices of the Charles Warren Center for Studies in American History, published as "The Quest for Concept," *Harvard Today*, Autumn 1967). Nonetheless, in keeping with his realist predisposition against judging morally, about the most he can bring himself to say about the "totality of our action in Vietnam" is that it "might well classify as a massive imprudence but scarcely as a deliberate crime" (*Democracy and the Student Left*, p. 139). In any event, as Rothstein observes, it is often "difficult to relate an individual Realist's position on policy to his philosophical convictions" ("On the Costs of Political Realism," p. 352).

82

THREE

REASON OF STATE, MILITARY
NECESSITY, AND DOMESTIC SECURITY

Viewed from within, each religious or national fanaticism
stands for a good; but in its outward operation it produces
and becomes an evil. —George Santayana

Political realism in twentieth-century American thought, as we
have seen, is primarily normative. It argues that morality *should*
be excluded from international relations, or at best given a limited
role. This sets it apart from the positivistic realism of those who
deny the very intelligibility of applying moral notions to the conduct of states.

I shall comment later upon the theological-metaphysical view of
human nature underlying much of this approach. Before that,
however, I want to examine the Niebuhrian view that groups are
incapable of achieving the same standard of mortality as individuals and that therefore a collective morality must be recognized
over and above the individual morality of persons.[1]

I

Niebuhr, we have seen, explains egoism in the morality of groups
by the alleged transmutation of altruism at the level of individual
morality into collective egoism at the group level. Though he gives
few details of how this comes about, others with similar accounts
have provided the rudiments of an explanation of how it works.
Robert Osgood, for example, says:

A citizen's dependence upon his nation assumes a distinct in-
timacy because he confers upon the object of his allegiance the

[1] Michael Walzer more recently seems to hold the view that the state is governed
by a different morality from that of individuals. Unlike Niebuhr, however, he appears to believe that it is higher morality, one that at times should override the
other. See his *Just and Unjust Wars* (New York: Basic Books, 1977), p. 254.

attributes of a person so closely identified with his own personality that he virtually acquires a second self, in whose behalf he can feel friendly, hostile, generous, selfish, confident, afraid, proud or humiliated almost as poignantly as he would feel these emotions for himself in his relations with other individuals.[2]

The state, in this view, comes to be regarded as though it were a superpersonality through this projection of attributes by its citizens. But this projection provides only part of the ground for the distinction between two moralities and only part of the proposed justification for preserving the illusion of a personified state. For the rest we need a variety of psychological and normative judgments.

So intimate is man's identification with his national group that national extinction, like the murder of one's family, would be equivalent to a direct depredation of the dignity of the individual personality, since it would destroy a virtually indispensable source of personal security and happiness, as well as the sum of all those personal satisfactions derived from the nation's "way of life." For this reason, those responsible for the nation's course in international affairs, although they may rightly feel the obligation to sacrifice their own lives, are no more justified morally than they are justified on grounds of expediency in committing national suicide.[3]

If the identification in question is indeed a "virtually indispensable source of personal security and happiness," and if, as Osgood seems to assume, what promotes personal happiness is right, then national egoism has a moral foundation. The individual can then, as he says in a continuation of the first passage, "manage with a sense of complete moral consistency to combine lofty altruism toward his own nation with extreme egoism toward other nations and thereby actively support a standard of ethics in foreign relations which he would not dream of tolerating in his private dealings."

Two moralities thus emerge, one governing the conduct of individuals, the other the conduct of states.[4] Add to this a commit-

---

[2] *Ideals and Self-Interest in America's Foreign Relations* (Chicago: University of Chicago Press, 1953), p. 11.

[3] Ibid., p. 12.

[4] Whether these two moralities are more accurately represented as individual and collective, or as public and private, is difficult to say. Since Osgood stresses the

ment to the preservation of the state above all else, and the doctrine of reason of state is then enshrined in this outlook as well.

If this view is correct, it means that the alleged inevitability of egoism in international affairs rests upon an illusion, a collective self-deception about the nature of the state. For the state is not in fact a superperson. It does not have feelings, thoughts, aims, or interests independently of those projected into it by individual persons. Nor as an imaginatively personified superbeing is it the fitting object of devotion, much less of the sacrifice of human lives. Only individual persons feel and suffer, live and die. Only their survival and quality of life can be of ultimate moral concern. To think otherwise is to generate myth from metaphor, to mistake the convenience of language by which we speak of nations deciding, choosing, and acting as though they were rational beings for a literal reflection of reality. Though it may be that whatever happiness a person derives from belief in a personified state is the same whether that belief is true or false, we have been given no reason to suppose that false beliefs provide a better foundation for the pursuit of happiness than true beliefs.

What is disturbing about such theories is not the importance Niebuhr and Osgood attach to the phenomena to which they call attention but rather their tacit recommendation about what to do about them. For rather than urging that we disabuse ourselves of such illusions, they urge instead, in net effect, that we reconcile ourselves to their perpetuation, acquiesce in the continued predominance of the collective egoism they generate, accept the inevitability of war which that virtually entails, and dismiss as idealistic the hope that we can ever change all of this and put an end to war. All in the name of realism.[5] If they believe that the state is indeed a superpersonality, we should see the argument for such a dubious metaphysics. If they do not, but think the illusion that it is should be perpetuated, we should see the argument for such a

responsibilities of individual governmental leaders when he speaks of the preservation of the state, and since public morality is a morality governing the conduct of individuals in the performance of specific roles—such as those of leadership in government or industry—I shall assume that the relevant distinction is that between public and private morality.

[5] This explanation of collective egoism can, of course, be accepted by those who reject political realism as well as by those who accept it. What is difficult to accept about the above account is the implicit judgment that nothing can be done to alter this state of affairs. Those, like Arthur Koestler, who offer accounts similar to the preceding, but based upon an analysis of man's phylogenetic heritage, do not maintain that this condition is irreversible. See his "Man—One of Evolution's Mistakes?" *New York Times Magazine*, Oct. 19, 1969.

dubious ethics. As it is, their outlook is an invitation to self-deception.

Once this theory is stripped of the claims about the personification of the state, however, it becomes plausible. People do identify with groups and do feel emotions of the sort Osgood and Niebuhr describe. This gives at least prima facie plausibility to the claims about the stake of human happiness in this phenomenon. Let us grant, therefore, that people often identify with the state. Central to the rest of Osgood's argument is the further claim that identification with one's national group is a "virtually indispensable" source of personal security and happiness. If one conjoins this with the view that we should promote happiness, it provides a basis for his conclusion that national leaders are obligated to preserve the state. This, in turn, provides a justification of reason of state.

What does one make of this further claim? This is a complex question on which ultimately depends the whole question of the legitimacy of the state. I shall for present purposes only consider certain aspects of it.

The link between happiness and the state might be either psychological or material. Osgood stresses psychological dependence. Even where there is no projection of personal attributes onto the state, loyalty and patriotism often give individuals a stake in its fortunes. This is true of its domestic as well as of its foreign dealings. Certainly the morale of a people is affected by a state's fortunes internationally, the most extreme cases being victory or defeat in war. Moreover, people frequently enjoy certain benefits because they live in a state, quite apart from whether they have confidence in it, much less identify with it. They may even oppose many of its policies. These benefits may include economic prosperity, civil liberties, and employment opportunities. Happiness may be thought to be materially dependent upon these conditions in the sense that their operation does not presuppose any favorable psychological attitudes towards the state.

The interconnection between these two kinds of dependence is highly complex, however. High levels of material prosperity may contribute little to happiness if there is a perceived injustice in the distribution of wealth. And, as the Vietnam experience attests, there can be widespread disaffection whatever the level of prosperity if a government is perceived to be involved in morally indefensible actions abroad. There is, in short, no simple correlation between the psychological and material factors.

Although Osgood stresses psychological dependence, let us assume that both material and psychological dependence are involved. What, then, can we make of his argument?

The argument, in brief, is that from the fact that (1) individuals identify with the state, and the claim that (2) their so doing is an indispensable source of personal happiness, one can conclude that (3) national leaders ought to promote the national interest. Assumed, presumably, is the normative principle that (4) one ought to promote personal happiness (as well as premises linking the identification in question with promotion of national interest). But we need to ask both *whose* happiness one is obligated to promote and *which* national leaders are referred to in (3).

Osgood clearly means that the happiness of Americans should be promoted and that U.S. leaders should promote U.S. interest. But is he saying, further, that the happiness of all peoples should be promoted and that all national leaders should promote the national interest of their respective countries? He must mean something like this if, as he sometimes seems to think (albeit, we should note, inconsistently with political realism), he is giving a moral justification of national egoism. Moral principles are for everyone alike, not just for certain nationalities. If it is right for some leaders to promote national interest on the grounds that it is for the good of their peoples to do so, then it is right for all. But if (4) is taken to prescribe the promotion of the happiness of all peoples, then (3) does not follow as a conclusion. That one ought to promote the happiness of people generally does not show that one ought to promote the interest of one's own state. To warrant such a conclusion one should need a further assumption to the effect that the happiness of all peoples is promoted by each nation's pursuing its own interest—a kind of international laissez faire. And such a thesis, given any usual interpretation of national interest, is surely false. The prosperity of any nation can be enhanced at the expense of others. Certainly nations think of their interest in this way, often exploiting and preying upon one another when they see some advantage in doing so. If this is correct, then Osgood's proposition (3) has not been established.

If, on the other hand, (4) prescribes only the promotion of the happiness of Americans, then it fails to be a moral principle. No principle that purports to be a basic moral principle can single out one person, group, nationality, or race as the sole beneficiary of the conduct it prescribes. Therefore, insofar as the argument purports to present a moral justification, it fails.

Let us suppose, however, that the argument is not intended to be a moral argument at all. This would be consistent with Osgood's political realism and would mean that the argument could still be evaluated in nonmoral terms. It would then simply hold that one ought to promote the happiness of Americans, that it is American leaders who are obligated to do this, and that therefore the survival of America should be put above all else. This would constitute the doctrine of reason of state.

Taking the argument in this way, let us see what we can make of premise (2), the claim regarding the indispensability of the state to the happiness of Americans.

It would be difficult, of course, to substantiate such a claim. To do so would require comparing the quality of life of persons living in a state, and who identify with it in the manner Osgood suggests, with persons who were not, and such judgments would be largely conjectural. It is true, of course, that the state so extensively determines the circumstances under which people live that most satisfactions are conditioned to some extent by those circumstances. But this is not at issue. What is at issue is whether the benefits deriving from identification with the state, as well as from other material benefits, render the survival of the state indispensable to happiness. And we have been given no reason to believe that it does, hence no good reason to accept premise (2). What gives this claim its initial plausibility is the easy confusion of it with the claim that *society* is indispensable to the happiness of individual persons. Many of the greatest goods are possible only in the context of cooperation, shared interests, and trust that are part of the fabric of society. Whether government plays a similar role is less clear, however. Simply to assume that it does is to beg the question against anarchism, which maintains that the optimal social conditions for the promotion of happiness are possible only in the absence of the state.

Let us assume, however, as Augustine and Hobbes maintain, that a state is necessary to the maintenance of society. Would this then justify reason of state?

It is doubtful that it would. First, if it is the maintenance of society that is of primary importance, it is possible that different states might perform this function equally well. While it might be true that the existence of *a* state is necessary to maximize human happiness, it would not follow that the existence of any *particular* state is necessary. What kinds of states are necessary would have to be argued independently.

Second, as others at least as far back as Rousseau have pointed out, the survival of the state cannot be identified with the survival of individual persons. Although the birth and demise of states is often accompanied by the destruction of human life, it need not be so, and in fact need be accompanied by no loss of life whatsoever. To create a state one need only institute the appropriate system of government, and to destroy a state one need only dismantle that system. This can in principle be done without the destruction of human life and without dislocating the lives of those in the society. This is not the way it most often happens. What people fear is the widespread destruction of persons and property—the destruction of a people's way of life. And this clearly does bear importantly upon human happiness. But if this is the concern, then the objection should be to the use of violence to achieve such ends, which after all is what occasions the wrong, not the possible replacing of one state with another.

It may be objected that even if this is so, and even if people perhaps should not identify so closely with the state as to have their personal happiness dependent upon its fortunes, nonetheless large numbers of them do, and the destruction of the state even by nonviolent means would still be a depredation against them.

Let us grant this for the sake of the argument. But in so doing we must weigh against it the fact that the state is also a source of unhappiness. Not only is there indignation and sometimes despair over perceived injustice within society but there may also be profound distress over misguided foreign policies. One need only review the history of race relations within America, or the trauma of the Vietnam War, to see this. On the material side, there is the restriction of the liberty of those conscripted to fight wars and the toll in lives and resources in the prosecution of those wars. If one argues for national egoism on the grounds of the benefits associated with identifying with the state, one must weigh into the scales the detriments from both identifying with and living within the state. And he must weigh into the scales the threat of nuclear annihilation from the pursuit of national interest by the major nations of the world. The growing threat of nuclear annihilation grows out of the workings of an international system in which, if many realists are correct, the promotion of national interest is the governing norm. And if, as many of them would also have it, national interest *ought* to be the guiding norm (either of some or of all nations), then we need some accounting of how such a judgment is justified in light of the apparent consequences of its implementation. If one places the highest value upon the survival of the state, and if that survival is jeopardized by the pursuit of national interest, it would seem that pursuit should be abandoned.[6]

I would suggest, on the basis of these considerations, that even granting the kind of psychological identification of which Osgood speaks, and the importance of not underestimating it in the assessment of policy decisions, one cannot extract from this account a justification of the collective egoism the account is meant to explain. And without that, reason of state and national egoism have not been justified.

What of the claim, finally, that the factors making for collective egoism give rise to two moralities?

I would suggest here, first of all, that the distinction between individual and collective morality collapses into the distinction between private and public morality. Collective morality supposedly governs the conduct of groups. But the conduct of the state is always translatable (though not necessarily without remainder) into the conduct of particular individuals. Thus while there is no reason to alter our usual way of speaking about the conduct of nations—speaking of them as acting, choosing, deciding, agreeing, and the like, as though they were entities on a par with persons—we should be mindful that this is merely a shorthand way of saying that the appropriately designated officials of those states are performing acts that constitute "acts of state" in those contexts. The question, then, is whether persons in their official roles are governed by a public morality different from the private morality governing their daily lives. I would suggest that they are not. That they undertake certain obligations in assuming their positions of

---

[6] This matter is actually more complicated. It is possible that the pursuit of what is *thought* to be in the national interest has led to the current world situation in which the major powers threaten one another with nuclear annihilation but that the pursuit of what is *actually* in that interest would not do so. It might be, for example, that what is in the national interest of one nation is in the interest of others, and vice versa. If true, this would represent a different conception of national interest from the usual one. It would require giving due regard to the interest of other nations, including—and perhaps especially including—those with whom one is most at odds.

If national interest were interpreted along these lines, one could then reconcile reason of state with the pursuit of national interest, hence with national egoism, and one could then also continue to adhere to political realism. For then realism would have become a very different sort of thing from what it is usually conceived to be, and its prescriptions would converge with those of morality. So while it is arguable that this is the only plausible defense of political realism, it is also clear that it is a defense that pulls its Machiavellian teeth.

90

responsibility is clear. That some of these are moral and not just legal obligations is also clear. In a democracy, for example, one may assume that a certain trust has been placed in elected officials. Though there are disagreements over the extent to which this requires doing only what one's constituents want, as opposed to exercising leadership, there *is* nonetheless an obligation to be responsive in some way to those who have placed this trust in you. This assuredly entails obligations that one would not normally have. But nothing in this warrants the postulation of a separate morality. Nothing in morality requires that all of one's decisions when representing others need be the same as those he might have made if not acting in that capacity, anymore than it requires that the decisions one makes after having made a promise need be the same as those he might otherwise have made. Nor, in either case, does it guarantee that in discharging an obligation one will be doing what he otherwise would prefer or even think best. When putting oneself forth as a candidate for governmental office, one, in effect, agrees to give weight to certain kinds of considerations that he might otherwise be under no obligation to consider. Morality can accommodate all of this, and unless reference to public morality is simply a shorthand way of saying these things, it is hard to know what is meant by it.

II

We have thus far considered the reasoning that leads to normative realism by way of the distinction between individual and collective morality as found in Niebuhr and transposed into public and private morality by Osgood. I have suggested that the claim that there is a kind of inevitability associated with the egoistic behavior of groups cannot be sustained by the sorts of arguments examined. That individuals do sometimes identify with the state and sacrifice themselves in its service is of itself no argument for concluding that they must do so, much less that they ought to do so.

It should be stressed, however, that as interwoven with the theological–metaphysical view as it often is, the historical strain in realism does not require that account and stands or falls by itself. It is, moreover, the more compelling of the forms of realism and for that reason merits further consideration.

Its central contention, again, is that the appeal to moral ideals in international relations has had (or does or would have) bad consequences and therefore should be foregone or at least subordinated to self-interest. This contention is assessable independently of the foundation that the Niebuhrian approach provides for it. It raises two questions: first, whether the realist's representation of the Wilsonian position prior to and during World War I is accurate; and second, whether, if it is, Wilsonianism can properly be charged with responsibility for the consequences alleged by realists. There is, of course, the further question of whether the consequences in question were (or are or would have been) as bad as realists contend, but I shall not deal with that here.

Although the realist's interpretation of Wilsonianism is challengeable, I shall confine myself primarily to the second question. For I do challenge the standard indictment of Wilsonianism. That indictment, we recall, charges that Wilsonianism consisted of self-righteous moralism: that it inadequately prepared the American people for entry into war, was uncompromising in its determination to settle for nothing less than victory once involved, and after the war left the country adrift on the seas of isolationism when it should have been steering boldly the course of national interest.

But it is arguable that Wilson's error lay not in failing to school the American people in national self-interest before leading them into war but rather in departing from principles that prescribed that we stay out of war in the first place. For if the events during and after World War I that realists perceive as consequences of Wilsonianism were indeed near-disastrous, it was no less a condition of their occurrence that the United States entered the war in the first place than that it did so from the motives realists disparage. Had Wilsonian idealism and its associated neutrality prevailed, *those* consequences—deriving from America's participation in the war—would not have taken place. Whether equally bad ones would have occurred in their place is a matter of conjecture, but it cannot simply we assumed that they would have.

It may be that far better than either the course that history in fact took, or the one it would have taken had we entered the war sooner from self-interest, is the one it would have taken had we stayed out of the war altogether, as Wilson originally intended and most Americans wanted. In short, the failure may have lain not with Wilsonianism but with Wilson the man; not with the principles but with the policies.[7] And it may have consisted less in the

---

[7] Wilson's critics urged entry into the war often from precisely the moralistic point of view that realists decry, claiming that it was a "supreme battle between right and wrong." See Arthur S. Link, *Wilson: The Struggle for Neutrality, 1914-1915* (Princeton, N.J.: Princeton University Press, 1960), p. 13. And by 1915 Wilson

fact that he held the particular moral perspective he did than in the fact that, rather than adhere to his own convictions, he yielded to the course advocated by his critics. It was, in fact, often his critics who viewed the war in heavily moralistic terms. When Wilson did enter the war, the official explanation, in Osgood's own words, "disavowed any hatred or rancor toward the German people and pledged the nation to eschew aggrandizement. . . . There was generally agreement that the U.S. had intervened for its own reasons and would fight for its own ends."[8] It was not Wilsonian idealism that bears responsibility for the subsequent course of history but the failings of a tired and beleaguered man of principle, who was unable to hold fast against the tide of events.

Such analyses of contrary-to-fact states of affairs are always partly speculative, of course. But unless we suppose that human history could not have been other than it has been—with all that would imply for the making of history at the present—one must consider such assessments worth making. The realist need not be conceded his assessment in the absence of such an undertaking and in the absence of reason to suppose that it would support his particular historical and value judgments.

Whether or not American's interest and security were actually at stake in those events in Europe, the important question is whether Americans could have been convinced that they were. If they could not, then it would have been unrealistic to try to justify entry into the war on that basis. Indeed, Osgood says of the military preparedness movement that it "failed to produce a dispassionate and realistic discussion of the fundamental bases of national self-preservation . . . because the circumstances of the war did not arouse any serious or widespread doubt about America's impregnable physical isolation. . . ."[9] Kennan concedes likewise that "people in general had no idea that our interests were affected by what was going on in Europe in 1913; they would never have dreamed of spending real money for armaments in time of peace, they would never have gone into a war deliberately, as a result of cold calculation about the balance of power elsewhere." He even concedes that they would not have gone to war if the effort could not have been clothed in high ideals and that such a course as he

---

shifted his emphasis from the broad moral one of humanitarian considerations to the narrower one of American rights on the seas. It is hard to see why this shift does not accord with the point of view urged by realists.

[8] *Ideals and Self-Interest*, p. 265.

[9] Ibid., p. 222.

advocates might not in retrospect have been "within the realm of practical possibility from the standpoint of domestic realities in our own country."[10]

If this is true, then even in terms of the realist's own analyses, the only way people could have been spurred to war was by an emotional appeal of the sort Wilson allegedly used and that supposedly led to the postwar disillusionment for which realists criticize him. And if the realists are also correct that it was a war we were properly involved in, the only course would seem to have been to delude people into supporting it on other grounds, a course that would have risked postwar disillusionment for having failed to achieve whatever objectives were set forth in the rationalization for the war. Such an approach led years later to the deceptions of the Vietnam War.

Even if it were Wilsonianism and not the waging of the war itself that led to a subsequent world war, this would not show that morality should be discounted in foreign relations. The most one could conclude is that Wilson's handling of American policy was an instance of bad judgment, one that subsequently had bad consequences. No one should be surprised that simply being motivated by the desire to act morally does not by itself suffice to produce good consequences; we all know which road is paved with good intentions. But the fact that *trying* to act morally sometimes has bad consequences does not show that *acting* morally has bad consequences. To act morally is to act in the way that has the best moral consequences. Those cannot be improved upon. *Trying* to act morally can have bad consequences because of bad judgments about what is right or errors in the execution of policies. The remedy in these cases, however, is not to cease trying to act morally; it is to make better judgments and to implement them more effectively.

The temptation to try to extract more than this from the realist's analysis of Wilsonianism reflects a number of misconceptions about the nature of morality.

One is the equation of morality with moralism. People can be as

[10] George Kennan, *American Diplomacy, 1900-1950* (Chicago: University of Chicago Press, 1951), p. 73. Osgood seems unsure whether the approach Kennan advocates would have worked even in World War II. He says that "one cannot know what the public and the Congressional reaction would have been had the President frankly disabused the American people of their hope of staying out of the war and forthrightly appealed to the nation, in terms of its own self-interest, to adopt all measures, defensive or otherwise, to resist German aggression" (*Ideals and Self-Interest*, p. 421).

self-righteous, dogmatic, and uncompromising about self-interest as they can about morality; or about interventionism as about isolationism. The doctrinaire toughness of the cold war realism in American foreign policy attests to this. By the same token, people can be as clear-headed, objective, and unemotional about the one as about the other. Neither these virtues nor these defects are the special province of the moralist, however much they may characterize the moralizer. To claim for political realism all of what is commendable among these attitudes and to impute to idealism all of what is deplorable is to stack the cards in advance.[11]

Nor can morality be identified with "principle" to the exclusion of "consequences," with a blind pursuit of righteousness to the disregard of facts.[12] Osgood represents this as the American attitude toward World War I, which he sums up by the motto, "Fear not the consequences when you know you are right." And it is in these terms that America's policy in the Far East prior to World War II is sometimes seen. Wilsonianism, now in the person of Cordell Hull, is again the culprit. "The policy of the United States," writes historian Paul W. Schroeder in this vein, "was avowedly not one of realism, but of principle." Regarding the U.S. response to Japanese depredations against China, Schroeder says:

> If the moral task of the United States in the Far East was to uphold a principle of absolute moral value, the principle of nonappeasement of aggressors, then the American policy was entirely successful in fulfilling it. The American diplomats proved that the United States was capable of holding to its position in disregard and even in defiance of national interests narrowly conceived. If, however, the task was one of doing concrete good and giving practical help where needed, especially to China, then the American policy falls fatally short. . . . Once most leaders in the administration and wide sections of the public became convinced that it was America's prime moral duty to stand hard and fast against aggressors, whatever the consequences, and once this conviction became

[11] Ironically, it was precisely the evenhanded, disinterested, accommodating spirit of neutrality—which constituted what Kennan calls the "nonsensical timidities" of neutralism—in 1914 and 1915 that Wilson's critics so deplored in him. The Wilson of 1915, coolly going about his usual golf game after the sinking of the *Lusitania* to avoid giving the appearance of being swept away on the tide of high emotion, contrasts with the near hysterical cries for action by some of his critics.

[12] As Henry A. Kissinger more recently seems to regard it. He says that "moral claims involve a quest for absolutes, a denial of nuance, a rejection of history." See *A World Restored* (London: Weidenfeld & Nicolson), 1957, p. 316.

decisive in the formulation of policy, the end result was almost inevitable: a policy designed to uphold principle and punish the aggressor, but not to save the victim.[13]

But there is nothing in the concept of morality to preclude a concern, even an exclusive concern, with consequences.[14] A concern with either principle or consequences, or both in varying combinations, may characterize any of the standard outlooks toward international relations. This is true equally of nationalism, internationalism, interventionism, and noninterventionism. It may also characterize realism as much as idealism. The point is that while one *can* subscribe to principles in the rigid, uncompromising way realists impute to moralists, one need not do so, and if one does do so the principles can as readily be nonmoral ones as moral. Any principle can be followed to the exclusion of consequences (excepting, of course, consequentialist principles themselves), and moral principles are probably so followed no more than any others.

Even the contrast between principles and consequences is misleading from the outset. Those, like utilitarians, who stress consequences in ethics, do not do so in lieu of subscribing to principle. They do so rather in accordance with a principle: that one should maximize value in the consequences of actions. It is not even possible to formulate utilitarianism other than as a principle. What distinguishes a consequentialist from a nonconsequentialist is that the former subscribes to a principle that prescribes the performance of one type of act only, namely, that which is conducive to the production of value; whereas the nonconsequentialist, if he subscribes to a principle at all (which he may or may not do), typically holds that there are many kinds of property that bring acts within the scope of the principle. Such properties include that of being conducive to goodness but also include properties like being

---

[13] "The Axis Alliance and Japanese-American Relations, 1941: An Appraisal of American Policy," in *Twentieth-Century America: Recent Interpretations*, ed. Barton J. Bernstein and Allen J. Matusow (New York: Harcourt, Brace & World, Inc., 1969), pp. 328-330.

[14] To his credit, Schroeder acknowledges that this preoccupation with principle to the exclusion of consequences is but one type of morality and not morality itself: "The policy . . . was bad not simply because it was moralistic but because it was obsessed with the wrong kind of morality—with that abstract 'Let justice be done though the heavens fall' kind which so often, when relentlessly pursued, does more harm than good" (ibid., p. 330). It is interesting to note that many interpreters of World War II would also have it that it was the failure to stand fast against aggression at Munich that was responsible for World War II in the first place.

an instance of promise keeping, whose verification requires no reference to consequences. He is, in short, typically a pluralist with respect to the kinds of properties bound up in the application of principles, whereas the utilitarian is a monist.

Those who contrast principle with consequences seem to intend to distinguish between one *kind* of principle that involves no reference to consequences and another kind that makes express reference to consequences. This is a legitimate and important distinction. But it neither coincides with the distinction between consequentialists and nonconsequentialists nor properly represents a distinction between "principle" and "consequences." And there is no more reason to associate advocates of morality in international relations with one side of either of these distinctions than with the other.

The upshot is that this strain in political realism proceeds from a fundamental misconception of the nature of morality. On the one hand, it treats self-righteousness, dogmatism, and utopianism, which do indeed often characterize moralism but often characterize other outlooks as well, as though they were part of the fabric of morality, which they are not. On the other hand, it implicitly judges the whole of morality to consist of rule following to the exclusion of consequences, which it does not. One suspects that historical realists have simply disagreed so strongly with the particular normative judgments of Wilsonianism that rather than merely reject the judgments themselves, they reject the whole perspective from which they issued. Their mistake has not been mainly an historical one—though I have suggested that their accounts are challengeable on that score—but a failure to understand the nature of morality.

III

If positivistic realism were correct, then the whole of the preceding discussion would be misguided. For then moral notions would simply have no applicability to international affairs. In that case there would be no point to the normative realist's judgment that morality ought not to be appealed to in foreign affairs. It makes sense to prescribe that one do or refrain from doing certain things only if one *can* do or refrain from doing them.

Positivistic realism, however, is untenable given the assumption, unquestioned by realists, that the concept of conduct applies to the behavior of states. For no conduct is in principle exempt from moral assessment. Indeed, nothing counts as conduct (as opposed to mere behavior) unless we can intelligibly ask whether it is right or wrong. In light of this, consider that "morally right" in the sense of "morally permissible" can plausibly be defined as meaning "not wrong." If the arguments for realism were correct, they would establish that it is not wrong to wage war. This is a central theme of a classical positivist like Hobbes. But if it is not wrong to wage war, then it is permissible to do so, hence (in this sense) right to do so, in which case certain moral concepts do apply to the conduct of states.

Defenders and critics of realism alike often confuse the question of the applicability of moral concepts to international affairs with the issue of whether the existing nations of the world *have* a morality. Hobbes, for example, argues that in the absence of a state there is no morality. Since nations exist in a virtual state of nature with no authority over them to compel obedience and punish disobedience, the notions of right and wrong have no applicability to their conduct. But this is a nonsequitur. Assuming the international system is a state of nature, the most this shows is that *a morality* does not exist among nations, not that their conduct cannot be judged by moral criteria. If the inhabitants of an island constantly war with one another, killing, raping, and plundering at will, they do not have a morality. A morality is a system of shared values and common interests in which there is general compliance with, or at least general conformity to, certain rules whose operation is for the good of everyone. Any collection of individuals may fail to have a morality in this sense. But this in no way precludes our judging their conduct morally, anymore than the fact that an amoral individual consistently disregards moral considerations precludes our judging his conduct morally. Indeed, if the conduct of a group of people should be as bad as that of the inhabitants of the island, it would be precisely for that reason that they should come together, recognize their common interests, and cooperate in ways that would enable a morality to come into existence among them.

By the same token, if nations behave in such a way that a morality cannot be said to exist among them, as arguably is true of the nations of the world today, they do not thereby exempt their conduct from moral assessment. Indeed, as with the inhabitants of the island, it is likely to be our moral assessment of that conduct which leads us to judge that they should move in the direction of greater cooperation, trust, and interdependence, which may in time bring a morality into being among them. All conduct is susceptible of moral assessment, whether or not one is responsive to moral considerations in the framing of it and whether or not it antecedently conforms to the standards of morality.

In addition to denying that morality has a role in international relations, political realism has a positive aspect as well, stating what is or ought to be the governing norm in international relations. In twentieth-century American realism, as we have seen, the norm is that of national interest. Embedded within national interest, moreover, is the idea of the survival of the state. National interest, as this notion is usually understood, requires such survival. Hence to take as a basic principle that one ought to promote national interest is to commit oneself to the survival and maintenance of the state. Because of this, national egoism and reason of state, while they are not logically entailed by political realism, characterize the versions that have dominated American thinking.

It is the implications of this marriage of views that I now want to consider. These center about the doctrine of reason of state. This doctrine lies behind the Machiavellian thesis, considered in the previous chapter, that the prince must be prepared at times to violate the tenets of accepted morality if he is to preserve the state. Although in saying this Machiavelli is concerned specifically with the individual who heads the state, and hence, strictly speaking, is setting forth the rudiments of a public as opposed to a private morality, we need only modify his position slightly to get the doctrine of reason of state; one need only affirm that one ought above all else to preserve the state, apart from whether doing so preserves the personal power that is Machiavelli's concern.

Though, as I have said, reason of state is seldom discussed as such today, it underlies most thinking on international politics. In fact, it is usually assumed without argument that survival of the state takes precedence over everything else in international relations. As Dean Acheson said in commenting upon the U.S. quarantine of Cuba in the 1960s, "the survival of nations is not a matter of law." Add to this that it is not a matter of morality either, and one has reason of state.

Preservation of the state can be at issue in the face of both external and internal threats. The external threat in its clearest form is that of destruction in war, in which the issue may be whether a people are to live under the domination of others. The clearest form of internal threat is that of destruction by revolution. The underlying issue in each case, however, is whether there are any moral or legal limits to what a government may justifiably do to try to preserve the state. The answer tacitly given by most governments is that there are none.

IV

Clausewitz contends that moderation in war is an absurdity, and there is a certain prima facie plausibility to this view. If you choose to engage in such a deadly undertaking as war, to exercise moderation may seem irrational, as though you have adopted the most extreme of measures only to deny them their full effect. Yet moderation is sometimes exercised in war, and counsels of moderation abound in the literature about it. They are even enshrined in the laws for the conduct of war. Is this consistent? It is not, I suggest, if one accepts reason of state. For that doctrine commits one to the principle of military necessity, and military necessity, as I shall argue, is incompatible with the rational exercise of any meaningful sense of moderation in war.

Moderation can be an issue either in the pursuit of chosen objectives or in the choosing of those objectives in the first place. One might set himself a limited objective in war—such as to drive an enemy back beyond a certain point—but then spare no means in the pursuit of that objective. In that case he would have exercised moderation in one area but not in another. On the other hand, one might conceivably have the unlimited objective of bringing about the unconditional surrender of an enemy, or even his complete destruction, and yet limit himself in the means by which that objective is pursued. In some wars of the ancient world an invading army would lay siege to a city, sometimes for years, in order to force its capitulation, even though it might have achieved the same end, albeit at greater cost, by an immediate attack.

Sometimes in limited war one of the objectives themselves may be to regulate violence in such a way as to keep it within controllable bounds. This may be done, for example, to keep the enemy from escalating the war, or to avoid provoking his allies into intervening on his behalf. One of the arguments against using the atomic bomb in the Korean War was that it might compel the Soviet Union to enter the war on the side of North Korea. The point is that insofar as moderation is indispensable to attaining one's objectives in war, it does not, to that extent, constitute an absurdity. This does not mean that it may not yet be an absurdity to *adopt* as ends in war any that entail limited objectives—as Douglas MacArthur thought of U.S. war aims in Korea and some thought of U.S. war aims in Vietnam. Whether that is so depends upon the rationality of waging wars.

My concern is with whether moderation in the pursuit of one's objectives—whether those objectives are limited or unlimited—is absurd. And this is the question of whether it is absurd to place any limits upon military necessity.

V

What exactly is military necessity? A persistent confusion runs through discussions of the topic. On the one hand, a key concern of many who deal with the subject is with whether acting in accordance with military necessity is or ought to be lawful from the standpoint of international law. In a 1921 address to the American Society for International Law, Secretary of State Elihu Root expressed concern that if there were no restrictions upon military necessity in the conduct of war it would spell the end of international law. More recently it was judged at Nuremberg that certain acts could be in violation of international law even though they were dictated by military necessity. Telford Taylor, on the other hand, implies that military necessity is lawful because attempts to restrict it are ineffectual and therefore invalid.[15]

According to the conception presupposed in these views, it is an open question whether military necessity accords with international law. According to the positions expressed by Root, and also by the judgment at Nuremberg, the two can conflict. Taylor's position is more complex. Although in a sense it allows that military necessity and international law can conflict, it seems to entail that there cannot be a long-standing conflict, since law that is regularly violated by all is ineffectual and eventually ceases to be law in any meaningful sense.

On the other hand, the most common accounts of military necessity define it in such a way that it is not an open question whether it accords with international law. Consider:

Military necessity, as understood by modern civilized nations, consists in the necessity of those measures which are indis-

---

[15] *Nuremberg and Vietnam: An American Tragedy* (Chicago: Quadrangle Books, 1970), chap. 1. There is no explicit argument to this effect in Taylor, but the tenor of his discussion suggests that this is his position, and I shall so interpret him for the purposes of this discussion.

pensable for securing the ends of the war, and which are lawful according to the modern law and usages of war.

Military necessity justifies a resort to all the measures which are indispensable for securing this object [to bring about the complete submission of the enemy as soon as possible by regulated violence] and which are not forbidden by the modern laws and customs of war.

[Military necessity is] that principle which justifies measures not forbidden by international law which are indispensable for securing the complete submission of the enemy as soon as possible.[16]

Some of these are statements only about the concept of military necessity but all seem intended either to formulate a definition or to express a principle.

What is significant about these accounts is that they implicitly or explicitly define military necessity in terms of both what is indispensable to the attainment of the ends of war *and* what is authorized by international law. According to such an account, only such means to the attainment of the ends of war as are lawful even count as militarily necessary.[17]

It is clear, for this reason, that this cannot be the sense intended when it is asked whether international law should place any limitations on military necessity, since such a question is pointless if military necessity is lawful by definition. Those who take seriously

[16] These three formulations are taken respectively from Francis Lieber, "Instructions for the Government of the Armies of the United States in the Field," in *Lieber's Miscellaneous Writings* (Philadelphia, J. B. Lippencott & Company, 1881), 2: 250; *Army Field Manual*, 1940; and *Army Field Manual*, 1956.

[17] Taylor seems aware of some of these distinctions but does not explicitly recognize them. For an analysis of his account and further consideration of these issues, see Marshall Cohen, "Morality and the Laws of War," in *Philosophy, Morality, and International Affairs*, ed. V. Held, S. Morgenbesser, and T. Nagel (New York: Oxford University Press, 1974), pp. 71-88. For a more robust account, see that of Meyers S. McDougal and Florentine P. Feliciano, *Law and Minimum World Public Order: The Legal Regulation of International Coercion* (New Haven, Conn: Yale University Press, 1961): "The principle of military necessity may . . . accordingly be said to permit the exercise of that violence which is indispensably necessary (proportionate and relevant) for promptly repelling and terminating highly intense initiating coercion against 'territorial integrity' or 'political independence'—indispensably necessary, in a word, for successful defense or community enforcement actions" (p. 528). An account that packs even more into the principle is that of William V. O'Brien: "Legitimate military necessity consists of all measures immediately indispensable and proportionate to a legitimate military end, provided that they are not prohibited by the laws of war or the natural law, when taken on the decision of a responsible commander, subject to review." See *The Conduct of a Just and Limited War* (New York: Praeger, 1981), p. 66.

this question must mean by military necessity something more nearly like: whatever is indispensable to the attainment of the ends of war. One can then intelligibly ask whether any given means necessary to attaining war's objectives are lawful.

Sometimes military necessity is stated in a way that deals with the further question of whether nations may go beyond the requirements of military necessity in the use of violence. Taylor quotes from the 1917 Army Field Manual that includes among the principles determining the laws of war the so-called principle of humanity. It says that "all such kinds and degrees of violence as are not necessary for the purpose of war are not permitted to a belligerent," and then affirms this to be part of the principle of military necessity. But the principle of humanity is a prohibitory principle and is best distinguished from military necessity, as it is in the Lieber Code after which the Field Manual is patterned. For not only the formulation but also the import of the principle of military necessity is controversial, whereas the principle of humanity is not. Whatever their practice, nations rarely claim any warrant to go beyond the requirements of military necessity. This betokens no great humanitarianism on their part; it is simply that violations of the principle of humanity serve no rational purpose in the conduct of war. To expend resources beyond what is required to attain one's objectives is pointless and may even be detrimental. The reason why the principle of humanity is of relatively little consequence is because it prohibits only what it would not be rational to do anyway.

Finally, we should note that the principle of military necessity in either sense—that is, the sense which includes conformity with international law by definition, and the sense which leaves it open whether the two correspond—can be taken in either of two ways. It can be taken to legitimize only what is required for the attainment of the ultimate objectives of war, which might or might not—and normally would not—require the success of each and every particular military operation. Or it might be taken to legitimize every individual operation as well. Clausewitz's claim regarding the absurdity of moderation in war clearly implies only the first of these positions, whereas many discussions of military necessity imply the second.

VI

As it is the weaker sense of military necessity—that which equates it simply with what is indispensable to attaining the objectives of war—that enables one most easily to raise the important questions about the relationship of military necessity to international law, it is the conception with which I shall henceforth be concerned.

There are two particularly important implications of accepting a principle of military necessity in this sense. One is legal, the other moral.

On the legal issue, whether or not we accept Root's claim that unrestricted acceptance of military necessity entails the end of international law, such acceptance would clearly undermine much of international law as pertains to the conduct of warfare. For given any legal limitation upon the conduct of warfare, it is easily imaginable—and will occur often enough in practice—that a nation find itself in a position in which military necessity requires the violation of that restriction.[18] Such was the case on both sides with regard to submarine warfare in World War II. The London Treaty of 1930, as Taylor points out, would have rendered submarine warfare ineffective by prohibiting submarines from sinking merchant ships without first making provision for the safety of their crews. The upshot was that rather than forego the advantages of submarine warfare nations chose to disregard the law. Even if we should accept the view that systematic violation of so-called laws of war renders them ineffectual, hence invalid, hence not genuine law, it would still be true that acceptance of the principle of military necessity would undermine the attempts to regulate the conduct of war by means of international law. What it would leave unaffected is only what is covered by the principle of humanity. And that line will gradually be pushed farther and farther back as the understanding of how much violence and destruction are allowable by military necessity (always a function in part of weaponry and technology) advances with glacial inexorability.

With regard to the moral issue, acceptance of military necessity would almost certainly conflict with two other widely held principles. The first is a principle of discrimination prohibiting the killing of innocent persons in wartime; the second is that one ought to pursue only those war policies that will result in the fewest lives lost. The former is typically appealed to whenever nations protest the killing of innocents by the other side; the latter—what we may

[18] Richard Wasserstrom develops much this same point in his "The Responsibility of the Individual for War Crimes," in Held et al. eds., *Philosophy, Morality, and International Affairs*, p. 50. On the difficulty of avoiding violations of the principle of discrimination even in an allegedly just war, see O'Brien, *The Conduct of a Just and Limited War*, chap. 3.

call the quantitative principle—is typically appealed to whenever they want to justify their own killing of innocents. For it is clear that sometimes the course which will result in the fewest lives lost may involve killing innocents. Such was alleged to be the case in the atomic bombing of Hiroshima and Nagasaki, which was justified in part by appeal to the quantitative principle.

The quantitative principle requires modification, however, before it can plausibly be thought to be actually held by nations. As formulated above, it might often dictate prompt surrender, since that could be the course which would minimize loss of life overall. Moreover, it might require accepting a greater loss of life on one's own side if by so doing one could achieve fewer deaths overall, and few nations would accept such an exchange. A qualified quantitative principle would assert that one ought to pursue those war policies consistent with eventual victory that will result in fewest lives lost on one's own side.

Now it is clear that the quantitative principle even in this modified sense may conflict with the principle of innocence: military actions that kill innocents might well minimize casualties on one's own side (this was also thought to be the case with the Hiroshima bombing). And both the quantitative principle and the principle of innocence may conflict with military necessity. It happened repeatedly, for example, that the success of military operations by the United States in Vietnam required violations of the principle of innocence, inasmuch as the Vietcong so pervaded the villages and countryside that it was impossible to destroy them effectively without killing innocents as well. In justification of such an approach theologian Paul Ramsey asks: "If the guerrilla chooses to fight between, behind and over peasants, women and children, is it *he* or the counterguerrilla who has enlarged the legitimate target and enlarged it so as to bring unavoidable death and destruction upon a large number of innocent people?"[19]—a question he answers in favor of the counterguerrilla.

The fact remains that the enlargement of "legitimate" targets, as Ramsey says, did take place. And while it is probably false that military necessity called for saturation bombing during World War

---

[19] "Is Vietnam a Just War?" *Dialog* 6 (Winter 1967): 19-29, reprinted in *The Just War: Force and Political Responsibility* (New York: Charles Scribner's Sons, 1968). William V. O'Brien makes much the same point when he says that "these U.S. violations of the *jus in bello* were in substantial measure the result of deliberate Communist policies of using the population as a shield. Often it was impossible to get at the enemy without risking disproportionate and indiscriminate action" (*The Conduct of a Just and Limited War*, p. 123).

II, it is arguably true that it called for it in Vietnam. It is in any event easily imaginable that there might be situations in which such deliberate killing of innocents would be indispensable to the winning of a war. And it might be as well that military necessity, calling as it does (in reference to the "ends" of war) for action to vanquish the enemy in the swiftest way possible, would dictate actions that would greatly increase the casualties on one's own side. That would bring the principle of military necessity and the quantitative principle into conflict.

Military necessity, then, can conflict with both international law and with some of the most rudimentary moral prescriptions regarding the taking of human life, innocent and noninnocent. Inasmuch as reason of state entails a commitment to military necessity in any conflict in which the state itself is in jeopardy, to subscribe to the doctrine commits one to a willingness to expend whatever lives are necessary—both on one's own side and on the enemy's—to achieve the ends of war. And because reason of state is entailed by national egoism, the same holds true of it. When, therefore, political realism is conjoined with national egoism, it imposes no limits upon the death and destruction the state may cause if necessary to preserve itself against external threats. State necessity then rules.

VII

But what of internal threats? If the overriding concern is with the preservation of the state, what does it matter whether a threat is external or internal?

Consider that during World War II, 120,000 Japanese residents of the United States, most of them citizens, were placed in internment camps without trial and without being charged with any crime. President Roosevelt simply signed Executive Order 9066 instructing the military to declare certain areas "military areas" and authorizing them to remove all persons from those areas. The appeal was to military necessity. The order stated that successful prosecution of the war against Japan "requires every possible protection against espionage and against sabotage." Then Attorney General Earl Warren, later to become Chief Justice of the United States Supreme Court, supported the internments.

At the same time the German government was herding millions of its own people into concentration camps. They were greater in number, of course, and met a far more ghastly fate. But in each

case certain persons—defined racially, politically, or ideologi-
cally—were declared and widely believed to be a threat to the
state. The Japanese Americans, it was feared, would engage in
sabotage on the West Coast. The Jews and Communists in Germany, Hitler had alleged in *Mein Kampf*, were bent on nothing less
than the destruction of the German nation. Even Lincoln, during
the Civil War, assumed vast dictatorial powers, including the sus-
pension of many civil liberties, when it appeared that these measures were necessary to preserve the Union. He said in a statement that is a good approximation of the principle of military
necessity, that "[a]s Commander in Chief of the Army and Navy
in time of war I suppose I have the right to take any measure
which may best subdue the enemy."[20]

The underlying issue is whether there are any limits—moral as
well as legal—to what a government may justifiably do to try to
preserve the state.

There is near universal revulsion at what the Nazis did in the
extermination camps. Such "final solutions" (as we may call any
attempt to resolve perceived problems by the extermination of
whole classes of persons) are regarded as having no justification,
morally or otherwise. Few judgments are as widely agreed upon
as this. But consider today that the U.S. government considers it
"acceptable" that scores of millions of Americans—far more than
were killed by the Nazis, and most of them innocent by any plausible standard—should die if a nuclear showdown with the Soviet
Union is deemed necessary. If a government considers it acceptable that millions should die under these circumstances, why
should it shrink from killing a fraction of that number—say six million, to think the unthinkable for a moment—if by so doing it
could remove no less a perceived threat to national security?

To be sure, there is a difference between deliberately killing a
certain number of your own people, as the Nazis did, and taking
an action that is known will result in their deaths. But the victims
are as dead in the one case as in the other, and ultimately for the
same reason, the interest of the state. The question is not whether
such a happening is likely in a country like the United States,
which has strong institutional and moral safeguards of individual
liberty; it is, rather, whether there is anything to preclude it in the

[20] Quoted in Clinton Rossitor, *Constitutional Dictatorship: Crisis Government in the
Modern Democracies* (New York: Harcourt, Brace & World, 1963), p. 233. Rossiter
cites Nicolay and Hay: *Abraham Lincoln: A History* (New York, 1890), 6: 155-156, for
the quotation.

logic that can justify nuclear war. I would suggest that there is not. Once one accepts the view that there are no limits to what governments may do to counteract external threats—and willingness to wage all-out nuclear war signifies the abandonment of such limits—there is no logical bar to the removal of all limits to counteract internal threats as well. There may be legal and constitutional bars. But just as military necessity rides roughshod over international law when the two conflict, so state necessity can be expected to do the same with constitutional guarantees in a severe enough crisis. All that is required is the conviction that the persons in question are a comparable threat to the state.

The issue for democracy was put by Alexander Hamilton in *The Federalist Papers* when he wrote that "[t]he violent destruction of life and property incident to war, the continual effort and alarm attendant on a state of continual danger, will compel nations the most attached to liberty to resort for repose and security to institutions which have a tendency to destroy their civil and political rights. To be more safe, they at length become willing to run the risk of being less free."[21] The paradox is that, the greater the perceived threat, the more drastic the measures believed warranted to meet it; but the more drastic the measures, the greater the threat to freedom.

Let us examine the progression of reasoning regarding national security that points directly to the extension of state necessity[22] to the domestic arena, which then opens the door to consideration of such drastic measures as final solutions. This reasoning moves through various stages, each of which has a particular model for national defense. As technology and improvements in weaponry render each successive model inadequate, thinking progresses to the next stage—except that, as I shall argue, one eventually reaches the point at which there are no more stages.

The first stage represents a fortress model. It is the conception of national security largely associated with isolationism. It holds that defense should consist of maintaining such strength on one's borders that one deters potential attackers from violating them and insures their defeat if they do. In stage two it is decided that security is best achieved by maintaining a defense perimeter extending beyond those borders. This stage, which represents something of a wagon-train model, is reached when it is concluded that

[21] *The Federalist Papers*, No. 8.
[22] In the use of this term I am following Geoffrey Best, *Humanity in Warfare* (New York: Columbia University Press, 1980), p. 49.

weaponry and the techniques of warfare are so sophisticated that it is imprudent to wait until an enemy has actually violated your borders before reacting. President Roosevelt set forth the rationale for this conception in the spring and summer of 1941 when he said that

> [m]odern warfare has given us a new definition for that word "attack." There was a time when we could afford to say that we would not fight unless attacked, and then wait until the physical attack came upon us before starting to shoot. Modern techniques of warfare have changed all that. An attack today is a very different thing. An attack today begins as soon as any base has been occupied from which our security is threatened. That base may be thousands of miles away from our own shores. The American government must, of necessity, decide at which point any threat of attack against this hemisphere has begun; and to make their stand when that point has been reached.
>
> Nobody can foretell . . . just when the acts of the dictators will ripen into attack on this hemisphere and us. But we know enough by now to realize that it would be suicide to wait until they are in our front yard.[23]

He then proceeded to announce that North Atlantic patrols by U.S. Naval vessels were being expanded and that Axis ships would enter waters considered essential to our defense only at their own risk.

But if it is reasonable to intercept your enemy before he enters your front yard, so to speak, is it not much more reasonable not to wait for him to come after you in the first place but to go after him instead?

This formulation leads to stage three, which was reached in American foreign policy thinking roughly during the Cold War era, with the Korean War marking the transition between the two. Prior to that time Korea had been considered outside of our defense perimeter and was so declared to be by Secretary of State Acheson. However, when war broke out, the decision was made to intervene anyway. As Kissinger writes of America's policy at

---

[23] Quoted in Charles A. Beard, " 'In Case of Attack' in the Atlantic," in *Causes and Consequences of World War II*, ed. Robert A. Divine (Chicago: Quadrangle Books, 1969), pp. 102, 101. The Beard article is reprinted from Charles A. Beard, *President Roosevelt and the Coming of the War, 1941: A Study in Appearances and Realities* (New Haven, Conn.: Yale University Press, 1948).

the time: "Secretary Acheson's speech of January 12, 1950, which excluded Korea from our defensive perimeter, was no more than an application of fundamental United States strategy." He then adds approvingly that "[i]t was a courageous decision to resist an aggression so totally at variance with all previous planning."[24]

One need only carry such reasoning through to its conclusion to regard events occurring *any place* in the world as constituting actionable threats to national security. The wagon train model, with its conception of a clearly defined defense perimeter, gives way to the model of world policeman, according to which it is the detection of threats to national security any place they may occur that is important.

The problem with having reached this stage is that there is no longer any perimeter to extend in the face of continuing threats. The whole world has already been encompassed. Thus, so long as the quest for absolute security persists, even more imaginative measures are called for. Here we move on to stage four. The reasoning here is that if it is reasonable to confront your potential assailant the moment he begins to march, it is even more reasonable to ferret him out before his designs reach the stage of execution. Thus one no longer confines himself to intervening against nations but undertakes, when necessary, to intervene *within* nations, either with or without the support of their governments, depending upon whether the threat emanates from the government itself or from forces within the country antithetical to the government. Considerations of economy, if nothing else, argue for snuffing out hostile flames before they ignite larger fires. This may require manipulating the internal politics of the country through bribery or threats, if possible, but through assassination and direct military intervention, if necessary.

There is, however, one final stage to be reached before this logic can be said to have run its course. If preservation of the state is of foremost importance, why distinguish between external and internal threats? A state can be as effectively destroyed from subversion as from external assault.

John Mitchell said when he was attorney general under the Nixon administration that "the threat to our society from so-called 'domestic' subversion is as serious as any threat from abroad. . . . You cannot separate foreign from domestic threats to the govern-

[24] *Nuclear Weapons and Foreign Policy* (New York: Published for the Council on Foreign Relations by Harper and Brothers, 1957) pp. 43-44.

ment and say that we should meet one less decisively than the other."[25] Lest this be dismissed as the viewpoint of a discredited administration, consider the words of soon-to-be Supreme Court Justice William Powell that same year: "There may have been a time when a valid distinction existed between external and internal threats. But such a distinction is now largely meaningless. The radical left, strongly led and with a growing base of support, is plotting violence and revolution. Its leaders visit and collaborate with foreign Communist enemies. Freedom can be lost as irrevocably from revolution as from foreign attack."[26]

How far such thinking is likely to progress remains to be seen. The point is that it supplies the key premise necessary for the extension of reason of state to the domestic sphere. As such, it completes the progression of the line of thought we have been examining, to the point where even the distinction between internal and external threats collapses—not in the sense that the distinction can no longer be made but in the sense that there is no longer a basis for treating the one less harshly than the other.

This final stage is complex, however, and contains within itself the same sorts of stages as are represented in the overall pattern. One can, for example, move from the position of waiting for overt acts on the part of supposed subversives to the position of anticipating such acts to the further position of anticipating conspiracies to perform actions—all the way to the point of banning those forms of speech and association that are preconditions of the very design of such acts. If one seriously believes there is no valid distinction between internal and external threats and is prepared to stop at nothing to counteract the one, why do any less to stop the other? If full use of the latest developments in weaponry is justified in the one case, then why not surveillance, wiretaps, harassment, kidnappings, and if necessary, mass arrests, incarcerations, and even killings against comparable threats in the other case? The relevant considerations from the standpoint of state necessity is the seriousness of the threat, not its origin.

The point, once again, is not that this will happen, or even that it is likely. It is that there is no bar to its happening once one accepts the logic that justifies nuclear war. We have adopted principles in international affairs that if applied consistently to domestic affairs would justify acts we all consider abhorrent—and abhorrent

[25] *New York Times*, June 12, 1971.
[26] *New York Times*, Nov. 1, 1971.

not just because the final solution of the Nazis was directed against innocent persons but because of the inherent immorality of such treatment of anyone. It would matter little if the millions Hitler exterminated had indeed been a threat to the German nation. It is not just the fallibility of a government that is at issue here. What is at issue is a whole way of thinking about how one may justifiably treat other human beings.

VIII

If this is correct, the philosophy of political realism, with its attendant national egoism and the state necessity entailed by it, is bankrupt. This is not because its advocates are bad men, and not because political realism invariably leads to consequences of the sort I have detailed (government officials frequently fail to see the logical extensions of their policies and pronouncements), but because in elevating the preservation of an abstraction—the state—above individual persons, it places no limits upon what may be done to achieve that objective. Only the perceived interests of the state limit one's conduct. Or, in wartime, the demands of military necessity. True, that may sometimes require considering the interests of other states; that is not ruled out. But only if there is an extraordinary concordance among the interests of the various states of the world (a concordance in which few really believe when their own country's interests are staked against those of another) are there any effective constraints. In a world of unevenly distributed resources, and in which the health and prosperity of everyone depends heavily upon access to such resources, it is naive to believe that laissez faire policies on the international scene can in the long run lead to anything but strife.

These considerations notwithstanding, nothing in political realism succeeds in showing that morality does not apply to international affairs, much less to war in particular. The actions of states cannot be understood apart from the actions of their officials, the agents of those officials, and the citizenry. Whatever their roles, they are morally accountable for what they do. *Their* acts are subject to moral assessment. There is no veil of neutrality that falls over them when they act as officials or agents of the state and that magically suspends the full relevance of morality to their acts. Whether we characterize wartime policies as the actions of such men, or as actions of the state itself (which in turn can ultimately only be understood by reference to the actions of such men), is immaterial. Morality can accommodate either way of speaking. No new "morality"—public as opposed to private, or collective as opposed to individual—is needed. All that is needed is sensitivity to the full range of obligations and responsibilities that changing circumstances impose upon us. These considerations, combined with the analysis of violence in Chapter One, suffice to establish the full relevance of morality to both the initiation and the conduct of war.

To maintain that morality is fully relevant to the assessment of war is not, however, to say anything about what that assessment should be. Most persons who would reject political realism in favor of applying the moral criteria of the just war tradition, for example, maintain that those criteria show that some wars are just.[27] Many of them think that wars are frequently justified. Some maintain that most American wars have been just. To show the relevance of morality to warfare, in other words, however conclusively that may be established, only sets the stage for the moral assessment of war. It does not advance that assessment. For that we need to examine the specific arguments to justify war.

[27] Charles Krauthammer, for example, rejects realism in the form in which it attacks the Reagan Doctrine of interventionism on behalf of anti-Communist insurgencies in such places as Afghanistan, Angola, Cambodia, and Nicaragua. What he calls the Reagan Doctrine and contrasts with realism, however, resembles closely the very doctrines realists advocated following World War II and called realism. See his "Morality and the Reagan Doctrine," *The New Republic*, Sept. 8, 1986.

FOUR

ST. AUGUSTINE ON THE
JUSTIFICATION OF WAR

Deeds which they would atone for with their lives if committed in peace, we praise them for having done under
arms.   —Seneca

If war is of the gravest moral concern, then it is important to understand the thinking of those who support it as well as of those
who oppose it. When I say "support" it, I do not mean necessarily
in the sense of advocating it, urging that nations wage wars and
claiming, say, with Treitschke or Hegel, that some abstract good
will somehow emerge if this is done. Few do this. Most people
believe that war is a terrible thing, that it should be avoided if at
all possible, and that we should try to create a world in which
there will be no war. That is, most people are for peace. Nonetheless they believe that *in some sense* the world is better off with war
than without; that some evils are worse than war and some values
worth fighting for. And they believe that being willing to wage
war when confronted with such evils is the best way to prevent
war.

Such a view may be called militarism, so long as it is distinguished from militarism in a narrower sense, which favors war
and the promotion of military values for their own sake or for ends
other than defense and the maintenance of peace. The militarist in
the sense I have in mind can be an advocate of peace as much as
the pacifist, and on moral grounds as well. It is just that he believes that military preparedness, and the fighting of wars when
necessary, is the best way to achieve peace.

This view is so deeply entrenched that for the most part it goes
unchallenged. Even the world's foremost socio-economic systems,
capitalism and communism, share it. In fact, considering the extent to which it shapes the values by which their respective policies are guided and competes for their human and natural re-

sources in their preparations for war, it may fairly be said to render them fundamentally more similar than dissimilar. Those who hold this view can agree that war would be wrong in an *ideal* world; that is, one in which everyone acted morally. In such a world the occasion for war would never arise and even the need for military preparedness would vanish. The moral problems emerge when one considers the *actual* world in which there is wrongdoing, cruelty, and injustice, for it is to combat these that most people think war is justified. Wrongdoing often takes the form of aggression by a nation seeking to appropriate the territory and resources of another nation. Such wars are now almost universally condemned, and the U.N. Charter allows recourse to war only in self-defense against aggression. But sometimes wrongdoing takes the form of oppression, as when a people are deprived of their freedom by their own government or by some group or class within society. According to Marxists, whereas economic exploitation may exist in a world that is technically at "peace," its existence justifies war, at least of a revolutionary sort, in order to redress the wrong of exploitation.

This, it should be said, is but one aspect of morality, since most of our dealings with people do not involve responding to wrongdoing. But it is an important aspect, for it is wrongdoing by others that tends to call forth the severest responses. People who would otherwise never think of harming anyone support the confinement of wrongdoers under conditions of deprivation and if the wrong is great enough approve their execution by the state. If the wrongdoing is by another nation they will support and, if they are of the appropriate age and qualifications, actively participate in the killing of countless other persons, the devastation of homelands, and the destruction of whole societies in order to combat the wrong. Those who do not actively participate honor and praise those who do. And most of them do all of this with scarcely a moment's hesitation and hardly a thought about whether what they are doing is right. It is the thinking that would justify such a response to wrongdoing that we want to try to understand.

I

I want for this purpose to begin with the thought of Saint Augustine, who lived in the late fourth and early fifth centuries A.D. Probably no single historical figure has been of greater importance in giving direction to the moral thinking about war in the Western world, and he is in fact often taken to be the founder of the just war theory.[1] His writing takes place in the context of an early Church undergoing a radical transformation.

It is difficult to read the New Testament with its emphasis upon loving one's enemies and turning the other cheek without suspecting that Jesus was opposed to war. He never says so, of course, and his prescriptions can be interpreted to apply only to conduct among individuals and not to that of groups—that is, to set forth only an individual and not a collective mortality, as we discussed these in the second chapter. But his message was interpreted by his early followers, a persecuted nonviolent minority in a militarized state, as counseling a way of life antithetical to war, and for years after his death Christians tended to be pacifistic.[2] This gradually changed as the movement gained adherents and Christianity was eventually accepted by the Roman ruler Constantine, who, though not actually baptized until his deathbed in A.D. 337, brought Christianity into accommodation with a militarized state. With the Edict of Thessalonica in A.D. 380 Christianity became the official religion of the Roman Empire. It grew rapidly thereafter until by the Middle Ages the Church had become one of the most powerful institutions in Europe, turning against heretics and infidels alike the very methods of violence that had been used against it in its fledgling years. Since that time, from the crusades and religious wars down to the twentieth-century's world

---

[1] Though it has been argued by James Turner Johnson, in his *Ideology, Reason, and the Limitation of War: Religious and Secular Concepts, 1200-1740* (Princeton, N.J.: Princeton University Press, 1975), and "Just War Theory: What's the Use?" *Worldview*, July-August 1976, that the "classic" just war doctrine, including both *jus ad bellum* and *jus in bello*, does not exist prior to 1500. He also stresses both the religious and the secular antecedents of the doctrine. Jenny Teichman in *Pacifism and the Just War* (Oxford: Basil Blackwell, 1986) sees the theory as developing between the ninth and thirteenth centuries (p. 13).

[2] This is the prevailing, though not universal, view among scholars. See, for example, Roland H. Bainton, *Christian Attitudes toward War and Peace: A Historical Survey and Critical Re-Evaluation* (New York: Abingdon Press, 1960), p. 14; Herbert A. Deane, *The Political and Social Ideas of St. Augustine* (New York: Columbia University Press, 1963), pp. 163-164; John Ferguson, *The Politics of Love: The New Testament and Nonviolent Revolution* (Nyack, N.Y.: Fellowship Publications, 1979), pp. 53-65; Adolf Harnack, *Militia Christi: The Christian Religion and the Military in the First Three Centuries* (Philadelphia: Fortress Press, 1981); James Turner Johnson, *Can Modern War Be Just?* (New Haven, Conn.: Yale University Press, 1984), p. 3; William V. O'Brien, *Nuclear War, Deterrence, and Morality* (New York: Newman Press, 1967), pp. 18-19; Robert L. Phillips, *War and Justice* (Norman: University of Oklahoma Press, 1984), p. 5; Paul Ramsey, *War and the Christian Conscience: How Shall Modern War Be Conducted Justly?* (Durham, N.C.: Duke University Press, 1961), p. xv; Frederick H. Russell, *The Just War in the Middle Ages* (Cambridge: At the University Press, 1975), pp. 18, 21.

wars, whose main participants (excepting Japan and the USSR in World War II) were predominantly Christian nations, Christians have wielded the sword against one another as well as against others with unparalleled intensity.

While no one person was by any means responsible for the whole of this transformation, Augustine stands out above all others. A convert to the Church who eventually became a bishop, he put Christianity on a new ethical footing by providing a rationale for Christian participation in war. In so doing he turned Christ's teaching on its head. What were among the foremost of those teachings, the counsels to love and not to return evil for evil, which early Christians took to proscribe war and the killing of human beings, he took to be compatible with war, torture, and capital punishment. This launched a tradition of sustained effort by Christians to justify war. And it makes Augustine Christianity's principal philosopher of war. Virtually every major writer in the just war tradition builds upon his work. In fact he looms in the scale of history as perhaps the single most important figure after Paul in the evolution of Christianity, surpassing even Luther by far in terms of his influence upon its ethical character.

The historical reasons for this undertaking on Augustine's part need not detain us. Suffice it to say that he sought not merely to justify Christian participation in war but also to show that Christians could have the full slate of civic responsibilities to the state. Rome had been attacked repeatedly by barbarians and was sacked by the Visigoths in A.D. 410, a calamity for which pagan critics blamed the Christian influence. They reasoned that in order for a people to survive they must be prepared to fight and that a religion which appears to forbid violence undermines the power of the state. Similar complaints had been brought against Christianity at least from the time of Marcus Aurelius in the second century. In his monumental work *The City of God*, Augustine responded by undertaking to reconcile Christianity with the existence of the state and the individual's responsibilities toward it. An important part of this involved showing the justifiability of Christian participation in war, an undertaking in which he had already been engaged for years.

The central problem in producing such a justification, of course, is to reconcile it with Christ's teaching. For Jesus had unmistakably taught loving one's enemies, turning the other cheek, and not resisting evil with evil. Yet Augustine noted that the biblical God sometimes commanded men to wage war, and he insisted that

117

God's commanding a war makes it just.[3] How were these to be reconciled? In a key passage dealing with this problem Augustine says: "If it is supposed that God could not enjoin warfare, because in after times it was said by the Lord Jesus Christ, "I say unto you, That ye resist not evil: but if anyone strike thee on the right cheek, turn to him the left also," the answer is, that what is here required is not a bodily action, but an inward disposition. The sacred seat of virtue is the heart."[4]

Of importance on this view is the adoption of the right attitude and cultivation of the appropriate dispositions, an outlook Augustine had found in earlier Stoic philosophy. The effect was to turn Christianity inward, emphasizing not so much outward action as purity of heart and motivation. Thus Augustine says of a virgin that if she has made a decision to submit to her seducer it matters little that her body has not yet been violated; her virtue, which resides ultimately in the soul, has already been lost. Behaving outwardly like the virtuous may conceal wickedness, but it does not change it. The other side of the coin, as we shall see, is that sometimes men may behave outwardly like the wicked provided in so doing their soul remains pure. They may even kill provided they do so in the right spirit. The way is then opened to one's being a Christian while acting outwardly in ways indistinguishable from those of non-Christians. How is that possible? How can one love his enemies and turn the other cheek and at the same time participate in the slaughter of warfare?

II

Augustine's answer to this is of the first importance, and it has been appealed to by generations of just war theorists, including prominent twentieth-century writers like Paul Ramsey and James Turner Johnson. Ramsey, for example, maintains that in Augustine's treatment of this topic we find the genesis of the idea of noncombatant immunity, which figures prominently in just war

[3] *Contra Faustum* 22. 75, in *The Works of Aurelius Augustine*, ed. Marcus Dods, Vol. 6, *Writings in Connection with the Manichaean Heresy*, trans. Richard Stothert (Edinburgh: T. & T. Clark, 1872). See also *De Civitate Dei*, trans. Marcus Dods (New York: Random House, 1950), 1. 21. On the rightness of God's commands in general see *Confessions* 3. 8.15, 9.17, in *A Select Library of the Nicene and Post-Nicene Fathers of the Christian Church*, Vol. 1, trans. J. G. Pilkington, ed. Philip Schaff (Grand Rapids, Mich.: Wm. B. Eerdmans Publishing Company, 1956).

[4] *Contra Faustum* 22. 76. See also *Letters* 138. 2.13, in *A Select Library of the Nicene and Post-Nicene Fathers of the Christian Church*, Vol. 1, trans. J. G. Cunningham.

theory and is the cornerstone of his own examination of the problem of the morality of war.[5] And he says of the problem of reconciling war with Christ's teaching that:

> Jesus did not teach that his disciples should life [sic] up the face of another oppressed man to be struck again on the other cheek. Out of neighbor-regarding love for one's fellow men, preferential decision among one's neighbors may and can and should be made. For love's sake (the very principle of the prohibition of killing), and not only for the sake of an abstract justice sovereign over the political realm in separation from the private, Christian thought and action was driven to posit this single "exception" (an exception only when externally viewed): that forces should be repelled and the bearers and close cooperators in military force should be directly repressed, by violent means if necessary, lest many more of God's little ones should be irresponsibly forsaken and lest they suffer more harm than need be.[6]

Though Ramsey does not refer specifically to Augustine in this passage, he has been interpreted as deriving the position from Augustine. And Johnson claims to find in Augustine's treatment of the issue a paradigm case of justifiable Christian killing.[7] This by extension provides a justification for warfare. He likewise makes Augustine's analysis the cornerstone of his argument for the recovery of the just war tradition for today's world. "Augustine," he says, "treated defense by means of a paradigmatic situation involving three persons: a criminal who is attacking or about to attack a second person, the innocent victim, and the third person, an onlooker, on whose behalf Augustine offers his thoughts. What should this third person do in such a situation?"[8] He then says:

> The proper action for the Christian, reasoned Augustine, is to intervene between the criminal and victim, defending the latter even at the risk of his own life against attack or threat of attack by the former. Such defense of the victim, argued Augustine, is mandated by the onlooker's love for him as someone for whom Christ died: yet Christ also died for the crimi-

[5] Ramsey, *War and the Christian Conscience*, chap. 3.

[6] Ramsey, *The Just War*, pp. 150-151.

[7] Cf. James Turner Johnson, *Just War Tradition and the Restraint of War: A Moral and Historical Inquiry* (Princeton, N.J.: Princeton University Press, 1981), pp. 145, 350, and *Can Modern War Be Just?* introduction and p. 176.

[8] *Can Modern War Be Just?* p. 3.

119

nal, and this limits what may be done toward him in defending the innocent victim.[9]

What is mandated, according to Johnson, is that the Christian use proportionate force to protect the innocent, "up to and including the possibility of killing the criminal, if he does not relent before that."

Even though Johnson concedes that Augustine does not extend this reasoning to the case of warfare, if this represents Augustine's view (and of course if it accurately reflects Christ's teaching in the first place), we can well understand how subsequent Christians have thought war could be justified. Even those who do not frame their arguments for the justifiability of war within the Christian perspective use very much the same kind of argument Johnson imputes to Augustine to justify their positions. They argue that violence is sometimes justified in defense of the innocent and that at the level of nations that may require resorting to war.[10] The notion of a right to self-defense is a strong one. The idea of defending others who cannot defend themselves is almost equally as strong. It reflects a deeply engrained moral sense about protecting the innocent.

Augustine leaves no doubt, in an early discussion of freedom of the will, that killing in self-defense by a private individual without public authority is impermissible.[11] To kill another person in defense of this earthly life represents an inordinate desire to cling to those things one ought not to love. This means that he does not avail himself of one of the most common ways of justifying war, which is to argue that the individual has a right of self-defense, and therefore the state, by extension, has a similar right. The justification of war must be found elsewhere. Because the passages in which Augustine deals most extensively with this issue are of such importance, and because they have been subjected to widely divergent interpretations, let us examine them in detail.

[9] Ibid., pp. 3-4.

[10] See, for example, Jan Narveson, "Violence and War," in *Matters of Life and Death: New Introductory Essays in Moral Philosophy*, ed. Tom Regan (New York: Random House, 1980), pp. 109-146.

[11] *De Libero Arbitrio* 1. 5., trans. Carroll Mason Sparrow (Charlottesville: Dietz Press, Inc., 1947). This leads some writers to speak of Augustine's "private pacifism" here. See, for example, Russell, *The Just War in the Middle Ages*, p. 18. For an excellent discussion of these and related issues, see also Richard Shelly Hartigan, "Saint Augustine on War and Killing: The Problem of the Innocent," *Journel of the History of Ideas* 27, no. 2 (April-June 1966): 195-205.

III

There are two parts to the argument, which is presented in the form of a dialogue between Augustine and his friend Evodius: the first to establish the nature of evil, the second to assess whether killing of various sorts is justified.

Augustine first establishes with Evodius that adultery, murder, and blasphemy are wrong and then asks what makes them so. In the case of adultery, for example, is it because it is forbidden by the law? No, says Augustine, rather it is forbidden by the law because it is wrong. Is it then wrong because it violates the golden rule (which Augustine takes in a negative form, as prescribing that one not do unto others what one would not have done to oneself). This will not do, he says, because a perverted man might take pleasure in offering his wife to another, in which case there would be no violation of the rule. Is it then because it is often condemned? This will not do either because there are many cases in which men have been known to suffer condemnation for doing what is right. "Is it not perhaps," Augustine then proposes to Evodius, "the concupiscence that is the evil thing in adultery, and you are having difficulty because you are looking for evil in the act itself, which can be seen?"[12] He then proceeds to explain that it is in sinful desire that evil consists. For if someone wanted to commit adultery and would do so if given the chance, he would be no better than one who had both the desire and the opportunity and in fact committed adultery. It is circumstance that provides or withholds the opportunity; it is one's character that determines the desire. But suppose a man should kill his master from fear of punishment? To live without fear is good and so to desire to live without fear seems not to be a culpable desire. But, argues Augustine, this desire can be had by bad men as well as good, and whereas good men seek freedom from fear by "turning their affections away from those things which cannot be held without the danger of losing them," the bad seek this end "in order that they may rest secure in their enjoyment of such things" and attempt to remove obstacles to its attainment.[13] What are those things? Worldly pleasures and possessions. These can be taken from us against our will. To cling to them inordinately reveals a love of earthly things. To love God, on the other hand, is to love eternal things. If one wants to be free of fear, he should turn away from those things he stands

[12] *De Libero Arbitrio* 1. 38.
[13] Ibid., 1. 4.10.

to lose against his will. So to kill another person to free yourself from such fear represents a sinful desire.

To understand evil, Augustine is telling us, it is not enough to look at a person's behavior; we must know the nature of his soul. The Stoics before him had stressed such inwardness for the understanding of virtue, and Kant after him gives such inwardness its paradigmatic philosophical expression in his notion that moral worth consists exclusively in the possession of a good will, one that is governed by the motive of duty.

Still, this by itself gives little reason for supposing that Christians may or should participate in war. It explains how a person can behave outwardly in a manner consistent with Christ's teachings and yet harbor an evil will within him, but it does not show how one can be virtuous within and yet act outwardly in ways that seem to conflict with those teachings. And this is what one must do if he is to show that Christ's teachings regarding love and nonresistance to evil are compatible with warfare. In fact the analysis thus far considered would seem to argue in the other direction. For if evil consists in concupiscence, and that reduces ultimately to loving earthly things rather than God, then why should Christians try to cling to life and possessions, the things men go to war mainly to preserve? Granting that evil is to be found in the heart rather than in outward action, why resort to the extremist of outward actions—the killing of other persons—in order to cling to those things one ought not to love in the first place and that can be taken away against one's will?

This is the more complicated part of Augustine's treatment of the problem, and his answer to it is less clear. It requires focussing upon killings that are fully sanctioned by law, like killing in self-defense, or defense of another, or by a soldier in warfare, rather than those like the preceding that are contrary to law. How can these fail to be evil? Let us look at Augustine's treatment of this, beginning with the observation of Evodius: "How can I deem them [who kill to protect life, liberty, or honor] without concupiscence, since they contend for those things which they may lose against their will; or if they can prevent loss, why go so far as to kill for their sake?" To this Augustine replies:

Then the law is not just that gives the wayfarer the right to kill a robber to save his own life, or that permits anyone, man or woman, to kill an attacking ravisher before he can accomplish his purpose? The law moreover commands the soldier to

122

kill the enemy; if he stays his hand he is punished by the emperor. Shall we venture to say that such laws are unjust, or that they are indeed not laws at all? For I think that a law that is not just is no law.[14]

He has shifted the question of whether such killings can take place without concupiscence to the question of what we are to make of laws that allow them. Are they just or unjust? And can anything properly be called a law that is not just? This is not the primary issue, and in the dialogue it takes a few moments for Evodius to get the discussion back on track.

But we should note an ambiguity in the first sentence of Augustine's reply. When he asks about the justice of the law in question, he may be concerned with one or the other of two possible cases. He is surely concerned with the case in which one kills such a person (a robber or ravisher) in *self*-defense. But he could mean to include cases in which one kills such a person in defense of someone else as well. In order to derive the Ramsey/Johnson interpretation of Augustine, cited in Section II, which holds that he unequivocally allows killing in defense of the innocent, one must take him to mean the second of these.

In any event, let us continue with Evodius's response to Augustine's apparent defense of the laws.

I see that the law is indeed safe enough from such a charge; for the law permits the people that it governs to commit lesser wrongs to prevent the commission of greater. For the death of one who lies in wait to kill another is a much slighter thing than that of one who would merely save his own life. And it is a far worse thing to force humiliation on a man than that the ravisher be killed by his intended victim.

Notice here, however, that the reference is clearly only to *self*-defense, not the defense of others. The "lesser wrong" in the first case is the killing of the robber as opposed to the death of him who would save his own life; in the second, it is the humiliation of a man as opposed to the killing of a ravisher by his intended victim. Evodius continues, turning now to the case of the soldier.

As for the soldier, in killing his enemy he is the servant of the law, and hence merely does his duty without any evil desire. Moreover the law itself, being made for the protection of the

14 Ibid., 1. 5.11.

people, cannot be accused of concupiscence. For he who made the law, if he made it by God's command—that is to say following the dictates of eternal justice—could do so without any concupiscence whatever; but even if he decreed it because of some evil desire, it does not follow that the law is necessarily tainted with concupiscence, because a good law may be made even by one who is himself not good. . . . Therefore that law which to preserve the state commands that the violence of an enemy be repelled with like violence, may be obeyed without concupiscence. And the same may be said of all officials who by rank and station are subject to any authority.[15]

Augustine affirms this view in the *City of God*,[16] and he has widely been interpreted as exempting from sin the killing that is done by public officials and their agents, like soldiers and executioners. If this is correct, it would mean that he is making a kind of distinction between private morality and public morality of the sort we considered in Chapter Two.

But we need to ask whether this passage represents Augustine's own considered opinion; he puts the words, after all, into the mouth of Evodius rather than that of the character of Augustine. So let us look at how Augustine has Evodius continue in what follows immediately upon the preceding passage: "But I do not see how these men, though blameless under the law, can be altogether blameless; for the law does not compel them to kill, but leaves it in their power. And so they are left free not to kill anyone for those things which they can lose against their will, and which therefore they ought not to love."[17] Here Augustine has Evodius bring the issue back from the question of the justice of the *laws* permitting such killing (which he says may be untainted by concupiscence even if decreed because of an evil desire) to the ques-

[15] Ibid., 1. 5.12.

[16] Trans. Marcus Dods (New York: Random House, 1950), 1. 21, 26.

[17] In analyzing this passage, Ramsey indicates in brackets following the words "these men" that Augustine means here those "who defend themselves privately" (*War and the Christian Conscience*, p. 36). But this seems unlikely. In the two immediately preceding sentences Augustine has (through Evodius) referred to the state's command to repel the violence of an enemy by violence, hence assuredly has referred to soldiers, since it is they who carry out such commands; and he has furthermore referred explicitly to "all officials" who are subject to public authority. It is unquestionably *all* of these to whom he refers when he raises the question of whether they can be altogether blameless, not merely those who engage in private self-defense.

tion of the possible concupiscence of the *individuals* who act in accordance with those laws. And he makes clear that, though blameless under the law (what he seems to mean by saying in the next to last sentence of the long quotation above, that the laws may be "obeyed without concupiscence") he cannot see how they are altogether blameless. Even public officials and soldiers when they kill are nonetheless free not to kill, particularly when to do so is for those earthly things that they can lose against their will and therefore ought not to love.

Augustine's continuation of the passage details the latter point. In explaining how it is that such persons ought not to love the things they try to cling to by killing, he has Evodius say:

As for the life of the soul, it is at least doubtful whether it can be taken away by killing the body. But if it can be taken, it is worthless; if not, there is naught to fear. As to chastity, who indeed doubts that it is in the soul, for chastity is a virtue. Hence it cannot be taken away by the violence of the ravisher. Whatever, therefore, he who is killed was going to take from us is not in our control, so that I do not understand in what sense it can be called ours. Wherefore, while I do not condemn the law that permits such people to be killed, I do not see how to defend those who kill them.[18]

That Augustine includes chastity among things that cannot be taken against one's will (the body can be violated against one's will but virtue resides in the soul) makes it clear that he intends this judgment to apply to individual self-defense as well as to public acts of killing. If we kill in order to cling to something that can be taken against our will (our money, our earthly life, the use of our physical body), and that we therefore ought not to desire, are we not acting from precisely the culpable desire that is of the essence of evil? Evodius sees no way to avoid this conclusion. Notice that no mention is made here of the justifiability of killing in self-defense or in defense of another. Not even in the case of public officials, it is affirmed, can a way be found to render them altogether blameless.

Now consider the exchange that follows. When Evodius says that he does not see how to defend those who kill in the above ways, Augustine replies: "Much less can I say why you seek a defense for men whom no law holds guilty." While agreeing with

18 *De Libero Arbitrio* 1. 5.12.

Evodius's initial defense, he demurs at the apparent afterthought that even those who act in accordance with such laws are not blameless. So Evodius proceeds to explain: "No law, perhaps, if you mean those public laws which men may read. But I know not whether they are not bound by some higher unwritten law, if all things are ruled by divine providence. For how are they free of sin before Providence, who for things that they should despise stain their hands with human blood?[19] This, then, is the clarification of the preceding analysis. The basis for holding that those who kill, though they are sometimes blameless in the eyes of temporal law, are nonetheless not altogether blameless, is that they are still subject to God's "higher unwritten" law. Of this Augustine observes, concluding the discussion: "I command and approve this distinction of yours. . . . For you see that the law that is made for the government of the states allows to go unpunished many things that yet are avenged by divine providence. And this is right; nor because it does not do everything should we find fault with what it does."[20]

Here, in the last analysis, Augustine accepts the preceding reasoning. He unquestionably accepts the distinction between human law and "higher unwritten" divine law. And he says that it is right that some things which go unpunished by human law nonetheless are avenged by divine law (a point urged later by Aquinas as an argument for the necessity of divine law). In light of what has gone before it is difficult to read this in any other way than as affirming that even those who kill in their capacity as public officials, or agents thereof, may nonetheless be sinning, and though blameless in the eyes of human law, may nonetheless eventually suffer punishment in the judgment of God. This does conflict with an earlier assent by Augustine to the claim that those who kill accidentally or while soldiering or in official capacities are free from sin.[21] But in the passages we have been examining, Augustine—in

[19] Ibid., 1. 5.13.
[20] Ibid.
[21] Ibid., i. 4.9. This may conflict also with what Augustine writes later in *De Civitate Dei* (1. 21) where he says that there are only two exceptions made by divine authority to its prohibition against killing, the one being justified by a general law, the other by a "special commission" to kill, as in a command by God. However, when he proceeds to discuss these, he deals only with examples of special commissions, citing the examples of Abraham, Jephthah, and Samson, and does not elaborate upon the issue discussed at such length in *De Libero Arbitrio*. Touching upon the matter again in chapter 26 of book 1, he says: "The soldier who has slain a man in obedience to the authority under which he is lawfully commissioned, is not accused of murder by any law of his state; nay, if he has not slain him, it is

a twist of irony that would have done credit to Plato's Socrates—reverses the roles of Augustine and Evodius within the dialogue, placing in the latter's mouth the job of bringing to bear the full weight of the previous reasoning.[22] What Evodius says is clear and consistent with all of what has gone before, as well as with what Augustine says elsewhere about the sinfulness of the love of earthly things. There can be little doubt that it represents the views of Augustine.

What is important to see in all of this is that not only does Augustine not justify killing in personal self-defense, he does not justify killing in defense of another either, and he furthermore is unwilling to say that even those who kill as "public" persons are blameless in the eyes of God for the killing they do. There simply is no paradigmatic situation here of the justifiable killing of one person by another in defense of a third of the sort to which Johnson appeals. The *law*, Augustine makes clear, permits all three types of killing. But he never says they are permitted by the "higher unwritten" law. Thus this passage, which has been taken as pivotal by some modern defenders of the just war theory, fails to provide a foundation for Christian justification of war.

Yet Augustine clearly defends Christian participation in war. And he clearly maintains the justifiability of some wars. The problem is that if one cannot kill as a means of clinging to earthly goods, whether in private self-defense, or defense of another, or in public actions, it is not easy to see that there is room left for the very conclusion that it is his central aim to establish.

---

then he is accused of treason to the state, and of despising the law. But if he has been acting on his own authority, and at his own impulse, he has in this case incurred the crime of shedding human blood." Here, however, it seems clear that he is talking about *legal* accountability, and this is not at issue in *De Libero Arbitrio*. Augustine consistently acknowledges that people are absolved of legal responsibility when they kill with authorization such as in warfare or self-defense. It should be noted that in a later translation of *De Civitate Dei* by Henry Bettenson (Middlesex: Penguin Books Ltd., 1986) it is made clear that killings authorized by law and by special commissions from God in book 1, chapter 21 do not have two essentially different warrants but are both instances of killing under God's orders: "There are some whose killing God orders, either by a law, or by an express command to a particular person at a particular time." So these later passages, while they weigh against the view Augustine expresses earlier, do not contradict that view, and in the one instance (chapter 26) are clearly consistent with it.

[22] In quoting this passage, Ramsey correctly takes the words of Evodius to represent the views of Augustine, as have others, but he stops before Evodius explains why he cannot hold blameless even those who kill in accordance with temporal law. See *War and the Christian Conscience*, chap. 3. Johnson does not quote the passage but cites Ramsey's interpretation, in *Just War Tradition and the Restraint of War*, p. 48.

IV

There is yet a basis, I believe, for that conclusion, albeit one that is slenderer than most just war theorists who appeal to Augustine have realized.

Let us remember that there is no problem where wars commanded by God are concerned. If one loves God, obedience to him will be unconditional. Then *whatever* one does, so long as it is from love of God (merely obeying God out of self-interest will not do), will be without sin. Aquinas later made explicit that even when God commands killing, theft, and fornication those things become right by virtue of God's command.[23] The problem concerns wars that are not commanded by God. To understand Augustine's reasoning here we must enlarge our concern to take in the broader perspective of his moral outlook.

A key to this as it relates to his account of warfare is expressed in his letter to Faustus of the heretical Manichaeans:

> What is the evil in war? Is it the death of some who will soon die in any case, that others may live in peaceful subjection? This is merely cowardly dislike, not any religious feeling. The real evils in war are love of violence, revengeful cruelty, fierce and implacable enmity, wild resistance, and the lust of power, and such like; and it is generally to punish these things, when force is required to inflict the punishment, that, in obedience to God or some lawful authority, good men undertake wars.[24]

The underlying Christian view that Augustine here assumes is a long-run view. Eventually everyone is going to die anyway, so deaths from war, whether they are justified or not, are not of par-

---

[23] "All men alike, both guilty and innocent, die the death of nature; which death . . . is inflicted by the power of God because of original sin. . . . Consequently, by the command of God, death can be inflicted on any man, guilty or innocent, without any injustice whatever.—In like manner, adultery is intercourse with another's wife; who is allotted to him by the law emanating from God. Consequently intercourse with any woman, by the command of God, is neither adultery nor fornication.—The same applies to theft, which is the taking of another's property. For whatever is taken by the command of God, to Whom all things belong, is not taken against the will of its owner, whereas it is in this that theft consists." Saint Thomas Aquinas, *Summa Theologica*, I-II, 94, art. 5, in Anton Pegis, ed., *Basic Writings of Saint Thomas Aquinas* (New York: Random House, 1944), p. 780. Strictly, of course, killing, intercourse with another's wife, and taking what is not yours do not, on this view, constitute murder, adultery, and theft respectively, since all things belong to God and it is God who has ordained natural death. By ordinary moral and legal standards, however, these designations remain accurate.

[24] *Contra Faustum* 22. 74.

amount importance to the assessment of war. Of importance is the necessity to avoid cruelty, enmity, and love of violence, where these, in keeping with the views we have just considered, represent inner attitudes, providing motives to action.

This long-run view is part of the basic Christian ethical orientation as Augustine conceives it. Morality according to his view deals with the way of life one must live to attain happiness, which in turn consists of salvation.[25] This means that the "end" of morality is not to be found in this life but in the hereafter. Its attainment, however, is not fully within man's power. Being corrupted by original sin, he requires the regeneration of divine grace to give him the capacity to attain the virtues of faith, hope, and charity, from which those of prudence, fortitude, temperance, and justice, as forms of charity, will follow. Since one must live virtuously in order to attain salvation, God's grace is needed to attain happiness. This sets Christian ethics radically apart from classical Greek ethics, whose cardinal virtues of wisdom, courage, temperance, and justice ("splendid vices" that never attain the status of virtues in Augustine's view) were held attainable by natural man through reason and self-discipline alone. And it means that only Christians can be truly virtuous. It also means that only they can achieve true justice in war. And as it is what is in one's heart that determines whether or not he is truly virtuous, we cannot tell from a person's outward conduct, however conspicuously religious it may be, whether the love of God impels him. We cannot in fact know, says Augustine, whether this is true of anyone; whether they have, as he puts it, and as Kant was to put it centuries later, a good will. Only God knows that. We have, then, a radical division among all of the souls of creation: one group, in their love of God, making up the City of God; the other, through their love of earthly things, making up the City of Man. Any temporal city or state may contain persons of both sorts. But there is no way of knowing for certain which are which.

From this there emerges a set of dualisms that inform Augustine's outlook on man and give the distinctive character to his philosophy of war. These grow out of the admixture of Christianity and platonism that came down to Augustine through the neo-Platonists.

When the increase in scientific knowledge in the sixth and fifth

[25] *On the Morals of the Catholic Church* 5. 8, in *A Select Library of the Nicene and Post-Nicene Fathers of the Christian Church*, Vol. 4, trans. Richard Stothert.

centuries B.C. seemed to threaten to relativize morality and values, Plato responded with a philosophy that partitioned reality into two dimensions: one the changing, temporal world of which we are aware through the senses; the other an eternal, immutable realm of essences knowable only through reason. With the latter providing the metaphysical foundation for values, particularly as it enshrined the Idea of Good, ethics was given a foundation that secured it from the vagaries of conventional morals as well as from the relativistic teachings of the sophists. But in so doing Plato instituted sharp dualisms between the soul and the body, true opinion and genuine knowledge, reality and appearance. Augustine adapts an equally thorough-going division in his conception of the world. Not only his distinction between the soul and the body but the very conception of divine and earthly cities reflects this. He also says, in a passage quoted earlier, that a law that is not just is not a law at all, implying that we must distinguish genuine laws from apparent laws. Moreover, he implies that a state that is not truly just is not a true commonwealth, which means that we have to recognize a distinction between true and apparent states as well.[26] A state without justice is little better than a great band of robbers.[27]

If all men are corrupted by original sin, and states are made up of men, no earthly state will be completely just. What is the role of the state then? It is, in Augustine's view, to maintain by force and coercion sufficient order to minimize the harms that sinful and ignorant men would otherwise inflict upon one another. By instilling fear, inflicting punishment, and waging wars, it also serves as an agent of God's design for the world in punishing man for his sins.[28] The ruler, then, whether he be good or bad, plays a role in the carrying out of God's will on earth. In this sense he rules by divine ordination. As he thus has legitimate authority, and as the state is an institution of God's agency in the world, individual citizens of the state owe nearly absolute allegiance to the ruler. Only if he should directly command them to do something contrary to God's will may they disobey him. Indeed, then they must disobey him, since to do otherwise would mean that they fear earthly pun-

---

[26] For a good discussion of this issue, see Deane, *The Political and Social Ideas of St. Augustine*, chap. 4.

[27] *De Civitate Dei* 4. 4.

[28] On these issues, see Deane, *The Political and Social Ideas of St. Augustine*, chaps. 4 and 5, and George J. Lavere, "The Political Realism of Saint Augustine," *Augustinian Studies* II (1980): 135-145.

ishment more than they desire to do God's will. All of this means that whether they are good or wicked at heart, men almost unavoidably suffer in this life, some more than others, without regard to whether it is personally deserved. That they should do so is the lesser of evils when compared with how they would live without the coercive apparatus of the state. And it serves God's justice, in any event, by punishing them for their sins.

The human condition, then, is this: no state possesses true justice; force, violence, and suffering are inevitable, both through the operation of the state in maintaining order and in the warfare in which it engages with other states; sin is pervasive as both individuals and states pursue temporal things in their love of this world; and, strictly, no one can know for certain who are the good and who are the wicked, who are the innocent and who are the guilty. As Augustine says at his most pessimistic:

> [A]s the judgments of God and the movements of man's will contain the hidden reason why the same prosperous circumstances which some make a right use of are the ruin of others, and the same afflictions under which some give way are profitable to others, and since the whole moral life of man upon earth is a trial, who can tell whether it may be good or bad in any particular case—in time of peace, to reign or to serve, or to be at ease or to die—or in time of war, to command or to fight, or to conquer or to be killed?[29]

All of this contributes to a moral skepticism in which it is virtually impossible for one ever to know anything beyond the testimony of his own heart, if indeed one's own motivation can ever be unmistakably certain.

This conclusion is virtually inescapable insofar as we are talking about true justice and virtue; or, if you like, about the "higher unwritten" law that is God's providence. But that is not all there is. For all of the corruption and evil that characterize human affairs it is nonetheless possible to distinguish what is just from what is unjust from the standpoint of the temporal realm. There are states of affairs that are better or worse, actions that are more or less harmful, conditions that are comparatively good or bad. If we cannot conform fully to God's law given our sinful nature, at least we can discern the traces of justice in our social life and within limits act accordingly. This provides the key to the possibility of just

[29] *Contra Faustum* 22. 78.

wars from a temporal or human perspective. Augustine tells us that just wars "are usually defined as those which avenge injuries, when the nation or city against which warlike action is to be directed or to restore what has been unjustly taken by it."[30] When a state has wronged another, either by failing to restore what it has unjustly taken or by refusing to punish wrongs committed by its citizens, one then has a just cause to punish that state, providing the decision emanates from a legitimate authority. This does not require that the ruler be a good man, for that cannot be known. Nor does it require that a state be truly just, for none is. The state need not even be nominally Christian; according to Augustine, the conditions of just cause and legitimate authority sometimes characterized the wars of pre-Christian Rome.[31]

The point is that there is implicit in Augustine both a strong and a weak sense of "just" in the discussion of war, what might be called respectively true justice and temporal justice, paralleling the distinction between Christian virtues and non-Christian virtues. Only the second of these provides an effective criterion by which sinful humans can make the difficult decisions regarding war in circumstances in which they do not have direct guidance from God. And because there is nothing in the idea of punishing wrongdoing that requires that a just war be defensive, one may justifiably initiate hostilities if he has a just cause and the appropriate authority. Augustine says that good men may justly initiate a war to eradicate *any* vices that a just government has a right to suppress. This suggests that wrongdoing of any sort is punishable by war, not just that which is suffered by the punishing state.[32] And, as we shall see, it has important consequences for the relationship of the just war theory to the contemporary distinction between aggressive and defensive war because it entails that some wars that are aggressive by modern standards may be just.

V

How can the Christian participate without sin in such a war in a way that does not violate Christ's apparent injunctions to the con-

[30] *Quaestiones in Heptateuchum* 6. 10, in John Eppstein, *The Catholic Tradition of the Law of Nations* (London: Burns, Oates and Washbourne, Ltd., 1935), p. 74.

[31] See *De Civitate Dei* 3. 10.

[32] "And in mercy, also, if such a thing were possible, even wars might be waged by the good, in order that, by bringing under the yoke the unbridled lusts of men, those vices might be abolished which ought, under a just government, to be either extirpated or suppressed" (*Letters* 138.2.14) in *A Select Library of the Nicene and Post-Nicene Fathers of the Christian Church*, Vol. 1, trans. J. G. Cunningham.

trary? This is the problem with which we began, and I want now to return to it. First consider that Augustine says:

> Since, therefore, a righteous man, serving [in a war] may be under an ungodly king, [he] may do the duty belonging to his position in the State in fighting by the order of his sovereign,—for in some cases it is plainly the will of God that he should fight, and in others, where this is not so plain, it may be an unrighteous command on the part of the king, while the soldier is innocent, because his position makes obedience a duty,—how much more must the man be blameless who carries on war on the authority of God?[33]

In light of our earlier analysis, we can now say that *if* the soldier participates in war without the feeling of cruelty, enmity, and love of violence that Augustine says constitute the evils of war but acts rather only out of duty to his temporal king, he is innocent. He is not, in so acting, motivated by the desire to cling to earthly things, hence is not trying to cling to that which he can lose against his will. Only in this way, in light of Augustine's analysis of evil, can one kill in warfare in a way that does not represent culpable desire. The soldier can, of course, be innocent of wrongdoing in the eyes of temporal law. In fact, he not only may but *must* kill if commanded to do so. But he cannot kill other than in the course of discharging such a duty. To do so is punishable. And if he is punished, he is so, as Augustine wryly notes, "for doing without orders the very thing he is punished for neglecting to do when he has been ordered."[34] Because a person acting in private self-defense does not have a similar duty, he cannot with moral impunity kill another person, whether to save himself or to save another. This does not mean that we can *know* for certain whether any given soldier is participating blamelessly in a war, anymore than we can know whether any given person is righteous in the eyes of God. He may be acting from fear, cruelty, or love of violence. But it is *possible* that his participation is permitted in the eyes of God, just as it is *possible* that a state acts from true as well as temporal justice.

This, as I say, provides a slender basis for Christian participation in war, but it provides a basis nonetheless. But one cannot help but wonder how realistic the account is, and whether it is humanly possible amidst the chaos of slaughter and gore that marks hand-

---

[33] *Contra Faustum* 22. 75.
[34] *De Civitate Dei* 1. 26.

to-hand combat to remain free of those things Augustine identifies as evil in war, the cruelty, enmity, and the like? And if one somehow remains free of these, is it even remotely plausible to suppose that he can remain free of the fear of losing his life? It is this that Augustine imputes to the man who kills his master in the earlier example and that he says exhibits a sinful desire to hang onto earthly things. And if men cannot free themselves of these fears and the covetousness they represent how can they be free of sin when they kill?

There is no convincing answer to this in Augustine. But we can shed light on the question and see some of the complexity of his philosophy.

Consider that the killing done by the executioner may be justified even if the executioner is a wicked man. If he is wicked he will be so judged when he comes before God. But in the meantime he plays a role in God's plan by helping to maintain order as authorized by public authorities. Just as a good law can be promulgated by a wicked man, and for sinful reasons (as in response to a bribe), so, we may presume, a person may perform a rightful *act* even though from an evil *motive*. *What* one does should be distinguished from what *motivates* him in doing it. Sin is a property of the individual soul. It arises with sinful desire and the motives it provides. And given Augustine's division between inner disposition and outward conduct, it may vary independently of the outward actions that produce changes in the world. If a guilty man is put to death by a legitimate order, that will be just in God's eyes and ultimately for the man's own good. But if the executioner takes pleasure in the man's suffering, then *he* is sinful even though he does not (in another sense) act wrongfully. If we extend this to the soldier we can say that even if he kills for the love of it, or from fear of punishment for failure to kill (both blameworthy motives), he may nonetheless be furthering God's will and in that sense be acting rightly. God's will is served by the existence of the temporal state; and the costs of the existence of the state (as with the blessing of free will for individual man) include the harm that it does and the opportunities for evil it affords. So at some level even the evils that men do is turned to God's purposes.[35]

---

[35] "[T]he reasons for the distribution of divine judgment and mercy, why one is in this condition, and another in that, though just, are unknown. Still, we are sure that all these things are due either to the mercy or the judgment of God, while the measures and numbers and weights by which the Creator of all natural productions arranges all things are concealed from our view. For God is not the author, but He

This does not, however, show that individual participants in (or perpetrators of) war act in accordance with Christ's teachings when they kill, even on Augustine's interpretation of those teachings. Quite the reverse. God can turn men's evil to his own purposes only if they act evilly. It shows at most how it is *possible* that they should act in accordance with those teachings. But if men are so sinful as to deserve the suffering inflicted upon them in this life, it is difficult to believe that when they turn to doing those things that seem most directly contrary to Christ's teachings they will somehow rise above their sinful nature and take up killing with pure hearts. Marching off on a crusade, as Christians were wont to do by the thousands after Augustine, is one thing; hacking someone to pieces who is trying to do the same to you on the battlefield is another. To expect men to be able to put aside feelings of enmity and fear for this earthly life when doing such things is to place an extraordinary high standard on the justifiability of their participation in warfare. Yet nothing less than this accords with Augustine's conception of what is sinless before God. That men should be under orders from a legitimate authority absolves them of legal guilt; they are innocent, in that case, whether that authority is vested in a good man or not and whether the war is just or not. And that the killing and destruction that results from their activities should serve some higher purpose in the divine scheme of things means that ultimately everything that happens in the whole of creation, from the particular acts of individual men to the sweeping events on the historical scene, is under the governance of God. But neither of these exempts one from sin in waging war. Only keeping one's heart free of the aforementioned evils does that.

If we suppose a good motive to be essential for a truly just war, then it follows that we can never *know* that any given war is truly just because we can never be altogether certain of anyone's motivation. Even in the case of a war commanded by God we cannot be certain that obedience springs from love of God rather than fear of punishment.

This creates a problem for any state proposing to go to war, for it complicates the matter of determining whether the outward acts one takes as meriting punishment actually spring from evil mo-

---

is the controller, of sin; so that sinful actions, which are sinful because they are against nature, are judged and controlled, and assigned to their proper place and condition, in order that they may not bring discord and disgrace on universal nature" (*Contra Faustum* 22. 78).

tives. It also raises a question that subsequent just war theorists discuss at length, of whether there can be justice on both sides in war, and that as we shall see in the next chapter, leads some of them to conclude that there may be at least simultaneous "ostensible" justice on both sides.

It is commonly thought that Augustine also requires a right intention as a condition for a just war; he is so understood by Aquinas and other just war theorists down to the present day. Sometimes he implies that there should, as when he says that in obeying commands soldiers should "perform their military duties in behalf of the peace and safety of the community."[36] But the passage Aquinas appeals to, citing cruelty, enmity, and love of violence[37] (see Section IV above), establishes only that it is evil to be *motivated* by such things. And intentions and motives should not be confused. Intentions are those states of affairs that it is one's purpose to bring about; motives explain *why* one undertakes to bring them about. Augustine says repeatedly that all states that wage war do so in order to bring about peace—peace, of course, to their liking. And insofar as peace is good, that in itself is a good intention. Sometimes he speaks as though the peace that should be sought consists of more than merely the absence of war and includes justice and tranquility as well. He does not, however, explicitly make the having of this intention a condition of one's being justified in going to war. If the survival of the state is threatened by an unjust attack, that presumably justifies going to war, whether or not in the course of so doing one has the further intention of bringing about the kind of just peace Augustine elsewhere makes clear is desirable. One does need to have a good motive in going to war if the war is to be truly just, lest one add to the evil of the wrong one hopes to punish. Presumably if one has a truly good motive and acts out of Christian love he will have a right intention as well, and Augustine says that a state guided by Chris-

[36] Ibid., 22. 75. He also says that in war, "[p]eace should be the object of your desire; war should be waged only as a necessity, and waged only that God may by it deliver men from the necessity and preserve them in peace." See *Letters* 189. 6, in *A Select Library of the Nicene and Post-Nicene Fathers of the Christian Church*, Vol. 1, trans. J. G. Cunningham. For a similar statement, see Cicero, *Offices* 1, 2, in *Cicero's Three Books of Offices, or Moral Duties*, trans. C. R. Edmonds (London: George Bell & Sons, York Street, Covent Garden, 1877).

[37] *The Summa Theologica of Saint Thomas Aquinas*, Dominican trans. (London: Burns Oates & Washbourne, Ltd., 1916), II-II q. 40, art. 1. Johnson follows Aquinas in attributing this to Augustine in *Ideology, Reason and the Limitation of War*, p. 40.

tian precepts would do so.[38] But it is not until Aquinas that a major just war theorist makes right intention an unequivocal condition for *jus ad bellum*, justice in the resort to war.

I have been speaking here of true justice. For a war that is temporally just, that is, from the standpoint of the human perspective, only the previously mentioned conditions are required: that it be undertaken by a legitimate authority and be done so for a just cause. This does not mean, as we have seen, that the authority must be a good person, or even that he be Christian. His being a ruler gives him a kind of legitimacy in that he then commands an institution (the state) that Augustine sees as instrumental to God's will. And unlike in the case of true justice, a good motive is not required. If it were, virtually no war could be known to be just. And while the goodness of a motive would ensure the rightness of one's intention in going to war (as well as in the conduct of war), the absence of such a motive leaves it open whether the intention will also be a right one. The justice of the cause, for these reasons, need be only, and almost invariably will be so far as can be known, only that of temporal standards. A state will normally have been wronged in order to have a just cause in going to war. The heart of *jus ad bellum* as a practical doctrine is the need to punish wrongdoing: it is not love or Christian charity, as has sometimes been maintained.[39] Love would suffice to ensure that the

[38] [I]f the commonwealth observes the precepts of the Christian religion, even its wars themselves will not be carried on without the benevolent design that, after the resisting nations have been conquered, provision may be more easily made for enjoying in peace the mutual bond of piety and justice" (*Letters* 138.2.14).

[39] Johnson, in *Just War Tradition and the Restraint of War*, takes Ramsey to be holding this view (p. 145). And Ramsey does indeed seem to hold it in *The Just War* when he says that for love's sake Christians may sometimes kill: "Thus, a love-inspired justice going into concrete action fashioned rules for practical conduct—at once justifying war and limiting it. The Christian is commanded to do anything for which such love commands, and he is prohibited from doing anything for which such love can find no justification" (p. 151). But in chapter 3 of *War and the Christian Conscience*, which Johnson specifically cites in support of his ascription of this view to Ramsey, Ramsey seems not to make Christian love the basis of the justification of war he finds in Augustine. There he says: "It is clear that supernatural charity is the basis of Augustine's judgment in the matter of private defense. . . . This confirms the conclusion . . . that he does not justify Christian participation in warfare on the grounds of intrinsic justice alone. . . . [T]he question remains whether instead it is from love that the Christian engages in public defense" (p. 37). He then seems to answer this in the negative: "It is not that he [the Christian], not at least explicitly, makes the ethical judgment that Christian love requires just this participating action, for it is a very earthly love that requires it; nor does he—he is even less in the position to do this than the ruler—make the ethical judgment that intrinsic justice requires it" (p. 39). What, then, justifies the Christian's participation in war? As Ramsey here reads Augustine, it is the fact that he is under orders and

agents of such punishment are good men in punishing the wrong, that is, that they are not acting evilly in so doing. But it is unnecessary. All that is needed is the appropriate authority and a just cause.

VI

This has discomfiting implications when one considers the twentieth-century's wars, particularly World War II. Hitler's rise to power, for example, compares favorably in legitimacy with that of most rulers throughout history, and his government arguably constituted a "legitimate authority" for purposes of declaring and waging war. And it is also arguable that at least some of Hitler's military ventures were to remedy wrongs inflicted upon the German nation at the end of World War I. If someone other than Hitler had engineered the same events in Germany up to September 1939, and if it were possible to view those events without knowledge of what followed, particularly in the concentration camps, many might concede that the German cause in 1939 was, if not a just one, at least no more clearly unjust by prevailing standards of international conduct than that of many other nations. It is easy to allow our revulsion at the extermination in the concentration camps to obscure this. It is also easy to allow it to stand in the way of an objective appraisal of Germany's international conduct up to the point of the outbreak of war. We need to remember that according to Augustine, as well as many traditional and contemporary just war theorists, the initiation of a war is compatible with its being just; and some just war theorists read Augustine as allowing

"the existing political authority has the responsibility for that combination of wills or agreements as to goods necessary to the earthly life of a multitude if it is a people" (ibid.). True justice, on Augustine's view, would indeed be a form of charity, as are the further virtues of prudence, fortitude, and temperance, and punishment by the true Christian, or the truly just state, would spring from love. But earthly or temporal justice need not be a form of charity. In any event, Ramsey does not there defend the further view Johnson imputes to him, that Augustine holds that the Christian may and should intervene to the point of killing in defense of an innocent person. This is the view that Johnson takes to constitute the paradigm, providing, by extension, the justification for war. He attributes this reading repeatedly to Ramsey (*Just War Tradition and the Restraint of War*, pp. 48, 145, 350) and eventually comes to advance it himself (*Can Modern War Be Just?* introduction and p. 176). In *Can Modern War Be Just?* (p. 19, n. 4), he cites *The City of God* 19. 7 and Ramsey, *War and the Christian Conscience*, chap. 2, in support of this view; but I can neither find in Augustine a defense of the view Johnson attributes to him nor in the reference to Ramsey a defense of the view that Augustine holds such a position.

at least some measure of justice on both sides.[40] As for the waging of the war itself, what took place in the concentration camps was for the most part directed against Germans and citizens of occupied territories and was not part of the conduct of the war; it was for this reason that the Nuremberg Tribunal felt the need to define a category of crimes against humanity as well as war crimes and crimes against peace to cover such atrocities. The point is that these atrocities, as abhorrent as they were, did not clearly represent violations of the standards (about which Augustine has little to say) of *jus in bello*, justice in the conduct of war.

And even if we were to assume that Germany's going to war in World War II failed to meet any of Augustine's criteria for a just war, still we must consider the possibility that on the sort of view Augustine held, God's purposes were furthered by the war. This is precisely what America's foremost political realist of the twentieth century argued. Though without expressly citing Augustine, Niebuhr wrote in 1942 that

> only the chastisements of a fairly long war can prompt a really thoroughgoing repentance and conversion from those sins of the democratic world which helped to produce the Nazi revolt against our civilization. We were much too soft and fat, much too heedless and indifferent to the ultimate issues of life to be changed by the only casual chastisements of a brief belligerency. This is not to say that war as such is the only possible source of repentance to nations. We must think not abstractly but historically about these questions. When we are guilty of sins that make a revolt against civilization possible, we can hardly repent of those sins until bitter experience has taught us what the consequences of the sins are and by what kind of sacrifices and change of heart the evils we have done can be overcome.[41]

He went on to attribute the problem ultimately to sinful human nature, remarking, as we noted in Chapter Two, that if moralists who find this conception abhorrent were to examine their own conduct "they would find evidences in it of this same reluctance and would learn to appreciate the tragic elements in history as

---

[40] See, for example, Ramsey, *War and the Christian Conscience*, chap. 2, and Russell, *The Just War in the Middle Ages*, p. 21.

[41] Reinhold Niebuhr, "Chastisement unto Repentance or Death," in *Love and Justice: Selections from the Shorter Writings of Reinhold Niebuhr*, ed. D. B. Robertson (Cleveland: World Publishing Co., 1967), p. 181.

manifestations of divine judgment, without which men would remain in the stupor of sin."[42] All of this is fully in keeping with the Augustinian outlook.

VII

The problem with this view lies with its attempt to found ethics upon motivation. Ethics is concerned ultimately with *conduct*; its aim is to provide guidance in what one does. There will always be motives for conduct, but they do not provide guidelines for action. To say that we should determine what it is right to do by considering whether, in doing it, we would be acting from a good motive is circular. Whether a motive is good or bad already presupposes the very criteria of right and wrong that the appeal to motives is supposed to provide. It is true that if people are governed by good motives they will then set themselves to *do* only what they think is right. But some sense of what this is antecedes one's being able to act upon the motive. No degree of commitment to do what is right can issue into right *conduct* unless one has some sense of what that is and what constitutes compliance with it. We cannot, in any event, choose our motives as we can our actions; at least not in the short run. We can over a period of time try to become responsive to considerations that previously did not move us and in that way cultivate traits of character that may then acquire motivating force. But we cannot just decide to do something from a certain motive; or decide to do something and then decide which of several motives to do it from. When we decide to perform one action rather than another we are governed by one motive rather than another. But that is not within our control. For the most part we simply have the motives we do and must strive to keep those that are manifestly ignoble from getting the upper hand of those that are good.

The risk in attenuating the connection between morality and conduct as Augustine does is that it takes only one last imperceptible snip to disconnect the two altogether, setting conduct (Augustine's "outward action") adrift to attach itself to whatever standards present themselves. In Augustine's case these are primarily the laws of the state. The problem is not unique to a religious-oriented ethic. Nor to Christianity in particular. One could excise Augustine's preoccupation with sin, and the problem

---

[42] Ibid., p. 183.

would remain. It is the fact that according to his view sin is an *act of the will*[43] that is crucial. Nothing that can be done to us by others constitutes sin on our part. And nothing we *do* in terms of outward conduct can by itself constitute sin. Only turning away from God—ultimately the sin of pride—constitutes sin. If people are motivated by the love of the world rather than of God, it does not matter what they do: they simply sin in one manner rather than another. The churchgoer who adheres to every detail of devotion sins as surely as the man who scorns religion, if he does this for love of the praise and esteem it brings rather than for love of God. Drop sin from the picture and require only that one act from the appropriate motive and the problem remains. If what is of ultimate importance is that one act from a good motive, nothing that one does, whatever its consequences for good or ill or its bearing upon others, will be right absent that motive. Nor will anything be wrong, given that motive.

It is as though Augustine were vaguely aware that his turning inward of Christ's teachings leaves no standard for actual moral conduct and that this is what leads him to emphasize so heavily conformity to the state. And then, sensing the need to provide some sort of justification for that conformity in its own right, he tries to establish a link between God's plan for the world and the role of temporal rulers and the state. The net effect, however, in terms of the actual prescriptions he extracts from this process, differs little from saying that it is the interests of the state that are paramount and that its laws, so long as they do not directly contravene divine law, should be obeyed unquestioningly. In this one can see the groundwork laid for Hobbes, Machiavelli, Hegel, and Tretischke in their accounts of the state, of Clausewitz in the philosophy of war, and of twentieth-century political realists in their insistence upon national interest as the only proper norm for international conduct.

Once the criteria for right conduct have been bound to the interests of the state, the gap between *true* justice and virtue, on the one hand, and *temporal* justice and virtue on the other, widens to the point of unbridgeability. Human ignorance effectively veils both the human heart and God's ultimate purposes, and with them the true moral character of human conduct, institutions, and practices. Appeal to earthly standards becomes the only alternative to skepticism. And of these none is better than those of the

[43] *De Civitate Dei* 14. 4.

state, even though they are none too good, and the attempt to implement them results in the harm, death, and destruction of war. But this is the lesser of the evils among which we must choose. We can know we should be motivated by love in all that we do. And we can know we should further God's purposes. But the former expresses a virtually impossible ideal (as Niebuhr was to call it later) in our own conduct, and one whose degree of approximation in others we can only dimly perceive. The other is an unfathomable mystery. The laws of the state, however, are clear. They are written or enunciated. They become, for all practical purposes, the only effective norms by which to conduct our affairs. In the last analysis, then, with respect to temporal (though not true) justice, Augustine becomes a political realist.

VIII

Where does Augustine stand with regard to the killing of innocent persons? Does his writing contain a bedrock prohibition against such killing, of a sort that many have come to think characterizes Christianity? And do we find in him the genesis of the notion of noncombatant immunity that plays such an important role in the just war tradition?

I suggest that the answer to these questions is no. There certainly is no absolute prohibition against killing the innocent in Augustine. According to his view, one not only may but must kill *anyone*, innocent or noninnocent, if God so commands. The Bible gives us an example of such a command in the case of Abraham and Isaac, and Augustine is unequivocal in defending Abraham's willingness to slay Isaac in obedience to God.[44] He is only slightly less unequivocal in defending Moses's killing of the Egyptian, an act not specifically commanded but arguably permitted by God.[45] The only question therefore concerns the warrant for killing that is not commanded or approved by God. May one ever kill the innocent under these circumstances? One may not do so in self-defense, as we have seen, if one is acting as a private person. If any such killing is justified it will be only that which is done by public officials or their agents. Now Augustine allows for capital punishment, which is the killing of one *found* guilty by the process of temporal justice. Whether such a person is actually guilty in the eyes of God we cannot know. Given that, it is possible that the

[44] Ibid., 1. 21; *Contra Faustum* 22. 73.
[45] *Contra Faustum* 22. 71.

practice of capital punishment will sometimes take the lives of innocent persons, just as the practice of torturing the accused in order to elicit the truth in a trial (a practice that Augustine finds regrettable but tolerable) will sometimes result in the death of an innocent person.[46] One may not knowingly kill innocent persons in either of these cases. But there is no prohibition against practices that are virtually certain to result in the deaths of some innocent persons by these means. To minimize the risk of killing the innocent would demand that we refrain from killing or torturing anyone. But Augustine does not say we should do this.

What, then, of killing in wartime? May one justifiably kill innocent persons then? Given Augustine's conception of man and the world, it is virtually inevitable that war will kill some innocent persons. Soldiers, as we have seen, may themselves be innocent. They are innocent before the law if they fight under orders from a legitimate authority, and some of them may be innocent in the eyes of God as well, provided they remain free of evil desires. So it is evident that soldiers on *both* sides may be innocent in the first sense, and some of them, at least may be innocent in the second sense as well. As some of either of these sorts are almost certain to be killed, this makes it virtually inevitable that innocent persons will die in war. And if some wars are justified, then the killing of innocents entailed by those wars will be justified—this notwithstanding the possible ancillary killing of non-combatants.

The upshot is that in the face of the virtual certainty that by human standards war kills innocent persons, and in the face of human ignorance about whether institutionalized killing (capital punishment, warfare) kills persons who are innocent by divine standards, Augustine elects to sanction the killing. There is virtually no basis, therefore, for the belief that he opposed the killing of innocents when the interest of the state in maintaining order and punishing wrongdoing is at stake. Nor is it easy to find a basis for Ramsey's contention that we find in Augustine the genesis of noncombatant immunity. Augustine's discussion of killing is not even framed in these terms. He speaks not of noncombatants and combatants but of innocent and the wicked. And it is clear from his contention that the soldier, a combatant, may be innocent that he does not think the two distinctions coincide. Those who maintain that the prohibition against killing the innocent is a bedrock prohibition of Christianity do not get this from Augustine.

[46] *De Civitate Dei* 19. 6.

IX

Thus we find in Augustine a proposed resolution of the conflict between the practice of men in arming and equipping themselves for war and engaging in the slaughter for which it prepares them, on the one hand, and the following of the teachings of Christ, on the other, which, depending upon one's understanding of the gospels, may or may not be possible in this life.

The warrant to wage war is the warrant to mete out punishment for wrongdoing. And this punishment is of the same kind that judicial authorities mete out to criminals within the state. The law, Augustine says in the passages we considered earlier, cannot punish everything; something must be left to God. He is committed to the same with regard to war. We can punish wrongful *acts* by another state, just as we can punish wrongful acts by private individuals. And we can legislate human laws prohibiting such acts. But we cannot know, hence cannot legislate against, much less punish, what is in men's hearts. Either, therefore, no wars are warranted, or we must settle for more modest criteria for waging them. We can punish wrongful *deeds* by war, but whether in so doing we are punishing only evil men we may not know. And whether we ourselves act evilly in God's eyes in so doing we may not know, because we are unsure how our conduct will be assessed when measured by the higher written law of God at the final judgment.[47]

This marks the turning point in Christianity. Having transformed Christian ethics into an ethics of motivation, and having been confronted by the fact that only God can fully know what motivates men, Augustine is left with virtually no effective criterion of right conduct in cases ungoverned by express commands of God other than what is prescribed by law. To be told to do what you do from the motive of love does not tell you *what* to do. It is hoped that the law will further God's purposes. But that too cannot be known.

The result is to build into Christianity an extreme moral conservatism. Christ's teachings marked a radical departure from the formalism of the Old Testament and the legalism of the Romans, which seemed to early Christians to call for a way of life different

[47] Augustine is not consistent throughout in maintaining this. In fact, he nowhere states all of it in systematic fashion. But this, I believe, represents the reading of his treatment of war that is most consistent with the overall picture he develops of the relationship of the individual to the state and of both the individual and the state to God.

from how men had lived in the past. But under Augustine these teachings, so far as they pertain to violence and the taking of human life, reduce *in practice* to little more than what is conventionally accepted. The only significant difference is the prohibition against killing by private individuals, and even that has given away over the centuries so that today it is generally accepted by Christians when done in self-defense. This enabled Christians to behave in ways that must have been scarcely imaginable to Christ and his early followers and at the same time to believe they were being true to his teachings to the point where today, if one were to reflect upon the conduct of civilized persons without regard to religious affiliations, he would be hard pressed to distinguish Christians from non-Christians.

While one cannot know what would have taken place had Christianity not charted for itself a new course after Augustine, the consequences of the course it did take holds increasingly grim prospects as they unfold in our modern world. It is as though belief in the pessimistic picture painted by Augustine has helped to bring about the truth of that belief. Not that Christianity is by any means solely, or even primarily, responsible for the state of the world today. But had it clung to the nonviolence of the early Church, much of the war and destruction the Western World has known in the past fifteen hundred years could not have taken place.

FIVE

CAN WAR BE MORALLY JUSTIFIED?
THE JUST WAR THEORY

[There are] men who assert that the contradiction between the striving and love for peace and the necessity of war is terrible, but that such is the fate of men. These for the most part sensitive, gifted men see and comprehend the whole terror and the whole madness and cruelty of war, but by some strange turn of mind do not see and do not look for any issue from this condition.   —Leo Tolstoy

Augustine makes a powerful case for the justifiability of war. Grant just a few of his premises, and all the rest follows, enveloped in a theological-metaphysical-eschatalogical wrapping that renders it impervious to countervailing evidence and argument. Virtually every major just war theorist in the Western tradition, as I have said, builds upon his work.

This is not to say there is not other important work on morality and war outside of the Western tradition. Both Judaism and Islam give attention to the issue, particularly to the question of how war should be conducted, as does some Eastern thought. It is clear, for example, from the Old Testament that wars commanded by God are considered righteous and that definite rules have been laid down for the conduct of war. These two considerations—the conditions under which one may have recourse to war and the manner in which war may be conducted—are components of any complete just war doctrine. And Islam, in the concept of *Jihād*, has a clearly developed just war doctrine that represents the war of Islam against the non-Moslem world as a permanent condition (at least until the establishment of a Moslem world). The war need not be, or at least need not be exclusively, military, and Moslems may participate in the *Jihād* "by the heart, the tongue, or the hands, as well as by the sword."[1] But it is seen as enjoined by

[1] Ali Raza Naqvi, "Laws of War in Islam," *Islamic Studies* 13, no. 1 (Mar. 1974): 25.

Allah, giving it much the same justification that Augustine saw in wars commanded by God, and it has as its mission the establishment of a universal Islamic state.

My concern, however, is with the just war doctrine in the Western tradition, where it has been heavily influenced by Christianity, and in particular with some of its more recent formulations. I shall not present a history of the evolution of the tradition; that has been done by others and would be beside the point of our present concerns. My aim, rather, is to examine those aspects of the tradition that bear most directly upon my central argument concerning the morality of war and to assess the just war theory as an approach to the morality of war.

Two principal objections have been brought against the just war approach to war, neither of which, in my judgment, is successful, but one of which helps to focus a third objection that I think is decisive.

The first concerns alleged consequences of the prevalence of just war theorizing in certain historical periods. It is sometimes said that the most terrible wars in history occurred during the ascendancy of the just war theory and that the longest periods of relative tranquillity occurred when the theory was in eclipse. This is sometimes taken, without further argument, to constitute a refutation of the theory. It is true that the sixteenth and seventeenth centuries, when the just war theory was extensively discussed among theologians and jurists, was a time of some of the most vicious wars in history, a fact that provided much of the impetus to try to humanize the conduct of war. It is also true that but for the Napoleonic wars and the American Civil War, both of which caused widespread devastation but were for the most part professionally conducted, much of the period from that time to the twentieth century (a time during which, contrary to the just war theory, it was generally held that nations could justifiably go to war for virtually any reason) was relatively free of the worst excesses of war.

But as tempting as it may be to dismiss the just war approach on these grounds, claims of the preceding sort are difficult to substantiate. We have seen this to be true with the related claim by political realists in their critique of U.S. policy during World War I. They argued that to allow morality to govern foreign policy leads in time of war to a crusading mentality that stands in the way of the cool, dispassionate assessment of self-interest that can limit war's excesses. They were not talking about the just war theory specifically, but in the sense in which that approach embraces any attempt to provide a moral justification of war, their arguments apply to it. Such claims require disentangling complex religious and moral elements in the thinking about war from other cultural, technological, and military developments that shape its character. This is a difficult task at best. Even if it could be accomplished, it would be hard to be certain that any resultant correlation between the acceptance of the just war theory in a given period and the documentable horrors of war in that same period represented a causal connection. To my knowledge, this has never been convincingly shown.

The second objection bears upon the changing character of war in the nuclear age. It holds that the nuclear age, with the threat of annihilation in the case of an all-out war between the superpowers, has rendered the just war theory obsolete. Michael Walzer, for example, speaks of the "monstrous immorality that our policy contemplates, an immorality we can never hope to square with our understanding of justice in war," adding that "nuclear weapons explode the theory of just war."[2] Various just war theorists, including James Turner Johnson, William V. O'Brien, and Robert L. Phillips,[3] defend the theory and argue that it is relevant to the contemporary age and, indeed, represents the only defensible way of thinking about the problem of morality and war.

I want to examine this second objection in greater detail. Before that, however, it is important to consider certain aspects of the evolution of the just war doctrine, since there are developments there that are important to understanding the newer forms of the theory as well as to understanding my own argument concerning the morality of war.

I

The second main stage in the development of the just war theory following Augustine comes with St. Thomas Aquinas in the thirteenth century, who takes over Augustine's requirements that a war be declared by a legitimate authority and be for a just cause but adds to them a third requirement his own.

What this is can best be appreciated by recalling Augustine's subjectivistic understanding of the morality of warfare. The real

---

[2] *Just and Unjust Wars* (New York: Basic Books, 1977), p. 282.

[3] See James Turner Johnson, *Can Modern War Be Just?* (New Haven, Conn.: Yale University Press, 1984); William V. O'Brien, *The Conduct of a Just and Limited War* (New York: Praeger, 1981); William V. O'Brien and John Langan, eds., *The Nuclear Dilemma and the Just War Tradition* (Lexington, Mass.: Lexington Books, 1986); and Robert L. Phillips, *War and Justice* (Norman: University of Oklahoma Press, 1984).

evils of war, he said, are "love of violence, revengeful cruelty, fierce and implacable enmity and the like." This, as we have seen, was part of the interiorization of Christian ethics, emphasizing purity of soul and motivation, and it is taken over by Aquinas. But he emphasizes something that is only implicit in Augustine, which is that any action may have bad consequences, whatever the intentions of the agent performing it. And this seems correct. Most actions have *some* bad consequences, particularly in the area of social and political affairs; the best of policies impose demands upon some persons or ask sacrifices of them. The relevant question is not whether those policies would benefit some individual or group but rather whether their benefits outweigh their costs—whether the good produced would outweigh the bad. In more general terms, from the perspective of morality discussed in Chapter One, the question for conduct is: How can one lead a fully moral life if he cannot help doing some bad in the ordinary course of things?

Aquinas proposes a solution in the third condition he adds to Augustine's requirements, which occurs in the context of an argument to show that one may sometimes justifiably kill another person in self-defense.

Nothing hinders one act from having two effects, only one of which is intended, while the other is beside the intention. . . . Accordingly the act of self-defence may have two effects, one is the saving of one's life, the other is the slaying of the aggressor. Therefore this act, since one's intention is to save one's own life, is not unlawful, seeing that it is natural to everything to keep itself in *being*, as far as possible.[4]

In the preceding chapter, we saw the importance of the distinction between intentions and motives. Here, more explicitly than Augustine, Aquinas calls attention to the further distinction between our intention—that which it is our purpose to bring about through an action—and what we merely foresee or expect as the outcome, and maintains that we may sometimes justifiably kill another person provided the killing is "beside the intention"—that is, merely foreseen and not intended (he also requires that one

[4] *The Summa Theologica of Saint Thomas Aquinas*, Dominican trans. (London: Burns Oates & Washbourne, Ltd., 1929), II-II, q. 64, art. 7. See also q. 40, art. 1. Aquinas is sometimes thought to have added a fourth condition, that there be a right use of means as well. See Austin Fagothy, *Right and Reason: Ethics in Theory and Practice* (St. Louis: The C.V. Mosby Company, 1953), p. 516.

have public authority for the act, use no more violence than necessary, and act for the common good).

In the case of the resort to war, it is expressly required that one have a right intention. This means that one must intend to promote the good and avoid evil; merely having a just cause and legitimate authority is insufficient. What constitutes a right intention during the conduct of war is less clear. It has been taken by subsequent writers to require that one not "directly" intend the killing of persons as persons but only intend the killing of them as combatants, or that one pursue peace and avoid unnecessary destruction, or that one protect rights.[5] In any event, the emphasis is subjectivistic, dependent upon inner purity. (There is a similar emphasis in Islam in the requirement that the *jihadist* fight with a good intention, specifically to promote Islam rather than, say, to achieve personal gain.)

II

The troublesome question of whether both sides can be just in a war arises here, however. For the first and third of the preceding conditions—legitimate authority and right intention—could easily be met by both sides. Even Hitler, as we saw in the preceding chapter, arguably had the legitimate authority to declare war in World War II. And it might just as easily be the case that both sides have a right intention in the required sense; good Christians and good Moslems will have no less, as the crusades attest. The crucial question concerns whether both sides could have a just cause, and this issue engaged just war theorists for years and led to some of the most significant developments in the evolution of the theory, particularly in its relationship to international law.

Vitoria in the sixteenth century came close to making explicit a distinction that has its origins in Augustine. He denied that war could be just on both sides, saying that "if the right and justice of each side be certain, it is unlawful to fight against it, either in offence or defence." But he qualified this by adding: "Assuming a demonstrable ignorance either of fact or of law, it may be that on the side where true justice is the war is just of itself, while on the

[5] See, for example, The Pastoral Letter on War and Peace of the National Conference of Catholic Bishops, *The Challenge of Peace: God's Promise and Our Response* (Washington, D.C.: United States Catholic Conference, 1983), p. 30; Phillips, *War and Justice*, chap. 2; Paul Ramsey, "Vietnam and Just War," *Dialog* 6 (Winter 1967): 19-29, reprinted in *The Just War: Force and Political Responsibility* (New York: Charles Scribner & Sons, 1986), pp. 497-512.

other side the war is just in the sense of being excused from sin by reason of good faith, because invincible ignorance is a complete excuse."[6] He said further, in the spirit of Augustine, that although a prince may knowingly carry on an unjust war, his subjects may not know that the war is unjust and "in this way the subjects on both sides may be doing what is lawful when they fight."

Two senses of justice emerge here: an objective sense designating the actual moral status of a war, which is unaffected by whether people *think* the war is just; and a subjective sense, according to which a war is just if it is believed through invincible ignorance to be just, even if in fact it is objectively unjust. In this way a war might be subjectively just on both sides but it could never be objectively just on both sides.[7]

This is a useful and important distinction, and it is elaborated by more recent ethical theorists. But an even more sophisticated handling of this problem is found in the eighteenth century in the writings of E. Vattel, whose influential analysis becomes the prevailing view into the twentieth century. Central to it is the distinction between legality and morality. While Hugo Grotius had clearly recognized the distinction in the seventeenth century, and

[6] *The Spanish Origins of International Law: Francisco De Vitoria and His Law of Nations*, pt. 1, app. B, *De Jure Belli*, in *The Classics of International Law*, ed. James Brown Scott (Oxford: Clarendon Press, 1934), pp. lx-lxi.

[7] A war that is truly just in the Augustinian sense would be objectively just in this sense, and vice versa. But a war that is subjectively just in this sense, that is, which is merely *believed* to be just, might or might not be temporally just in the Augustinian sense. The sixteenth-century writer A. Gentili is sometimes thought to have maintained that justice can reside with both sides in war. But despite some misleading statements, his position is not far from Vitoria's. He maintains, for example, that the Israelites, led by the voice of God, justly made war against the Canaanites and that the latter nonetheless justly resisted in self-defense, through ignorance of divine law. But even he distinguishes between "that purest and truest form of justice, which cannot conceive of both parties to a dispute being in the right" and justice as it appears from man's standpoint, and asserts that "therefore we aim at justice as it appears from man's standpoint." As undeveloped as the point is, he has tacitly invoked a similar—though not identical—distinction to that made by Vitoria. He hedges still further by adverting to his normative definition of war as "a just and public contest of arms" and claims that if one side is contending "without any adequate reason, that party is surely practicing brigandage and not waging war"; and thus he says that "if it is doubtful on which side justice is, and if each side aims at justice, neither can be called unjust." For quoted material see Alberico Gentili, *De Jure Belli: Libri Tres*, in *The Classics of International Law*, ed. James Brown Scott, trans. John C. Rolfe (Oxford: Clarendon Press, 1933), pp. 31-32. Hugo Grotius, sometimes thought of as the father of international law, clearly recognizes different senses of justice in his treatment of this topic in the seventeenth century. See Hugo Grotius, *De Jure Belli ac Pacis Libri Tres*, in *The Classics of International Law*, ed. James Brown Scott, trans. Francis W. Kelsey (Oxford: Clarendon Press, 1925), pp. 565-566.

some awareness of it can be found in Vitoria and possibly even in Augustine, Vattel brings it to bear upon international problems in a way that sheds important light on the interrelationships between law and morality in connection with war.

Let us consider first the nature of international law, after which we will be in a better position to appreciate Vattel's argument.

III

Philosophers and jurists are not fully agreed as to precisely what international law is, but they largely agree that its modern origins lie in the rise of the nation-state in the sixteenth and seventeenth centuries. It was at that time that diverse and often tenuous loyalties to monarchs, princes, and feudal lords began to congeal around larger, politically and territorially definable units having a monopoly of force. The command of such a monopoly came to be a defining characteristic of the state in later writers like Weber. Not only did this process establish nation-states as the principal actors in the interrelationships among peoples but it also added new fuel to the furnace of war. For by the time of the Napoleonic wars between 1792 and 1815 patriotism became an added ingredient in the mixture of emotion, fear, hope, and courage that was to impel peoples to fight and die for the state, a factor that, combined with the advance in weaponry brought by the industrial revolution, made possible the unprecedented capacity for warfare possessed by the industrial nations of the twentieth century.

Both the emergence of states and the increased destructiveness of war contributed to the development of modern international law, but they did so in different ways. The emergence of states altered the character of the entities, or "juristic persons," who are subject to that law. In antiquity the subjects of such rudimentary international law as there was were peoples: the Athenians, the Corinthians, the Romans, the Vandals, and so forth. Today they are states, and it is their conduct that international law seeks to regulate. It is also their rights and obligations that are largely at issue in disputes over international law. I say largely because the Nuremberg trials challenged that view and attempted to extend international law to the conduct of individual persons as well as to states. This raises questions about what sorts of entities states are, what it is for a state to "act," how they can have rights and obligations, and what those rights and obligations are—questions that underlie many of the problems of contemporary international law as it bears upon the problem of war.

The destructiveness of war, on the other hand, contributed to the development of international law by creating a perceived need to mitigate war's horrors. We saw in the preceding chapter the warlike footing Christianity was put on by Augustine. By the seventeenth century the militarization of Christianity had progressed to the point where Grotius, in explaining his reasons for writing his major study on the laws of war and peace, lamented:

> Throughout the Christian world I observed a lack of restraint in relation to war, such as even barbarous races should be ashamed of; I observed that men rush to arms for slight causes, or no cause at all, and that when arms have once been taken up there is no longer any respect for law, divine or human; it is as if, in accordance with a general decree, frenzy had openly been let loose for the committing of all crimes.[8]

The concern for the most part was not to do away with war; it was rather to civilize it and bring it into line with humanitarian ideals. This led to efforts to formulate so-called "laws of war."

Early discussions of the laws of war had two concerns. One, dealing with *jus in bello*, was to establish rules for the conduct of war once it had begun. It dealt with such issues as the legitimacy of killing noncombatants, the treatment of prisoners, the use of poisons, appropriation of property, and the use of especially terrible weapons. The other, dealing with *jus ad bellum*, which in its moral dimension was the primary concern of Augustine, was to establish rules governing the resort to war in the first place and to lay down conditions under which war could justifiably be waged at all. On this view war, no matter how scrupulously waged, could be unjust depending upon how and why it began. The distinction between these concerns is central to Vattel's analysis.

I have been speaking of international law as though there were a clearly specified body of rules comprising such law. But there is not. There is an International Court of Justice (World Court) but no world legislature that enacts legislation and sets penalties for its violation. Nor has there ever been. International law has other origins. What these are is a matter of disagreement among scholars, but three alleged sources stand out: natural law, custom, and convention.

---

[8] Prolegomena, *De Jure Belli ac Pacis Libri Tres*, p. 20.

Natural law dates back at least as far as the Stoics, and perhaps to Anaximander. The Stoics conceived of nature as a rational manifestation of God and took rightness and duty to be determined by what accords with it. "This, then, . . . has been the decision of the wisest philosophers," Cicero wrote in one of the clearest classical statements of this idea, "that law was neither a thing contrived by the genius of man, nor established by any decree of the people, but a certain eternal principle, which governs the entire universe, wisely commanding what is right and prohibiting what is wrong."[9] Natural law so conceived contains the criteria for judging moral rightness and wrongness. It is unchangeable and transcends man-made laws. It provides a natural standard by which to judge human, or "positive," law as well as the conduct of peoples of different countries who may not be bound together by positive laws. Sometimes such law is represented as taking the form of precepts impressed by common sense upon the minds of all persons, sometimes as taking the form of natural inclinations that are a part of human nature. Aquinas, who Christianized the concept, represents it in both ways. In his view natural law is part of eternal law, God's plan for the governance of the whole of creation, and as such it perfects man unto well-being and happiness in his relation to the natural world and his fellow men.

This sets natural law theory in a metaphysical or theological framework concerning the nature of man and his relationship to the cosmos. The theory varies according to the underlying philosophies of those giving accounts of it. In a more general sense, however, natural law theory is simply the view that moral considerations are or should be the governing considerations behind positive law. In this sense it need not have the implications associated with the formulations of Cicero and Aquinas, and may simply represent an appeal to morality in the formulation and assessment of laws.

Custom, or customary law, on the other hand, designates practices that develop of their own accord without benefit of design or legislation. It represents a kind of international common law, which in turn represents legal norms for the conduct of states. Needless to say it is always an open question whether the practices of people and states are right from a moral standpoint, which means that what is prescribed by natural law and what is dictated

[9] *The Treatises of M.T. Cicero*, trans. C. D. Yonge (London: George Bell and Sons, York Street, Covent Garden, 1876), p. 431.

by customary law may diverge. Grotius in effect recognized both sorts. Natural law provided the foundation of his account, but the better part of his discussion concerns the practices and customs surrounding warfare. In fact, he takes the law of nations, which along with municipal law is part of human law, to be rooted in "unbroken custom and the testimony of those who are skilled in it."[10]

Conventional law, finally, refers to enactments by treaty and convention. Although binding only upon states that are a party to the particular treaty or convention, they play a role in the establishment and acceptance of the rules that states recognize and must take account of in their dealings with one another.

Any one of these might be claimed to be the prime source of international law. The philosophy underlying international law has undergone change depending upon which has been emphasized. Natural law gradually gave way after Grotius and his followers to customary law, which is widely regarded today as the major source of international law, as it is in this statement by Hans Kelsen:

> [T]he general norm which obligates states to behave in conformity with the treaties they have concluded . . . is a norm of general international law, and general international law is created by custom constituted by acts of states. The basic norm of international law, therefore, must be a norm which countenances custom as a norm-creating fact, and might be formulated as follows: The states ought to behave as they have customarily behaved.[11]

This view takes customary law to be more basic than conventional law, since it represents the latter as merely codifying what is contained in the former. It leaves natural law out of the picture altogether. It also conflates the "is" and the "ought" of international conduct by taking custom to be prescriptive.

Despite the preeminence of customary law, natural law can be seen to underlie the Nuremberg Charter and the Human Rights Declaration of the United Nations. In connection with warfare natural law was implicit in a statement by the prosecution at Nuremberg: "The law of war is to be found not only in treaties, but in the

---

[10] Grotius, *De Jure Belli ac Pacis Libri Tres*, p. 44.

[11] *Principles of International Law* (Berkeley: University of California Press, 1952), p. 417, as cited in William W. Bishop, Jr., ed., *International Law: Cases and Materials*, 3d ed. (Boston: Little, Brown and Company, 1962), p. 9.

customs and practices of states which gradually obtained universal recognition, and from the general principles of justice applied by jurists and practiced by military courts. This law is not static, but by continual adaptation follows the needs of a changing world."[12] If "principles of justice" is taken to refer to moral principles rather than merely to the conceptions of justice held by jurists and military courts, this formulation blends all three of the preceding sources. Along with explicit references to natural law by the prosecution during the trials, this suggests a reemergence of natural law in the thinking about international affairs. Crimes against peace were taken by the tribunal to pertain to the initation of war, hence to belong to that aspect of international law dealing with recourse to war. Crimes of war, or simply war crimes, were taken to pertain to the conduct of war. Crimes against humanity were defined as consisting of various inhumane acts against "any civilian population, before or during the war, or persecutions on political, racial or religious grounds in execution of or in connection with any crime within the jurisdiction of the Tribunal." (In its judgment the tribunal issued guilty verdicts on this score only in connection with inhumane acts committed after the outbreak of the war, and insofar as those acts were not also war crimes, issued them on the ground that they were committed in connection with an aggressive war. The implication is, though the tribunal did not draw it, that virtually all mistreatment of civilians in the course of an aggressive war is a crime against humanity.)

Lest it be thought that the foregoing distinctions and the question of what priority to assign to the various sources of international law are of merely theoretical interest, it should be noted that men have been put to death as a result of differences over the nature, scope, and authority of international law. The defendants at Nuremberg were charged with crimes against humanity as well as with war crimes and crimes against peace. In addition they were charged with conspiracy to commit such crimes. The principal basis for the charges was the London Charter, officially known as the Agreement for the Establishment of an International Military Tribunal, concluded at London, August 8, 1945, which specifically identified the aforementioned as crimes. This fact gave rise to one of the central issues in the trial, namely, whether the London Charter constituted retroactive law, inasmuch as the acts for which

[12] *International Military Tribunal, Trial of Major War Criminals, Proceedings* (Nuremberg, Germany, 1948), 22: 464.

the defendants were indicted occurred before that charter existed. The prosecution seemed at times to concede that new law had been created, or at least that existing law had been supplemented, but for the most part it argued that all the charter did was to codify existing law. Here it appealed to the League of Nations Covenant, the Kellogg-Briand Pact, and the Hague Conventions. Germany, of course, had withdrawn from the League of Nations in 1930 and had renounced the Kellogg-Briand Pact.

The defense argued that even if the relevant laws had been in effect, they would not apply to individuals but only to states. They called attention to the fact that only states had customarily been considered the subjects of international law. The reasoning was that, even though it was true, as the prosecution pointed out, that acts of states are acts of men, nonetheless individuals are not personally responsible for such acts and should not be punished for them. They pointed out that at the conclusion of World War I the United States had argued against punishing the Kaiser on the ground that such punishment would imply a limitation upon the sovereignty of the state to punish its citizens for acts performed by them in their capacity as its agents.

The defendants argued that they had been under orders with regard to at least certain of the alleged crimes. The orders were embodied in the *Führerprinzip*, according to which Hitler's orders were binding upon the citizens of Germany. These defenses were repudiated by the prosecution. While the tribunal did not accept the plea of having acted under superior orders as exculpatory, it did allow that it might mitigate punishment in some cases. Nearly all of the major figures among the accused were found guilty, and most were executed.

IV

Vattel recognizes each of the preceding sources of international law. In addition, following Christian Wolff, he recognizes voluntary law, which along with conventional and customary law makes up what he calls positive law. According to natural law, a war cannot be just on both sides. In this he agrees with Vitoria. But he holds that natural law dictates a number of more specific rules to govern the conduct of nations in light of their nature and the circumstances in which they act. The particularly relevant circumstance is that they are free, independent, and sovereign moral persons, and in a state of nature such as exists among nations none can dictate morally to others. These rules make up what he calls the voluntary law of nations. And thus it is that "the necessary [or natural] law prescribes what is of absolute necessity for Nations and what tends naturally to their advancement and their common happiness; the voluntary law tolerates what it is impossible to forbid without causing greater evils."[13] Nations are presumed to consent to voluntary law whether they do so in fact or not because otherwise they would be violating the liberties of all.

One of the rules of voluntary law holds *"that regular war, as regards its effects, must be accounted just on both sides."*[14] A regular war is one that is authorized on both sides by the sovereigns and is accompanied by appropriate formalities. This does not mean that from the standpoint of natural law both sides *are* in the right; only that from the standpoint of legality they should both be accounted in the right. It is the consequences of failing to do this that concern Vattel: "If an unjust war can give rise to no legal rights, no certain possession can be obtained of any property captured in war until a recognized judge, and there is none such between Nations, shall have passed definitely upon the justice of the war; and such property will always be subject to a claim for recovery, as in the case of goods stolen by robbers."[15] This suggests that territorial acquisitions through war, even if the war is unjust, should be regarded as legitimate lest there be continuing claims for recovery. Because such acquisitions cannot effectively be prohibited, tolerating them will have better consequences than denying their legitmacy.

This would seem to give carte blanche to nations to take what they want whenever they can get away with it. But this, in fact, is the way most nations have conducted themselves throughout history, including the period of European colonialism and the appropriation of North America from the Indians. They have done so to such an extent that if existing territorial boundaries, not to mention the ownership of various kinds of national treasure, were to be subjected to review from the standpoint of historical justice, few claims to legitimacy would survive. Except perhaps in the Middle East, where memories are longer than elsewhere, time generally legitimizes the results of war—at least from the stand-

---

[13] E. de Vattel, *The Law of Nations or the Principles of Natural Law: Applied to the Conduct and to the Affairs of Nations and of Sovereigns*, in *The Classics of International Law*, ed. James Brown Scott, trans. Charles G. Fenwick (Washington: The Carnegie Institute of Washington, 1916), 3: 306.

[14] Ibid., p. 305. Cf. Hugo Grotius, *De Jure Belli ac Pacis Libri Tres*, p. 644.

[15] E. de Vattel, *The Law of Nations*, p. 304.

point of legality—if the acquiring nation consolidates its position and is able to achieve stability. For better or worse, this tends to be the accepted principle of international affairs.

Thus, paradoxically, in Vattel's view the very law of nature according to which at least one side in a war must be acting unjustly dictates that for the good of all peoples it is best from a legal standpoint that both sides be considered just. This marks a clear separation of the conditions for a morally just war from those for a legally just war. It establishes that nations may wage war for any reason without violating international law. This view prevailed into the twentieth century when, following World War I, with the League of Nations Covenant and the Kellogg-Briand Pact, international law was taken once again to govern recourse to war as well as the conduct of war, a conception reaffirmed at Nuremberg and built into the United Nations Charter.

V

Renewed attention to *jus ad bellum*, the justice of going to war, has, however, brought some changes in the thinking about war.

Classical just war theorists, as we saw in the case of Augustine, believed it was sometimes just to initiate war. The question of who initiates a war was not in itself of particular concern to them. However, in the League of Nations Covenant, the Kellogg-Briand Pact, and the London Charter (Charter of the International Military Tribunal), the emphasis is upon aggression. The crimes against peace for which the defendants at Nuremberg were tried covered "planning, preparation, initiation or waging of a war of aggression." And it is the notions of aggressive and defensive wars that have come to dominate the discussions of war throughout much of the twentieth century. Whenever hostilities break out, each side accuses the other of aggression and proclaims that it, on the other hand, acts only in self-defense. Aggression is commonly regarded as a criterion of the illegality of war as well as the immorality of war.

This means there have emerged two sets of distinctions: one between just and unjust war, the other between defensive and aggressive war. Their interrelations are complex in light of the fact that both are subject to different interpretations.

If aggression is understood in a neutral sense (let us call it aggression$_1$), as standing simply for the initiation of hostilities without regard for the rights or wrongs of so doing, then it is clear that a just war in the traditional sense can be either aggressive or defensive. Who initiates a war is irrelevant. What is relevant is whether he has a just cause, is acting from legitimate authority, and so forth. This, however, is at odds with the more recent use of these notions according to which an aggressive war is unjust virtually by definition. In this normative sense (call it aggression$_2$) aggression stands not simply for the initiation of hositilies but for the *unjustified* initiation of hostilities. To call something a war of aggression is not only to classify it; it is to judge it as well.[16]

But even a third use of the notion can be discerned. In Michael

[16] For a somewhat different way of drawing the distinction among kinds of aggression, see Yehuda Melzer, *Concepts of Just War* (Leyden: A. W. Sijthoff, 1975), pp. 86-87. Aggression$_2$, I have suggested, is the sense found most often in discussions. A theoretical basis for a somewhat similar account is provided by David Luban in his essay "Just War and Human Rights," *Philosophy and Public Affairs* 9, no. 2 (Winter 1980): 160-181. He argues that aggression should be regarded as a crime against individuals, not states. States, he reasons, have a right against aggression only insofar as they enjoy legitimacy, where legitimacy must be understood in terms of the honoring of human rights. Thus he believes that unjust war can be defined as a war subversive of human rights. Aggression, though it does not figure explicitly in the characterization of a just war, is then understood in terms of the subversion of human rights. This makes it an evaluative notion, though not one that entails the initiation of hostilities. In any event, his characterization of a just war as "(i) a war in defense of socially basic human rights (subject to proportionality); or (ii) a war of self-defense against an unjust war" (p. 175) enables him to say, in keeping with classical theorists, that aggression is not the sole crime of war.

The Pastoral Letter of the National Conference of Catholic Bishops similarly characterizes just war in terms of human rights. In setting down the requirements for a just cause it says: "War is permissible only to confront 'a real and certain danger,' i.e., to protect innocent life, to preserve conditions necessary for decent human existence, and to secure basic human rights" (*The Challenge of Peace: God's Promise and Our Response*, p. 28). Though the bishops seem not to recognize this, such a characterization leaves open the possibility that a just war could be an aggressive$_1$ war, that is, one in which the just side initiates hostilities. It is easily conceivable that protection of innocent life and the security of human rights might require initiating hostilities; this, after all, was among the rationales given for the U.S. invasion of Grenada in 1983. "The present-day conception of 'aggression,' " Elizabeth Anscombe says on this issue, referring pretty clearly to aggression$_2$, "like so many strongly influential conceptions, is a bad one. Why *must* it be wrong to strike the first blow in a struggle? The only question is, who is in the right." See "War and Murder," in *War and Morality*, ed. Richard Wasserstrom (Belmont, Calif.: Wadsworth Publishing Company, Inc., 1970), pp. 43-44. In a similar vein, Paul Ramsey observes, "There is really no reason to be found in the justice of war itself for forbidding aggressive war and allowing only the right of self-defense or for forbidding the use of certain weapons systems as such." See "Tucker's Bellum Contra Bellum Justum," in *Just War and Vatican II: A Critique*, by Robert W. Tucker, with commentary by Paul Ramsey et al. (New York: The Council on Religion and International Affairs, 1966), p. 100; reprinted in Ramsey, *The Just War*, chap. 17. See also Johnson, *Can Modern War Be Just?* pp. 177-178, and Tucker, *The Just War: A Study in Contemporary American Doctrine*, p. 15.

Walzer's *Just and Unjust Wars*, it is used in a way that does not even require the initiation of hostilities. Walzer contends that

> aggression can be made out not only in the absence of a military attack or invasion but in the (probable) absence of any immediate intention to launch such an attack or invasion. The general formula must go something like this: states may use military force in the face of threats of war, whenever the failure to do so would seriously risk their territorial integrity or political independence. Under such circumstances it can fairly be said that they have been forced to fight and that they are the victims of aggression.[17]

Such an implicit definition as this (let us call it aggression$_3$) enables one to render just and unjust wars virtually coextensive with defensive and aggressive wars. It expands the notion of aggression to cover cases of mere threats, provided the threats are serious enough. If one assumes further that such threats provide a just cause for going to war in self-defense, this would enable one to hold that it is possible to initiate a just war. In this way, the apparent proscription of the initiation of war in the League of Nation's Covenant, the Kellogg-Briand Pact, the London Charter, and the United Nations Charter is overridden in favor of an approach more in keeping with the traditional just war theory.

This is at some cost, however. For as one moves from aggression$_1$ to aggression$_2$ to aggression$_3$, the conceptual content of the notion changes. In aggression$_1$ there is an objective and neutral criterion for deciding when aggression has occurred, namely, when someone fires the first shot. It may not always be easy to apply in practice, but it is simple and clear. In aggression$_2$ the idea of initiating hostilities is retained, but whether aggression has occurred requires showing that the initiation of hostilities was unjustified. Reference to the initiation of hostilities drops out altogether in aggression$_3$ and is replaced by reference to a "threat of war," where this does not even require an immediate intention to attack. Aggression$_1$ has the shortcoming that many people, including heads of state, some just war theorists, and experts in international law, feel there are circumstances in which one is justified in initiating war; in other words, that aggression$_1$ is sometimes justified. Israel's attack upon Egypt initiating the 1967 Arab-Israeli War is a case in point. This means that to incorporate this sense of the

[17] Page 85.

concept in laws defining criminal action in the resort to war is to render illegal some wars widely held to be just. Aggression$_2$ and aggression$_3$, on the other hand, leave discretion to potential initiators of war to determine when hostilities are warranted. Since virtually every nation that starts a war believes it does so justifiably, this enables nations to go to war pretty much when they want and for whatever reasons they want and to call it a response to aggression. Since, furthermore, to respond to aggression by force is understood by all to be self-defense, and to wage war in self-defense is recognized by all except pacifists to be legitimate, this provides a rationale for virtually every war.

Some of these difficulties figured in the protracted effort by the United Nations to define aggression. If to call something an act of aggression is to imply that it is wrong, no nation will settle for a definition according to which its past or future actions are rendered aggressive. This made agreement on a definition by the United Nations difficult to achieve. The one finally adopted affirms that "[a]ggression is the use of armed force by a State against the sovereignty, territorial integrity or political independence of another State, or in any other way inconsistent with the Charter of the United Nations, as set out in this definition." However, the second of eight Articles following the definition asserts:

> The first use of armed force by a State in contravention of the Charter shall constitute *prima facie* evidence of an act of aggression although the Security Council may, in conformity with the Charter, conclude that a determination that an act of aggression has been committed would not be justified in the light of other relevant circumstances including the fact that the acts concerned or their consequences are not of sufficient gravity.[18]

This qualification so dilutes the definition as to render it of questionable value. But it does make clear that aggression$_1$ is not the sense the U.N. Special Committee proposing the definition had in mind, since the first use of force is taken to represent only prima facie evidence of aggression. Defensive wars, once begun, are often directed against the "sovereignty, territorial integrity or political independence of another State." The situation is less clear

---

[18] This and the above definition are cited in Melzer, *Concepts of Just War*, pp. 29-30. Melzer's book contains an excellent discussion of these and related issues. See further, Julius Stone, *Conflict through Consensus: United Nations Approaches to Aggression* (Baltimore: The Johns Hopkins University Press, 1977).

regarding aggression$_2$. But then Article 4 states that "the acts enumerated above are not exhaustive and the Security Council may determine that other acts constitute aggression under the provisions of the Charter." This opens up still further the possibility that acts which do not involve the imminent or actual first use of force might nonetheless constitute aggression, which is the essential idea contained in aggression$_3$. It also suggests that the U.N. attempt to define aggression is hopelessly muddled.

The legality of war is, as we have seen, but one concern of *jus ad bellum*; the main concern is with the morality of war, and parallel problems arise here. Does one, for example, treat the concept of aggression as neutral for purposes of moral judgment, implying nothing one way or the other about the justifiability of the use of force it represents, or does one require as part of the definition that the use of force in question be unjustified? And does one allow that aggression may be committed without the use of force, as allowed by aggression$_3$? In the absence of the resolution of these and related issues, neither the legal nor the moral dimensions of the just war theory can provide adequate criteria for *jus ad bellum*.

VI

Most modern theorists, however, devote little attention to the question of *whether* war is justified; they assume that it is and ask only under what conditions it is justified and how it is to be conducted justly. Their actual prescriptions, in fact, differ little from those of political realists, and apart from the underlying rationales they provide for them it would be difficult to tell them apart. If anything, the just war theorists may be more hardline than political realists, which suggests that adopting a moral perspective does not per se make it less likely that one will be militaristic. They tend to be strongly anticommunist, particularly anti-Soviet, to be pro nuclear deterrence, and to feel that one is sometimes justified in initiating a war. All of them agree, however, that *jus in bello* requires that the conduct of war be limited, and most of them favor a counterforce as opposed to a countervalue (or countercities) policy with respect to the targeting of nuclear weapons.

No single statement of the conditions of just war would do justice to all of the just war theorists, since the number of conditions vary from writer to writer, ranging from about five to ten for both *jus ad bellum* and *jus in bello* combined, and their interpretation often varies as well. But they all include just cause for *jus ad bellum* and principles of proportion and discrimination for *jus in bello*.

A fairly representative statement is that of the National Conference of Catholic Bishops in their pastoral letter on war and peace. For one to be justified in resorting to war, they say, the following conditions must be met:

1. Just Cause: "War is permissible only to confront 'a real and certain danger,' i.e., to protect innocent life, to preserve conditions necessary for decent human existence, and to secure basic human rights."
2. Competent Authority: "[W]ar must be declared by those with responsibility for public order, not by private groups or individuals."
3. Comparative Justice: In recognition of the fact that there may be some justice on each side, "[e]very party to a conflict should acknowledge the limits of its 'just cause' and the consequent requirement to use *only* limited means in pursuit of its objectives."
4. Right Intention: "[W]ar can be legitimately intended only for the reasons set forth above as a just cause."
5. Last Resort: "For resort to war to be justified, all peaceful alternatives must have been exhausted."
6. Probability of Success: This criterion is not precisely stated, but the bishops affirm that "its purpose is to prevent irrational resort to force or hopeless resistance when the outcome of either will clearly be disproportionate or futile."
7. Proportionality: "[T]he damage to be inflicted and the costs incurred by war must be proportionate to the good expected by taking up arms. . . . This principle of proportionality applies throughout the conduct of the war as well as to the decision to begin warfare."

Two principles, finally, govern the conduct of war, even when justifiably resorted to:

8. Proportionality: as above.
9. Discrimination: "[T]he lives of innocent persons may never be taken directly, regardless of the purpose alleged for doing so. . . . Just response to aggression must be . . . directed against unjust aggressors, not against innocent people caught up in a war not of their making.[19]

[19] See the Pastoral Letter of the National Conference of Catholic Bishops, *The Challenge of Peace: God's Promise and Our Response*, pp. 28-34.

We find here an elaboration of the conditions set forth by Augustine, with explicit recognition that justification must be given both for the resort to war as well as for the manner of conducting it. There is also recognition here of the problem of whether there can be justice on both sides during a war. The bishops imply there may at least be degrees of justice, that these must be compared, and that war must be kept limited in light of this possibility. Finally, it is notable that the notion of innocent life plays an important role in both areas of *justum bellum*, its protection being a central element in the constitution of a just cause and the prohibition against taking it being a central condition of the just conduct of war. In this, modern just war theorists depart from Augustine, for whom the importance of protecting innocent life is at best implied in the notion of a just cause and virtually absent in the few things he says about the conduct of war. In fact, the idea of protecting innocent life has today become one of the chief justifications for resorting to violence in general. By extension it has come to play an imporatnt role in most accounts of *jus ad bellum*. What it is for innocent lives to be "directly" taken, however, is crucial to understanding *jus in bello*, for in most accounts it is only the direct taking of innocent life (and of the lives of noncombatants, as it is about equally as often put) that is prohibited. I shall examine this question in the next chapter.

Although just war theorizing has been closely identified with the Catholic tradition, there has been wide interest in it among Protestant and secular writers as well in more recent thought, with Paul Ramsey leading the way among Protestants.[20] He is one of the relatively few to devote much attention to the origins of the just war tradition, and we have considered in the preceding chapter his analysis of Augustine on the matter of noncombatant immunity. We may add here that he breaks with tradition on the issue just considered and reads Augustine as allowing that there may be justice on both sides in war. However, he seems to regard the sense of justice involved in this claim as a subjective one, representing the good will and intentions of a people bound together by agreement on common aims, this constituting a form of political justice. In this he is more in the tradition of Vitoria and Gentili. But he is skeptical about the possibility of discerning true or "universal" justice in war, and in this his orientation is strongly Augustinian, as the distinction between true and temporal justice was

[20] See his *War and the Christian Conscience: How Shall Modern War Be Conducted Justly?* (Durham, N.C.: Duke University Press, 1961) and *The Just War*.

central for Augustine. This leads Ramsey to give limited attention to *jus ad bellum* and to concentrate almost exclusively upon *jus in bello*. His thought also marks a return to another important feature of the classical just war theory in that he allows that sometimes an aggressive (or offensive) war can be just or, at the very least, that a fast adherence to the distinction between aggressive and defensive war is unreasonable. Finally, he virtually identifies just war in the modern age with counterforce war (that is, war targeting only military forces and installations) as opposed to countercities or countervalue war. But although he attaches great importance to noncombatant immunity, he does not see this as precluding the use of nuclear weapons or the destruction of homes that may be used as sanctuaries by the enemy. We shall in the next chapter examine the principle of double effect to which he subscribes, which allows such acts so long as the intention is not to kill innocent persons.

James Turner Johnson likewise focusses almost exclusively on the question of the conduct of war, saying that his concern is with "the *jus in bello* of the just war tradition, the broad cultural consensus on the appropriate limits to force that has developed over Western history."[21] The problem as he sees it is how to limit the violence of war. The assumption is that certain values are so important that their defense sometimes requires going to war; as he says, "[I]t is sometimes necessary to oppose evil by force unless evil is to triumph."[22] The just war tradition, he contends, has full relevance to the contemporary situation, and he examines the applicability of *jus in bello* criteria both to nuclear deterrence and to such conventional conflicts as the Falklands War and the Israeli invasion of Lebanon. Indeed, he claims that the ideas contained in the just war tradition represent the "only way actually open for persons in our culture to think about morality and war."[23] Although he thinks an all-out nuclear war between the superpowers would strain the limits of a just war conception of proportionality, he believes there are sufficient restraints operating in the international situation to make such an outcome unlikely.[24] Nonetheless, he favors the strengthening of conventional forces and the development of weapons that can be used effectively with minimum risk to noncombatants. "In this regard," he says, "the continued

[21] *Can Modern War Be Just?* p. 3.
[22] Ibid., pp. 31, 84.
[23] Ibid., p. 29.
[24] Ibid., p. 186.

existence and enhancement of nuclear deterrent forces, including the progressive development of less massively destructive means of deterrence and alongside the provision of effective means of defense and warfighting capability, is the lesser evil not only politically and militarily, but also morally."[25]

VII

This issue is important for the just war theory. For however justifiable war is taken to be, one cannot help but wonder whether waging it all-out with nuclear weapons can ever be justified. And if it cannot, can the just war theory remain relevant in the nuclear age?

William V. O'Brien, like Johnson, believes it can, arguing that limited nuclear war need not necessarily escalate into all-out war. But the deeper issue is whether the conditions that make for justice in the recourse to war, whether it be conventional or nuclear, can justify violations of moral constraints in the conduct of war; that is, whether *jus ad bellum* can override *jus in bello* in circumstances in which they conflict. Michael Walzer maintains there may be such violations in the case of what, following Churchill, he calls supreme emergencies, such as was represented by the Nazi threat in World War II. If this should be correct, it would at least open the way (though Walzer does not argue this) to justifying such violations in the case of nuclear war as well. And that is crucial to showing that the just war theory can demonstrate the permissibility of war in the nuclear age, since it is virtually certain, as I shall argue in the next chapter, that one cannot wage modern war of any sort, much less nuclear war, without killing innocent persons.

Walzer's appeal to supreme emergencies has been taken by O'Brien to represent an alternative to the just war theory, and O'Brien argues that the just war approach is the more defensible of the two.[26] I believe it can be shown, however, that there is no significant difference between the ethics of supreme emergency, as O'Brien characterizes it, and the just war theory as he conceives it. This requires taking a closer look at Walzer's theory.

Walzer devotes rather more attention to *jus ad bellum* than do most recent writers, but he also assumes with little argument that

---

[25] Ibid., p. 104.
[26] See his "The Future of the Nuclear Debate," in O'Brien and Langan, eds., *The Nuclear Dilemma and the Just War Tradition*, pp. 223-248.

war is justified. Although he sometimes speaks as though aggression only creates a presumption in favor of armed resistance, he usually affirms that aggression suffices to justify the resort to war. He says, for example, that "[a]ll aggressive acts have one thing in common; they justify forceful resistance"; and again that "[a]ggression is a singular and undifferentiated crime because, in all its forms, it challenges rights that are worth dying for."[27] He states unequivocally, however, that *only* the defense of rights can justify war.

His analysis of aggression centers about the legalist paradigm. He analogizes the international order to the civil order, except that the international order "is unlike domestic society in that every conflict threatens the structure as a whole with collapse. Aggression challenges it directly and is much more dangerous than domestic crime, because there are no policemen."[28] Because of the gravity of aggressive violations of the international order, the violation of those rights must be vindicated; the members of international society have not done enough if they "merely contain the aggression or bring it to a speedy end."

The theory of aggression as he construes it consists of six points: (1) that "[t]here exists an international society of independent states"; (2) that this society has a law establishing the rights of individual members, above all to territorial integrity and political sovereignty; (3) that "[a]ny use of force or imminent threat of force by one state against the political sovereignty or territorial integrity of another constitutes aggression and is a criminal act"; (4) Aggression justifies a war of self-defense by the victim and a "war of law enforcement" by the victim and any other member of society; (5) "Nothing but aggression can justify war"; and (6) "Once the aggressor state has been militarily repulsed, it can also be punished."[29]

Walzer then proposes revisions to take account of the disanalogies between domestic and international society. I shall mention only the one of these that bears most directly upon our preceding discussion. It is the revision of (3) above, to count as aggression certain acts that fall short of the first use of force or even an immediate intention to initiate hostilities. It is this which commits him to the concept of aggression$_3$. He finds this revision justified by the 1967 Arab-Israeli War. Though the Israelis launched the initial attack, he believes that circumstances justified the attack be-

[27] *Just and Unjust Wars*, pp. 52-53.
[28] Ibid., p. 59.
[29] Ibid., pp. 61-62.

cause of Egypt's threat to Israel's security. This he believes effectively made Israel a victim of aggression.

Although his emphasis upon aggression has a modern ring, and his insistence that only aggression justifies resort to war seems to place him in the legalist tradition developed since World War I, in certain respects Walzer's position actually lies closer to that of the traditional just war theorists. With Augustine, he emphasizes that resort to war is justified only to vindicate the violation of rights, and his expanded conception of aggression enables him to justify the initiation of war, as Augustine did. In these respects his position is a restatement in modern dress of a basically traditional theory. But in certain other respects, as I shall point out, particularly in what he says about supreme emergencies, it resembles political realism.

It is in his exploration of the relationship between *jus ad bellum* and *jus in bello* that he appeals to supreme emergencies. He contends that justice in these two domains may sometimes conflict. When it does, rules governing the conduct of war may in some circumstances be violated in the promotion of a just cause. Thus he holds that nazism was such a menace that one could have done anything to defeat it,[30] including violating the rights of the innocent. But he stops short of saying that one is justified in doing this. Rather, he says that the rights violated remain in effect even as one violates them.[31] Johnson, it should be noted, takes this issue to be so important that he says: "The problem of just warfare in the contemporary age is not the problem of warfare in this age as such; rather, it is the problem of how to avoid what Michael Walzer terms 'supreme emergency' situations."[32]

Walzer's last contention is as important as it is puzzling. There are two ways of reading it. According to the first, individual rights sometimes have to be overridden in the interests of a just cause, namely, in circumstances of supreme emergency. The rights remain "in effect" only in the sense that they remain prima facie claims to certain sorts of treatment. According to the second interpretation, the rights remain fully in effect, and their violation is wrong even though it is morally justified by the supreme emergency. This, however, would seem to render some actions both right and wrong at the same time, and as this is incoherent, I shall assume that Walzer intends the first interpretation. The first, in

---

[30] Ibid., pp. 248-249.
[31] Ibid., p. 231.
[32] *Can Modern War Be Just?* p. 185.

any event, is consistent with the few remarks he makes about the moral theory underlying his position.

That theory is a morality of human rights, with considerations of utility secondary.[33] But when it comes to justifying the violation of the rights of the innocent—apparently to the point of being willing to kill them[34]—the situation is reversed. In a tantalizingly equivocal passage, Walzer says first that the rights of innocent people "cannot simply be set aside, nor can they be balanced, in utilitarian fashion, against this or that desirable outcome," and then:

> And yet the case for breaking the rules and violating those rights is made sufficiently often, and by soldiers and statesmen who cannot always be called wicked, so that we have to assume that it isn't pointless. Anyway, we know its point all too well. We know how high the stakes sometimes are in war and how urgent victory can be. . . . The very existence of a community may be at stake, and then how can we fail to consider possible outcomes in judging the course of the fighting? At this point if at no other, the restraint on utilitarian calculation must be lifted.[35]

As though unable to let stand a decision on the dilemma he has posed between collective security and individual rights, he then adds: "Even if we are inclined to lift it [the restraint on utilitarian calculation], however, we cannot forget that the rights violated for the sake of victory are genuine rights, deeply founded and in principle inviolable."[36]

He seems, in the last analysis, then, to say that utilitarian considerations sometimes override rights. But whatever the justification, the appeal in the above passage is to the survival of the "community," presumably meaning the nation or state; which suggests that national survival, or more basically, national egoism, is the governing norm. He does not always speak this way; sometimes he speaks of opposing "immeasurable evil" and the like. But repeatedly it is the survival and well-being of the state that is his ultimate appeal, which means that reason of state begins to show itself in the guise of the just war theory. The survival of the state becomes the ultimate end (with no clear underlying moral justifi-

[33] Walzer, *Just and Unjust Wars*, p. xvi.
[34] Ibid., pp. 259-260.
[35] Ibid., p. 228.
[36] Ibid.

cation of that end), and one is willing to do anything to promote that end.

O'Brien contends that Walzer's position, though resembling that of the German doctrine of *Kriegsraison* during World War I (basically, an unqualified principle of military necessity), differs from that position in that Walzer allows that measures warranted by supreme emergencies are justified only so long as the emergency lasts.[37] When they are no longer necessary one must conform once again to moral constraints in the conduct of war. The allies during World War II failed to recognize this limitation, O'Brien argues, in their bombing of cities; hence although their policies differed from those of the German proponents of *Kriegsraison* of World War I in that their justification was much more plausible, "they resembled the Germans in their propensity to use exceptional and morally impermissible means beyond the point where they could be justified by even a bona fide argument of necessity."[38]

Whatever the actual practice of the Germans in World War I and the allies in World War II, there is nothing in the notion of military necessity to authorize killing and destruction beyond what is militarily necessary; while it does not preclude going beyond that, military necessity provides no authorization for doing so. And in circumstances of supreme emergency, exceptional measures are called for precisely *because* they are militarily necessary; there would be no warrant in Walzer's view for violating the rights of innocent persons were that not the only way to preserve the community or to combat "immeasurable evils." As circumstances change, those measures may no longer be justified. But that is because they are no longer *necessary*. By the same token, measures that are militarily necessary in one set of circumstances may cease to be so in others. Their justification on grounds of military necessity then likewise ceases. So whatever the end for which one is fighting, and however justified the resort to war in the first place, Walzer's supreme emergency provisions justify the same measures as military necessity. For this reason, *if* Walzer believes that it is the preservation of the state that justifies the resort to war and the resort, when in war, to the extraordinary measures called for by supreme emergencies, his position begins to look indistinguishable in practical import from that of political realism.

O'Brien points out that *Kriegsraison* as advanced by Germany

[37] In "The Future of the Nuclear Debate," in O'Brien and Langan, eds., *The Nuclear Dilemma and the Just War Tradition*, p. 235.
[38] Ibid., p. 233.

171

during World War I held that "the German state possessed superior worth and had the right to greater latitude in self-preservation and self-advancement than other states.[39] He discounts this claim, saying that "Germany would be eligible for a supreme-emergency claim if its very existence and its fundamental values were at stake, but no more eligible than any other state." This is an important observation. It reflects the fact that if a principle is to have any claim to being moral it must extend equally to all and be equally usable by them in the same sorts of circumstances. But would one be willing to acknowledge the right of Nazi Germany to make such a claim? Few even consider the kind of justification the Nazis gave for their policies; as O'Brien says, "I take it that it is unnecessary to discuss justification for the conduct of the Third Reich in World War II."[40]

But *Mein Kampf* represents the German nation (meaning the German people, not the state) as confronting the very kind of threat to its survival and values that Walzer takes to justify supreme emergencies and that just war theorists almost universally take to constitute a just cause. Hitler saw the German nation as threatened by a Marxist-Jewish conspiracy of diabolical proportions, sapping its life, poisoning its blood, and dragging it down from its prior heights of cultural achievement. Reason of state demanded strong measures. This led to the Nuremberg Laws of 1935, to increasing persecutions of Jews and Communists (and others considered undesirable for other reasons), and eventually to exterminations of both as war broke out. That many more Jews were exterminated than non-Jews should not obscure the fact that in Hitler's mind Jews and Communists were part of the same threat. That he was mistaken in these views is beside the point. One acts necessarily upon what he *believes*. People can only apply principles that seem to them relevant. And this allows for error. So, if one lays down such requirements for a just war as that one have a just cause, what this means in practice is that nations may resort to war when they *believe* they have a just cause. By the same token, to justify the killing of innocent persons when necessitated by a supreme emergency is to say, in effect, that nations may resort to such measures when they *believe* they confront such an emergency. And in Walzer's account, as well as those of just war theorists, it is always the nation proposing to resort to war that is

[39] Ibid., p. 231.
[40] Ibid.

172

the judge of whether it has justice on its side or whether a given emergency is supreme. There is no correcting mechanism by which to detect errors. (Augustine had a better sense of this than some contemporary theorists because he recognized that one can never know when true justice is present.) It also does little to argue that Hiltler did not really believe these things. The evidence is that he did. To imply otherwise is to underestimate the seriousness of the threat he posed and the sense of conviction he imparted to followers. And in any event one *could* believe equally vile things and convince himself that equally severe measures were justified for the survival of the state or of a particular people. If claims of supreme emergency, or appeals to military necessity, are to have even a prima facie warrant to being moral, they must be available equally to all to use.

Do Walzer and O'Brien differ sufficiently on these issues to warrant saying that their analyses represent different approaches to the morality of war? I suggest they do not. Their accounts will likely justify precisely the same sorts of acts and in the same sorts of circumstances, with only the rationales differing in certain points of detail.

Walzer contends that in supreme emergencies one may override the rights of innocent persons. And O'Brien says repeatedly that violations of the principles of proportionality and discrimination by the allies during World War II and by the United States in Korea and Vietnam did not prevent those wars from being just.[41] The violations were *wrong*; unlike Walzer, he is unequivocal about this. It is just that they were offset by the overwhelmingly just causes for which the United States was fighting. But to say that a war can be just *overall* despite violations of *jus in bello* criteria differs little from saying that a war can be just even though supreme emergencies justify violating these criteria. It is just that in the one case the rights of the innocent are violated, in the others they are "overridden." The overwhelmingly just cause and the supreme emergency become practically equivalent. Both Walzer and O'Brien think war may be a justifiable response to aggression, and both think that response may necessitate violating the moral constraints upon the conduct of war (with O'Brien holding further that such a war may be just even if such violations occur but are not necessitated). That is, both believe that there may be conflicts between *jus ad bellum*

[41] See his *The Conduct of a Just and Limited War*, chaps. 4 and 5.

173

and *jus in bello* and that when they occur *jus ad bellum* may override *jus in bello*.

If now we return to the second of the objections considered at the outset of this chapter, concerning the relevance of the just war approach to the nuclear age, we may observe that for all of this O'Brien may nonetheless be correct in saying in response to that objection that a limited use of nuclear weapons would not necessarily escalate into an all-out war. No one can know for certain. If *that* is what is meant by saying that the just war theory is relevant to the nuclear age, the point can be granted and the second objection considered met.

But there is another reply to the objection that is more telling. It is that even if O'Brien and others should be wrong about the possibility of keeping a limited nuclear war limited, all that would follow is that by just war criteria themselves an all-out war would be unjust. The fact that a certain type of war turns out to be unjust does not show that the just war theory is inapplicable to it; it shows only that it yields a certain outcome when applied to that type of war.[42] So if the question is whether the nuclear age has rendered the just war theory obsolete in the sense of showing that its criteria are no longer appropriate for the assessment of war, the answer is that it has not. Whether some, or all, or no nuclear wars turn out to be just by just war criteria is immaterial. That those assessments can be made shows the relevance of the theory to nuclear war in the sense its advocates intend.

The preceding discussion suggests a third and more serious objection to the just war doctrine. We have seen that there are serious problems in reconciling the claims of *jus ad bellum* with those of *jus in bello* with regard to whether a just cause sometimes warrants, or at least excuses, violations of moral constraints in the conduct of war. A more fundamental question is whether even a war that is just according to both *jus ad bellum* and *jus in bello* criteria will still unavoidably involve the violation of moral constraints; whether, that is, there is something in the very nature of war that renders it wrong and that is not dealt with directly by the just war theory. The just war theory says that if certain conditions are met, it is permissible to go to war; and it says further that if certain other conditions are met, one's manner of conducting the war is moral. What it does not do is to ask whether there are things that one unavoidably does even when *all* of these conditions are met

---

[42] This point is well made by Phillips in *War and Justice*, p. xi.

which cannot be justified morally. If there are, then the just war theory is defective in a far more serious way than suggested by either of the first two objections.

I believe that there are, and that is what I shall argue in the next chapter. But the issue is complex and requires an examination of the relationship between *jus ad bellum* and *jus in bello*.

VIII

A war, once again, is justified if it is characterized by *jus ad bellum*: if, that is, the conditions constituting justice in the resort to war are met. These include but are not limited to a just cause. Traditionally, as we have seen, one had to have legitimate authority and a right intention as well, with various other requirements often added, such as that the war be a last resort, have a likelihood of success, that the use of force be restrained, and that there be proportionality in the resultant good and evil.

A justified war, however, is not necessarily a just war. To be fully just a war must be characterized by both *jus ad bellum* and *jus in bello*. A war obviously cannot be just if one is unjustified in entering upon it in the first place, but neither can it be just, however just the cause and right the intention, if it utilizes indefensible means.[43] Even those like Walzer who think that normally indefensible means may sometimes be used affirm this. Though the earliest just war theorists gave insufficient attention to this issue, there must be rules or principles governing the conduct of war as well as governing the decision to enter into it.

Notice that I am concerned here with what is morally justified in the conduct of war, not with what is legally justified. There exist certain rules, known as the laws of war, generally accepted as governing the conduct of warfare on all sides. These, as we have seen, are part of international law. Individual soldiers, whether fighting for a just cause or not, are not considered accountable for their participation in a war so long as they observe these rules. This, however, is not my concern at the moment. My concern is with what is morally justified in warfare, whether or not it coincides with what is legally permissible. The laws of war, as Grotius recognized,[44] might as a matter of fact allow many things that in the last analysis cannot be justified morally.

---

[43] On the issue of the relationship between *jus ad bellum* and *jus in bello*, see Melzer, *Concepts of Just War*, esp. chap. 2.

[44] *De Jure Belli ac Pacis Libri Tres*, bk. 3, chap. 10.

In the eighteenth century William Paley proposed a principle to govern the conduct of war in his *Principles of Moral and Political Philosophy*, writing that "if the cause and end of war be justifiable; all the means that appear necessary to the end, are justifiable also."[45] Súarez before him had written even more simply that "if the end is permissible, the necessary means to that end are also permissible."[46] Except that they are intended to apply only to just wars, and that Súarez expressly added a prohibition against the killing of innocents, these formulations resemble the principle of military necessity. If one is justified in going to war, they say, he is justified in doing whatever is necessary to win. Moderation in the prosecution of a just war, in the sense of refraining from doing what is necessary to achieve your objectives, would be no less an absurdity on this reasoning than Clausewitz thought it to be in the prosecution of any war.

Let us call the principle that one may do whatever is necessary to prosecute a just war a principle of just necessity. Though only occasionally expressly formulated, it probably has many adherents. One often hears that it is wrong to send men to fight and be killed unless you are willing to fight to win. If one adds to this the qualification that it applies only to justified wars, as often seems the intent, one has just necessity.

According to this view, then, whatever justifies resorting to war in the first place justifies the means necessary to winning it (or achieving one's objectives, if they fall short of victory). There are no independent moral constraints upon the conduct of war. This represents what may be called an internalist view of the relationship between *jus ad bellum* and *jus in bello*, in the sense that the standards for judging *jus in bello* are already, as it were, contained in the standards for judging *jus ad bellum*.

Distinguished from this, however, is an externalist view, which holds that there are independent standards for judging *jus in bello*—independent, that is, of *jus ad bellum*. Whatever the justice

---

[45] *The Principles of Moral and Political Philosophy* (London: J. Faulder, 1814), 2: 425.

[46] *Selections from Three Works of Francisco Súarez*, specifically *On the Three Theological Virtues: On Charity* (disputation 13: On War, sec. 7, p. 840), in *The Classics of International Law*, ed. James Brown Scott (Oxford: Clarendon Press, 1944). See also Hugo Grotius, *De Jure Belli ac Pacis Libri Tres*, p. 599. In a more recent approximation, Robert W. Tucker says that "the ethics of war may justify the use of almost any weapons and the employment of any methods which realize the ends or purposes of the just war" (*The Just War: A Study in Contemporary American Doctrine*, p. 75). Walzer considers much this same principle in responding to possible criticisms of his own view of combat equality (see *Just and Unjust Wars*, p. 230).

of one's resort to war, there are in this view limits to what one may do in conducting it. The most prominent of these concerns the treatment of innocent persons, with writers like Ramsey, Phillips, and Anscombe maintaining that there is an absolute prohibition againist the intentional killing of such persons.[47]

The issue between internalism and externalism in the theory of *jus in bello* is important because whatever undesirable consequences follow from the principle of military necessity also follow from the principle of just necessity in a justified war. Any action that one principle legitimizes the other will also.

It is easily imaginable that the only way to win an otherwise just war (assuming there may be such) would be to demoralize the civilian population by terror bombing. This, indeed, was much the rationale for the saturation bombing of German cities during World War II, except there the bombing was probably thought necessary only to hasten victory, not to achieve it. But if World War II was a just war on the side of the allies, and if such bombing *had been* necessary to win, just necessity no less than military necessity or supreme emergency would have dictated it. If, moreover, Elihu Root was correct that adherence to military necessity would spell the end of international law, then one should expect the same to be true of adherence to just necessity; or at least that it would have a strong tendency to that end (unlike military necessity it will be implementable only by the side acting justly, and hence its bad effects may reasonably be thought to be less than in the case of military necessity). Circumstances can bring military necessity into conflict with international law. These may have nothing to do with the justice of the war and can arise as easily in a just war (meaning for the side that is warring justly) as in an unjust one.

To justify the pursuit of victory in war requires showing that the necessary means to that end are justified. The permissibility of going to war provides no assurance they will be. One may not even know fully what those means are until the war has progressed, perhaps nearly to its conclusion. Yet, according to the usual thinking in just war theory, one may know in advance of going to war whether or not he is justified in so doing. If that is true, then the standards for *jus ad bellum* cannot by themselves, determine the standards for *jus in bello*.

This means that the internalist position, and with it the principle

---

[47] See Anscombe, "War and Murder," in Wasserstrom ed., *War and Morality*, pp. 42-53; Phillips, *War and Justice*, chap. 2; and Ramsey, *The Just War*, especially chap. 7.

of just necessity, must be rejected. It is not the end that justifies the means but the means (among other things) that justify the end.[48]

This has even more far-reaching implications. Both the internalist and the externalist assume that war may be just; they differ only over the criteria for *jus in bello*. But if the impermissibility of the means necessary to win a war means that one may not justly pursue victory in that war, then the impermissibility of the acts necessary to the very *waging* of war mean that one may not justly wage war, whatever one's objectives. Waging war requires justifying the means of so doing as much as winning a war requires justifying the means to that end.[49]

To justify going to war, then, that is, to establish *jus ad bellum* in the first place, requires showing that what one would be doing by waging it is justified. If a war is justified, then the necessary means to waging it will indeed *be* justified—but not because they are legitimated by the justice of the war assessed independently of those means. They will be justified because to be justified in going to war requires establishing antecedently that those means are permissible. Again, it is not the end that justifies the means but the permissibility of the means (including the killing and destroy-

[48] One is justified in performing an act only if he is justified both in employing the means necessary to its performance and in performing any subsidiary acts constitutive of it. I cannot be justified in watering my garden unless I am justified in attaching the hose and turning on the water; or in mowing my lawn unless I am justified in cutting the grass. The justification of the act is not one thing and the justification of the means another. What one justifies in the first place *are* those means; to justifiy the act *is* to justify the means (and/or the constitutive acts). This is the truth in the saying that the end does not justify the means.

Some, of course, would argue that if the end is justified, then so must be the means. And this is true, if properly understood. But it does not follow from it that the end justifies the means. For there is an asymmetry here. One must justify the necessary means before one can justify pursuing the end, whereas the reverse is not the case. I do not need to justify watering my garden before I justify hooking up the hose and turning on the water; I may do these things as a means to a different end, such as washing the car. If the end is justified, the means will in fact *be* justified. But that is because one must justify them in the course of justifying the end, not because the justification of the end in isolation somehow justifies them.

[49] I am, for the sake of simplicity, speaking here as though what one must do in order to wage war constitutes the means to waging war. In actuality, those acts are constitutive of waging war. There are two related but distinguishable relationships here. One is that of means to end. It figures in the argument to show that the internalist position is incorrect. It involves showing that the means to victory in war must be justified in their own right; their permissibility does not follow automatically from the fact that the resort to war may be justified. The other is that of constituent to whole; it is central to the present argument regarding the justification of the resort to war, which involves pointing out that to be justified in resorting to war one must be justified in doing all those things that make up the waging of war.

ing that are part of the nature of warfare) that, along with satisfaction of the other requirements of *jus ad bellum*, justifies the end.

The point is that killing and destruction are inherent in warfare, and unless they can be justified, war cannot be justified. It will by its very nature be wrong.

Two conclusions follow from this. First, the issue of a possible conflict between *just ad bellum* and *jus in bello* is more complicated than it first appears. There cannot be a conflict between the two on the internalist view because the standards for the former constitute the standards for the latter. Satisfaction of the conditions of *jus ad bellum* (just cause, right intention, and the like) in the light of the principle of just necessity entails satisfaction of the conditions of *jus in bello* as well—at least so long as one does only what is necessary to achieving one's objectives and does not engage in gratuitous violence. But there can be a conflict on the externalist view if one assumes, as much of the just war tradition does, that it is possible to justify the resort to war independently of consideration of the constraints upon its conduct. For then one might adopt unjustifiable means to the attainment of otherwise justifiable ends. But there are compelling reasons for dropping this latter assumption. One does not just go to war. One goes to war for certain reasons, to achieve certain ends or objectives. The very act of embarking upon war presupposes them, as does the selection of certain means by which to try to achieve them. This means that to justify going to war requires justifying the selection of means from the outset. There are not two separate acts here, the embarking upon war and the implementing of chosen means. To embark upon war *is* to implement chosen means. What one justifies doing, in applying the standards of *jus ad bellum*, is inseparable from the conduct of war. Not that there cannot still be a conflict between *jus ad bellum* and *jus in bello*; as I have said, one may not always know in advance precisely what means the successful prosecution of a war will require. As events unfold, to prevail in a war may require the resort to morally impermissible tactics that could not have been foreseen at its outset. This notwithstanding, one can never justify the resort to war without justifying the means by which one proposes to fight the war.

On the other hand, there is no presumption at all that a war that meets the conditions of *jus in bello*, as these are usually conceived, will meet those of *jus ad bellum*. I am speaking here of the usual conditions that comprise the rules of war (regarding noncombatant immunity, treatment of prisoners, and the like). War is not a game. Following the rules is not exculpatory if you should not be involved in the enterprise in the first place. Even when the conditions are intended to be moral, like those of proportionality and discrimination, they do not ensure the justifiability of resorting to war. It would be different if they included *all* of the morally relevant considerations pertaining to the treatment of persons. For then, if those conditions were met, a war could hardly fail to be just, since everything one did in the course of fighting it would be permissible. To say one might still be acting wrongly by fighting it would then be vacuous. So, if *jus in bello* were understood in this way (which it is not by just war theorists), the satisfaction of its standards would virtually guarantee the satisfaction of those of *jus ad bellum* as well.

The relevant question, then, is whether all of what one does in the course of fighting a war can be morally justified (by which I mean, all of what one does that is associated with the nature of war; obviously one can do many gratuitously barbarous things that are unessential to the aims of war and that are morally prohibited). This is why I say that in addition to justifying the *means* of conducting war as part of justifying the resort to war, one must also justify those acts which are *constitutive* of the waging of war by whatever means. War by its nature is organized violence, the deliberate, systematic causing of death and destruction. This is true whether the means employed are nuclear bombs or bows and arrows. Often it is the doing of psychological violence as well. And, as we saw in Chapter One, it is presumptively wrong to do violence to persons in these ways. So given that one can know to a virtual certainty that he commits himself to doing these things in going to war, fully to justify going to war requires justifying these acts as well. A necessary condition of the justifiable pursuit of *any* objectives in war, by *any means* whatever (hence a necessary condition of the satisfaction of the criteria of both *jus ad bellum* and *jus in bello*), is that one be justified in engaging in such killing and violence in the first place.

Second, and relatedly, this means that most attempts to justify war from the early just war theorists to the present day are inadequate. For they do not meet this necessary condition.

Discussions of *jus in bello*, if they deal with the conduct of war in moral rather than just legal terms at all, talk mainly about whom one may kill and in what proportions one may cause destruction, not about whether that which they seek to regulate should be taking place at all. That is supposedly the province of *jus ad bellum*.

But discussions of *jus ad bellum* mainly require both certification that an appropriate wrong has been committed, that is, that one has a just cause, and satisfaction of other conditions (like legitimate authority, right intention, probability of success, etc.) which are appropriate if one assumes *in advance* that killing and violence are justifiable responses to wrongdoing but which do not establish that. It is as though the only question were what violence is acceptable and the only issue were to specify when it is acceptable—with little recognition of the fact that, as we saw in Chapter One, to establish that wrongdoing has occurred does not suffice to establish what one's response to it should be, that the response is a separate act and needs justifying in its own right. Most just war theorists proceed, in short, as though they assume that one can justify the resort to war independently of, and antecedently to, justifying both the necessary means to conducting it and the acts constitutive of waging it.[50]

If this is correct, it means that attention in *jus ad bellum* must be shifted away from the almost exclusive concern with the offenses and ancillary conditions commonly thought to justify war to a consideration of the precise nature of what one is doing in the waging of it; not, as in traditional accounts of *jus in bello*, starting from the assumption that war is justified and needs only to be waged humanely, but rather starting with an open mind about whether it is ever justified in the first place. *Unless one can justify the actions necessary to waging war, he cannot justify the conduct of war and the pursuit of its objectives; and if he cannot do this, he cannot justify going to war.*

So what we might call justice in the waging of war (by which I mean the justifiability of the violence and killing and destruction that are part of the nature of warfare) is a necessary condition of both justice in the conduct of war (*jus in bello*) and justice in the resort to war (*jus ad bellum*).[51] This means further that as interesting and important as many of the historical and contemporary issues are in the just war tradition—issues concerning what consti-

[50] This is not, I should say, true of all just war theorists. Among classical theorists, Grotius is notable for trying to specify with some precision the conditions under which an individual person's life may be taken. See *De Jure Belli ac Pacis Libri Tres*, bk. 3, chap. 11. And both he and Augustine, as well as others, deem it important to try to rebut interpretations of the New Testament that would seem to block the way to justifying the violence of war.

[51] The American Catholic bishops show an awareness of this when they acknowledge the presumption against war and ask: ["D]o the rights and values involved justify killing? For whatever the means used, war, by definition, involves violence, destruction, suffering, and death" (*The Challenge of Peace: God's Promise and Our Response*, p. 29).

tutes a just cause, what constitutes aggression, whether nuclear war can ever be justified, and so forth—their satisfactory resolution can never by itself justify the resort to war. In short, the just war theory in its historical and contemporary forms fails to do justice to the central moral problems in war's justification.

S I X

THE KILLING OF INNOCENT PERSONS
IN WARTIME

> But of course one can't just say to a million mothers: "I want your sons," and then six months later: "Sorry, they're all dead." If war is to be made tolerable, the romantic tradition must be handed on. "Madam, I took away your son, but I give you back the memory of a hero. Each year we will celebrate together his immortal passing."
> —A. A. Milne

If the means necessary to waging war cannot be justified, then war cannot be justified and no war can be just. Not only must there be moral constraints upon the *conduct* of war even if the war is in all other particulars justified; the possibility must be recognized that there are moral constraints upon the treatment of persons that prohibit the *waging* of war in the first place, that is, even engaging in the limited killing and destruction that otherwise just wars entail.

Although Augustine gave this little attention, most just war theorists impose limitations upon the conduct of war. As we have seen, some recent theorists deal almost exclusively with the conduct of war in their preoccupation with *jus in bello*. The limitations deal with such things as the treatment of prisoners and with the use of certain kinds of weapons, whose violation constitute war crimes in international law; but the most prominent of the concerns is with the killing of noncombatants and innocent persons. My concern shall be with the killing of innocent persons. Nothing is more central to the moral assessment of war, and this issue is at the heart of the question whether the waging of war can be justified, whatever other limitations are imposed upon its conduct. As we saw in Chapter One, there is no stronger moral presumption than that against the doing of violence to innocent persons. And knowingly killing them against their will is to do violence to them.

183

This does not, as I have said, of itself mean that such killing is never justified; whether that is so is beyond my present concerns. But it does mean that the burden is upon those who would kill innocent persons to justify so doing, not upon those who believe it wrong to show that it is wrong.

Virtually everyone agrees that innocent persons are killed non-consensually in wartime, though they do not all agree that war necessarily kills such people or that it kills them in substantial numbers. But if it is presumptively wrong to kill innocent persons, and if, as I shall maintain, war should *inevitably* involve such killing, then war itself is presumptively wrong. This also does not mean that war may not yet be justified. But it does mean that the presumption in question must be defeated and war's justification demonstrated if one proposes to engage in it.

I

Whether war, or at least modern war, which shall be our concern henceforth, inevitably entails the killing of innocent persons cannot be answered independently of a consideration of what constitutes innocence. Here one encounters disagreement. Some argue that virtually everyone in wars between states is noninnocent, others that nearly everyone in such wars is innocent. The most common strategy is to substitute the categories of noncombatancy and combatancy for innocence and noninnocence and to ignore the problems associated with the killing of innocents.[1] But I shall maintain that this will not do.

[1] Robert L. Phillips argues in his discussion of the just war that "I have refrained from making any reference to 'the innocent,' despite the fact that most of the current debate on the morality of war has been about treatment of innocent parties. This seems to me to represent a major confusion which has quite unnecessarily complicated the issue." See *War and Justice* (Norman: University of Oklahoma Press, 1984), p. 56. His reasons consist principally of the claim that "[it] is *combatants* who are the objects of attack in war, and, therefore, moral distinctions will center upon that notion rather than innocence. This is necessarily the case, since war is a contest of strength, an arbitrament of arms carried out under the direction of moral and political aims" (p. 58). It is unclear, however, why this particular characterization of war, even if it should be accepted as something approximating a definition, entails or even implies that noncombatancy is of sole moral importance. In wartime, innocent people are knowingly and often deliberately killed. That fact establishes the relevance of innocence to the assessment of war. If, further, as I have argued in Chapter One, to kill innocent persons is to do violence to them, and to do violence is presumptively wrong, then that suffices to establish that killing innocent persons in wartime is presumptively wrong. And as it is with what is right and wrong in war that morality is concerned, such killing cannot fail to be of the first importance. Phillips contends that to focus upon innocence is to fail to

If one is pronounced guilty by a duly established court in accordance with the laws of the land, he is legally guilty. But moral guilt may not coincide with legal guilt. To be morally guilty is to have engaged in moral wrongdoing. One may fit either of these descriptions whether or not he is legally guilty. With regard to war, moral wrongdoing is relative either to the initiation of war or to the conduct of war, or both. The relevant concern is not with *personal* guilt or innocence in the general conduct of one's life. A person may lie, cheat, steal, and otherwise violate all standards of moral decency and yet be completely innocent of any wrongdoing so far as war is concerned. Another may be upright in his personal conduct but guilty of grievious wrongdoing in the initiation or conduct of war, say, in his capacity as a political leader or military commander. Regarding the killing of innocents in wartime the relevant concern is with innocence pertaining to the particular war in question.

I have spoken of innocence and guilt, but it is useful to take the more basic distinction to be between innocence and noninnocence, since there are some relations of conduct to wrongdoing that, though they do not render one guilty in any strict sense, nonetheless do not leave one altogether innocent either. If one person robs a bank, another keeps the car running, a third provides the gun, and a fourth knows of the robbery but does nothing to stop it, the first is clearly guilty, the others culpable in varying degrees. The second and third are closer, as it were, to the wrongdoing of the principal agent and accordingly share greater responsibility for it; the fourth is farthest removed and bears least responsibility. All of them, however, are noninnocent and are to be distinguished from other persons who have no knowledge of, or involvement with, the intended crime and its perpetrators. Guilt is a strong notion, and we usually reserve it for the actual performance of serious acts of wrongdoing. Responsibility or culpability we reserve for those whose conduct is farther removed from wrongdoing but not so far removed as to render them innocent. Noninnocence encompasses both guilt and responsibility.

Matters are complicated in the case of war, however, because those *most* responsible for wars are usually least involved in the actual killing. Nearly all of the consequences of the actions of state

distinguish between the whole person, to whom the notions of guilt and innocence are appropriate (p. 61), and the *role or function* of the person as combatant, to which they are not. But I hope to show that we can both recognize that distinction and see that the notion of innocence applies in each case.

leaders who order armies into combat are mediated by the responses of those who carry out the orders. Those who do the actual killing have little say in the overall enterprise in which they are engaged; they are usually young conscripts who have no part in decision making and little grasp of the issues over which they are asked to fight. Frequently they are lied to by their governments. Although they nonetheless bear ultimate responsibility for what they do, circumstances often attenuate that responsibility, to the point where in international law ordinary soldiers are not held legally responsible so long as the killing they do conforms to the accepted rules of war.

Assume for the moment that some wars are justified. In any such war, one side will be acting justly. However much both sides may *think* they are in the right, as both sides do in most wars, it cannot be the case that both sides *are* in the right. (If one side acts justly, it can only be because the other side acts unjustly, and vice versa, so to say that both sides are acting justly would be to say that both are acting rightly *and* wrongly, which is incomprehensible.) This is hardly controversial, and most just war theorists would agree. Now if at least one side acts unjustly (it may easily be the case that both sides act unjustly, of course), then *all* of the killing done by that side, whether of soldiers or civilians, will be wrongful. This point was made as far back as Grotius and reaffirmed at Nuremberg. And if the other side acts justly, then in addition to being wrongful, the killing done by the unjust side will be the wrongful killing of innocent people. The killing of *anyone* who has done no wrong relative to the war in question is, in the relevant sense, the killing of an innocent person. This suffices to show that the distinction between combatants and noncombatants, however deeply enshrined it is in various codes of war, and however common it is in discussions of more recent just war theorists, is neither equivalent to the distinction between innocents and noninnocents nor adequate for framing the central moral issue in the assessment of war. If a war is just, the soldier who fights on that side is as innocent as the civilian who stays behind. And so are government leaders, even though it is they who send armies into combat.[2]

[2] The exception to this would be the case, unlikely in practice but imaginable in theory, in which both sides act unjustly and only those responsible for the war participate in it, perhaps removing themselves to some remote corner of the earth to do battle. What they do in that case might be imprudent or irrational or even immoral if they neglect obligations to others who depend upon them for support

Members of a nation that is justly warred against will fall roughly into one or more of six categories: (a) initiators of wrongdoing (government leaders); (b) agents of wrongdoing (military commanders and combat soldiers); (c) contributors to the war effort (munitions workers, military researchers, taxpayers, etc.); (d) those who approve of the war without contributing in any significant way; and (e) noncontributors and nonsupporters (e.g., young children, some active opponents of the war who refuse to pay taxes, the insane, etc.). Those in the first category, and perhaps some of those in the second as well, will properly be said to be guilty in the relevant sense; those in categories (b) through (d) will be involved in a wrongful activity in increasingly attentuated ways, and those in (e) will be uninvolved, though some of them— children, for example—may be potential contributors, agents, supporters, and so on, if the war should continue until they mature. Even in a view that regards responsibility for national policy as diffused throughout society (and even if we assume the aggressor nation is a democracy so that much of the adult population can be presumed to have had a say in the choice of leadership) it seems clear that those in category (e) are innocent. It also seems clear that many of those in the other categories at most share limited responsibility for the war, so limited in some cases as to be negligible. Someone whose livelihood involves work that in some way contributes to the war effort will fall into category (c). But such a person might in fact oppose the war. He might contribute to dissenting groups and even participate in antiwar activities. Though he undeniably contributes to the war effort, if only as a taxpayer, he is surely innocent of the wrongdoing represented by the war and arguably should not be held responsible for it. The same may be true even with regard to soldiers. When the penalty for refusing to serve may be imprisonment or even death, responsibility for service, particularly if one opposes the war and makes known that opposition, may be sufficiently mitigated that we should call such a person innocent, or at least not guilty. Even in category (a) this may be true. If the government as a whole is responsible for initiating the wrongdoing, there may nonetheless be persons in government who oppose the war but who stay on in the conviction that they may be able to influence policy for the better. Such per-

---

or love. But they would not be killing innocent persons. This is the one type of case in which the question of innocence is irrelevant to judging the justness of war, since, by hypothesis, all parties are noninnocent.

sons may have had no more say in the initiation of the war than the ordinary citizen.

Modern warfare, therefore, will inevitably kill innocent persons, most likely even on the side that acts unjustly in the initiation of the war. Not only the character of modern weaponry but also the principles on which most nations conduct war make this clear. Military necessity, just necessity, and the quantitative principle, discussed in Chapter Three, if not constrained by an express prohibition against the killing of innocents, legitimize such killing in circumstances in which the aims of war, or of limiting casualties to one's own side, dictate it. Indeed, governmental and military leaders have often judged that killing innocents is better than abiding by such a prohibition. We see this readily when it is put as starkly as by the Kaiser during World War I:

> My soul is torn, but everything must be put to fire and sword; men, women, and children and old men must be slaughtered and not a tree or house be left standing. With these methods of terrorism, which are alone capable of affecting a people as degenerate as the French, the war will be over in two months, whereas if I admit considerations of humanity it will be prolonged for years. In spite of my repugnance I have therefore been obliged to choose the former system.[3]

We do not see it so readily in the terror bombing of German cities during World War II that was expressly calculated to break the will of the German people. Nor do we see it in the following revelation of the early adoption of what is in effect the quantitative principle by the United States in the Pacific War during World War II:

> America answered Japan's attack on Pearl Harbor by an order for total and unrestricted submarine warfare against the enemy, and as a result shortened the war and saved thousands of lives, the Navy Department revealed last night. . . . Pointing out that it "took moral courage of the highest order to release the dispatch 'execute unrestricted air and submarine warfare against Japan' " the Navy said that "the conditions under which Japan employed her so-called merchant shipping

---

[3] Quoted from the dissenting opinion of Judge Pal of India in the Judgment of the Tokyo War Crimes Trial, 1948, in *Crimes of War*, ed. R. Falk, G. Kolko, and R. Lifton (New York: Vintage Books, 1971), p. 135.

were such that it would be impossible to distinguish between 'merchant ships' and Japanese Army and Navy auxiliaries.''

Turning what by international law was a war crime into a virtue, the report continues: "The Navy added that it would have been the easy course to have insisted on submarine warfare in accordance with international treaties, shifting to other shoulders the responsibility for the inevitable increase in the length of the war and for the longer casualty lists that would have resulted.' ''[4] Here we see the effects of implementing principles of the sort we have discussed in Chapter Three. And here we see the force of the warning by Elihu Root of the danger to international law from military necessity.

Given the presumption that killing innocent persons is wrong, the fact that war inevitably kills such persons means, in light of our argument that war can be neither just nor justified if the means necessary to waging it are not justified, that modern war is presumptively wrong.

II

We have examined attempts to show that morality does not apply to war (hence that war cannot be adjudged morally wrong) and to show that *jus ad bellum* can be established independently of the conditions for *jus in bello*, and more specifically independently of a justification of the acts entailed by the very waging of war.

Can the presumption of the wrongness of war be undercut by defeating the presumption that killing innocent persons in wartime is wrong? Most attempts to justify such killing maintain either that there are clear cases in which it is permissible or that there are circumstances, however ambiguous, in which overriding considerations allow it. We shall consider shortly two of the strongest arguments, one in Section III, the other in sections IV through VIII.

But first let us look at a unique argument, which concedes that killing innocents is wrong but denies that that fact renders war wrong even if war inevitably involves killing innocents. Though the argument is not offered by Walzer, it would, if sound, make sense of his view that although killing innocent persons is wrong,

[4] *Washington Sunday Star*, Feb. 3, 1946, p. A7. Quoted in William W. Bishop, Jr., *International Law: Cases and Materials*, 3d ed. (Boston: Little, Brown and Company, 1971), p. 975.

sometimes wars in which one has to do that are justified; and it would call into question the position for which I have argued, that *jus ad bellum* and *jus in bello* cannot be separated. The argument claims that although war may inevitably involve killing innocent persons, so long as it does not do so on a large scale that fact does not necessarily render the entire war wrong. Richard Wasserstrom poses this question when he speculates whether "the occurrence of even a single instance of immorality [e.g., the killing of innocents] makes the entire act of fighting the war unjustifiable." Though he thinks that wars in fact do not kill just an occasional innocent person, he nonetheless believes that at least theoretically the argument is sound. "Given," he says, "the number of criteria that are relevant to the moral assessment of any war and given the great number of persons involved in and the extended duration of most wars, it would be false to the complexity of the issues to suppose that so immediately simple a solution [as concluding that war is wrong] were possible."[5]

The issue is not whether the accidental killing of innocents in wartime renders war wrong. That would no more show that war is immoral than accidental auto deaths would show that highway construction is immoral. It is whether knowingly killing innocents renders war wrong, where by this I mean killing them intentionally or foreseeably, and where we are assuming, as the objection presupposes, that such killing is itself wrong. What grounds might there be for denying that it does?

Two stand out. One turns upon some points of logic, the other reintroduces a general position discussed in Chapter Three in connection with political realism.

The first alleges that it is fallacious to argue that war is immoral simply because some acts which inevitably occur in war are immoral. It represents what has traditionally been called a fallacy of composition, that of supposing that because a certain characteristic can properly be assigned to a part of a thing it can also be assigned to the whole. If, for example, my car's brakes are new, it would be fallacious to infer that my car is new; and if the second hand on my watch works, it would be fallacious to conclude that my watch works. My car *might* be new and my watch *might* work, but I would not be entitled to infer either of these on the strength of the indicated fact alone. So, it might be argued, to say that certain acts

[5] "On the Morality of War: A Preliminary Inquiry," in *War and Morality*, ed. Richard Wasserstrom (Belmont, Calif.: Wadsworth Publishing Company, 1970), p. 100.

of war (the killing of innocents) are immoral does not mean that the whole activity of which they are a part (the war itself) is immoral. War might inevitably kill innocent persons but nonetheless itself be permissible.

If successful, this argument would undermine my earlier analysis of the relationship between *jus ad bellum* and *jus in bello*. It would challenge my contention that an action or an activity can be justified only if the necessary means or constitutive acts associated with it are justified. For one could then have moral acts that entailed either as means or as constituent parts other acts that are immoral. This would be a stronger position even than that which claims that the end justifies the means, because in this case it is conceded that the means (or constituent parts) are unjustified. They are acknowledged to be immoral.

But notice that it is not always a mistake to ascribe to a whole a property of a part. If a car's brakes are untrustworthy then the car is untrustworthy; and if the gin is poisoned then the martini is poisoned. These are perfectly good inferences in the appropriate contexts. In other cases the inference is problematic (for example, if someone's brain is dead it may be an open question whether the person is dead). The inference from the presumptive wrongness of certain acts of war to the presumptive wrongness of war itself cannot, therefore, simply be dismissed because of the character of the inference. Though such inferences are not formally valid, they are sometimes perfectly proper in the broader context of assumptions in which they take place.

The second ground for denying that the wrongful killing of innocents makes war wrong consists of the claim that notions like "is immoral," "is right," "is wrong," and so on do not intelligibly apply to phenomena like war in the first place. This, we recall from Chapter Three, is the position of the positivistic realist. He might argue, in line with the above quotation from Wasserstrom, that war as a whole is simply a set of acts, or perhaps a unique, complex, and nonintentional phenomenon, and that moral concepts designed to apply to particular acts are inapplicable to it. It is not, he might say, that wars can be said to be moral, either, but rather that they are simply neither moral nor immoral. If this should be true, one could agree that war inevitably kills innocents and that killing innocents is wrong but consistently deny that war is wrong.

This is a forceful objection, and if one considers the *whole* of a modern war in all its complexity—the mobilization of whole societies and the millions of lives caught up in it—it presents itself as a vast and unique phenomenon far removed from the individual acts of persons for whose assessment our moral concepts are tailored; so much so as to make one wonder whether moral categories can indeed be extended to it. It was considerations like these that led Tolstoy to imply at the end of *War and Peace* that wars do not even have causes in any ordinary sense. Matters would be simpler if nations were persons, as Treitschke considered them to be, for then there would be no problem in regarding their doings as susceptible of moral assessment in a fairly straightforward way. But they are not. So that model will not do. There is no problem, as we have seen, with applying *evaluative* concepts like "good" and "bad" to war. Anyone who holds that war is justified can agree that wars are bad; most advocates of the just war theory would say that. Wars by their nature entail killing and destruction, and these are bad even if one thinks they are sometimes necessary. What Anatol Rapoport calls the cataclysmic philosophy of war lends itself particularly to this mode of analysis in that it conceptualizes wars as happenings not unlike natural disasters.[6] We apply evaluative concepts to natural phenomena, as when we speak of a good rainfall or a bad storm, but we do not speak of them as right or wrong. If war were like a natural catastrophe, that fact would indeed be good grounds for withholding moral assessment from it. The whole of the just war tradition would then be wrongheaded.

But as I have said, war consists at its core of acts of men. The prosecution at Nuremberg rebutted the claim of some of the defendants that theirs were acts of state rather than acts of men by pointing out that acts of state *are* acts of men. There is much more than we associate with war—pain and suffering, for example. But it is *actions* that are at the heart of it. To wage war is to *do* something. And acts that make up war are for the most part calculated and deliberate. The crucial ones among them, those whose success the others are designed to ensure, are acts of violence. And they inevitably involve killing innocent persons. That killing need not be intentional, though much of it no doubt is, but that it will occur is foreseeable. In virtually any modern war innocents will be killed. No accounts that give full weight to these facts can proscribe moral considerations from war's assessment.

The positivist may still insist that wars cannot be immoral, and

[6] "Introduction" to *Clausewitz on War*, ed. A. Rapoport (Baltimore: Penguin Books, 1968).

there would be little harm in granting this if everything that goes along with it were granted as well. For then the concession that wars are not wrong would provide no warrant for the waging of wars; indeed, its practical effect would be the same as to show that war is wrong. If, as the argument we are considering concedes, war inevitably involves killing innocents and killing innocents is wrong,[7] then whatever one's analysis of the nature of war and the applicability of moral concepts to it, the moral course dictated by the conjunction of these views would still require that men cease waging wars. In other words, if one respects the prohibition against killing innocent persons, he will not kill innocent persons; and if not killing innocents means not waging war, he will not wage war. It is immaterial whether one says in addition that wars are immoral; knowing that one cannot wage them without killing innocent persons is sufficient. So while this last consideration does not refute the positivistic view, it does deprive the militarist of any advantage from it.

III

Can one nonetheless avoid saying that war is presumptively wrong by showing that in wartime the presumption against killing innocents can be defeated?

The most notable attempt to show this is mounted by just war theorists by means of the principle of double effect. That principle enables them to regard the killing of innocents as wrong but at the same time as justified under certain conditions. Use of the principle is not restricted to Christian ethicists, but it derives from that tradition and is in keeping with the Christian moorings of the just war theory. Although we saw in Chapter Four that Augustine did not do so, Christianity is often understood to prohibit absolutely the shedding of innocent blood.

[7] Meaning here *actually* and not merely prima facie wrong. One might say that all things being equal—that is, prima facie—killing innocents is wrong, but that in some circumstances, such as those of warfare, or in very special cases of warfare, such as to save other innocents, killing innocents is permissible. In that case the conjunction of views in question would not necessarily dictate that people cease waging wars; it would require saying only that all things are not equal in the case of warfare. Here I intend the judgment that killing innocents is wrong to mean that it is *in fact* wrong in circumstances that include those of warfare. This does not require saying that killing innocents is absolutely wrong, a claim I reject in the next section, because one might consistently hold that it is in fact wrong to kill innocents even while conceding that there may be logically conceivable circumstances in which it is not wrong.

The "double effect" referred to is that we saw noted by Aquinas in the previous chapter. Acts may sometimes have both good effects and bad, and what is important from a moral standpoint is to intend only the good. This by itself is usually not thought sufficient to make an act right, and other conditions are commonly incorporated into the notion of double effect, such as that the act itself be good or at least indifferent, the bad effect not be a means to the production of the good, and the good of the good effect be proportionate to the bad, in the sense of being greater than it or at least not less. The principle expanded in this way constitutes virtually a moral theory unto itself, and our concern shall be only with the requirement that the intention be good, that is, be to promote the good rather than the bad.

Writing in this tradition, Elizabeth Anscombe brings out the importance of this distinction for Christian ethics:

> The distinction between the intended, and the merely foreseen, effects of a voluntary action is indeed absolutely essential to Christian ethics. For Christianity forbids a number of things as being bad in themselves. But if I am answerable for the foreseen consequences of an action or refusal, as much as for the action itself, then these prohibitions will break down. If someone innocent will die unless I do a wicked thing, then on this view I am his murderer in refusing: so all that is left to me is to weigh up evils. Here the theologian steps in with the principle of double effect and says: "No, you are no murderer, if the man's death was neither your aim nor your chosen means, and if you had to act in the way that led to it or else do something absolutely forbidden." Without understanding of this principle, anything can be—and is wont to be—justified, and the Christian teaching that in no circumstances may one commit murder, adultery, apostasy . . . goes by the board. These absolute prohibitions of Christianity by no means exhaust its ethic; . . . But the prohibitions are bedrock, and without them the Christian ethic goes to pieces. Hence the necessity of the notion of double effect.[8]

The point usually extracted from such reasoning, though Anscombe does not do so in this passage, is that one can prohibit the killing of innocent persons, even prohibit it *absolutely*, and yet proceed to kill such persons provided in so doing their deaths are

[8] "War and Murder," in Wasserstrom, ed., *War and Morality*, pp. 50-51.

merely foreseen and not intended. It is this application of the principle of double effect that we want to examine.

The claim that it is wrong to kill innocents conceals an ambiguity. To ask whether it is ever right to kill innocent persons in wartime might be to ask whether it is ever *in fact* right, given the world as it is or is ever likely to be. Or it might be to ask whether it is right *under any conceivable circumstances*, however absurd or contrived. One might answer these questions differently. One could believe it is never right to kill innocent persons in the world as we know it but concede that if the world were radically different that would change—if, for example, to kill innocent persons meant they would be reborn to a life of heavenly felicity whereas otherwise they would suffer an eternity of torment. Or one might ask whether it would ever be right to kill innocents under conditions that are likely to obtain in the future, or under conditions that could possibly obtain but are improbable, and so on. The point is that the prohibition against killing innocents (as, incidentally, with other moral prohibitions as well) can be understood in ways that yield a plurality of principles.

If one takes the prohibition to rule out the killing of innocents in all conceivable circumstances, it is an absolute prohibition and can consistently be held only if one is prepared to defend the most absurd of moral judgments in wildly hypothetical cases. Absolutism of that sort borders on fanaticism. Those who subscribe to it usually have in mind a different principle, one that absolutely prohibits only the *intentional* killing of innocent persons. This is sometimes misleadingly put as the "direct" killing of innocents. It is understood in this way that Anscombe regards the prohibition as central to Christian ethics, and it is the importance of the principle of double effect to this understanding that she sees as making it essential to that ethics.

One can adhere to this principle while at the same time supporting or even engaging in extensive killing of innocents. This comes out in a discussion by Paul Ramsey of Vietnam and the just war doctrine. "The objective of combat," he writes, "is the incapacitation of a combatant from doing what he is doing because he is this particular combatant in this particular war; it is not the killing of a man because he is this particular man. The latter and only the latter would be murder."[9] More particularly, the principle can

[9] *The Just War: Force and Political Responsibility* (New York: Charles Scribner's Sons, 1968), p. 502.

be used to justify the killing of noncombatants. "The deaths of noncombatants are to be only *indirectly done* and they should be *un*intended in the just conduct of war whose actions may and should be, and are intended to be, directed upon combatants and legitimate military objectives. This aiming of intention and of action is entirely compatible with *certain* knowledge that a great number of civilian lives will be unintendedly destroyed."[10] He argues that the only justified war is a limited war that recognizes noncombatant immunity in accordance with the principle of double effect. Although one may permissibly kill noncombatants, one may not direclty intend to kill them. If, therefore, the prohibition against killing innocents applies only to intentional killing, and one can knowingly kill innocents without intending to do so, the way is open to saying that it is absolutely wrong under all circumstances to kill innnocent persons and at the same time to supporting wars that kill them without limit. The sacred seat of virtue, Augustine said after all, is the heart, not one's bodily actions, and so long as one's motives and intentions are good, one's heart is pure.

Technically this is an externalist position. It does impose a restriction upon what one may do in the conduct of war. But in effect it is internalist, since it enables one to wage war in ways indistinguishable from those sanctioned by just necessity, which legitimizes all means necessary to the prosecution of a justified war; it is, as we saw in the preceding chapter, military necessity adapted to a justified war. And double effect legitimizes every action legitimized by just necessity, provided only that one not intend the harm that he does. In fact no action whatsoever is prohibited by the principle of double effect so long as one acts from a good intention (remembering that I am now speaking of the principle in its narrower form and not as expanded to include other conditions).

This approach violates a fundamental requirement of rationality, however, namely, that one be consistent. This requirement has received various formulations in ethics under the heading of a principle of universalizability. Consistency here requires that we judge similar cases similarly or, better, that we judge cases similarly unless there are relevant dissimilarities between them. One cannot

---

[10] "Tucker's *Bellum Contra Bellum Justum*," in *Just War and Vatican II: A Critique*, by Robert W. Tucker, with commentary by Paul Ramsey et al. (New York: The Council on Religion and International Affairs, 1966), p. 75. Reprinted in Ramsey, *The Just War*, pp. 391-424.

perform virtually identical acts and judge them differently unless they differ in morally relevant respects. Nor can one judge differently the actions of two or more persons unless one can point to morally relevant differences in their actions. If it is wrong for Jones to steal candy from a baby, it is wrong for Smith as well, unless there are relevant dissimilarities in their two cases.

But double effect allows virtually identical acts, either performed by different persons or by one person at different times, to be judged differently. Why? Because in the one case the act may be performed with a good intention, in the other with a bad. Thus if two soldiers fire upon the enemy, one with the intention of killing human beings qua human beings, the other with the intention of killing combatants qua combatants, as in the Ramsey example, the second killing will be justifiable, the first not (assuming that other conditions making for a just war and for the application of double effect are met). Or suppose two pilots fly over a military target surrounded by schools, hospitals, and recreation areas. Both have orders to destroy the military target. But one drops his bombs intending only to destroy the target even though he knows that in the process he will kill innocent persons, the other does so intending as well to kill those persons. They perform virtually identical acts. But the one act, according to double effect, is permissible, the other impermissible.

It might be objected that the intentions are a part of the acts themselves, and hence that in these cases the acts in fact differ. But this would fly in the face of much of our common-sense understanding of acts. We can often know and identify acts apart from their intentions; indeed, we often do not know what those intentions are. When we ask whether someone did something with such-and-such an intention, we know in advance *what* he did, which would be difficult to explain if intentions were a part, particularly an essential part, of acts. It is true that every act *has* an intention. Behavior that does not have an intention is not an act for purposes of moral assessment. And it is true that to understand conduct fully requires understanding intentions. Acts are the means by which we try to realize the purposes our intentions embody. But acts do not themselves include the intentions. Much of the discussion of double effect by its defenders reflects this, as when they speak of requiring that the evil intention be "withheld" from the act or "directed" or "aimed" in the appropriate way. The assumption is that the act can be performed either with or without that intention, or with or without its being aimed or directed in the manner indicated. And this makes sense only if one and the same act can be accompanied by different intentions.

In any event, whether or not they are understood to be part of the acts with which they are associated, intentions are of questionable relevance to the moral assessment of acts. They are relevant to the assessment of *persons*, but that requires a different sort of judgment. Conduct we judge to be right or wrong, obligatory or prohibited; persons we judge as good or bad, praiseworthy or blameworthy. Although we base judgments of persons partly upon their actions, we look mainly to their character for this purpose, specifically to their motives and intentions (as Augustine saw in his emphasis upon inner purity). It is this that makes the *person* deserving of praise or blame, commendation or condemnation. If someone averts the collision of two trains by switching one to a different track, and we learn that he was merely toying with the controls, or worse yet, intended to cause a collision but mistakenly threw the wrong switch, we give him no credit morally for what he did even though what he did was objectively right. Intentions and motives do not figure into our judgment of the rightness or wrongness of the act itself. If they did, we could not without circularity cite a person's actions as a basis for our judgment of the person. In judging the act we would already have judged the person.[11]

[11] This issue is actually more complicated than this. If one distinguishes consequentialist and deontological moral theories, it seems clear that according to consequentialist theories intentions are irrelevant to the assessment of acts, since they make no difference to consequences (other, of course, than insofar as they make a difference to which acts are performed). There is nothing in a deontological view, however, that prevents intentions from being considered a part of acts. But the fact that so doing would render circular the citing of a person's actions as a basis for a judgment of the person makes it implausible to do so. This is not to say that one *cannot* describe actions in such a way as to include reference to the intention. If asked what I am doing, I can reply "boiling water so as to make coffee." The point, rather, is that we need not so describe actions (and even when we do so describe them, nothing more follows than that actions have intentions, not that the intentions are part of the actions), and moral theory becomes less confusing if we do not.

Although it is difficult to be certain, Phillips seems to regard intentions as a part of their associated acts. Thus he says that "there are cases where two quite different actions are identical with respect to result, observable behavior, and foreknowledge of the result; and the *only* way to distinguish the two is by reference to intention." As an example he says that if we did not so regard intentions, we should, in the matter of suicide, be unable to distinguish between the death of an officer who shoots himself and that of another who fights a rear-guard action "in such a way that he knows he will not survive." This, he says, is absurd. It is indeed absurd, but the two cases do not represent otherwise identical actions. One's behavior in shooting himself is radically different from that of fighting in combat in which one

Thus we might judge the two *pilots* differently if we believe one acted with a good intention, the other with a bad. But the fact of their different intentions would not affect the moral assessment of *what* they did. People can with good intentions perform horrendous actions, just as they can with the worst of intentions do exactly the right thing. Thus including intentions in acts would show that double effect does not conflict with universalizability in the assessment of persons, but it would not show that it does not conflict with it in the judgment of acts. Even in the absence of a principle of universalizability and its possible conflict with double effect, double effect—even in this restrictive sense—fails to provide an adequate ground for judging acts.

These theoretical considerations notwithstanding, the principle of double effect suffers from a serious practical shortcoming, which is that it lends itself to the justification of virtually any action its user wants. On the assumption that we can "direct" or "aim" intentions as we please, any action whatever can be performed with a good intention or, at any rate, can be described as being performed with a good intention (whether any given individual, or people generally, can perform the action with that intention is an empirical and psychological matter that is not usually of primary concern to theoreticians justifying acts of war by the principle). This is as true of pillage, rape, and torture as of killing. One suspects that defenders of the principle find that it invariably justifies just those actions they are antecedently disposed to believe are right.

So, while theoretically the principle is intelligible (as a condition of the goodness or virtue of the agent, not of the rightness of actions), from a practical standpoint it is vacuous. The morally artful can turn it to whatever purpose they want. This means that when it is accompanied by other conditions (once again, such as that the act itself be good or at least indifferent, that the good produced outweigh the bad, and that the bad not be a means to the good) one's moral assessment might just as well be made by appeal to these conditions from the outset. The principle of double effect is otiose.

---

is shot by someone else. Suicide is causing one's death by one's own hand. He says further that "failure to take account of intention means that we are unable to make the difference between doing x in order that y shall result and doing x knowing that y will result" (*War and Justice*, p. 34). If by this he means that unless we think of an act's intention as *part* of the act we shall be unable to make this distinction, it is unclear why this should be so. One need only say that acts *have* intentions, and that in the one case that intention is that y shall result, and in the other it is not.

If this is correct, then the particular externalist position we have been examining fails. If one prohibits the killing of innocents, he cannot then invoke good intentions to justify proceeding to kill them.

IV

It is sometimes said that in some circumstances one has to kill persons, and the only question is whether to kill a larger or smaller number. If all of the persons happened to be innocent, this would be an instance of justifiably killing innocent persons, since the killing would be unavoidable.

As common as it is, this view is mistaken. One never *has* to kill anyone. One may sometimes have to kill someone or let others die. And sometimes letting people die is as bad morally as killing them (watching a child drown when with minimal effort one could save it would be a case in point). But one need never kill another person. Inaction is always an option, even if that should be to let someone die.

But there is another argument that merits consideration in this connection, which makes explicit use of this distinction between killing and letting die. Though it lends itself readily to a utilitarian justification, there is no single formulation of it, and any number of different rationales can underlie it. I will not attempt to detail all of them but will instead focus upon the one that seems to me strongest.

The reasoning goes like this: killing innocent persons in wartime is terrible and can be justified by one and only one consideration, and that is that sometimes it is the only way to prevent other innocent persons—perhaps in greater numbers—from being killed. Some aggressors will pursue their objectives at any cost. As terrible as the casualties to innocents were in World War II, if Germany had not been stopped, many times that number would have died at the hands of the Nazis. This is why the Nazi threat constituted a supreme emergency in the eyes of writers like Walzer. It is a false and self-righteous virtue that would persuade itself that killing innocents is worse than letting them die at the hands of others. Terrible times demand terrible remedies, and precisely because they are terrible they take courage to apply. Better to humble ourselves in the thought that we live in an imperfect world than to let conscience make cowards of us.

One can see possible permutations to this reasoning. One might concentrate solely upon the threatened loss of life to innocent persons in one's own country, if it is they who are threatened by an aggressor. The reasoning would then overlap with that which appeals to national self-defense, which is itself another possible ground upon which to try to justify killing innocents. Or one might focus upon the innocents of another country threatened by a third nation that one's own is in a position to oppose. In any event, the underlying consideration approximates the quantitative principle, except that its emphasis is not upon the number of lives likely to be lost per se but only upon the number of innocent lives.

Let me make clearer the points we want to focus upon. The reasoning is that *if* a consequence of refusing to wage war would be to let innocent persons die, and if there is no moral distinction between "killing" and "letting die," then the fact that one would inevitably be killing innocents by waging war is by itself an inconclusive reason not to do so. Innocents are going to die whatever you do. So better to resist evil as best you can than to maintain what is only the appearance of clean hands.

Two assumptions are central here: the first holds that there is no moral distinction between killing an innocent person and letting an innocent person die (between "killing" and "letting die," for short), which is part of a larger claim that there is no distinction between killing and letting die in general; the second holds that the consequence of refusing to fight is that innocents will be killed by the aggressor. It is not as though you have the luxury of pursuing a course in which no innocents at all will die. And you are, it is held, as responsible for deaths you could have prevented as for those you cause yourself.

V

Let us begin with the second assumption, that in situations of the sort described the deaths of innocents will be among the consequences of our actions whatever we do. It is this that provides the basis for the judgment that we are responsible for such deaths whether we cause them or merely allow them to happen. Is this assumption correct?

Notice that the problem could be alleviated if the principle of double effect were adequate for the use to which it is put. For then one would need only to be careful that the foreseeable deaths of innocent persons at the hands of others is never part of one's intention in refraining from saving them. Though she does not relate

201

it specifically to letting innocents die at the hands of others, the general point is put in the earlier passage by Anscombe when she says that if one is answerable for the foreseen consequences of an action or refusal as much as for the action itself, the absolute prohibition against killing innocent persons breaks down.

Interestingly, some of those who argue most vigorously for the principle of double effect refuse to extend its use to those, like pacifists, who refuse to kill innocents in order to save other innocent persons, or who refuse to take up arms to save innocent persons. Thus Robert L. Phillips argues that although the pacifist and the adherent of the just war doctrine "are in agreement that direct attacks upon other people are morally wrong, . . . the pacifist will not accept the distinction between intentional and unintentional killing in war." He then states that

> if the pacifist does make this argument, then surely he is open to his own criticism. For in a war between pacifists and ruthless aggressors, such as the Nazis or the Soviets, the pacifists would also have perfectly clear foreknowledge that *their* refusal to bear arms would result in the deaths of a great many people who could have been saved if they had been prepared to use force to save them. The difference seems to be that the pacifist will not "dirty his hands" by countering force with force.[12]

This is part of a common objection that pacifists are concerned mainly about their own moral purity and do not really care much what happens to others, including innocent persons, so long as they personally keep their hands clean by refraining from violence.

What is unclear, however, is why it should be thought that double effect, were the pacifist to appeal to it and were it an adequate principle for the purposes to which it is put, would not be as exculpatory for the pacifist as for those who use it to justify killing innocents. If, that is, I may *personally* kill another person and not be held accountable, provided I do not intend to kill him but merely foresee that I will cause his death in my effort to incapacitate him as a combatant (as Ramsey puts it), why should I be held accountable if *someone else* kills that same person in circumstances in which I could foresee that by refusing to kill yet another person his death would result? In the one case I am absolved of respon-

[12] *War and Justice*, p. 107.

sibility, in the other I am held blameworthy, even though the killing was done by someone else. If double effect justifies killing innocent persons by one's own hand, its use cannot be denied to those who refuse to kill innocent persons but foresee that if they do other innocent persons will die.

This assumes, of course, that the death of an innocent person at the hands of someone whose killing I might have prevented, either by killing him or by killing others, is a consequence of my inaction, hence accountable to me. And it is true that the fact that my act is one of omission is irrelevant. We can sometimes *do* things as much by refraining as by acting. But is it true that in such circumstances the death of the innocent person at the hands of another is properly considered a consequence of what I do? It is commonly assumed that it is, particularly in the critique of pacifism or nonviolence. Thus Phillips says that "[t]he unwillingness of the pacifist to dirty his hands is no doubt the source of the charge that he is more concerned about the state of his soul than with the preservation of life. The unwillingness to kill or injure may be part of the pacifist's very being, but what happens to his 'respect for life' defense when his refusal to fight causes loss of lives which could have been saved?"[13]

I want to question this. For if this assumption cannot be sustained, then whether or not pacifists make use of the principle of double effect the ground will be removed for saying that preventable deaths of innocent persons are accountable to them.

VI

Notice at the outset that moral responsibility must be distinguished from causal responsibility. A nurse is causally responsible for a patient's death if he gives him the wrong medicine. But he is not morally responsible if he does so because someone mislabeled the bottle. On the other hand, people are often morally responsible for things for which they are not (directly at least) causally responsible. Adolf Eichmann operated no gas chambers, gave no lethal injections, and very likely (though he was accused of so doing) never personally killed anyone. Yet as a conscientious bureaucrat he facilitated the extermination of countless persons during World War II and accordingly shared moral responsibility for their fate.

[13] Ibid., p. 104.

Nonetheless, helping to bring about a state of affairs, even if it is not the direct effect of one's actions, is a necessary condition of being morally responsible for it. This makes the question of responsibility in social matters a complicated one. For given any reasonably complex social problem, different "causes," direct or indirect, can be singled out for various happenings according to inclination or bias.

Consider the Kent State shootings during the Vietnam War. Students at Kent State University protested the bombing of Cambodia. The National Guard was called in. Under circumstances that have never been fully clarified, they fired upon the students, killing four. Those who favor a hard line on campus unrest argued that, tragic as the incident was, the students brought it upon themselves by being out demonstrating when they should have been at their books. Those who approved of the protest claimed that the tragedy was precipitated by the calling in of the National Guard—or before that, by the bombing of Cambodia. Both sides are correct in a sense. In the absence of the actions to which they call attention, the killings would not have occurred. And both sides can agree on certain basic facts, such as that it was National Guardsmen who aimed the rifles and pulled the triggers and that it was students who were killed. But what "caused" the shootings, students or National Guardsmen (or, to carry things further, permissiveness, disrespect for law and order, capitalistic imperialism, etc.)? One can have it either way by selectively emphasizing certain aspects of the situation to the exclusion of others.

Is it possible to give morally neutral causal accounts of social phenomena; not just accounts that do not logically entail moral judgments but ones that do not reflect the value-orientations of the persons giving them? Those who believe that social and political issues can be dealt with in a scientific fashion usually think so. But there has been no convincing analysis of causality in social, political, and international affairs that precludes the operation—often in subtle and decisive ways—of normative convictions in the selection of so-called "causes." And it is hard to see how there could be. Closer to the truth is John Dewey's claim that what the facts are, especially in social matters, is often a matter of interpretation. And interpretation in the context of highly controversial problems almost invariably reflects the values of those making the judgments. This means that the underlying "factual" bases from which opponents on controversial issues argue their positions are often founded from the outset upon normative convictions rather than vice versa. Nowhere is this more evident than in ideological debates between Marxists and capitalists, whose perceptions of the world often differ so radically as to give them little agreement even about the basic facts that they are discussing, much less about matters of policy.

This is the more general problem of which the one that concerns us is a part. It has to do with the extent of one's responsibility in decision making to take account of the probable responses of others to those decisions. More specifically, to what extent must the responses of others be reckoned among the consequences of what we do?

VII

Any plausible moral theory, to be sure, must take some account of consequences, even if it does not place exclusive emphasis upon them. This presupposes at the least that one knows what sorts of things to count as consequences.

But two kinds of candidates present themselves: those that depend upon the mediation of some choice, decision, or judgment—some cognitive *response*, let us say—on the part of other persons to the act in question and those that do not. These may be called respectively *mediated* and *unmediated consequences*. A person's death is an unmediated consequence of his being shot by a firing squad; once the triggers are pulled, the laws of physics and biology alone determine the outcome. No decision, choice, or action by anyone is necessary to mediate between that act and its consequence. But his death can be said equally correctly to be a mediated consequence of his having been sentenced to death by a court. Once a death sentence is issued, many persons must respond cognitively in the chain of events leading from that moment to the execution in order for the death to result. These include those who pass the sentence on to the appropriate commanding officer as well as the members of the firing squad who respond to the command to fire by the officer in charge.

Clearly, unmediated consequences must be counted among the consequences of our actions, but should mediated consequences be counted as well? And if so, should they always or only sometimes?

This constitutes a central problem for ethics and social philosophy. If we limit consequences to those that are unmediated (and accordingly absolve persons of moral responsibility for all else that issues from their doings), we are forced to deny some of our most common causal and moral judgments. We are prevented from saying that a person who cries fire in a crowded theater is responsible for the ensuing panic, or that an officer who orders the execution of civilians is responsible for their deaths. In neither case would the subsequent happenings be any part of the consequences of their respective actions. On the other hand, to allow all mediated consequences to count would be equally undesirable, since no one can reasonably be held accountable (either causally or morally) for *everything* that others do in response to his actions. Otherwise we should be committed to an extreme moral conservatism that would place in the hands of authorities the power to render actions wrong by making the consequences of their performance invariably worse than those of nonperformance. Governments, for example, would need only attach severe penalties to the performance of actions they prohibit as, in varying degrees, they tend to anyway. It is not simply that they could make it imprudent to perform them; they could actually make it morally wrong to perform them, and could do so even after the performance of the actions and with or without advance knowledge of the agent. It was much these sorts of considerations that Thoreau had in mind when he spoke of those who think that "if they should resist [unjust laws], the remedy would be worse than the evil." He pointed out that "it is the fault of the government itself that the remedy *is* worse than the evil. *It* makes it worse."[14]

Both views are reflected in our thinking about social and political issues. When it is argued that reformers should proceed slowly lest they create a backlash that could lead to repression, the assumption is that they share responsibility for the response of others to what they do—even if the reformers' position is reasonable and the response to it unreasonable. When Vietnamese villages were bombed during the Vietnam War, it was said that responsibility for the resultant deaths of innocents lay with the Vietcong for choosing to mingle with the civilian population. Likewise, some people blamed the PLO for the ensuing civilian casualties when the Israelis bombed South Lebanon during the 1982 invasion, on the grounds that the Israeli action was in response to PLO terrorism. In each case the killing of innocents is treated not principally as a consequence of the acts of those who do the actual

[14] "Civil Disobedience," in *The Portable Thoreau*, ed. C. Bode (New York: The Viking Press, 1947), p. 119.

killing but as a consequence of prior acts of those to whom those doing the killing allegedly are responding (or, in the Vietnam case, prior acts of those who have helped to create the circumstance resulting in the deaths of innocents). At the same time we often commend as persons of principle precisely those who forge ahead when convinced they are right, to the disregard of both the opinions and likely responses of others. We admire them for not compromising themselves. Thus when Socrates reviewed his decision to forego the chance to escape an unjust death, he said that no need should be paid in such a review to the opinions of the multitude.

It seems clear that no determination of moral responsibility for what is done in the context of the state can be made without at least an implied judgment of the relative weights of mediated and unmediated consequences. This is because those who wield power rarely effect any of its consequences directly. They personally collect no taxes, make no arrests, fight no wars. Their power is transmitted through the wills of thousands, and sometimes millions, of other persons. This makes the politically and morally relevant consequences of their actions almost exclusively mediated.

Where, then, should the emphasis be placed in our judgments of moral responsibility, upon mediated or unmediated consequences?

The only possible answer is that we should sometimes stress one, sometimes the other. There is no neutral criterion for settling once and for all what should count as consequences (or, alternatively, of settling once and for all which type of consequence should be regarded as morally relevant and in what degree). Although one could arbitrarily draw a line at some point in the sequence of events following upon the performance of an action beyond which he would exclude everything from counting as a consequence, to do so would be convincing only to the extent that its results coincided with plausible judgments about what ought to be counted as consequences. *The question of whether we ought to stress mediated or unmediated consequences, and with what comparative weight, is itself a moral question.*

This does not mean that it is just a matter of preference which we do, anymore than the fact that one cannot determine on scientific grounds whether it is right to harm another person means that it is just a matter of preference which we do. It does mean that the making of moral judgments in the area of social affairs requires sensitivity to a greater range of considerations than is often supposed. It requires as extensive a knowledge of psychological, sociological, political, economic, moral, and other matters as one can command. Whether what one does eventuates in a morally satisfactory social state of affairs depends to a considerable extent upon the character, moral and factual beliefs, and personality of those affected by it. It is these considerations, far more than the more easily calculable disbursements of material goods, or even the pleasures and pains emphasized by traditional utilitarians, that are the chief determinents of the effects of actions upon persons.

Sometimes we rightly give high priority to mediated consequences. If one knows that a wrong word, or even a wrong look, can lead an emotionally unstable person to act rashly, or that an inflammatory speech may incite a crowd to riot, these should be weighed among the possible consequences of one's actions. Other times we may disregard mediated consequences. Unconventional sexual behavior elicits negative responses in some communities, as do bizarre dress and interracial marriage. Sometimes the responses can be harsh. Yet, though we might want to counsel prudence to persons contemplating engaging in such practices in those circumstances, we do not consider that the rightness or wrongness of what they do depends upon how others respond. Interracial marriage is no more rendered wrong by the reaction of bigots than Christianity was rendered wrong by the feeding of Christians to lions.

VIII

Returning now to the question of the killing of innocents, the fact that it is a moral question what to include among the consequences of actions means that it cannot simply be assumed that preventable deaths at the hands of others are a consequence of the inaction of those in a position to prevent those deaths. More specifically, one cannot simply assume that preventable deaths of innocents at the hands of an aggressor are among the consequences of the refusal of others to respond violently to the aggression. More specifically still, one cannot simply assume that the deaths of innocents at the hands of an aggressor are among the consequences of the refusal of others *themselves* to kill innocents in the course of responding violently to the aggression. This does not mean that sometimes one ought not to include such deaths among the consequences of our actions, only that it is an open question morally whether to do so and that the moral issues involved in the controversy over *killing* versus *letting die* cannot be settled by an antecedently nonmoral determination of consequences.

What, then, do we make of the second assumption, that, morally speaking, there is no distinction between killing innocent persons and letting them die?

We should first distinguish between saying that allowing a particular person to die is indistinguishable from killing *that* person and saying that allowing a particular person to die is indistinguishable from killing someone else. Gandhi once observed that to withhold medication from a dying man is no different from murdering him. Even if this is true it does not mean that allowing that particular person to die is no different morally from killing someone else. During World War II, some people favored bombing the Nazi extermination camps even though it would have killed many inmates. The thinking, no doubt, was that it would be no worse to kill those persons than to allow them to be killed, and it would actually be preferable if by so doing one could save other innocent lives by destroying the camps. In most wartime cases, however, the issue is whether to kill some innocent persons in the course of waging war in order to save other innocent persons.

If you can save an innocent person but do not do so, there is a sense in which you are "letting" that person die. To let someone die is to refrain from intervening in processes that, if allowed to run their course, will bring about his premature death. But these processes may be of two sorts. There are those that involve human agency and those that do not—what we may call respectively human and natural processes. Gandhi had in mind the case of someone dying of disease or injury, where the processes whose unimpeded operation would effect death are natural ones. If, on the other hand, someone were under a death threat and the question was whether to intervene on his behalf, they would be human; it would be someone's action that, if uninterrupted, would bring about his death. When we ask about the comparative morality in wartime of allowing innocents to die as opposed to killing them, the question is whether we should kill some innocent persons so as not to let *others* die; whether we should alter the death-threatening conditions to some by ourselves killing others.

Is allowing the deaths of innocents in this sense no different from, or perhaps worse than, the killing of other innocents in order to save them?

It is difficult to think of any plausible ground upon which it could be argued that *in general* killing and letting die are morally indistinguishable. All of us continually "let" others die all the time, in the sense that there are countless persons the world over suffering from hunger, disease, exposure, and malnutrition whose deaths we could avert by prompt and sustained effort. It might require that we sacrifice the interests, and in some cases even the lives, of those who depend upon us, and it would alter the whole character of our own lives, but we could do it.

Apart from whether each of us should make a concern for the world's poor and hungry an abiding concern of our lives, morality does not require the sacrifice of virtually everything for the sake of others. There are some who do this—the Mother Theresas of this world—and they are esteemed for it. But theirs are acts of supererogation and not part and parcel of the ordinary requirements of morality. Yet if killing and letting die were indistinguishable, then they should be so in the case of the person sacrificing all for the suffering souls of the world. But surely it would be wrong to kill those persons whom we might save by heroic efforts and extraordinary personal sacrifice and whom we might now be said to let die.[15] The mere fact that it is at least problematic whether it is wrong to let them die in circumstances in which that outcome can be avoided only at the sacrifice of virtually all other undertakings, including the discharge of obligations to family and friends, indicates that in this case the two are distinguishable.

In other words, if we do let others die in this sense, we do not similarly countenance the killing of them. We have, as Jeffrie Murphy has argued,[16] a greater obligation to refrain from killing innocent persons than we do to save them (i.e., not to let them die). Leaving aside children and dependents, no one has a *right* to be saved by others—to expect as a matter of obligation that they go out of their way, perhaps sacrificing their interests or even their lives, to preserve him. But everyone has a right not to be harmed or killed by others. To kill someone (other than inadvertently or accidentally) requires doing something knowingly and, in the clearest cases, deliberately causing his death; and we have a strong prima facie obligation to refrain from doing that. It is, as I have said, presumptively wrong to treat persons that way. Letting others die, on the other hand, may involve nothing more than going about one's everyday activities; it may even result from en-

---

[15] This same argument has been used by D. W. Haslett in "Is Allowing Someone to Die the Same as Murder," in *Social Theory and Practice* 10, no. 1 (Spring 1984): 81.
[16] "The Killing of the Innocent," *The Monist* 57, no. 4 (Oct. 1973): 527-551.

gagement in moral and self-sacrificing undertakings. To devote one's life to the care of one person would be to let countless others die. And even if we should say that each person has a right to be saved by others, and they a corresponding obligation not to let him die, the right is surely not an imprescriptible one, and the obligation is less stringent than the obligation to refrain from killing.

The killing of innocents by an aggressor is no worse *as such* than the killing of innocents by those who would oppose him by waging war. Human beings have as much right to be spared destruction by good people as by bad. If an aggressor poses a threat to innocent persons it is presumably because killing them will be a means to achieving certain ends, or because killing them is at least a byproduct of adopting those means. If I choose to kill innocent persons in order to prevent the deaths of others at the hands of an aggressor, I, no less than and perhaps even more than he (if his killing of innocents is only incidental to his attaining his ends) am using innocent persons as a means to an end. If this is correct, the presumption against killing innocents is not defeated by this reasoning.

IX

Let me draw together our main conclusions at this point. I have argued that doing violence to persons is presumptively wrong, and that war by its nature does such violence. Because realist attempts to insulate war either wholly or partially from moral consideration do not succeed, this fact must be at the center of the assessment of war. It means, if I am correct, that attention needs to be focussed away from the standard conditions dealt with in the just war tradition and upon the nature of what one is doing in the very *waging* of war, however just one's cause and however carefully one otherwise abides by the standard rules for its conduct. This reveals, I maintain, that modern war inevitably kills innocent persons. And this, I contend, makes modern war presumptively wrong. What I consider the strongest arguments to defeat that presumption, by way of trying to defeat the presumption against the killing of innocent persons, also do not succeed. If that is the case, then war has not been shown to be justified, and if it has not been shown to be justified, then it is unjustified. This does not of itself mean that modern war *could* not be justified; to show that something has not been justified and that the main attempts to justify it are inadequate can never logically foreclose the possibility that a justification might someday be forthcoming. But that justification must be produced. And unless or until it is produced, war should cease to be in our repertoire of responses to world problems.

Although I have emphasized the killing of innocents, it should not be thought that this means that it is all right to kill the noninnocent. In fact, I think both sorts of wartime killing are wrong. But this is a stronger conclusion than I believe is necessary to establish the unjustifiability of war and one that would require a different kind of analysis from the one I have sought to provide. Moreover, as it is a conclusion that fewer people are predisposed to accept, to proceed from it would narrow considerably the common ground from which most persons could begin consideration of the problem of war. Militarists and pacifists alike, on the other hand, can for the most part agree that killing innocent persons is wrong.

In saying this, it is important to stress that I have by no means tried to take account of all of the possible arguments that might be (or even have been) advanced to try to justify the killing of innocent persons, partly because many of them do not bear directly upon the problem of wartime killing and partly because many of them are plausible only if taken to be directed against an absolutist prohibition against the killing of innocents, hence, by implication, against an absolutist antiwar position. And I have defended neither of these. Once one enters the realm of highly speculative counterexamples, one can readily make a case for war and killing of all sorts, as one can for almost any other type of action whose wrongness is not part of its very definition from the outset. Wars as they are waged today, have been waged in the past, and are likely to be waged in the future are complex enough in the issues they raise. What the proper understanding is of all of the theoretically imaginable wars that might be waged I do not know. And except where it is clear that consideration of them advances our understanding of the wars humankind actually faces, time spent analyzing them seems to be time diverted from more urgent problems.

It should also be noted, finally, that I have not taken up directly the many possible utilitarian arguments that might be given for war and the killing of innocents (except insofar as they are implied in some of the just war criteria, the principle of double effect, and so on). This is because I am convinced that if the analysis of consequences in sections VII and VIII of this chapter are correct, it means that utilitarianism (and consequentialism generally) is inadequate as a basis for moral theory. I have not tried to detail this, but I believe it can be shown insofar as such theories presuppose that it is possible to make an antecedently nonmoral determination of consequences as a basis for making moral judgments. This means, I should add, that the moral personalism with which we began, and that has provided the moral point of departure for our discussion, turns out to be a deontological position.

X

The nuclear age has, however, complicated the assessment of the killing of innocent persons. For although all-out nuclear war would kill innocents on an unprecedented scale, it is widely thought that the threat of such war is precisely what can prevent it from occurring, by deterring the very use of the weapons comprising the threat. Not that people might not continue to die in more limited wars; but the large-scale, indiscriminate destruction of life threatened by nuclear war need never take place. Even the vast destruction of a major conventional war can be avoided, on this view. For the basic principles of deterrence can be extended to conventional as well as nuclear conflicts. In short, some would say that the very horror of nuclear war is precisely its virtue, guaranteeing that it will never occur and confirming that strength and firmness are the surest ways to deal with threats of any sort.

Although I have given reasons in the Introduction for believing the main problem we must come to grips with is war itself and not just nuclear war in particular, there are aspects of the threat of nuclear war that deserve special attention. For not only does that threat put at risk more persons, innocent and noninnocent, than any wars in past history, and not only does it raise questions (as we considered in the preceding chapter) with regard to whether the just war theory is relevant to the nuclear age, it also raises questions concerning the rationality of some of the conventional thinking about war in the nuclear age, specifially with regard to the idea of nuclear deterrence. For this reason I want to examine those aspects of the theory of deterrence that bear most directly upon the issues before us.

S E V E N

NUCLEAR DETERRENCE: THE ILLUSION
OF SECURITY

The logical consequence of the preparation for nuclear war
is nuclear war. —Helen Caldicott

John Foster Dulles once called deterrence "one of the great advances of our time." The thought behind this, as elaborated by Robert W. Tucker, is that deterrence provides an alternative to traditional notions of defense, so that "peace-loving nations may realize the purposes otherwise frequently realized only through a defensive war though without ever having to engage in such a war."[1]

In other words, nations once had to *defend* themselves to ward off aggression. This meant fighting, killing, and dying. It was the business of the just war theory to spell out the conditions under which this was supposedly justified. But if you can avoid the need to fight, so much the better. Nuclear weapons are relatively inexpensive, and they are so destructive one should in principle be able to deter aggression with relatively few of them. And unlike other weapons, if they function properly they will never have to be used.

Some analysts contend the notion of deterrence goes back at least as far as the Romans, others that it is as old as warfare itself. In other words, the idea is not unique to the nuclear age. Even in modern dress it has many dimensions, depending upon what is threatened and what the threat is intended to deter. Nuclear weapons can be used to try to deter nuclear attacks. But they can also be used to try to deter conventional attacks or virtually any sort of aggression one chooses to define. And they can be used to try to deter attacks upon the United States (basic deterrence) or

[1] *The Just War: A Study in Contemporary American Doctrine* (Baltimore: The John Hopkins University Press, 1960), p. 67.

214

upon other nations as well (extended deterrence). Even the very existence of such weapons without any declaratory threat is said to be capable of acting as a deterrent (existential deterrence). Conventional and chemical/biological weapons can likewise be used to deter the use of similar weapons or weapons in general or the pursuit of ends to which the deterrer objects. The *concept* of deterrence, however, remains the same throughout all of these cases.

Deterrence clearly has not prevented war in general, even during the nuclear age. Nor has it prevented nonnuclear forces from warring with nuclear forces, as in the case of China against the United States in Korea, Afghan rebels against the Soviet Union in Afghanistan, and Argentina against Great Britain in the Falklands. And it certainly has not deterred either superpower from intervening in other countries, as witnessed by the Soviet Union in Hungary, Czechoslovakia, and Afghanistan and the United States in Vietnam, the Dominican Republic, and Grenada. A major theme in much of strategic thinking, moreover, is that deterrence has not slowed Soviet expansionism, which is why some analysts have long argued that the United States must have a form of military response intermediate between acquiescence and all-out nuclear war. If these were the objectives of deterrence, it would be documentably false that it has worked.

The usual claim, however, and in any event the central claim, even where it is held that deterrence has other objectives, is that it has deterred a first-strike by either of the superpowers. A massive use of nuclear weapons by either or both of the superpowers is what people most want to avoid. Throughout the many permutations in the idea of deterrence, the core idea in Western thinking is that the United States must first of all deter a first-strike by the Soviets and do so by credibly threatening to annihilate them should they ever launch such an attack. It is assumed the Soviets reason in the same way.[2] Irrespective of whether deterrence works

[2] Though it is not in fact known that they reason in this way. Much of Soviet writing about war in the nuclear age stresses defense and views peaceful coexistence as an alternative to deterrence. Typical is Soviet military historian Daniil Proektor, who contends that Soviet military forces are intended solely for defense. " 'Deterrence'," he says, "is based on the postulate that men and states have only the worst intention against each other, that ours is a world in which there is neither mutual respect nor culture and where other states are regarded only as predators. . . . But the importance of 'deterrence' began gradually to decrease as the Cold War period drew to a close and the concept of a balance of forces gained increasing authority as a means of achieving security." Both deterrence and the balance of forces approach, he maintains, will eventually be superseded historically by peaceful coexistence, a higher form of international relations. See *The Choice Facing Europe*

in any of the other ways policy makers intend (such as to deter a conventional attack upon NATO), if it does not deter a massive first-strike by either side, the system does not work. For this reason I shall examine primarily this core idea.

The conventional wisdom has been that deterrence not only works but that it enjoys moral justification as well. Such thinking concedes that we must be willing to wage nuclear war but contends that we will never have to do so if that willingness is conveyed unmistakably to potential enemies. Deterrence, in fact, it is said, is the only thing that has so far kept the United States and the Soviets from a confrontation. As one writer puts it, "the paradox of peace in the nuclear era is precisely that one can only prevent war by evoking the horrors of the destruction of humanity."[3]

The stakes in such thinking are high. If the reasoning is sound, we need only maintain the balance of terror to guarantee security; threatening the unthinkable will prevent the unthinkable from happening. But if the reasoning is unsound, it risks catastrophe of unprecedented proportions.

I hope to show that, contrary to conventional wisdom, we have no good reason to believe that threatening the unthinkable will prevent the unthinkable from happening and that unless we actively set ourselves to develop alternative conceptions of security, the likelihood increases that we will bring upon ourselves the thing we most want to avoid.

Before that, however, I want to examine a more fundamental aspect of the problem concerning the rationality of this whole approach to war. It cannot be rational to fight a nuclear war unless it is possible to win, or at least to achieve rational objectives by so doing; and it is not possible to do that unless it is possible to survive.

I

The view that nuclear war would represent annihilation for both sides was challenged by Herman Kahn in 1960. His magnum opus, *On Thermonuclear War*, appeared during the early years of the era of deterrence—the "Golden Age" of strategic thinking, as

---

(Moscow: Novosti Press Agency Publishing House, 1981), p. 84. As Colin S. Gray points out, on the other hand, much of American planning until the late 1970s regarded defense and deterrence as inconsistent notions. See *Strategic Studies: A Critical Assessment* (Westport, Conn.: Greenwood Press, 1982), p. 22.

[3] The Rev. Gerard Defois, *New York Times*, July 9, 1983.

it has been called[4]—and was extolled as a model of the objective, rigorous thinking that should be done on the topic. Indeed, he might with some justification be called the father of deterrence theory. It is instructive for that reason to examine his reasoning.

The book, it should be said, is not a defense of war, much less of nuclear war in particular. But it does defend certain theses essential to the justification of nuclear war, one of which is that it is possible to survive such a war. If nuclear war is not survivable, then it cannot be justified, morally, legally, militarily, or in any other way. And if it cannot be survived, then what Kahn regards as "defeatist" attitudes—giving top priority to abolishing war, or thinking that there is no point to planning tactics for fighting such a war or for preparing for a postwar period—would all seem to be reasonable ones.

But Kahn believes that those who think this way have not done their homework, and he sets about to do it for them. This is the task of his chapter "Will the Survivors Envy the Dead?"

That task is variously represented as being to establish: (1) "that the view so prevalent in the mid-'fifties, that any nuclear war automatically entailed world annihilation, [is] probably wrong"; (2) "that a country might be able to survive a very large thermonuclear attack"; and (3) *"that if proper preparations have been made, it would be possible for us or the Soviets to cope with all the effects of a thermonuclear war, in the same sense of saving most people and restoring something close to the prewar standard of living in a relatively short time."*[5] These presumably add up to the conclusion that the survivors would not envy the dead.

Probably no one has ever seriously defended thesis (1) in the form Kahn states it, but many people do believe that an all-out nuclear war would mean the end of civilization and that it is possible it would destroy all human life. But Kahn is correct to point out that this is not *necessarily* the case. No one can prove that every last man, woman, and child in every corner of the earth would be killed by any nuclear war. Kahn advises us, however, that there are persons—mostly scientists and engineers—who favor the creation of a device capable of destroying all of mankind. It is known

[4] Colin S. Gray, *Strategic Studies and Public Policy: The American Experience* (The University Press of Kentucky, 1982), p. 45. For a more critical assessment of Kahn's work, as well as of the theory of deterrence, see Philip Green, *Deadly Logic: The Theory of Nuclear Deterrence* (New York: Schocken Books, 1966).

[5] *On Thermonuclear War* (New York: The Free Press, 1969). The first two quotations are from p. xviii, the third from p. 71.

as a doomsday machine. And it supposedly would deter any country from ever initiating a nuclear war. Though he himself takes a dim view of the feasibility of such a machine, he allows that "it is quite possible that technical validity may be given the common pictures of a war in which both sides can easily be destroyed—irrespective of the preparations that are made before the war . . . Even then, unless we are willing to surrender we must at least make preparations to fight wars carefully."[6] In the absence of such a device, however, or of reason to believe that any likely use of existing nuclear weapons would have a comparable effect, it cannot be proven that even an all-out nuclear war would, as Kahn puts it, automatically mean the annihilation of all mankind. At the same time, he concludes that nobody can prove survival," either,[7] which means that we can neither prove nor disprove that total annihilation would result from a nuclear war, a claim that, though it entails that (1) as stated is unsubstantiated, establishes neither (2) nor (3) nor answers the questions whether the survivors of a nuclear war would envy the dead.

A scattered collection of destitute survivors would not, of course, constitute a society, much less a country or a state or a nation. Would such survivors reestablish anything that could plausibly be called a society? The closest one can find to an argument on this point is the following: "[N]o matter how much destruction is done, if there are survivors, they will put *something* together. The creating (or recreating) of a society is an art rather than a science; even though empirical and analytic 'laws' have been worked out, we do not really know how it is done, but almost everybody (Ph.D. or savage) can do it."[8] This seems to say, in short, that if there are *any* survivors at all, then a society will survive or be quickly created—the apparent basis for this optimism being Kahn's view that men never live in a Hobbesian state of nature and that there is always a society of some sort. Mankind has never, of course, been plunged directly into a state of nature after having known only a state of advanced civilization, and no one knows what the psychological effects alone would be of so traumatizing an event as a nuclear war, a point that Kahn at times concedes.[9] Even the shock experienced by the survivors of Hiroshima is not a reliable gauge, since they at least had the benefit of

[6] Ibid., p. 561.
[7] Ibid., p. xix.
[8] Ibid., p. 77.
[9] Ibid., p. xviii.

emerging into an essentially intact and functioning society, with food and medical care soon available.

Suppose, however, that there would be survivors and that they would somehow reconstitute a society. This would not be enough to show that the country or nation had survived. In the sense in which these are thought to be part of the state, at the very least some government must be presumed to have survived. It is possible that people would not take kindly to a government that had involved them in a war that cost 50 or 100 or 200 million lives plus the country's major cities and that this would stand in the way of successful implementation of plans for recuperation. Kahn, however, does not see this as a serious problem.

It is my belief that if the government has made at least moderate prewar preparations, so that the most people whose lives have been saved will give some credit to the government's foresight, then people will probably rally round, especially if the government has the organization, equipment, and manuals that it needs for recuperation and survival activities, and (most important of all) if the overall plan for recuperation looks sensible and practical. It would not surprise me if the overwhelming majority of the survivors devoted themselves with a somewhat fanatic intensity to the task of rebuilding what was destroyed.[10]

One has the image here of government officials emerging unscathed from their subterranean hideaways, distributing manuals, and talking up sensible schemes for recovery while the president goes on TV assuring people we gave worse than we got and announcing the creation of a presidential commission to investigate the causes of nuclear war; during all of which time the plucky survivors, for their part, pick themselves up, dust themselves off, and turn with renewed dedication to hard work, thrift, and the American Way of Life. The hitch in all of this, of course, is that "if there is a fantastic disparity between the government's preparations and the problems to be solved, then none of this would hold. Quite the contrary. There would probably be a complete rejection of the prewar government, and possibly the prewar ideals and institutions as well."[11] This means that Kahn sees survival and recuperation as dependent upon the credibility and munificence of gov-

[10] Ibid., p. 90.
[11] Ibid.

219

ernment. If either should be lacking, his projections for survival collapse. And it may be a large assumption to maintain that both credibility and munificence can be sustained.

It is one of Kahn's criticisms of the government that it has not undertaken adequate preparations for a postwar period and has not taken seriously enough the need for careful thought about what it would actually be like to wage nuclear war—in short, has not thought sufficiently about the unthinkable. Even granting that since the early 1960s there has been greater thought given to some of these things, it has mostly been in the way of securing the safety of top government, military, and business leaders, not the general public. It has been claimed, for example, that the top corporations have underground headquarters in case of nuclear attack, replete with duplicate company records, air conditioning, and piped-in music. One oil company advisor has been quoted as saying that "it is possible for our nation to survive, recover, and win, and that our way of life, including free enterprise, the oil industry, and the Socony Mobil Oil Company, can survive, recover, and win with it."[12]

But it is the survivors among the population at large whose confidence the government must have and whose well-being must be provided for if the conditions necessary for survival and recuperation as Kahn sees them are to obtain. The issue of confidence cannot be overemphasized. One cannot help but wonder by what reasoning it can be adjudged likely that the black and the poor, many of whom under the best of circumstances have little enough confidence in government, will rally around and "credit the government's foresight" following the devastation consequent upon that government's policy. In the case of the United States, a government that had more than a decade to sell a foreign war in Vietnam, with all of the advantages of money, television time, presidential press conferences, not to mention covert obstruction of critics of that policy, is supposed to market successfully a nuclear war at home.

What Kahn primarily deals with, however, as I have indicated, is not whether the country would survive but whether it could recuperate if it survived. And this, as we have seen, is an alto-

[12] Quoted by John H. Rothchild in "Civil Defense: The Case for Nuclear War," *Washington Monthly* 2, no. 8 (Oct. 1970): 23. See also "Civil Defense Wins More Corporate Converts, But Industry Is Still Vulnerable to Nuclear Attack," The *Wall Street Journal*, June 17, 1981.

gether different issue, one that has little bearing upon the question of survival.

Let us consider the argument for the possibility of recuperation. It is framed in the context of two different hypothetical attacks, the first an early, or small attack, comprising 150 targets, 500 bombs, 1,500 megatons total fission yield; the other a large attack consisting of 400 targets, 2,000 bombs, 20,000 megaton fission yield. With regard to the smaller attack, Kahn is optimistic:

> Would the survivors live as Americans are accustomed to living—with automobiles, television, ranch houses, freezers, and so on? No one can say, but I believe there is every likelihood that even if we make almost no preparations for recuperation except to buy radiation meters, write and distribute manuals, train some cadres for decontamination and the like, and make some other minimal plans, the country would recover rather rapidly and effectively from the small attack.[13]

Not that we would enjoy the process, he says; only that a successful outcome would be likely. He then hypothesizes that the top fifty-three metropolitan areas of the country are completely wiped out, "every stick and stone," and inquires whether the above conclusion could still be sustained. He concludes that it could. As tragic as the loss of fifty-three metropolitan areas would be, it is still far short of "total destruction." As he puts it in Appendix V, "One can almost hear the President saying to his advisors, 'How can I go to war—almost all American cities will be destroyed?' And the answer ought to be, in essence, 'That's not entirely fatal, we've built some spares.' "[14]

It might surprise some people to learn that we should be back on our feet so quickly after a nuclear attack. Fifty-three metropolitan areas totally wiped out seems like a lot. But notice the assumptions underlying this projection.

1. That we have not lost the war (not that we necessarily have won it); "only that no one is seriously interfering with the reconstruction effort."
2. "That society has started to function again—that, where necessary, the debris has been cleared up, minimum communications restored, the most urgent repairs made, credits and markets re-established, a basic transportation system pro-

---

[13] *On Thermonuclear War*, p. 74.
[14] Ibid., p. 642.

vided, minimum utilities either set up or restored, the basic necessities of life made available, and so on."

3. "That [p]reparations for survival and patch-up should include provisions for continuity of government, improvised postattack radiation shelter at work and home, food supplies for those communities where food will be in short supply, manuals and instructions to aid adjustments to the new conditions of life, trained cadres, and radiation meters."

4. That no unforeseen bottlenecks develop that presuppose that the enemy has not deliberately attacked our recuperation potential.

5. That people "would be willing to work at reconstructing the country and would have a productivity at this task about equal to that of their prewar work."

6. "[T]hat it would be possible to adopt 'workable' postwar health and safety standards."

7. "[T]hat the economic and social cost of dealing with 'other' postwar problems will not be catastrophic."[15]

This is a remarkable set of assumptions, for they virtually entail that recuperation is taking place. To say that if there remains a functioning society, willingness to work, lack of interference from the enemy, health and working conditions, basic communications, credit and markets, and so on, then recuperation is possible is redundant. In the very stating of the assumptions one has said, in effect, *that* recuperation is taking place. Anyone who seriously questions whether the country can survive and recuperate from a nuclear war is questioning these very assumptions themselves, not whether, if they are granted, survival and recuperation then follow.

Kahn's procedure is capped by one further methodological assumption, which is that *each of the effects of nuclear war is regarded as occurring by itself, in the absence of the others*. He notes that they considered the effects of radiation, blast, economic dislocation, genetic damage, and so on but "did not look at the interaction among the effects we did study." And then he adds: "But if all these things happened together and all the other effects were added at the same time one cannot help but have some doubts."[16] This is a little like saying that although people have been known to survive heart attacks, kidney failure, cancer, cholera, malaria,

[15] Ibid., pp. 84-91.
[16] Ibid., p. 92.

typhus, fractured skulls, broken arms, legs, ribs, third-degree burns, etc., if a person suffered all of these at once one could not help but have some doubts. Kahn then continues:

Some of these interactions are researchable and should be studied even though we did not do so. However, I believe, though admittedly on the basis of inadequate evidence and subject to caveats I have already pointed out, that none of the problems encountered in the small attack would prove to be annihilating or even seriously crippling. No such judgment can be passed about the heavy attack without more research effort.[17]

The upshot, then, is that if we separate out the elements of a small nuclear war, consider their effects one at a time in the absence of other effects and in the absence of any further effects of their interaction, and if we make all of the assumptions stated previously, including those regarding postwar attitudes towards the government, then, we are told, a small attack would not prove annihilating or even seriously crippling.

This, I submit, tells us nothing about whether we would *in fact* survive a nuclear war, or having survived, could recover. It tells us almost nothing of relevance to estimating what a nuclear war would actually be like (as against what it might be like to experience the curious, science-fictional phenomenon he describes), hence provides no basis for saying whether or not the survivors would envy the dead. Survivors of the phenomenon Kahn characterizes might well not envy the dead; they, after all, have an ongoing society with adequate working and health conditions, no serious external interference, a willingness to work, etc.—things that many people do not have normally. Discount further the suffering they may experience, and one can readily agree that they might well rather be alive than dead. One might as well hypothesize the sprinkling of vanishing powder on the nations's top fifty-three metropolitan areas and then ask the rest of the population whether it is glad it survived.

Suppose, however, that we grant that the survivors of a nuclear war would not envy the dead. What would this show? Only that the survivors are just as glad to have survived, and this is hardly surprising. People's lives can be pretty bad before they prefer to be dead. Kahn seems to believe that such a consideration will help

[17] Ibid.

in the determination of what would be "acceptable" in the way of losses from a nuclear war. He asks: "If 180 million dead is too high a price to pay for punishing the Soviets for their aggression, what price would we be willing to pay?"[18] Though this is never made clear, he apparently thinks that establishing certain conditions under which survivors would not envy the dead helps to indicate what would, or might, be considered acceptable in the way of losses.

Insofar as the problem of nuclear war is addressed to those of us living here and now, however, one does not get an accurate estimate of what is "acceptable" by asking only how the survivors would view the situation, much less by asking whether they would envy the dead. For one thereby omits in his calculations the preferences of those now living who would not be living as the result of a nuclear war; that is, the ones who stand to lose the most. If, say, 50 percent of a population survived a war, and "most" of those did not envy the dead, that might mean no more than that 51 percent of the survivors, or 26 percent of the original population, are glad to be alive—not much of a basis for judging the acceptability of nuclear war.

To make plausible a judgment about what would be acceptable in the way of losses to a given population, one must suppose the population to consist of living persons, not some who are living and some who are dead (even though, by hypothesis, many of the living would be dead if the casualties on whose acceptability they are passing judgment were ever inflicted). If the living did envy the dead, then the dead, if they could be polled, might be just as glad to be dead. But if, as Kahn maintains, and we are now granting for purposes of argument, the survivors would not envy the dead, then it is not unreasonable to suppose that the dead, if they could express a preference, would prefer to be alive.

Now obviously one cannot consult the dead after such a war about whether or not they would prefer to be among the survivors. What one can do, however, is to consult them before they are dead and ask whether they find the risks of nuclear war acceptable. One might find they would prefer that such a war not take place in the first place. To gather the pertinent data on this question one would have to act before the event, and it is surprising that among the various studies described in the book, there is not a nationwide survey of just this sort. It would have to be care-

[18] Ibid., p. 29.

fully designed, but a few observations, about how it might proceed may be in order. Although you would not know precisely which people would die, you would know that for certain sorts of wars, those in the heavily populated urban areas stand the greatest chance of being killed, and that for other sorts of wars, persons in the vicinity of missile silos and so forth would stand the greatest chance. One might therefore randomly select 10, or 50, or 100 million persons (according to the size of the attack hypothesized) and ask them whether they personally would be willing to die in order, as Kahn puts it, to "punish aggression."

Further, to see that they not get by without thinking about the unthinkable, both the "survivors" and the "dead" should be fully informed about what a nuclear war would actually be like. Not only should they be acquainted with the various statistics Kahn deals with—quantitative material, the assumptions, probabilities, and so forth—but also, as nearly as possible, with the reality of war. For that percentage of the survey who are selected to "die" from burns within the first few weeks they could be informed about what it is like to die from burns, those predicted to die from fallout could be informed what it is like to die from radiation sickness, those who would die from leukemia in coming years, what death by leukemia is like. One might also select certain percentages who would survive blinded or maimed by the blast, a reasonable number of women who would give birth to deformed children, and so on. None of this need be done emotionally; it can be done in plain, factual terms. When one had completed this educational task—which is essential if the notion of "acceptability" is to have any meaning at all—one would then ask people whether or not they would consider nuclear war acceptable. One might then have some slender empirical basis for judging what would be acceptable to informed people. In a democracy, if nowhere else, one would expect government to undertake such a study before adopting policies that could have farther-reaching consequences for the country as a whole than anything else it could possibly do. To do less than this is not to think responsibly about the unthinkable.

II

These latter considerations are unaffected by the widely varying estimates of the effects of nuclear war that have appeared since Kahn's analysis. But many of the other shortcomings of his analysis have been minimized or eliminated by subsequent calculations that have had the advantage of new data and more sophisticated computers. I shall not attempt to survey all of these. But it may be useful to consider certain of them, beginning with a report prepared for the Senate Committee on Foreign Relations by the Office of Technology Assessment. That report, published in 1980, projected the effects of four possible nuclear attacks: one in which only one city is destroyed (Detroit), a second in which oil refineries alone are attacked, a third in which ICBM silos, bomber bases, and submarine bases are attacked, and a fourth in which urban-industrial, strategic, and other military targets are struck. It attempts also to assess the effects of a comparable attack on the Soviet Union. The first three represent decidedly limited nuclear wars, the fourth a large one, using a major portion of the attacking country's nuclear arsenal.

Of particular interest are the second and fourth of these cases. In the second, the attack on oil refineries, it is hypothesized that the Soviet Union attacks with only ten missiles with multiple warheads. The attack, it is projected, would destroy 64 percent of U.S. oil-refining capacity and result in 1 to 5 million immediate deaths, with millions more eventually dying of cancer if surface bursts are hypothesized.[19] This is assuming that 10 percent of the population in large cities had already evacuated and that the remainder is distributed among fallout shelters, home basements, and buildings. Even though the report acknowledges that "[a]ll economic damage was not calculated from this attack, because no existing data base would support reasonably accurate calculations," it maintains that such an attack would "shatter" the U.S. economy.[20] It apparently does not, however, believe that such an attack would prevent recovery, even though such recovery would be difficult.

Indicative of the evolving and widely discrepant predictions in this area, a four-year study at M.I.T. through computer simulations of nuclear attacks concluded in 1987 that an attack on U.S. oil facilities using only 1 percent of the Soviet Union's nuclear weapons would virtually destroy the U.S. economy and result in death by starvation of most of the population owing to disruption of transportation and energy-producing facilities. It would, on this projection, take the country at least a quarter of a century to re-

[19] Office of Technology Assessment, Congress of the United States, *The Effects of Nuclear War* (Montclair, N.J.: Allanheld, Osmun, 1980), p. 65.
[20] Ibid., p. 69.

store a third of its economic productivity.[21] It is interesting to note that Kahn did not consider U.S. petroleum-refining capacity to be a problem in the attacks he considered.

In the fourth case described by the Office of Technology Assessment, the Soviets launch a large attack, targeting mostly urban-industrial areas. The results are described as devastating. From 20 to 160 million are killed immediately, and "[i]t cannot be said whether the productive facilities that physically survived . . . would be adequate to sustain recovery."[22] Although the report makes clear that the country's national leadership would have evacuated to outlying areas (and presumably survived) if there were advance warning, there is a possibility that during a recovery period "the country might break up into several regional entities," adding that [i]f these came into conflict with each other there would be further waste and destruction."[23] What the report does not say is that if this should happen, the country as a social unit has not survived.

Two of the assumptions underlying these calculations also raise questions regarding survival. One is that the Soviets did not deliberately target the U.S. population but rather killed people only as a "side effect" of attacking economic and military targets. Were the intention specifically to kill people, the casualties would be 20 to 30 million higher. But second, the report makes clear that its calculations reflect only the deaths that would take place in *in the first 30 days*. "Additional millions," it says, "would be injured, and many would eventually die from lack of adequate medical care. In addition, millions of people might starve or freeze during the following winter."[24]

Conspicuously absent in these calculations is any estimate of damage to the environment and longer-term deaths which that might cause. Indeed, the report makes clear that all of their estimates presuppose "no significant ecological damage."[25] It allows that "the incalculable effects of damage to the Earth's ecological system might be on the same order of magnitude as the immediate effects" but says that "it is not known how to calculate or even estimate their likelihood."[26]

[21] The *International Herald Tribune*, June 22, 1987.
[22] *The Effects of Nuclear War*, p. 98.
[23] Ibid., p. 99.
[24] Ibid., p. 8.
[25] Ibid., p. 100.
[26] Ibid., p. 115.

An attempt to make some estimate of the effects of environmental damage following a major nuclear war was undertaken in 1983 by the Royal Swedish Academy of Sciences. As part of this study, which hypothesized a war utilizing 14,737 warheads, or about half the megatonnage of the 1985 arsenals, Paul J. Crutzen and John W. Birks in estimating the effects upon the atmosphere of such a war report that "[u]nder such conditions it is likely that agricultural production in the Northern Hemisphere would be almost totally eliminated, so that no food would be available for the survivors of the initial effects of the war."[27] Economist Yves Laulan projects, as part of the same study, that if 50 percent or more of the population of advanced industrial countries were killed, that "could be the end of these particular societies or civilizations as we know them."[28] Given the interconnectedness of international commercial and monetary systems, the collapse of commercial and monetary exchange would have dire consequences for Third World countries as well. "Most of these countries," he says, "cannot now produce enough food to feed their teeming populations; they are heavily dependent on massive imports of food and technology to keep their people fed and their economics running."[29] Some of them are heavily dependent upon revenues from the sale of oil to the large industrial nations. If the M.I.T. report is even approximately correct, this source of revenue would virtually cease, owing to the devastation of the petroleum industries in large countries. The resultant deaths in the tropical regions (from a war waged primarily in the northern hemisphere), he projects, would be 1 to 3 billion.

These projections were followed by further efforts to assess accurately the climatic effects of nuclear war. This led in 1983 to a controversial report regarding the so-called "nuclear winter." Scientists advancing the theory of nuclear winter contend that even a relatively small nuclear war could send smoke, dust, and soot into the atmosphere in sufficient amounts to block the sun's rays and alter drastically the earth's climate, not only in the northern hemisphere, in which nuclear war is presumed to take place, but in the southern hemisphere as well. With the failure of crops added to a severing of the lifeline of food and technology imports from na-

[27] *The Aftermath: The Human and Ecological Consequences of Nuclear War*, ed. Jeannie Peterson for AMBIO (New York: Pantheon Books, 1983), p. 90.
[28] Ibid., p. 142.
[29] Ibid., p. 144.

tions involved directly in the war, a nearly worldwide crisis in agriculture could ensue, resulting in famine for millions.

Carl Sagan, one of the authors of the report, writes that it is likely "that nations having no part in the conflict . . . might be reduced to prehistoric population levels and economies, or worse. . . . Thus, the very survival of nations distant from any likely nuclear conflict can now be seen to depend on the prudence and wisdom of the major nuclear powers. India, Brazil, Nigeria or Saudi Arabia could collapse in a nuclear war without a single bomb being dropped on their territories."[30] Even a first-strike by one side or the other might have such effects, even if the other side did not retaliate at all. This leads Sagan to observe that "[a] major first strike may be an act of national suicide, even if no retaliation occurs."[31] In the worst case, it is claimed, the extinction of all human life cannot be excluded.

The more drastic of these projections have since been challenged. Writing in 1986, Starley L. Thompson and Stephen H. Schneider of the National Center for Atmospheric Research contend that three main theses of the nuclear winter theory cannot be supported. They are that the onset of a nuclear winter might result in the extinction of all mankind, that there is a threshold in the size of a war that would trigger a nuclear winter, and that it might be national suicide for a country to launch a first-strike. But while discounting the more disturbing claims about the relatively short-term nuclear winter effects, they acknowledge that the longer-term, chronic climatic effects are uncertain.

The previously discovered chronic environmental problems of global radioactive fallout and ozone layer depletion continue

---

[30] "Nuclear War and Climatic Catastrophe: Some Policy Implications," *Foreign Affairs* 62, no. 2 (Winter 1983/84): 280-281. The main report, of which Sagan's article is a summarization for lay readers, was authored by Richard Turco, O. Brian Toon, Thomas Ackerman, James Pollack, and Carl Sagan and entitled "Nuclear Winter: Global Consequences of Multiple Nuclear Explosions," *Science*, Dec. 23, 1983, pp. 1283-1292.

[31] Ibid., p. 292. There is evidence that the Soviet leadership may think this as well. In announcing an extension of the Soviet Union's unilateral moratorium on nuclear testing in a television address to the Soviet people on August 18, 1986, Mikhail Gorbachev said "[o]ne must learn to face the facts with courage: Experts have estimated that the explosion of the smallest nuclear warhead is equal in radioactivity to three Chernobyls. Most likely, this is true. If that is so, the explosion of even a small part of the existing nuclear arsenal would be a catastrophe, an irreversible catastrophe. And if someone still dares to make a first nuclear strike, he will doom himself to agonizing death—not even from a retaliatory strike, but from the consequences of the explosion of his own warheads" (*Soviet Life*, Nov. 1986).

to be studied. It now appears that the trend to smaller war-heads has made the intermediate-term (days to weeks) and global fallout problems somewhat more serious, but the ozone problem has become less serious. As noted earlier, neither problem *considered separately* is thought to pose a global threat that is substantial compared to the direct effects of a nuclear war. But considering all the chronic, indirect effects of a large nuclear war separately may be a misleading exercise; all the chronic effects would, to some degree, act synergistically with each other, and with the direct weapons effects, to produce unprecedented worldwide human misery. . . . Therefore it is still quite plausible that climatic disturbances, radioactive fall-out, ozone depletions and the interruption of basic societal services, when taken together, could threaten more people *globally* than would the direct effects of explosions in a large nuclear war.[32]

This possibility is more or less in line with the estimate by Laulan. It is also in keeping with the claim by Mark Harwell, one of the coauthors of a 1985 study by a special committee of the International Council of Scientific Unions, that although several hundred million persons would be killed directly by a nuclear war itself, from one to four billion would eventually die of famine.[33]

Some of these calculations may be grossly inaccurate. Others may be more or less on target. But we do not know which are which. This gives considerable latitude both to those who would minimize the consequences of nuclear war as well as to those who would exaggerate them. Nuclear blast effects can pretty well be calculated because there is some experience to go on, with the atomic bombings of Hiroshima and Nagasaki. But as one moves from the more immediate effects of blast and fire and short-term radiation to broader environmental and global effects, and from these, considered in the short term, to consideration of them in the long term, the complexities become too great to inspire much confidence that anyone really knows what the world be like after a large-scale nuclear war, or even after a fairly limited war. We do not, in particular, know whether nuclear war would extinguish all human life.

But as important as that question is from the most general of

[32] "Nuclear Winter Reappraised," *Foreign Affairs* 64, no. 5 (Summer 1986): 997-998.

[33] From a news conference reported in the *New York Times*, Sept. 13, 1985.

moral and religious standpoints, it is relatively unimportant from the standpoint of the issues of greatest concern to persons living here and now, who want to live, to enjoy a reasonable quality of life, and to have security for themselves, their friends, and their children. For the consequences of a nuclear war can be monstrous without killing every last person on earth. And even if we knew to a certainty precisely what all of the effects of a nuclear war would be, both short term and long term, and knew the secondary and tertiary effects of the interactions of all of these effects, that would not (so long as it did not entail the extinction of humankind) tell us whether we would survive a nuclear war. The reason it would not is that whether the United States (or any other country) survives is not altogether a factual question. It is partly conceptual and partly evaluative. The criteria for deciding whether a given individual is alive or dead have become increasingly problematic with the advances in science and medical technology. The criteria for deciding whether a country, a nation, or a state (and these all differ from one another in various ways) has survived are even less clear. Does the survival of a handful of government leaders constitute the survival of a country? Or of those leaders plus 100, 1,000, 1 million, or 10 million of the population? Or of 100 million of the population but not the government? Or of various other possible combinations with or without the survival of the top one hundred or two hundred cities, and so on? These are conceptual questions, in part. But they are also partly evaluative, because whether a social or social-political-cultural unit can be said to survive depends upon value judgments about the quality of life it affords those individuals who have survived.[34] And that depends in part upon the survival of property, transporation facilities, energy-sources, and the like, which lend themselves to quantitative calculations, but also partly upon unquantifiable effects of catastrophe upon the morale and psychological health of those who physically

[34] This requires taking account of the value of cultural, historical, and artistic things that would be destroyed, as well as losses to human and animal life. As Douglas P. Lackey says in arguing that nuclear war probably would not result in the end of the world: "What nuclear war *will* do is so bad that the news that it will not destroy the world provides little relief. A full scale nuclear exchange will kill hundreds of millions of innocent people and the survivors will face a world barely capable of supplying their elementary physical needs. It is hardly likely that democracy could survive the shock or serve the needs of the survivors. As for the art and architecture destroyed by nuclear war, that will be gone forever. Those who speak optimistically of reconstruction after nuclear war should note that no one has ever reconstructed a Rembrandt or revived the dead." See *Moral Principles and Nuclear Weapons* (Totowa, N.J.: Roman & Allanheld, 1984), p. 94.

survive. Their behavior, how they react to what has happened, and how they deal with one another are major factors in whether or not what remains after a nuclear war can be said to constitute survival of the country or the nation in any meaningful sense. Increasingly sophisticated studies based upon computer models can be useful in helping to project the resultant physical state of things, but they cannot themselves yield those assessments.

When I say that "we" do not know the answers to these questions, I include, and include specifically, government and military leaders who are responsible for the policies that have generated this situation. They do not know either. Prior to the 1980s they did not even have plausible projections of the environmental effects of a nuclear war. As Sagan says, "[E]very American and Soviet leader since 1945 has made critical decisions regarding nuclear war in total ignorance of the climatic catastrophe."[35] Nor did they have plausible estimates of the amount of death and destruction to which their policies could lead for millions of persons (*billions*, if the higher of the estimates are correct) in other nations of the world who would be killed or adversely affected, with or without a nuclear winter, in the event they decide to go to war. The most momentous of decisions by democratic and nondemocratic nations alike, jeopardizing civilization itself and possibly even the survival of humankind, have been made in abysmal ignorance.

Where does this leave us, then, on the question of whether we would survive a nuclear war? The answer is that we do not know. We almost certainly would survive some nuclear wars. We almost certainly would not survive others. But we do not know what sort of war we would have to endure, or whether, if we survived such a war, there would be another in ten or twenty or one hundred years and whether we would survive that one or the one after or the one after that.

One could, of course, always define "country" in such a way that it is nearly impossible for it not to survive. There is, for example, a way of thinking that would have it that if the president, the joint chiefs of staff, some cabinet members, and perhaps a few members of Congress survive in some mountain hideaway, then the "country" has survived—even if virtually everyone else has been killed. But such reasoning at the same time diminishes the threat to the country's survival. For if that counts as survival, then

[35] "Nuclear War and Climatic Catastrophe: Some Policy Implications," *Foreign Affairs* 62, no. 2 (Winter 1983/84): 285.

little that most enemy powers are likely to do seriously threatens the survival of the country. A government can survive even though close to 100 percent of the population has been destroyed. By the same token, a state can cease to exist without the loss of a single life—as by annexation by another state or break-up into two or more separate states. It would be mad to favor the survival of the country in the first sense to its destruction in the second. The point is that in the absence of the relevant specifications regarding what counts as the survival of a country, calculations of the sort we have been considering, as important as they are for the answering of many questions, are of limited value for answering the question about national survival.

III

I have said that it cannot be rational to wage nuclear war unless it is possible to survive. By that I mean it is a necessary condition of such a war's being rational that we be able to survive it and/or achieve some rational objectives by fighting it.

But such a condition is surely not sufficient. And, indeed, most commentators agree that an all-out nuclear war between the superpowers would be irrational. One does not need to assume the destruction of all humankind to see that. Even on the more optimistic calculations, an all-out exchange by the United States and the Soviet Union could not possibly leave either country better off than if it did not engage in such a war, and would surely so devastate both that no plausible social, political, or moral objective could be attained thereby.

Indeed, this was the general supposition by most analysts beginning sometime in the 1960s.[36] As the Soviets acquired a signif-

[36] Russian dissidents Roy A. Medvedev and Zhores A. Medvedev place it in the late 1960s and early 1970s. See "A Nuclear *Samizdat* on America's Arms Race," *The Nation*, Jan. 16, 1982. On the other hand, W. Scott Thompson contends that "nuclear war had never been remotely possible prior to the time in the mid-1970s when Moscow achieved at least parity with the United States. . . . Moscow had simply lacked the power to wage war on the United States." See Thompson, ed., *National Security in the 1980s: From Weakness to Strength* (Calif.: Institute for Contemporary Studies, 1980), p. 9. In any event, as Joseph S. Nye, Jr., points out, it is important to distinguish between MAD as a doctrine and as a condition. See *Nuclear Ethics* (New York: The Free Press, 1986), pp. 110-111. MAD as a doctrine—if ever it was actual, as opposed to so-called "declaratory," U.S. policy—seems pretty clearly no longer to be U.S. policy, and it was never the official policy of the Soviet Union. In the view of many defense analysts the whole concept is contrary to Soviet thinking. Colin S. Gray says, for example, that [t]he idea of mutual deterrence through a reciprocated threat to punish societies is politically anathema to Soviet civilian of-

icant nuclear capability against the U.S. mainland, it was assumed that all-out war meant certain destruction for both, a state of affairs aptly dubbed by the acronym MAD, Mutual Assured Destruction. This, however, was deemed to make it rational to threaten to retaliate if attacked. According to this view, all-out nuclear war would be irrational. But to *threaten* such war would not be irrational because it would virtually ensure that the irrational will never happen. Indeed, the policy of deterrence would appear to be preeminently rational given the common conception of rationality as choosing the most effective means to one's ends. For that reason it represents a "rationality of irrationality strategy."

There is however, a long-recognized problem for this theory. It is that if deterrence should fail, there would be no point to retaliating. If nuclear weapons are meant to deter and an attack occurs, they have failed in their purpose. Destroying tens of millions of Soviet citizens (or Americans, if one is Soviet) in return would not prevent our own destruction.[37]

The underlying assumption here is that it is the sole purpose of our nuclear weapons to deter. As Robert McNamara says, "Nuclear weapons serve no military purpose whatsoever. They are totally useless—except only to deter one's opponent from using them."[38] But this makes little sense. It cannot plausibly be said to be the *sole* purpose of nuclear (or for that matter any other) weapons to deter. If it were, an adversary could initiate an attack at any time, knowing that by so doing he would have rendered the use

---

ficials and is judged to be militarily irresponsible by Soviet soldiers" (*Strategic Studies and Public Policy*, p. 154). See also Klaus Knorr, "Controlling Nuclear War," *International Security* 9, no. 4 (Spring 1985): 79-99. Secretary of Defense Caspar W. Weinberger said, however, in a 1985 speech, that mutual assured destruction was "still the basis for the nuclear standoff," but that it had been abandoned by the Soviet Union. This, he said, was why the administration was proposing an alternative in the Strategic Defense Initiative. (*New York Times*, Oct. 4, 1985).

[37] As Edward Luttwak puts it: "In the formal sense: killing x percent of the Russian (or Chinese) population in the wake of a nuclear attack upon the United States would not in any way improve the material position of the nation. On the other hand, the *ability* to inflict retaliation could be used to extract reparation from an aggressor. Hence the act of retaliation—if it follows directly the attack that provokes it—can only be irrational, since means are not aligned with goals." *Strategy and History: Collected Essays* (New Brunswick, N.J.: Transaction Books, 1985), 2: 33, n. 16. See also Robert W. Malcolmson, *Nuclear Fallacies: How We Have Been Misguided since Hiroshima* (Kingston: McGill-Queen's University Press, 1985), p. 26.

[38] Quoted by Arthur Macy Cox in "End the War Game," *New York Times*, Nov. 8, 1983. Similarly, a group of Soviet and American military men, following a week of discussions sponsored by the Center for Defense Information, issued the statement that "[n]uclear weapons cannot be used for any rational or political purpose." *New York Times*, April 28, 1987.

of those weapons pointless. If their sole purpose is to deter, and they have failed in that purpose, then there is no point—*absolutely no point*—to using them thereafter. So on the assumption that we would not destroy millions of other persons for no reason at all (and the theory of deterrence, to have even initial plausibility, assumes rationality on both sides), an adversary could confidently do whatever he pleased, knowing that he could render such a "deterrent" useless any time he wanted.

Moreover, it cannot be the purpose of the *use* of nuclear weapons to deter at all. At most it can only be the purpose of *threatening* to use them that can deter.[39] For once an attack has occurred it is no longer possible to deter that attack, no matter what you do (it might be possible to deter subsequent attacks, of course, but even then it is the use of those weapons that does the deterring; and if one has retaliated to a limited attack by a limited response, it is the threatened continued use of nuclear weapons that deters). I am here and throughout talking about a large-scale deliberate first-strike and massive retaliation; for if that occurs, deterrence has failed. The use of nuclear weapons in that case must either be senseless, because devoid of any purpose, or irrational because intended to achieve a logically unachievable objective. For deterrence to be rational there must be a purpose both to *threatening* to use nuclear weapons and to actually *using* them if the threat fails.

But punishment or revenge are about the only candidates for objectives for the actual use of such weapons, and neither has convincingly been shown to have any moral justification when one considers the millions of deaths their pursuit would inflict upon essentially innocent persons. One could, of course, have as an objective to prevent an adversary from ever attacking anyone else again. And while this arguably would be an achievable objective, to pursue it would be to purchase the certain destruction of one set of innocent persons for the possible salvation of others at some indeterminate time in the future; its consequences, in fact, would be precisely the same as those of punishment or revenge (only the motives, and possibly the intentions, would differ). But even this objective would be unattainable if it brought on a nuclear winter, with the worst of its possible consequences. The pursuit of any of these objectives in the circumstances under consideration would

[39] By the "use" of nuclear weapons here I am referring to the exploding of them. As pointed out in the Introduction, one uses them (in another sense) when he threatens to explode them or relies upon an adversary's uncertainty as to whether he will explode them to try to achieve his ends.

likely involve the mutual annihilation of both countries and perhaps the whole of civilization as well. It would, by removing forever the capacity of either country and perhaps all humankind to achieve *any* objectives ever again, signify madness by any plausible criterion. If nuclear war is irrational and we would gratuitously be participating in such a war by retaliating (retaliation would simply convert what otherwise would be a unilateral attack *into* a nuclear war), to do so would be irrational.

Some who consider this problem accept this conclusion. They say there would indeed be no point to retaliating and that we might as well use cardboard missiles or not hook up the wires to our real missiles.[40] Others, and so far as we have reason to believe, the U.S. and Soviet governments, believe this would not work and that in order for the *threat* of the use of nuclear weapons to be credible one must intend to carry it out. A specious threat, they say, would be found out.[41]

This casts the whole theory of deterrence in a different light. Though I shall argue that there is little reason to believe that deterrence has worked in the past, or if it has that it will continue to work in the future, it is at least conceivable that it *could* work; that the threat of nuclear war could in fact deter either side from ever attacking the other. But that would not justify *waging* nuclear war. It would at best only justify *threatening* to wage it. To threaten to perform an act is itself an act, a different one from the act threatened. Because the two may have different consequences they need separate justifications. In the thinking under consideration the two are linked by the intention to carry out the threat; it is believed that for a threat to work it must be credible, and for it to be credible one must intend to carry it out. That is, for the first act to succeed

---

[40] Jerome Frank, in *Sanity and Survival: Psychological Aspects of War and Peace* (New York: Vintage Books, 1967), notes that "[c]ardboard ICBMs would be as effective as real ones if the enemy believed that they were real and would be used under certain provocations" (p. 142).

[41] "Deterrence requires a complex bureaucratic machinery to which it would be impossible to convey the intention of bluffing without disclosing the bluff to the adversary and thus defeating the strategy" (Nye, *Nuclear Ethics*, p. 53). To the same effect, see David Fisher, *Morality and the Bomb: An Ethical Assessment of Nuclear Deterrence* (New York: St. Martin's Press, 1985), p. 75. Thomas C. Schelling had argued earlier that one could make a threat credible by removing its execution partially from one's control. Thus: "The acknowledged purpose of stationing American troops in Europe as a 'trip wire' was to convince the Russians that war in Europe would involve the United States whether the Russians thought the United States wanted to be involved or not—that escape from the commitment was physically impossible." See *The Strategy of Conflict* (Cambridge: Harvard University Press, 1960), p. 187.

one must intend to perform the second act if the first fails. Is it rational to do this?

This is not a moral question per se, but it is the most basic of the nonmoral questions about the strategy of nuclear deterrence.

It is, however, a moral question whether it is right to intend to do something you know to be wrong (and the assumption is that waging nuclear war would be wrong as well as irrational). Many just war theorists, as we have seen, argue that if one's intention is good (and other conditions associated with the expanded principle of double effect are met) then the intended act is permissible. But here is a case in which both the act *and* the intention are bad (or, if you like, in which the act is wrong and the intention bad). So, the proposed way out by modern-day casuists is to argue that *if* by intending to do the evil act (which, by hypothesis, is necessary to making one's threat to do it credible, which in turn is necessary to making deterrence work) you will bring it about that you never have to do it, then so intending is itself morally permissible.

There are two issues here: first, whether intending to do what is irrational is rational, second, whether, intending to do what is immoral is immoral. As I shall assume that an act is moral only if it is not irrational, I shall focus upon the first issue. Its resolution requires examining what is implied by intending.

To intend to do something under certain circumstances is *to do* it under those circumstances (assuming that one is able or has not changed his mind, and so on).[42] I cannot be said to intend to do something if now is the time to do it and I know it is the time and am able to do it but do not do it.

Since doing a certain thing under the appropriate circumstances is what it is to intend to do it under those circumstances (this is not all that it is, but it is essential to intending), it cannot be rational to intend to do it under those circumstances if the thing in question is irrational. That would be knowingly to intend to do what is irrational, and *that* is irrational. Since (we are assuming) credibly threatening to do something is to intend to do it, this means that it cannot be rational credibly to threaten to do something if that thing is irrational; for that would make it rational to

[42] Although sometimes we say indeterminately that we have always intended to do something, like write a novel or study classical guitar, where there is no special time or circumstance for doing it. While it is arguable that we do not really intend to do such things (as opposed to fantasizing about doing them, or hoping we will do them), they are in any event a very different sort of intention from that bound up in deterrence, where there are clearly specifiable circumstances in which we are resolved to do what we threaten to do.

do the irrational. It cannot, in short, be rational credibly to threaten to do the irrational.[43]

This means that if nuclear war is irrational and one threatens to engage in it and intends to carry out that threat if put to the test, he is not acting rationally. It is not just that he may *appear* to be acting irrationally, an impression strategists think it may sometimes be useful to give one's enemy; it is that he will in fact *not* be acting rationally. This does not mean that credibly threatening to wage nuclear war could not deter an attack. It conceivably could do so. People can sometimes be deterred by irrational behavior. But that only attests to the kind of circumspection one understandably displays in the face of threats by madmen. It does not make the threat rational. To whatever extent both sides are wary of one another in the balance of terror—and for reasons I shall explain, it cannot even be assumed that this wariness makes them more cautious than, or necessarily even as cautious as, they would otherwise be—it is either because each senses the irrationality of the other (though not of itself) or, worse yet, does not sense it but imagines they are both engaged in simply a more sophisticated than usual version of power politics.

IV

This fact does, however, bring us back to the issue posed at the outset of this chapter, which is whether the balance of terror is a guarantee of security.

Some would contend that even if the balance of terror is irrational, it works; both sides are deterred, and that is what counts. Some would go further and say that if deterrence works, then, rational or not, it is moral. Even if credibly to threaten to retaliate is irrational, and even if in fact to retaliate would be both irrational

---

[43] A case could be made for saying that it is not possible knowingly to intend to do what is irrational because that would imply a degree of comprehension of the nature and intention of the proposed act that would be incompatible with its *being* irrational. Acts by themselves are neither rational nor irrational; they just are. It is only from the perspective of how they cohere with beliefs, intentions, and perhaps other acts, either of the agent in question or of some larger group, such as society, that they can be said to be rational or irrational. But if it is not possible knowingly to intend to do the irrational, then it follows even more directly that the theory of deterrence as represented by MAD is irrational. For its central idea is that it is eminently rational knowingly to threaten to do the irrational and to intend to carry out that threat if circumstances warrant. And that would mean that it assumes it is possible to do the impossible. For a discussion of deterrence and intentions, see Fisher, *Morality and the Bomb*, chap. 6.

and immoral, to threaten to retaliate is moral because of its consequences. It prevents nuclear war.

There are typically two parts to this thinking. The first holds that nuclear weapons have been a deterrent thus far; the second holds that they will continue to be a deterrent in the future.

The first claim has come to be virtually an article of faith among those who think about the nuclear issue. It is usually assumed without argument and then used as a premise in the argument for the second claim. Consider the following:

> Since the dawn of the atomic age, we've sought to reduce the risk of war by maintaining a strong deterrent and by seeking genuine arms control. . . . This strategy of deterrence has not changed. It still works.[44]

> Everywhere I have gone, leaders and ordinary citizens alike have voiced one concern above all others: the need to avoid nuclear war. Our Government has set policies in place that, if adhered to, will keep such a war from ever taking place. . . . Our first aim has been effective deterrence. We have made certain that our adversaries understand that a nuclear strike against us or our allies would result in retaliation. That sounds chilling, but by keeping our deterrent forces strong enough to be credible, we have avoided the need to use them.[45]

> [T]his exclusive reliance on the Great Deterrent to cope with the dangers of nuclear war has impressive arguments in its favor. First, it seems to have worked in the past. For twenty-five years, the nuclear arsenals of several powers have grown, yet nuclear weapons have not been used again.[46]

> The problem with deterrence is not that it doesn't "work"—it is, I am sure, a very effective (though far from infallible) way of restraining the superpowers from attacking one another should they be inclined to do so—but that we must pay an inconceivable price if it fails.[47]

It is a curious paradox of our time that one of the foremost factors making deterrence really work and work well is the

[44] President Ronald Reagan, address to the nation, March 23, 1983.
[45] Vice-President George Bush, *New York Times*, Nov. 21, 1983.
[46] Fred Charles Iklé, *Every War Must End* (New York: Columbia University Press, 1971), p. 121.
[47] Jonathan Schell, *The New Yorker*, Jan. 9, 1984.

lurking fear that in some massive confrontation crisis it might fail.[48]

Indeed, in the world as it is we might well hesitate even to wish for the abolition of nuclear weapons. For it is the existence of these weapons on both sides that, under circumstances of extreme conflict and strain, has so far prevented the outbreak of a Third World War.[49]

Even opponents of the arms race, including so-called "nuclear pacifists," rarely question this reasoning. But it contains a nonsequitur. That the United States and the Soviet Union have threatened one another with annihilation is incontrovertible. That war between them has not yet broken out is also incontrovertible. But that the second state of affairs obtains because of the first does not follow.[50] To establish that someone has been deterred from doing something requires more than simply showing that he has not done it. It requires explaining *why* he did not do it. One must know, therefore, not only what the other would have done if things had been different but also why he did not do it.

Let us make this clearer by considering exactly what deterrence is.[51]

---

[48] Bernard Brodie, *War and Politics* (New York: The Macmillan Company, 1973), pp. 430-431.

[49] Louis J. Halle, "A Hopeful Future for Mankind," *Foreign Affairs* 58, no. 5 (Summer 1980): 1131. For a more cautious view of the role of deterrence in preventing war, see Nye, *Nuclear Ethics*, p. 61.

[50] Where there seems to be some awareness of this, it is advanced almost as an article of faith that deterrence works. Thus George H. Quester maintains: "The normal justification of deterrence is, of course, the unprovable (but very plausible and probable) proposition that it works, that the number of conventional wars that would have been fought in Europe and elsewhere since 1945, with American and Russian sponsors locked in combat, would have been greater if nuclear weapons had never been invented." See "The Strategy of Deterrence: Is the Concept Credible?" in *Deterrence in the 1980s: Crisis and Dilemma*, ed. R. B. Byers (London: Croom Helm, 1985), p. 77. For a good discussion of this and related issues in understanding the notion of deterrence, see Patrick M. Morgan, *Deterrence: A Conceptual Analysis* (Beverly Hills, Calif., Sage Publications, 1977), particularly chapters one and two.

[51] Some representative characterizations of deterrence are illustrated in the following quotations. "Deterrence is concerned with the exploitation of potential force. It is concerned with persuading a potential enemy that he should in his own interest avoid certain courses of activity." (Schelling, *The Strategy of Conflict*, p. 9). "To be deterred is to prefer the situation which will result from inaction to that which would result from action, when the latter would produce the anticipated consequences—that is, on the level of international relations—the carrying out of implicit or explicit threats." See Raymond Aron, *Peace and War: A Theory of International Relations* (New York: Praeger, 1967), p. 414. "Military deterrence simply means the process of convincing a potential enemy, by the threat of force, that he

Deterrence is the state of deterring or being deterred. One deters someone from doing something, and one is deterred by someone from doing something. To be deterred is to refrain from doing something in order to avoid something else, that something, loosely speaking, being the consequences of what one has refrained from doing. To deter someone is to cause him to refrain from doing something in order to avoid those consequences. But deterrence can be either circumstantial or agential. If I know the ice is thin, that may deter me from skating. It is my knowledge of the circumstances likely to produce the undesired consequence that deters. On the other hand, if *someone* does the deterring, the deterrence is agential. And in that case it may be either intentional or inadvertent. If I overhear you remark that the ice is thin then you have deterred me if I refrain from skating for that reason. But you may have had no intention to deter me, or even been aware that I was deterred. On the other hand, if you know I intend to skate and warn against it, then your deterring of me has been intentional.

This points to another distinction, however, in that deterrence can be either punitive or nonpunitive. If you would in no way be involved in the production of the undesired consequences if I fail to refrain from what you have sought to deter me from doing, the deterrence is nonpunitive; if, for example, I go ahead and skate after your warning, my falling through the ice is no part of anything you have done. But deterrence is punitive if you would knowingly be involved in the production of the undesired consequences if I fail to refrain from doing what you have sought to deter me from doing (and if you would be involved for the purpose of seeing me punished for that failure). Thus, if you threaten to tell the police if I skate where it is prohibited, and report my violation when I ignore the warning, my subsequent apprehension and prosecution is something you have helped to bring about. The deterrence in that case is punitive.

is better off if he does not use military force against you." See Albert Carnesale et al., *Living with Nuclear Weapons* (New York: Bantam Books, 1983), p. 32. "Nuclear powers A and B are mutually deterred from attacking each other if and only if: (i) Each side has the ability, if attacked by the other, to inflict on the attacker sufficient harm to outweigh any conceivable gain to be secured from the attack. (ii) Neither side can rule out that the other might use this ability, if attacked" (Fisher, *Morality and the Bomb*, p. 6). For some perceptive discussions of the shortcomings of the notion of deterrence as an explanatory concept, see Robert Jervis, Richard Ned Lebow, and Janice Gross Stein, *Psychology and Deterrence* (Baltimore: The Johns Hopkins University Press, 1985).

This enables us to say in general that someone has deterred someone else from doing something if and only if, first, he has made it known that if that person does the thing in question certain undesired consequences will follow, and, second, the person has refrained from doing it in order to avoid those consequences. If, in addition, the person doing the deterring would have been involved in the production of those consequences (where they consist of something he does in retaliation or of something he helps to bring about in response), then the deterrence is punitive.

This also shows the importance of distinguishing deterrence from a number of things with which it is sometimes confused. Intentional deterrence is deliberately bringing it about that someone not pursue an intended objective. But there are other ways of doing this. One is *prevention*. I can stop you from doing something by tying your hands or locking you up. But I may succeed equally well by reasoning with you and convincing you not to do it, or by pressuring you or bribing you. That is, *dissuasion, coercion*, and *bribery* are other ways of achieving that objective which may in some circumstances be equally as effective as prevention. Deterrence requires choice on the part of the person deterred. And choice is precisely what one is deprived of in the case of prevention (that is why capital punishment cannot deter those upon whom it is inflicted; killing can prevent someone from doing something, but it cannot deter him). Moreover, punitive deterrence, which is the mode of international deterrence that primarily concerns us, requires an implicit or explicit threat to inflict harm or injury (or more generally some undesired consequence) upon a person if he does what you would deter him from doing. Such a threat need be no part of dissuasion, coercion, or bribery, though it may sometimes be associated with the first two, in which case there may be an element of deterrence in them. Notice that in the case of bribery, dissuasion, and coercion, a choice of yours mediates between what I do and the eventual outcome, your nonperformance of the intended act. This, I say, is important. For like dissuasion and bribery (and sometimes coercion), but unlike prevention, deterrence requires choice on the part of the person deterred. It is always a mediated consequence of what the deterrer does. This means that deterrence can be present in ordinary interpersonal relationships as well as in military matters. It has nothing to do with nuclear warfare per se.

We can now define the relevant sense of deterrence for purposes of understanding the nuclear issue. It is that someone has deterred someone else from doing something if and only if he has threatened something undesired if the person does it and the person has refrained in order to avoid that consequence.

Notice what this means. To know that someone has been deterred from doing something requires knowing both that he has *refrained* from doing it and why he has refrained. The mere fact that I have threatened to do x if you do y and you have not done y does not mean that I have deterred you. Simply not doing something is not to refrain from doing it. I have never attempted to scale the Empire State building. But I have not refrained from doing it. That is because I have never had any inclination to do it. To refrain from doing something is to choose not to do it when you otherwise would have. It is not enough in the case of deterrence even that you refrain *because* of the threat; you must refrain for a specific reason. If I threaten to step on your blue suede shoes if you whistle Dixie, you have refrained if you choose not to do it because of my threat. But if you refrain because a third person dissuades you, then I have not deterred you, even if that person would not have dissuaded you but for my threat. Simply refraining, even if because of the threat, in other words, is not enough. Only if you refrain *in order to avoid* the execution of the threat have you been deterred.

In the case of nuclear deterrence, then, to know whether deterrence has worked over the past several decades would require knowing that but for our threatened retaliation the Soviets would have attacked us and/or that but for their threatened retaliation we would have attacked them.[52] And we simply do not know this.

So far as the Soviets are concerned, it is difficult enough to know what determines their foreign policy in general, considering the secrecy in which those decisions are shrouded; it would be doubly difficult to know what they would have done if circumstances had been different—if, that is, we had not possessed nuclear weapons and threatened to use them if attacked. Nothing in the philosophy of Marxism supports the view that communism will come to ascendancy through national conquest, nor do official statements of

[52] Once again, I mean both implied and expressed threats. As Brodie points out (in this case with regard to tactical nuclear weapons, but with a point applicable to strategic weapons), "[w]e do not need repeatedly to threaten that we will use them in case of attack. We do not need to threaten anything. Their being there is quite enough. (Brodie, *War and Politics*, p. 404). Morgan makes the point with regard to what he calls pure deterrence, that if "the threat of retaliation prevents an attack, then surely the implication is that in the absence of the threat an attack would occur" (*Deterrence: A Conceptual Analysis*, p. 34).

the Soviet government indicate they have ever had any such intention. This leaves, then, only the conduct of Soviet foreign policy as an area in which to look for evidence of such an intention, and there the evidence is negligible. Even if one thinks the Soviet Union is bent upon global conquest rather than the pursuit of national interest and security, that would not show that it ever had or has now an intention to launch a nuclear attack upon us. In fact, if that were its aim, it would have an interest in not devastating and contaminating the very land it hoped to claim. On the other side, if we are to believe the U.S. government, it has never had any intention to attack the Soviet Union. In the absence of such evidence, one cannot conclude that deterrence has "worked" because nuclear war has not yet broken out.

V

But there is a different notion people sometimes have in mind in discussing deterrence, which is suggested by the Schell quotation cited earlier: "[T]he problem with deterrence is not that it doesn't 'work'—it is, I am sure, a very effective . . . way of restraining the superpowers from attacking one another, should they be inclined to."

In this sense (which may or may not be exactly what Schell had in mind), it is unnecessary that one have intended to do the thing in question and have refrained in order to be said to have been deterred; it is enough that he *would have* refrained had he intended or even been inclined to do it.[53] In this looser sense, which I shall call deterrence$_2$, one can be said to have been deterred if he would have been deterred in the first sense had he been going to perform the act, apart from whether he ever was so inclined or is so now. In this sense it might be claimed that both sides in the Cold War have been deterred by nuclear weapons, in that if either *had* in-

[53] When I include inclination here, it should be understood that what is meant is an inclination that would have eventuated in an attempt to launch such an attack; otherwise the alteration of such an inclination would not count as refraining from initiating the attack. One has not *refrained* from doing something unless but for his refraining he would have done it (or, if you like, attempted to do it; he could be prevented from doing it by factors out of his control). That is why one cannot be said to have refrained from using nuclear weapons because of threatened retaliation unless he otherwise would have used those weapons. Morgan's analysis of what he calls general deterrence situations captures one element in what I am calling deterrence$_2$, when he says that in such situations "[r]elations between opponents are such that leaders in at least one would consider resorting to force if the opportunity arose" (*Deterrence: A Conceptual Analysis*, p. 40).

tended to attack the other it would have refrained, which might be true even if deterrence$_1$ has not been in effect.

This looser sense of deterrence might be put by saying that you have deterred someone from doing something if and only if you have threatened retaliation if he does it, the person has not done it, and he *would have* refrained from doing it if he had intended to do it.

But as initially plausible as this might seem, it would stretch the notion of deterrence out of all reasonable proportion. Every possible act that one does not perform but that he would have refrained from performing (in order to avoid the consequences thereof) had he been inclined to, including countless acts one has never thought of, one would be said to have been deterred from performing. Suppose someone is obsessed with lawn care and wants to insure that a neighbor does not cross his lawn, despite the fact that in ten years the neighbor has never shown the slightest inclination to do so. To that end he stakes a vicious dog in the yard. Predictably, the neighbor does not cross the lawn. Has he been deterred? Clearly not in the sense of deterrence$_1$; the necessary intent is absent. Almost certainly in the sense of deterrence$_2$ for if it *had* entered his mind to cross the lawn he almost certainly would have refrained. The point is that to establish deterrence$_2$ is to establish very little indeed. There are innumerable things each of us may never have had the slightest inclination to do (like leaping from the Matterhorn or trying to swim the Atlantic) but that we would have refrained from doing had it ever crossed our minds to do them. And while it is not conceptually vacuous to speak of deterrence in these cases, it is devoid of practical significance to do so in the absence of reason to believe that but for the probable consequences we would have seriously considered doing them. In other words, to establish deterrence$_2$ *simpliciter* is to establish something of monumental inconsequence.

Deterrence$_2$ might be of considerable significance, however, if there is reason to believe that but for the probable consequences the agent in question would have performed the act in question. Or, to turn the matter around so as to bring it in line with intentional deterrence, understanding that significance requires specifying precisely what one has refrained from doing as a result of the threat (one cannot be said to have been deterred in any sense unless there is something he has refrained from doing). In the nuclear case the act deterred cannot be, as it was for deterrence$_1$, initiating a nuclear attack. Otherwise there would have to have been an intention to attack that was altered in light of the threatened retaliation, and deterrence$_2$ (in referring to what *would* have been the case if there had been the appropriate intention) implies that this was absent.

What deterrence$_2$ might have deterred, however, is the *consideration* by either side of the possibility of launching an attack (or the further consideration if it had already considered it at the time the deterrent threat was made).[54] So to give even minimal plausibility to deterrence$_2$ we need to add that the agent has refrained from considering (or further considering) performing the act in question because of the deterrer's threat.

Whether or not deterrence has worked in this sense would, of course, require knowledge of thoughts and intentions that would normally be as inaccessible as in the case of deterrence$_1$, possibly even more so. Do we have the requisite evidence? Even assuming that if either side had been tempted to attack it would not have done so, is there reason to believe that each has been deterred from even seriously considering such an attack?

I am unaware of any such evidence, though there may be some. There was some consideration of initiating nuclear war against the Soviet Union during the 1950s when it as yet had no significant nuclear arsenal. Certainly if Bertrand Russell could seriously have mentioned such a possibility[55] it is not unlikely that the thought crossed the minds of government leaders. And if either or both had considered a first-strike, whether they have been deterred from further considering one is difficult to say, and in fact it seems unlikely that they have. To have been deterred from *considering* the possibility of a first-strike, each would have to have refrained in order to avoid the consequences of such consideration. But there are no deleterious consequences of considering an attack.[56] The

---

[54] A person might be undecided as to whether to perform an act. If then you threaten to punish him if he does, and he, for that reason, decides not to do it, one could not say, strictly, that he would have performed it but for your threat; even he may not know for certain what he eventually would have decided. In that case, we would not know whether he had been deterred. Strictly speaking, he has been deterred from further considering the possibility of performing the act, not from performing it.

[55] Though he later explained that he recommended threatening war in the belief that the Soviets would yield to Western demands. See his *Common Sense and Nuclear Warfare* (New York: Simon and Schuster, 1959), app. II, and *The Autobiography of Bertrand Russell*, vol. 3 1944-1969 (New York: Simon and Schuster, 1969), pp. 7-8.

[56] At least there are none so long as it is not known that one is considering it. If one assumed that serious consideration of a first-strike was likely to become known to the other side, and that such knowledge might prompt it to consider a preemptive strike, that might lead him to refrain from such consideration; for then the

deterrent threat is against an *attack*, not against consideration thereof. Neither side threatens to do anything if the other side only considers an attack. So, if either side has refrained from considering a first-strike, it probably has done so because of the pointlessness of considering it in the absence of any inclination actually to launch it, rather than from fear of the consequences of considering it. And if each side's nuclear arsenal is (or were) meant as a deterrent, then there would be no such inclination in the first place. In that event, the fact that each has refrained from considering a first-strike (and we do not know this to be true) would not mean that each had been deterred from such consideration. Nor would it mean that their refraining had even significantly diminished the probability of nuclear war by deliberate attack, since that probability, on this hypothesis, would have been close to zero in the first place.

But if I am wrong in this, and either side *has* considered (or is considering) a first-strike, then it obviously has not been deterred from doing so, in which case deterrence₂ has failed. It would seem, then, that if either side has refrained from seriously considering a nuclear attack, it has likely done so for reasons other than fear of retaliation for considering it, in which case its refraining was not a case of its having been deterred; and if it has *not* refrained for this reason, then deterrence₂ has not worked. So, just as it is possible that deterrence₁ has worked, it is possible that deterrence₂ has worked; but in neither case do we know that to be true, and in the second case it seems likely that it is false.

We may not even know if deterrence in either of these senses fails. In fact, deterrence₂, if ever it was in effect, may already have failed. Failure of deterrence₂, remember, does not signify that the missiles have been launched; it consists only of at least one side's seriously considering a first-strike. And while the side responsible for any such failure will know if that has happened, the other side

---

preparations by the other side would be among the mediated consequences of his own consideration of an attack, and he would surely prefer to avoid those consequences. In that case, one would have been deterred not by a declaratory threat but by knowledge of the likely consequences of his act in the circumstances, which would make the deterrence circumstantial. This would point up a flaw in the system of deterrence, however. For it would mean that the side considering the attack believes that if it could achieve complete surprise the attack might well be worth launching. But it could believe that only if it is undeterred by the prospect of retaliation, and if fear of retaliation does not deter an attack, deterrence₁ is not working, whether or not war occurs.

may not.[57] In the case of deterrence$_1$, we will assuredly know if a nuclear war occurs, and most people assume that would signify the failure of deterrence$_1$. But it might not. Since, as I shall point out below, a nuclear war may start for reasons other than a deliberate decision to strike first, even the onset of a nuclear war would not show conclusively that deterrence$_1$ had failed.

It is, in other words, one thing for a system of deterrence to have been in effect, another for it to have worked, and yet another for it to have failed. We have no problem in the case of deterrence$_1$ in knowing that the system has been in effect; the threats are real, and the means by which to carry them out are known. Matters are less clear in the case of deterrence$_2$. But assuming that both have been in effect, we do not know that either of them has worked, and in the case of deterrence$_2$, we do not know but what it may already have failed.

VI

Still, some may say, even if we do not know that deterrence has worked, it *may* have worked, and may have avoided war for all those years, and is it not worth it for that reason alone? Considering the calamity that a nuclear war would represent, is it not worth maintaining our deterrent forces if there is even a chance that it will prevent such a war? This expresses an understandable concern. For it certainly is true that, the scarcity of evidence notwithstanding, deterrence may have worked in the past.

But suppose it could be shown that nuclear deterrence (by which I shall henceforth mean deterrence$_1$, the more usual of the two notions) has in fact worked. Would that be good reason to believe that it will continue to do so in the future?

It is worth noting at the outset that estimates of the effectiveness of conventional deterrence throughout history do not lend much support to the idea that nuclear deterrence, if it has worked, will continue to do so indefinitely. Those estimates show that militarily weaker powers repeatedly have attacked militarily stronger powers.[58] If I am correct in my analysis of deterrence, of course, one

[57] Some persons in the Soviet government may know whether it has worked over the years on their side and the same with some present or past members of the U.S. government; but it is unlikely that any one person has that knowledge about both sides, which is necessary to knowing whether the system has worked.

[58] As Kissinger observes, "[T]he frequency of warfare since the Middle Ages demonstrates the difficulty of achieving deterrence with conventional weapons alone." See "Limited War: Conventional or Nuclear? A Reappraisal," in *Arms Con-*

would need to show considerably more than this to show that deterrence had failed. In the absence of the requisite counterfactual knowledge, establishing that deterrence had been in effect in the first place (which is required whether the deterrence be nuclear or conventional), the most one could conclude is that such empirical studies establish a necessary condition of knowing that deterrence has failed. Nonetheless, even a cursory review of the historical evidence provides little basis for optimism that military deterrence works very often or for very long at all. In fact, sometimes the very circumstances constituting the supposed deterrent actually provide an incentive to wage war. I shall maintain that the same may very well be true of nuclear deterrence.

But, that aside, suppose deterrence has worked. Will it continue to do so?

The time frame in which nuclear weapons have been around has been too short to warrant much confidence in such a judgment. It was not until somewhere between 1965 and 1975 that the Soviets had a significant nuclear capability to strike the continental United States. Before that mutual deterrence by threat of massive retaliation was not even a possibility. Kahn has even argued that U.S. nuclear weapons probably were not a deterrent in the 1940s and 1950s when we enjoyed a monopoly of them.[59] And historian Barton Bernstein has indicated that one reason nuclear weapons were

---

trol, Disarmament, and National Security, ed. Donald G. Brennan (New York: George Braziller, 1961), p. 142. In line with this, anthropologist Raoul Naroll reports on a pilot study to determine the effectiveness of military deterrence, choosing twenty historical periods "covering several civilizations, thousands of years, and hundreds of countries." For each period one decade was randomly chosen, and for each decade it was asked whether the leading nation was stronger than its leading rival and whether it wanted to avoid war, the expectation being that when both of these conditions were met, one would find less war. But that was not the case. In fact, satisfaction of these two conditions made no difference at all. "Three times," he reports, "our random sample picked up great powers fighting long wars with weaker rivals, wars the stronger did not want. England against France, 1776-1785, Spain against the Dutch, 1576-1585, China against Tibet, 776-785." These, he says, were as many times as deterrence seems to have worked (New York Times, Aug. 1, 1975). A still more recent study maintains that conventional deterrence is likely to fail if one side has the capacity to wage blitzkrieg warfare, and argues that it has in fact failed repeatedly in the twentieth century, from Germany's initiation of World War II to the 1956 and 1967 wars in the Middle East. See John J. Mearsheimer, Conventional Deterrence (Ithaca, N.Y.: Cornell University Press, 1983). Others have pointed out that Japan attacked a militarily superior power in initiating war against the United States in 1941, as did Egypt in attacking Israel in 1973. See Jervis et al., Psychology and Deterrence.

[59] "Strategy, Foreign Policy, and Thermonuclear War," in America Armed: Essays on United States Military Policy, ed. Robert A. Goldwin (Chicago: Rand McNally & Company, 1961), p. 45.

not used by the United States in Korea was the fear that their use might bring the Soviet Union into the war—this at a time when the Soviets did not yet have a significant nuclear capability.[60] There has, moreover, been a proliferation of nuclear weapons and capabilities. The Stockholm International Peace Research Institute contends that before the end of the century more than thirty-five nations are likely to have a nuclear capability. When that happens (and given, what seems clear, that without new direction the nations of the world will continue to resort to war against each other) nuclear war will be virtually inevitable; not necessarily between the superpowers, and not necessarily a large-scale nuclear war, but one that will very likely eventually involve the superpowers. That the superpowers, with their growing worldwide entanglements, would long be able to stay removed from such conflicts is doubtful.

Beyond this, there have been shifts in nuclear strategy that cast doubt upon whether deterrence, even if effective in the past, could be expected to work in the future. As noted, in the early years of the nuclear age it was believed that both the United States and the Soviet Union could inflict such devastation upon one another that neither would dare launch an attack. But the worry developed that the Soviets would exploit this situation other than by outright attack; specifically through subversion and takeovers under the guise of wars of national liberation. Kissinger had warned as early as 1957 in *Nuclear Weapons and Foreign Policy* that the Communists would nibble us to death unless we found some mode of response between acquiescence and all-out nuclear war. Confinement to those options would result in a paralysis of our will.

Two proposed answers emerged to this problem, even before the Soviet Union possessed anything like the U.S. nuclear capability.

One answer was given by Kahn, who argued that the United States should be prepared not only to retaliate if attacked but also to initiate a nuclear attack under some circumstances. Otherwise the Soviets might "manipulate our fear" of nuclear war to their advantage—precisely the concern expressed by Kissinger. This fear of being perceived as weak and afraid is a strong one. Policy makers continually try to avoid being maneuvered into positions in which they are forced to choose between all-out war and acceding to Soviet demands over relatively minor issues; for in such sit-

[60] "New Light on the Korean War," *The International History Review* 3, no. 2 (April 1981): 262.

uations accommodation will always seem to be preferable to nuclear war. Even in the Cuban missile crisis, as it turned out twenty-five years later, President Kennedy was prepared to make a major concession to the Soviets by withdrawing U.S. missiles from Turkey in exchange for the withdrawal of Soviet missiles from Cuba in order to avoid war. Kahn's proposal grows out of his apparent conviction that nuclear deterrence not only might fail (as he urges against the naive and unrealistic) but also (as he might well urge against the squeamish) that in some circumstances it should fail; that in some circumstances we should be prepared to initiate a nuclear war ourselves. The worst of all situations, he says, would be that in which we had not made preparations for the failure of deterrence and the Soviets provoked us and we were forced to initiate a war in retaliation. "Long before the day of crisis, and peace-loving as most of us are, we must understand that unless we have confidence in our ability to initiate and terminate a war under some "reasonable" conditions, the Russians can with safety do almost anything they want in the way of preparations to launch an attack."[61] Iron-clad deterrence would be equivalent to a de facto "nonaggression treaty" with the Soviets, and Kahn thinks this would be undesirable. This means that the balance of terror should not be too reliable or too stable; in short, it should not be a balance at all but should be tipped in our favor.

Notice the implications of this. For deterrence to work, there must be a balance of terror; both sides must fear a nuclear war, if not to exactly the same degree at least to approximately the same degree. Moreover, in order for this balance to be effective, it must be stable. To achieve a balance of terror for a few months or even a few years would be inconsequential if in the end it fails. In order for stability to be achieved, moreover, there must be a high degree of certainty on each side, where this encompasses both specificity (knowledge of at least the sorts of situations in which the other side is prepared to attack) and credibility (believability of the threats on each side). Otherwise neither side will know under what circumstances the other is likely to use nuclear weapons.

Kahn advocates a policy that has uncertainty deliberately built into it. This uncertainty is supposed to work to the U.S. advantage by holding open the possibility that we *might* strike first, that we *might* not act rationally.[62] This is supposed to enable us to seize the

---

[61] *On Thermonuclear War*, p. 214.

[62] Thomas C. Schelling makes much the same point when he says: "Another paradox of deterrence is that it does not always help to be, or to be believed to be,

initiative from the Soviets. But its effect would ultimately be to undercut deterrence. The strategy is not one of mutual deterrence at all but of what we might call preferential deterrence—attempting to deter the enemy without being deterred oneself. The aim is to achieve preferential stability, in which neither side in fact uses nuclear weapons, not because both are deterred but because one side is deterred and the other simply elects not to use them, counting on achieving its objectives without their use. This, of course, is precisely the strategy that Kahn and Kissinger ascribed to the Soviets.

There are two questions for any theory of deterrence: (1) who is supposedly deterred? and (2) deterred from what? Mutual deterrence theory answers the first question by saying that both sides are deterred and the second by saying that they are deterred from launching a first-strike. Preferential deterrence theory says, on the other hand, that it is the "other" side that is deterred and deterred not only from a first-strike but also from various other sorts of actions that the undeterred side presumes to define. This means that according to preferential deterrence theory there is no balance of terror and is not intended to be. The aim is to direct the inhibitory power of nuclear weapons against the other side in a way that allows one's own side to gain the advantage. To the extent that both sides attempt to achieve this position, what passes for mutual deterrence is in actuality preferential deterrence, which in principle is unstable.

If one combines a willingness to launch a first-strike with the maintenance of uncertainty in the enemy, he has a volatile mixture—doubly so if both sides hold this view, since then each holds open the possibility of a first-strike and knows that the other does also. This means that you may give the impression of saying to an enemy not only that if he engages in certain provocations you may strike first but also that if he interferes with various of your initiatives you may strike first anyway. One suspects that whether we are talking about a balance of power in general, or a balance of terror in particular, most nations, their protestations to the contrary notwithstanding, really do not favor such a balance so much as they favor some form of preferential deterrence in which they have the advantage.

The other proposed answer to the problem by Kissinger, as we

fully rational, cool-headed, and in control of oneself or of one's country." See *Arms and Influence* (New Haven, Conn.: Yale University Press, 1966), p. 37.

saw in Chapter Two, was presumed to lie in the development of a capability for limited war in order to provide us with flexibility. Though Kissinger speaks of the possibility of limited nuclear war, the first priority came to be to develop a capability for limited conventional war. The West, in Raymond Aron's words, was to wield the conventional sword beneath the nuclear shield.

This the United States did in Vietnam. And the results were disastrous. Partly because of the duration of the war, partly because of the number of casualties, and partly because of heightened awareness of the reality of the war through television coverage, most Americans showed little conviction that the stakes were such as to warrant that kind of commitment. Domestic support for the war eroded, and America's fighting role ended in 1973.

There were predictions that if the United States met defeat in Vietnam that might lead to emphasis in the future upon tactical nuclear weapons rather than manpower, as in Vietnam. This would add even greater flexibility to America's war-fighting potential. Intimations in the Nixon Doctrine of greater emphasis upon tactical nuclear weapons in American Asian policy fit with such an idea. Just as a limited (conventional) war capability was sold as insurance against having to use nuclear weapons, so tactical nuclear weapons may also have looked attractive not only as an alternative to strategic weapons but also as an alternative to massive commitments of ground troops as in Korea and Vietnam. Whether or not they will be so used in future conflicts not involving the Soviet Union remains to be seen.

But another dimension of flexibility has clearly become a part of U.S. policy. That is the targeting of military and command installations, not just, or perhaps even primarily, urban areas, in the event of nuclear war with the Soviet Union. There was always theoretically the possibility of a limited nuclear war in the sense that each side could limit the number of cities it destroyed. With the option of not targeting cities, yet another type of limited nuclear war would be possible.[63]

This had a certain humanitarian appeal. All things being equal, given the choice between destroying cities and destroying military targets the moral course seemed to many clear. Moralists and theologians debated the ethics of using nuclear weapons against cities as opposed to using them against enemy forces (countervalue ver-

[63] It is not, of course, possible to target military installations without destroying cities, since many military installations are in or around cities.

253

sus counterforce strategies). In 1970 President Nixon put the question to Congress: "Should a President in the event of a nuclear attack," he asked, "be left with the single option of ordering the mass destruction of enemy civilians, in the face of the certainty that it would be followed by the mass slaughter of Americans?" This issue had been raised in the early 1960s, and it seemed resolved in 1974 when Defense Secretary Schlesinger indicated that we would no longer rely exclusively upon massive retaliation. But it was not until 1980, after two decades of simmering, that the issue was resolved conclusively by the Carter administration. Presidential Directive Fifty-Nine made clear that U.S. policy would henceforth include development of a capacity for limited nuclear war.[64] The targeting of missile sites and command posts was to be stressed in addition to the targeting of cities.

When one looks beyond the humanitarian gloss covering this, it is clear that it represents a decision to develop what has all the appearance of a first-strike capability. With the development of the MIRV (Multiple Independently Targetable Re-entry Vehicle) system in the early 1970s it was assumed by some that the shift in policy had already quietly taken place. But whether this development represents a first-strike capability or merely a strengthened retaliatory capacity, it is intentions alone that make it what it is. It is perceptions, as I have said, that determine how people respond to situations, and the Soviets have said they believe we are developing a first-strike capability.

And one can well see why they might. The United States has repeatedly refused to renounce a possible first-use of nuclear weapons. It has been made clear that it might resort to nuclear

[64] There is considerable disagreement as to the exact chronology of the evolution of U.S. strategic policy. The Stockholm International Peace Research Institute, for example, sees U.S. policy as based primarily upon mutual assured destruction (MAD) until 1973, with increasing emphasis upon counterforce capabilities thereafter. See *Armaments and Disarmament in the Nuclear Age* (Atlantic Highlands, N.J.: Humanities Press, 1976), chap. 2. On the other hand, Robert C. Aldridge suggests that "counterforce has been the Pentagon's clandestine military doctrine since at least the 1950s, even when the announced policy has been deterrence." See *The Counterforce Syndrome: A Guide to U.S. Nuclear Weapons and Strategic Doctrine* (Washington, D.C.: Institute for Policy Studies, 1978), p. 4. Colin Gray sees counterforce targeting rising to "official prominence" in the period 1961 to 1965 in *Strategic Studies and Public Policy*, chap. 8. Albert Carnesale et al. maintain that U.S. nuclear weapons were targeted primarily against Soviet military forces throughout the 1960s, despite a declaratory policy that increasingly emphasized assured destruction, and contend that the era of MAD arrived at the end of that decade (*Living with Nuclear Weapons*, chap. 4).

weapons if necessary to repel a Soviet attack upon NATO.[65] Kennedy, moreover, hinted that we might use strategic nuclear weapons for a first-strike against the Soviet Union during a radio and television address during the Cuban missile crises, saying that "it shall be the policy of this nation to regard any nuclear missile launched from Cuba against any nation in the Western Hemisphere as an attack by the Soviet Union on the United States, requiring a full retaliatory response upon the Soviet Union."[66] Moreover, President Reagan's Strategic Defense Initiative, or so-called "Star Wars" proposal of March 23, 1983, contributed to Soviet fears. The idea of a defense system that would intercept and destroy Soviet missiles seemed contrary to the very principle of deterrence, which was supposed to provide an alternative to defense.[67] And it is indisputable that if one side has the capability to nullify the effectiveness of the other's strategic nuclear arsenal, that side has an enormously expanded potential to attack the other with relative impunity.

[65] While it is almost universally assumed among analysts that this is necessary to deter an attack upon NATO, Douglas Lackey has challenged this reasoning: "The main funcion [sic] of NATO nuclear weapons is to deter Soviet attack with the threat of escalation to nuclear war. If the Soviets launch a conventional attack on Western Europe, NATO nuclear weapons will have failed to achieve their primary purpose. Nor does it seem likely that they will achieve their secondary purpose of preventing Soviet conquest once the Soviet invasion begins. Should NATO use nuclear weapons against a Soviet conventional attack, the Soviets can reply with their own battlefield nuclear weapons. . . . The use of tactical nuclear weapons cannot save Western Europe from conquest, except in the sense that it will make parts of Western Europe not worth conquering. Thus, it hardly seems that NATO use of nuclear weapons in these circumstances will do more good than harm" (Moral Principles and Nuclear Weapons, p. 173).

[66] Dept. State Bull. 715-718 (1962). Quoted in William W. Bishop, Jr., ed., International Law: Cases and Materials, 3d ed. (Boston: Little, Brown and Company, 1971), p. 927.

[67] It is not altogether clear what the relationship of the Strategic Defense Initiative is supposed to be to the theory of deterrence. When President Reagan spoke in 1983 of "rendering these nuclear weapons impotent and obsolete" as part of the SDI proposal, it sounded as though SDI was intended to replace deterrence. But a subsequent White House Paper, "The President's Strategic Defense Initiative," represented the purpose of SDI as to provide "a better, more stable basis for enhanced deterrence." See The Nuclear Predicament: A Sourcebook, ed. Donna Uthus Gregory (New York: St. Martin's Press, 1986), pp. 215-224. Then Caspar Weinberger, in an October 1985 speech, accused the Soviets of already having abandoned deterrence based upon mutual assured destruction and seemed to imply that SDI, in removing the threat of mutual destruction, was an alternative to deterrence (New York Times, Oct. 4, 1985). In any event, insofar as deterrence was once, or is now, thought of as an alternative to defense, SDI represents at the least a serious modification of that view. For an argument on behalf of a "defensive deterrent" see Colin S. Gray and Keith B. Payne, "Nuclear Policy and the Defensive Transition," Foreign Affairs 62, no. 4 (Spring 1984): 820-842.

What this means, of course, is that in a piecemeal and somewhat roundabout way, the United States came to adopt a position that but for stated intentions, is virtually what Kahn had recommended twenty years previously. It is a policy that if successfully implemented would *in fact* give the United States a first-strike capability against the Soviet Union. Whether that is, has been, or would ever become the use to which the U.S. government would put it is immaterial to its effect upon the system of deterrence.[68] It is *perceptions*, once again, that determine how each side responds to the other. And if the Soviets believe we are seeking a first-strike capability, the consequence so far as their behavior is concerned will be exactly identical to what they would be if we were in fact seeking such a capability. And it is the beliefs and behavior of each side, not the actual facts, that determine whether deterrence (still assuming that it has worked in the past) will continue to work in the future.

The point is that once either side believes—correctly or not—that the other has a first-strike capability, a capacity to strike first and inflict such devastation as to be able to win a nuclear war, the very foundation of deterrence collapses; there is no longer a balance of terror. Some in the United States believe the Soviets already have or are seeking a first-strike capability;[69] the Soviets, who view our intentions as darkly as we do theirs, believe the same of us. Even on the assumption that deterrence has worked in the past, only the naivest of optimists can believe it will work indefinitely in the future.

VII

Suppose that even this is incorrect, however. Suppose not only that deterrence has worked in the past but also that it can be pre-

[68] Although this would seem to be the use that strategists Gray and Payne have in mind when they say: "There should be no misunderstanding the fact that the primary interest of U.S. strategy is deterrence. However, American strategic forces do not exist solely for the purpose of deterring a Soviet nuclear threat or attack against the United States itself. Instead, they are intended to support U.S. foreign policy. . . . Such a function requires American strategic forces that would enable a president to initiate strategic nuclear use for coercive, though politically defensive, purposes." Colin S. Gray and Keith Payne, "Victory is Possible," in Gregory, ed., *The Nuclear Predicament*, p. 119; reprinted from *Foreign Policy* 39 (Summer 1980): 14-27.

[69] Defense Secretary Weinberger asserted this in his 1985 speech. *New York Times*, Oct. 4, 1985.

sumed to work in the future. Would this guarantee, as is almost universally assumed, that we will avoid nuclear war? It would not.

Deterrence, even if 100 percent effective, deals with only one of the ways in which nuclear war might start, namely, by a deliberate first-strike. To avoid war one must deal with all of the ways.[70] *And it is the system of deterrence itself which increases the probability that war will begin in one of these other ways, specifically through miscalculation or accident.*

Consider that the other side of the deterrent coin is that whatever deterrent value nuclear weapons are assumed to have, they also serve as a provocation, increasing the fear that their possessor will use them to initiate an attack, and thereby increasing the likelihood that an adversary will seek to counteract that threat by acquiring a deterrent of the same or greater magnitude. That is, whatever deterrent value nuclear weapons may have is offset by their provocation value.[71] Weapons designed to deter, if perceived by an adversary not as a deterrent but as a threat to his own security, will provoke him to increase his armaments and thus intensify suspicions that he is indeed providing himself with the first-strike capability that the weapons are meant to deter. The response by the initial deterrer will predictably be the same in order to strengthen his deterrent against the perceived threat by the other. As each responds in kind, the result is a never-ending escalation of threats. With rising tensions and decreasing margin of error entailed by advances in technology, the risk increases that one side will eventually take precisely the action each wants to deter in the belief that it is necessary to preempt the attack it perceives in the other's threat; either that, or that through computer or human error it will attack in the mistaken belief that it is retaliating against an attack already begun by the other side. In the spiraling arms race we have, I suggest, better evidence that nuclear weapons are effective as a provocation than we have that they are effective as a deterrent.

[70] For a good discussion of closely related issues, see Janice Gross Stein, "Deterrence in the 1980s: A Political and Contextual Analysis," in Byers, ed., *Deterrence in the 1980s*, chap. 2.

[71] Indeed, some experts speculate that the United States would like to provoke the Soviet Union into an accelerated arms race in the belief that it cannot support such a race economically and that by such means the United States can exploit growing weaknesses in the so-called "Soviet Empire." The Soviets, in any event, seem to believe that this is the U.S. aim. In a televised address to the Soviet people on October 14, 1986, Mikhail Gorbachev said that the "United States wants to exhaust the Soviet Union economically through the buildup of sophisticated and costly space weapons." *Soviet Life*, Dec. 1986.

Equally importantly, with the proliferation of nuclear weapons there is increasing risk of war through accident. The likelihood of a nuclear bomb's accidentally exploding is small. The chances of a nuclear war's starting over an accidental detonation is no doubt smaller. But over time the likelihood increases. It has been estimated that the chances of a nuclear weapon's exploding accidentally before the year 2000 may be as high as three in five, based on an assumed one in a million probability that one will explode accidentally in a given year. And that represents only a calculation for the near future. If our concern is for posterity as well as ourselves, we must look at the long run as well as the short run. In any event, as between accident and miscalculation, the chances are vastly greater that an unintended war will begin through misjudgment. The experts insist that *because* nuclear weapons are so terrible they will not be used and *because* no rational person would start a nuclear war there will not be one. But history is one long record of man's misjudgment and of the eventual use of weapons once thought too terrible to be used. It never happens that both sides win in war; hence in nearly every war—and there have been an estimated three thousand of them in history—at least one side has miscalculated. Here, unlike in the case of deterrence, the evidence is clear. And it inspires little confidence that today's leaders can do any better.

Thus even if, contrary to my earlier argument, it could be shown that deterrence has worked thus far, it does not follow that it will avoid war in the future. Even if it should be true that had either side been tempted to attack it would have refrained because of threatened retaliation, the very circumstances rendering that true would have increased the probability that at some point, whether through miscalculation or computer error, one side or the other will come to believe that the other has either launched an attack or is about to and believing that will launch its own weapons. That can happen even if deterrence has provided an iron-clad safeguard against a deliberate unprovoked first-strike by either side. One cannot assume that if deterrence "works," it prevents war. It can both work and *cause* war.

To assume, moreover, that but for deterrence (by which I mean the system of deterrence—the possession, deployment, and willingness to use nuclear weapons by both sides) nuclear war might have occurred or might occur in the future is unintelligible. But for deterrence a nuclear war *could not* occur; it is the possession, deployment, and willingness to use those weapons that makes nuclear war possible. It could not even conceivably occur otherwise (it could not, strictly speaking, even occur if only one side possessed such weapons, since that would make possible only a unilateral attack, not a nuclear war). Not only is it not true, then, that but for deterrence a nuclear war might have occurred; it is the case that but for deterrence a nuclear war could not have occurred. One cannot justify deterrence on the grounds that it minimizes the risk of war created by the system of deterrence itself.

The upshot is that the theory of nuclear deterrence, far from being one of the great advances of our time, and despite the fact that it is the cornerstone of U.S. policy and the subject of countless earnest and learned studies by scholars and strategists alike, is so little understood in its conceptual foundations and so thoroughly confused in its implementation as to be practically useless from the standpoint of the rational, not to mention moral, guidance of policy. It may, in fact, ultimately prove disastrous. The mode of warfare for which the superpowers have prepared themselves fails to provide even a rational approach to the avoidance of war. If nuclear war is irrational and we intend to live as sane and rational beings, we must refuse to engage in it. Not if others do, not after treaties and agreements, not at some time in the future. But now. It must cease to be in our repertoire of possible responses to international conflict.

E I G H T

THE ALTERNATIVE TO WAR

No effort in this world
is lost or wasted.
—*Bhagavad Gita*

The problem is not ultimately with nuclear weapons. The problem is with the belief that security can be achieved through armaments. So long as this belief is clung to, the limitation, reduction, and even elimination of nuclear weapons—as desirable as that would be—will not solve our problems.

We turn to armaments for national security. But what is it that we are trying to preserve? What constitutes security?

John Stuart Mill characterized security as a higher-order interest, present when the essentials of well-being are adequately protected. We should consider this carefully. We have become accustomed to identifying security with the preservation of the state, often with the preservation of a specific form of government or even a particular government itself. Partly we are led to this, as we saw in our discussion of political realism, through language—the fact that we speak of states as though they were living organisms, acting, choosing, coming into being, and going out of existence. Partly we are led to it through the misidentification of government with a country or people. But states are simply abstractions; there actually exist only human beings organized in various ways, with different institutions, values, customs, and traditions. It is their lives, their well-being and happiness that is important, not the "lives" of states. The latter have value only insofar as they contribute to the former.

There are two kinds of ethics operating here. What I shall call macroscopic ethics takes the ultimate concern of ethics to be with the survival and well-being of abstract or collective entities—states, countries, religions, classes, etc. Microscopic ethics takes the ultimate concern to be with the survival and well-being of living, conscious, sentient beings—persons and perhaps animals.

260

These concerns are not exclusive, of course. Micro ethics can have a regard for the survival of states and other collectivities insofar as that is important to the survival and well-being of individuals, and macro ethics can have a concern with individual persons insofar as they are important to the survival of the collectivity—as indeed the survival of at least some persons invariably is. But in each case this other concern is secondary. When there is a conflict between the survival of the principal object of concern and that of the object of the secondary concern, it is the former that takes precedence.

In the preponderance of cases macro ethics supercedes micro ethics. That this should be so is built into some of the leading social and political philosophies. It is found in Treitschke, who regards the state as an actual person, whose "ethical health," as Hegel characterized it, takes precedence over the lives and well-being of individual persons; it is found in fascism, with its view that the state or the nation is supreme (Italian Fascists emphasizing the state, Nazis the nation), overriding the individual in cases of conflict between their two interests; and it is found in at least some versions of Marxism that would subordinate individual interests to the collective interest of the working class. There is even a strong whiff of it in John F. Kennedy's rhetorical flourish: "Ask not what your country can do for you; ask what you can do for your country."

When one speaks of self-defense on the international scene the concern is with the defense of the state; it is *its* security that is deemed paramount, *its* survival that must be ensured at all costs. And when a state goes to war it is usually to punish what is perceived, or at least represented, as aggression by another *state*. This is why it is easy to kill countless persons in warfare, including, as we have seen, innocent persons. Instead of focussing upon the reality of warfare, which is the killing of human beings, one concentrates upon the interaction of collectivities, struggling like the Homeric gods on the world's battlefields. We think we are punishing *an* aggressor, a single, self-willed, personified being. It is the *state* that stands tall in the face of threats from evildoers. Notions like self-defense and security, which derive their significance from interpersonal relations, are carried over to the macro level as though they had precisely the same significance there, which they do not.

American leaders say from time to time that Americans have no quarrel with the Soviet people, only with their leaders. Soviet leaders express similar sentiments about the American people. Yet it is the *people* on both sides that the governments are prepared to annihilate; people who, as the governments' own characterizations imply, are innocent. We have no quarrel with them, each says, yet it is they we will destroy if need be in our quarrel with their leaders.

Moral considerations aside, if one's quarrel is with the leadership of a country, and one believes in the use of violence, the more rational course would be to engage in selective assassinations— something that with the marvels of modern science and technology governments could almost certainly do more easiy and less expensively than by pitting armies against armies. It would, moreover, force government leaders to bear directly the major risk for their policies, which today they do not. It might even cause them to be a shade more careful in the setting of those policies. As it is, government leaders stand the least chance of being killed in the event of war, since they do not do the fighting and have their hideaways to enable them to maintain command even if the rest of the country is devastated.

There is nothing of intrinsic value in government. Its sole value lies in contributing to the preservation and enhancement of the lives of individual persons. If it can do this on balance better than people could do it themselves by means of voluntary associations, and without inflicting a morally intolerable cost upon others, and if it is, moreover, something that people choose for themselves, then it is justified. If it cannot, then it is not. But *its* preservation and security understood in any other terms is not worth a single human life. Governments of the major nations of the world today no longer promote the security of individual persons; that is, they do not protect the essentials of well-being. Where they are not themselves a direct threat to individual security through economic and political oppression, their commitment to weapons of mass destruction for national defense creates a world situation that threatens the security of everyone.

While this is easy to see of other countries—Soviets can see it of Americans, for example, and Americans of Soviets—it is psychologically difficult to see of one's own. People identify with their country, as we have seen, and tend to identify the country with the government, at least to the extent of thinking that loyalty to the former entails loyalty to the latter. No offense is deemed more heinous and punished more swiftly than attempting to overthrow the government, as though that were *by itself* a threat to the country and people. A change in government often means a change in a way of life of a people. But it need not do so and can be effected without interrupting the rhythm of everyday life. When security is identified with the preservation of the state, people come to regard it as the highest of virtues to sacrifice their own interests, including, if necessary, their lives, for its preservation, not noticing that in the process their own security and that of others like them—the only thing worth preserving—has utterly vanished. Political leaders in both democratic and totalitarian states encourage them to do so. They are the high priests of this collective idolatry. It enables them to harness the energy of patriotism in the service of virtually whatever causes they choose. They need only represent those causes as furthering the interests of the state (or the nation or the proletariat or whatever is taken to be the relevant collectivity) and people will sacrifice themselves by the thousands for them as well as inflict untold destruction upon others.

The greatest threats to security are often the least visible to the naked eye. A pack of wolves loose in the streets would cause great alarm; television crews would be out and the newspapers would run headlines. But the threat would be a minor one compared with the threat of war. On the other hand, a country can be armed to the teeth with nuclear weapons and that fact rarely penetrates one's consciousness. The B-52s fly too high to be seen or heard; the missiles are hidden in underground silos; and the submarines prowl out of sight beneath the sea. Relatively few people have ever so much as seen a nuclear bomb. The ordinary person in both the United States and the Soviet Union is surrounded by destructive force that, though intended for defense, contributes to his insecurity. Yet people live on in the delusion that they are secure. It is as though humankind has created for itself a world situation for which intellectually and morally it is unprepared to cope.

The need now is to supersede this whole approach. The very security long thought to dictate the need for armaments now dictates that we surpass the war system. There must be a new conception of how to get along in the world, a recognition that only the individual person is of ultimate value—not governments, not abstractions, not collectivities—and that if we do not cherish the life embodied in such persons there is no point to our other pursuits, much less to contention over ideologies, economic systems, and political policies.

I

This requires in the first instance abandoning the view that human nature is corrupt—that, as Kennan says in a passage quoted ear-

lier, "the decisive seat of evil in this world is not in social and political institutions, and not even, as a rule, in the will or iniquities
of statesmen, but simply in the weakness and imperfection of the
human soul itself." For this view virtually forces the pessimistic
conclusion that war is inevitable.

The early Greeks saw human misfortune as the result of external
forces, the workings of fate. Plato internalized this view with his
contention that man has an immaterial soul within a physical
body; this, as he saw it, made man's misfortune the result of his
own doing and made it principally his own responsibility. But
even this was qualified with the conviction, which came to be
characteristic of much of Greek thought, that wrongdoing is ultimately from ignorance and that had we but a better perspective on
the good we would conduct ourselves accordingly; and it was believed, in any event, that we have within ourselves the resources
to lead a good life, provided only we put reason to work as it was
intended. Christianity reversed all of this. With the conception of
a good, omnipotent and omniscient God, evil was, as it were,
crowded out of the external world. Being God's creation, the
world could contain no evil attributable to God's hand lest it reflect
upon his goodness. Evil, as we saw in Augustine, was accordingly
seen to derive from the human soul, not through ignorance, as
Plato thought, but through willful, prideful disobedience to the
will of God. Man was thought to have been so corrupted from the
time of Adam as to be deprived of the capacity even consistently
to choose good over evil. The corrupt human soul thus became the
convenient explanation of all the wrong that men do.

But to locate the source of man's problems in human nature is,
in effect, to reconcile oneself to their perpetuation. For then all that
is left is to participate in evil and to confess one's own guilt in the
process. You may then proceed in Christian love to slaughter your
fellow men by the thousands. Wars then do indeed become inevitable. The most that one can hope for is, as most just war theorists
argue, to try to minimize the horrors of war and to devise rules to
limit the carnage. If wars are inevitable, it makes little sense to ask
whether they are justified; only their conduct is open to assessment. To ask more is to ask the impossible.

To indict all of human nature, of course, makes it hard to justify
condemning one's enemies; after all, they are just doing what you
would expect. What one must do is to concede one's own sinfulness but insist that others—the enemies of the day—are even
worse. You can then wage warfare against them and write it off to

the human predicament. Niebuhr, in the spirit of Augustine, took this tack in 1942 in analyzing the U.S. role in World War II, as we saw in Chapter Four.

> The experience through which we have already gone in a few months of belligerency suggests a different thesis about the relation of our war efforts to democracy. The thesis is that only the chastisements of a fairly long war can prompt a really thoroughgoing repentance and a conversion from those sins of the democratic world which helped to produce the Nazi revolt against our civilization. We were much too soft and fat, much too heedless and indifferent to the ultimate issues of life to be changed by the only casual chastisements of a brief belligerency. . . . When we are guilty of sins that make a revolt against civilization possible, we can hardly repent of those sins until bitter experience has taught us what the consequences of the sins are and by what kind of sacrifices and changes of heart the evils we have done can be overcome.[1]

One supposes that the 50 million dead of World War II constituted more than a "casual" chastisement and that it should have been enough to cause us to repent. Yet it was little more than a decade after that war that Niebuhr was himself warning against new military ventures in South Vietnam; and more than forty years after the end of the war the social inequalities in the American economic system, which Niebuhr predicted the war would greatly reduce, were such that 35 million Americans were living in poverty. But whether or not such prophecies were fulfilled and the hoped-for repentance realized, it is the grim pessimism of this outlook that is my present concern. What does one make of such sweeping claims as that the whole of human nature is corrupt, "literally every soul" flawed, as Kennan put it? We understand easily enough what it is for this or that individual person to be evil. But in the sense in which that is the case it is false that everyone is evil. It is precisely because the conduct of the occasional evil person contrasts so sharply with what we observe of the conduct of people in general that we assess it as we do. Remove those differentiating conditions and the clear cases at the heart of our understanding of good and evil disappear. And if it is said that the claim means only that, being corrupted, every individual soul is

[1] "Chastisement Unto Repentance or Death," in *Love and Justice: Selections from the Shorter Writings of Reinhold Niebuhr*, ed. D.B. Robertson (Cleveland: World Publishing Company, 1967), pp. 180-181.

capable of evil, then we must ask what evidence there is for this. And inevitably the evidence turns out to consist of little more than such facts as that we all sometimes make mistakes, sometimes yield to temptation, sometimes do wrong, and sometimes are basely motivated—incontrovertible facts that only those bent upon thinking the worst of human beings could suppose add up to the conclusion that the whole of human nature is corrupt; facts, moreover, that can readily be accepted by those who think that human nature is basically good as well as by those who regard the evidence as inconclusive either way. Hannah Arendt said of guilt in another connection that when everyone is guilty no one is guilty, and much the same applies here. If everyone is sinful and corrupt, the very distinctions that enable us to tell good from evil are obliterated.

One cannot, of course, prove that this outlook is mistaken. We can only choose between different ways of conceiving the world; choose which set of values seem most rational and humane, which strike the deepest chord in our inner being and seem to promise more hope than despair. At stake in this choice is our most fundamental conception of the value of the human person—whether to regard the human person as we find and experience it here and now as so sinful that it can be justifiably used as a means, an instrument to serve the ends of those who wield social, political, and military power, or to regard it as something of infinite worth, to be cherished when close to us, respected when at a distance, and always regarded for what it is, the source of what is known to be good in this world. To adopt this latter outlook requires changing the emphasis in our moral thinking about social and political matters, and calls for a new understanding of the problem of conflict resolution.

II

Let us recall that war is usually thought to be justified as a response to wrongdoing of one or the other of two sorts, aggression or oppression. It is when one believes he has been aggressed against that considerations of self-defense, or in the case of the state, national security, come into play. When other peoples are oppressed or aggressed against, either by their own governments or by the governments of other states, revolutionary wars or wars of national liberation are often thought to be justified. As both aggression and oppression represent conflict of different sorts—

one of the overt use of violence by one nation or people against another, the other the assertion of the interests or will of one group or class over another—we may say that conflict resolution is the primary concern of the aspect of morality concerned with wrongdoing.

There are basically two approaches to conflict resolution. One assumes that in a dispute one side is correct, the other incorrect, and that the "correct" side should prevail. The assumption is that this will represent the best solution to the problem. The further assumption is that, however much use one might make of discussion or negotiation, he must be willing to apply all necessary force to achieve the desired outcome if such methods fail. Force, it is thought, is the only language wrongdoers understand, and one must speak that language clearly to deal with them effectively. This means, in our contemporary world, being ready to wage war—nuclear, if necessary—to combat aggression.

War is simply the extreme of this mode of conflict resolution. In more rudimentary form it is found in personal relations when a person seeks to prevail over others in discussions, to dominate or manipulate others in situations calling for attention to conflicts of interest. It can be utilized fairly or unfairly, and the parliamentary rules of order represent the codification of a fair set of rules for the resolution of conflicts in this manner. Under such rules you can marshall all the support you want in trying to get your position accepted, but you have to abide by a clear set of rules in the process. Even in war there are generally acknowledged rules, though ones, as we have seen, that give way before the demands of military necessity when the two conflict. And often the rules are abandoned altogether, either because of the exigencies of war or the emotional heat generated by its waging, or in nuclear war simply because of its unavoidably indiscriminate character.

The other approach, which I will mention only briefly now and return to later, assumes that in any conflict there may be truth on both sides. It strives to see that the best solution emerge whether or not it is the one to which you were initially predisposed, and even if it should require abandoning views to which you might originally have been committed. According to this approach, there is no interest in seeing either side prevail; only in seeing that the truth, in a sense that includes acknowledgment of the legitimate interests of both sides, be the final outcome of the process.

Now, if nuclear war as a mode of conflict resolution is irrational, and conventional war increasingly so because of its growing destructive power, and if neither has a moral justification so long as they kill innocent persons, what is the alternative?

The alternative, I suggest, is to cease waging wars.

People say, treaties have failed to prevent wars, so let us be done with treaties; they do not say, war has failed to prevent wars, so let us be done with war. Yet that is what they must say if they are to be serious about war's abolition.

To be done with war means being done with the war system. For that system has a force that will pull apart the best-intentioned of agreements. Train dogs to kill, accustom them to the savagery of the pit, the shouts of spectators, the crunch of bones, and the smell of blood. Then put them face to face under the lights and expect them not to fight. "Unrealistic," skeptics will scoff, "it's in the nature of dogs to tear each other to pieces." And indeed they will be correct—if, that is, one grants the whole system of values and practices leading up to the dogs being placed in the ring in the first place. What is not in the nature of things is that system itself, the institution of dogfighting. Dismantle it and organized dog-fights will cease. Occasional dogs will still scrap, but the bloody, systematic brutalization of dogs and men entailed by that practice will be ended.

So with war. The problem is not so much a lack of desire for peace as it is a commitment to institutions that make peace impossible.

Consider the United States for example. Millions of persons earn their livelihood in defense industries; roughly 40 percent of scientists and engineers work at military related jobs; colleges train military officers and appoint men in uniform to professorships to instruct them; corporations seat retired military officers on their boards of directors; Congress regularly votes billions of dollars for military expenditures; and highest officials accept violence as a means of resolving international disputes. With due allowance for the differences in the systems, the same is true in Communist countries. Both the people and perhaps the leaders want peace. But in countless ways nonmilitary institutions and practices serve military ends—as though Adam Smith's invisible hand were at work to maximize, not the common good, but human destructiveness. When this happens a society becomes hostage to military values as surely, if less conspicuously, as by a military takeover. There remain, to be sure, those who wear uniforms and those who do not, but they simply serve the war system in different ways.

It is not surprising, then, that violence erupts when the nations of the world, virtually all of which are committed in one degree or another to the perpetuation of the war system, confront one another in the ring of international conflict. To expect the signing of documents outlawing war to change that is naive.

This state of affairs can be changed only by reconstituting societies.[2] We need to make peace education a priority; to make development of alternatives to violence a priority; to begin to take seriously the values we profess to cherish. Not least of all, economies need to be converted to peaceful ends. This would have to be gradual, and in a country like the United States would require the cooperation of government, industry, unions, and local communities. But there is no reason it cannot be done. And there are pressing economic reasons, if no others, why it should be done.

Consider just one of the economic costs of the war system, inflation. Inflation is the major nonmilitary threat to the Western economies today. And if war is not its sole cause, it is nonetheless one of its principal causes, and the removal of the occasion for war would be a major step toward world prosperity. Yet the myth persists that military spending is a boon to a country's economy. "What we need is another war," people say only have in jest during times of economic crisis. But the vaunted economic benefits of military spending are largely illusory. Military spending presently creates fewer than half the jobs it did in 1964, and it is estimated that each billion dollars of tax monies is now capable of creating more civilian jobs than military jobs.

More importantly, military spending is economically wasteful and on a large scale ruinous. It puts money into the hands of consumers without a commensurate increase in consumer goods (few consumers buy tanks or fighter planes). When, in addition, governments print money to finance their wars—as they have a least as far back as the Roman emperors who, without benefit of the printing press, debased the coinage instead—the money supply is inflated. With more dollars chasing fewer goods, price inflation follows, as happened in the United States in the 1970s as a result of Vietnam. When an economy the size of America's becomes inflationary, moreover, it exports inflation to other countries as well, disrupting currency markets and straining the world economy as a whole.

Historically, even the gold standard did not restrain this phe-

[2] Ronald J. Glossop, *Confronting War: An Examination of Humanity's Most Pressing Problem* (Jefferson & London: McFarland, 1983), pt. 4, "Proposals for Solving the War Problem."

nomenon. Nations simply went off the standard during wartime and then returned to it afterward. In fact, it is suspected that the fifty- to sixty-year Kondratief cycles in capitalist countries (named after a Russian economist) are the result of deflation and depression following reimposition of the gold standard after major wars. Though the gold standard no longer exists and the existence of K-cycles is disputed, it is likely that the United States will either have to drastically reduce its money supply, and thereby risk a depression, or face continuing and possibly eventually rampant inflation. It may be an overstatement to say that nothing short of a nuclear war can be as devastating as uncontrolled inflation. But in flirting with the one to maintain our capacity for the other we currently risk both.

III

Many who agree basically with the foregoing nonetheless feel that while it would be fine if everyone renounced war in one grand gesture, the consequences could be grievous if only some do while others do not. Nonviolence it is reasoned, is fine as an ideal, but in an imperfect world we must reluctantly take up the sword when it is forced upon us. Thus at the same time that people profess to abhor violence they perpetuate institutions geared to preparation for its use and, for the most part, if they are male and young enough become its willing purveyors first hand—all on the ground that we must be "realistic."

But the alternative to war is not passive acceptance of evil. It is resistance and defense, but of a nonviolent sort. This requires not only conversion to a peace-oriented economy but also the development of alternative means of national defense.

This thought occasions smiles from the experts. They want to know how you stop an enemy tank by going limp. Or melt the heart of a Hitler by turning the other cheek. Fair enough questions. At least as fair as asking them how you defend yourself against a nuclear bomb about to explode overhead.

The answer is that you cannot. Hypothesize situations in which an advocate of nonviolence confronts someone armed and committed maniacally to violence, and the outcome can abstractly always be made to favor the advocate of violence. Let that be conceded. Still, such questions betray a lack of imagination about the potential of nonviolence. Just as it is a mistake to adhere to concepts of defense and security derived from simple models of inter-

270

personal relations that do not apply to the international level, so it is a mistake to evaluate nonviolence solely on the basis of cases of the sort presupposed by these questions.

To see this requires attention to the concepts of power and effectiveness. For here is the key to understanding both the potential of nonviolence and the failure of the war system.

Power, from a social standpoint, is the ability to achieve one's objectives. And while capacity to use violence in one measure of power and may be effective in some contexts, it is demonstrably ineffective in others. That virtually every war has at least one loser attests to this. Destructive force does not automatically add up to social power.

Moreover, beyond a certain point increments in the capacity for violence cease to yield increases in power. Beyond that point, in fact, power may decrease, however much destructive force one commands.

The United States discovered this in Vietnam, where it proved incapable of attaining its objectives despite overwhelming military superiority. The Soviets did the same in Afghanistan. With sufficient superiority one can of course always annihilate one's opponent. But that rarely constitutes power in the sense at hand. The objectives in terms of whose attainment power must be understood rarely consist simply in destruction. They consist in securing benefits for oneself or those one cares about, or, often, in bringing about what one believes would be a better world (as distorted as his conception of such a world was, this was true even of Hitler). It is as a means to these ends, or because they are perceived as obstacles to the attainment of these ends, that human beings are usually killed.

But attainment of the objectives for which people wage wars is incompatible with destruction that exceeds certain limits. We could, for example, have destroyed North Vietnam in a matter of hours with nuclear weapons, but that would not have deterred the Vietcong in the South (though it would have reduced the scale of their struggle and protracted the war). And though we similarly could have destroyed the Vietcong as well, we could not have done so without annihilating South Vietnam in the process. That, however, would have defeated the very objective of creating a showcase anti-Communist government in Southeast Asia for which we were fighting. As it was, the destruction of village life, the ravaging of the countryside with bombs and defoliants, and the alienation of the people made the attainment of that objective

271

impossible anyway. When the U.S. officer at Ben Tri immortalized the words "[W]e had to destroy the town to save it," he not only unwittingly epitomized the thinking that had come to govern our Vietnam policy, he also revealed the absurdity of thinking you can ultimately achieve your objectives by mere destruction.

That American power is diminishing in the world is not, as militarists argue, because we are becoming militarily weaker than the Soviet Union. It is because we have misidentified power with the capacity to cause destruction. Theorists of war like Clausewitz, and more recently Mao and Giap, as committed as they are to violence nonetheless have seen this better than we in their emphasis upon the social and human dimensions in the attainment of one's objectives. Increased military spending will not alleviate the situation because there is a basic misunderstanding of what the problem is in the first place.

Nonviolent power, on the other hand, increases in proportion to increases in the instruments of power—namely, the nonviolent actions of individual persons—to the point where, as even critics of nonviolence agree, it would obviously be a better world if everyone acted nonviolently. As one moves from contrived cases like that of a solitary Gandhi assuming the lotus position before an attacking Panzer Division, to cases in which millions of persons are hypothesized as confronting an actual adversary pursuing credible objectives, new sources of power can be seen to come into being. They are generated by a quantitative increase in the number of persons committed to nonviolence.

People fear, of course, that if the United States were to renounce the use of violence—in effect to disarm unilaterally—the Soviet Union would immediately attack. But there is little reason to believe this would happen, inasmuch as we would no longer constitute a threat to them; and there are many reasons to suppose it would *not* happen, considering the needless detriment to themselves such an attack would represent from worldwide fallout and environmental damage. Some scientists, as we have seen, even think such an attack would be an act of national suicide. Even if their ultimate aim were to take over America—and perhaps especially if that were their aim—it would be self-defeating to devastate and contaminate the very territory on which they had designs. They could indeed be expected to assert themselves more aggressively in the world. In the worst case they might even invade us— although to do so would have no warrant in Marxist ideology, and history provides no evidence of their so acting against a nation outside their sphere of influence.

But suppose they did? This is a legitimate concern.

Consider a population of 240 million persons committed to nonviolent resistance against an invading army bent upon ruling the country. A large industrialized society like ours cannot be run, much less be run with the efficiency necessary to make it worthwhile to try to do so, without the cooperation of its population. People are needed to run factories, grow food, collect trash, and perform thousands of other essential tasks. In fact, it is difficult enough to run the country *with* the cooperation of the people. Deny to an invading army that support—as one can through passive resistance, strikes, boycotts, civil disobedience, and other nonviolent techniques—and you render it virtually incapable of attaining its objectives.

An invading Soviet army, for example, could hardly perform all of these tasks itself. How many millions of persons would it have to transport to the United States to keep this country functioning economically? Meanwhile, what happens to the Soviet Union's own economy, which desperately needs revitalizing in its own right? And how would an army that had morale problems in Czechoslovakia and Afghanistan cope with a nonthreatening but noncooperating population day in day out, perhaps for years? Governments can lie to their soldiers. But when the soldiers are face to face with the people themselves those lies no longer work and new ones must be produced. If, in addition, the people resist in ways that show consideration for the plight of the soldiers themselves, most of whom would rather be with their families and loved ones than where they are, it will take more and more lies to maintain the image of an enemy that deserves to be repressed. Lies work only when people can be kept from seeing the truth for themselves. A government that strives to keep its own people insulated from Western influences could hardly welcome the pervasive effects of an occupation that would maximize those influences.

A people who have sought security through arms alone are defenseless once their military forces have been defeated. They are a conquered people. A people committed to nonviolence may be deprived of their government, their liberties, their material wealth, even their lives. But they cannot be conquered.

True, nonviolence could be effective on such a scale only with the concerted effort of tens of thousands of well-trained persons willing to sacrifice and perhaps die for what they believe in. But no less is true of violence. That is why we now put millions of persons in uniform and train them to kill. It is also true that non-violence is no guarantee against bloodshed. No system has such a guarantee. But the use of violence not only allows situations to develop in which bloodshed is inevitable, it entails the shedding of blood. And if we are to use considerations like these as a criterion of adequacy in the one case, we must use them in the other as well.

Consider the notion of "effectiveness" further. Effectiveness has no meaning in the abstract; it is always effectiveness in achieving some purpose, end, or goal. As such it is always in part a function of existing conditions. Thus, from a moral standpoint one must ask not only whether what is adjudged to be effective is in fact so but also whether, if it is, the ends or goals to whose realization it is a means are morally defensible. This means that one must ask further whether in comparing violence and nonviolence with regard to effectiveness the two are presumed to have the same ends. If they are, the matter of effectiveness can be considered decisive and the issue resolvable at least in part on empirical grounds. If not, then attention must be shifted to the moral assessment of their respective ends.

These ends may overlap, but unless nonviolence is considered merely a tactic, they will diverge at some point; and certainly the basic ends of violence and nonviolence differ radically. The facile comparison of violence and nonviolence as tactics led to the gradual erosion of support for nonviolence in racial matters, since non-violence, as preached by Martin Luther King, Jr., failed to achieve many of its specific short-range goals, whereas violence, especially in the form of riots, sometimes elicited a more prompt and constructive response from the white community. If nonviolence is thought of as a way of life, however, then its end is not a far-off state of affairs but an ongoing process of infusing a certain quality into one's day-to-day engagement with the world. To live nonviolently and to encourage others to do the same *is* the end, and the question is not whether nonviolence is effective (though one might ask whether it is effective in achieving other ends) but whether this or that person or society is successful at living nonviolently. Here means and ends collapse into one another because it is in part the particular means one adopts in pursuing the many short-range ends in life that go to make up the ends. Rather than being steps on a ladder to a lofty and remote destination, means in this view are more akin to ingredients in a recipe, the end or final product of which consists of what one puts into it.

IV

To take effectiveness to be relevant to the assessment of nonviolent versus violent ethical philosophies is to have to come to grips eventually with the problem of Nazi Germany. World War II—the "best of all possible wars," as it has been called—is the closest thing there is to a test case in matters of this sort.

Most people regard World War II as a just war. Many who opposed the war in Vietnam say they would have fought against Hitler. The question is whether anything short of violence could have been effective against as ruthless a tyranny as Hitler's and, if not, whether this is not decisive against nonviolence?

To assess the comparative effectiveness of violence as against nonviolence one must specify the relevant ends or goals to whose attainment the war against Hitler is said to have been instrumental. What were they? To halt Nazi aggression? To eradicate fascism? To secure world peace? Defenders of the war usually do not make clear what it was the war was effective in accomplishing, but it usually has something vaguely to do with "stopping Hitler."

Now whether or not nonviolence could have stopped Hitler once the war began, had enough German citizens acted responsibly with or without a commitment to nonviolence, but particularly with it, say, in the 1920s and early 1930s, fascism could never have advanced to the stage where it could be deemed necessary to reverse it by military means. Had German industrialists not financed Hitler's rise to power; had German youths refused to serve in the military; had conservatives not supported him and communists deluded themselves that anything would be better than the liberal democratic Weimar regime, Hitler might have remained the frustrated and ineffectual architect he was in his early years and very nearly remained despite all. He was considered washed up in 1923 following an attempted putsch, his imprisonment, and the crushing of the German Workers party that he headed; again in 1928 when the growing prosperity of the Weimar Republic temporarily deprived the Nazis of much of the discontent upon which they fed; and still again as late as 1932—the year before his rise to power—following setbacks at the polls and the loss of much-needed financial backing. Despite the strong-arm methods and street violence we usually associate with the Nazis, Hitler worked primarily through legal institutional channels, and his future hung precariously in the balance more than once. Compared with what it took to stop him years later when he had consolidated his position, he could easily have been denied power in the first place by concerted nonviolent (particularly political) action.

So while nonviolence obviously could not have pushed German armor back on the battlefield once the institutions of militarism had been allowed to mature and the self-propelling mechanism of a military state put into motion, it might have been effective at an earlier stage in preventing the rise to power of those responsible for all of this. If historical fact is that military means stopped Hitler once he began to march, it is also an historical fact that reliance upon such means on the part of the world's nations did not prevent his rise to power in the first place.

The militarist may reply that it would have been all well and good if people had stopped fascism nonviolently years earlier, but the fact is they did not. They were neither ready nor willing in sufficient numbers to act, and it is precisely this fact that led to the crisis that eventually called for a military solution.

This cuts both ways, however. The advocate of military violence cannot make a plausible case for *its* effectiveness unless it is presumed that there are tens of thousands of well-trained and equipped persons wiling to make the ultimate sacrifice in the service of the cause for which the action is undertaken; not to mention millions more in the society at large who are willing to support this effort financially and often through direct participation in the maintenance of the machinery necessary to war. Military action cannot, in other words, hope to succeed without armies, guns, money, and equipment. By the same token, nonviolence cannot be imagined to succeed when the basic conditions necessary to its success are similarly absent. These may well include, at least if it is contemplated on a grand scale, a willingness to sacrifice and a degree of discipline and training on the part of tens of thousands comparable to that required in the military; and it will require extensive background research into techniques of nonviolence against various forms of aggression. In short, one cannot make a case for the effectiveness of nonviolence any more than for that of violence in hypothetical situations in which certain obviously necessary conditions of any prospect of success are presumed absent. To point out, therefore, that nonviolence would not have succeeded if tried in a context in which these conditions were absent may refute simplistic versions of the theory, but it will not tell against versions that hold, among other things, that these conditions ought to be promoted.

We have been assuming, of course, that nonviolence could not have been effective against Hitler at the time the war broke out and that violence was successful. Both assumptions require some qualification.

Some of the most effective forms of nonviolent resistance in the twentieth century were undertaken, mostly without advance preparation and coordination, against the Germans in World War II—a fact consistently overlooked by those who reply to the examples of Gandhi and King by saying that they could not have done it against the Nazis. One could profitably speculate on what might have been the consequences if whole nations had been geared in advance for such action. Any attempt to conquer and rule a modern nation must in the long run be a multifaceted one of which what takes place on the battlefield is but one aspect. For only by enlisting the support or cooperation (willing or coerced) of whole populations can dictators remain in power. Mass strikes and boycotts can cripple the administration of a country far more quickly and effectively than all but the most devastating of military means. The key lies in concerted action by large numbers. It is with regard to its potential for devising ways of withholding necessary support and making such concerted action possible that nonviolence must be assessed.

The second assumption, however, is doubtful. That Hitler was stopped is true, and if among the possible aims of the war this were the only relevant one, then the war succeeded. But considering some of the other ends mentioned, it is either questionable that they were accomplished or clear that they were not. It is arguable, for instance, that fascism in Germany and elsewhere was not eradicated but merely temporarily suppressed. Neo-Nazi groups have continued to thrive in both West Germany and the United States (and elsewhere), and it is significant that following the death of Rudolf Hess, the last of Hitler's close associates, Spandau prison in which he had been held was torn down so it could not be turned into a shrine by Nazi sympathizers. A more realistic assessment is suggested by the following:

They tell us we had to fight, we had to win the war against Hitler. We haven't won the war against Hitler. He's still around; he's just hiding behind other men's faces. You can't defeat Hitler with guns. As long as you have to have guns to

277

keep him off, he's not defeated. Hitler will be defeated when we could let him come back, reincarnated, with all the charisma and all the hate; when we could let him make speeches in the public square, and people would pass by, stop and listen for a minute to see what he was saying, then laugh a little and go on their way.[3]

In this sense, Hitler has not been defeated. He himself said you could not defeat a philosophy by violence alone—that to do so required a superior philosophy.[4] That has not yet been provided by the governments of the world, at least where the use of violence is concerned. Beyond this, it is incontrovertible that with regard to the broader aim of securing lasting peace, World War II failed abysmally. Power was redistributed and enemies redefined. But injustice and oppression remain, and the clouds of nuclear war forebode a possible devastation greater than any the war averted.

The comparison, in any event, should not be of nonviolence with some ideal of conflict resolution in an ideal world but with our present methods in the actual world. And our present methods have brought us to the brink of disaster. If ever they had a usefulness, they have outlived it. Nor should the comparison be of nonviolence in its present embryonic form, in which it has only been tried occasionally, with a system of violence that is in an advanced stage of development and deeply entrenched in the socioeconomic systems of the world. This would be as though one had compared air travel with rail travel at the time of the Wright brothers and said, "Look, we have only two pilots, no airports, and one plane that can fly a few hundred yards but we have thousands of miles of railroads and a nation accustomed to rail travel," and then argued on that basis against the development of the airplane. It is the potential of nonviolence that must command our attention. *The comparison should be of our present system of violence with nonviolence as it might realistically be developed.* Humankind has given violence a chance; it has dealt with conflict repeatedly through bloodshed; it has waged wars with all the energy and passion it can muster and devoted its time, energy, and resources into perfecting its capacity for destruction. And it has in the process only increased the insecurity of persons throughout the world. The time now is for a

[3] Nancy Davis, "Pacifism: Some Objections to Some Objections," a term paper for a seminar on morality and war at the University of Rochester, 1972.
[4] Adolf Hitler, *Mein Kampf* (Cambridge: The Riverside Press, 1962), p. 172.

change. Nonviolence may not only be a better way of getting along in the world; it may be the only way.

In short, vast resources of power lie untapped within the people of a country. These sources remain to be explored with all the determination that presently goes into the study of war and the refinement of techniques for waging it. Just as we need alternative sources of energy for the future, we need alternative sources of national power. And we should be developing the one as assiduously as the other.

V

We have too long conceptualized war as a problem of "us" against "them"; as something we engage in because of the bad conduct of others (the Soviets if you are American; the Americans if you are Soviet; the Arabs if you are Israeli; the Israelis if you are Arab, etc.—with periodic reshuffling of friends and enemies), rather than as an affliction of all humankind. By overlooking that we are precisely that "other" to others, our behavior as threatening to them as theirs is to us, we maintain a climate of mistrust that elicits from each of us the very conduct others then take as confirming their worst suspicions.

This is nowhere more evident than in relations between communist and capitalist countries, particularly the United States and the Soviet Union. There are many reasons for this, of course. But a central one is lack of understanding that derives from deep-seated differences between the two systems. These differences should not be minimized. In fact is is important to try to identify and understand them. Such an undertaking must be part of any serious attempt to defuse tensions in the nuclear age, and must particularly be part of any attempt to deal nonviolently with the problem of war. It is a larger project than can be carried out here. But it can be started. To that end I want to detail what seem to me to be some of the more formidable obstacles to understanding between the peoples of communist and capitalist countries generally, but much of it will be specific to the United States and the Soviet Union.

The differences I shall be concerned with are conceptual, ideological, and philosophical. And they are rooted in competing perspectives, that, interestingly, can be profitably illuminated by considering different ways of understanding American society itself.

The issues are complex, and I shall simplify them for present purposes.

The central question is whether what is sometimes called classical or individualistic liberalism represents an adequate philosophy for understanding American society.[5] More than that, it concerns whether liberalism in that sense *ought* to be the governing outlook for America in the future. In short, the issue is not simply whether the outlook is *descriptively* accurate (both sides generally agree that it was accurate for America in the nineteenth century) but whether it is *normatively* justified as well.

Those who maintain that it is contend that society is composed of basically self-contained, self-interested individuals who have come together to better enable each to satisfy his needs and interests. For this purpose it is in their mutual interest to have the safeguards and protection of the state: a system of organized power to maintain order and defend the association against external threats. This comes legitimately into existence only as individual persons voluntarily surrender to it some of their liberties. War making and maintenance of law and order are the state's primary functions. If the liberties of individual persons are to be safeguarded, they must be its sole functions. Individuals will then have the maximum opportunity to pursue their own interests in whatever manner they choose, so long as they do not interfere with a similar pursuit by others. The spirit of this outlook was well-put by the nineteenth-century British philosopher Herbert Spencer when he said that "[e]ach shall have as much liberty to pursue his ends as consists with maintaining like liberties to pursue their ends by others; and one as much as another shall have the enjoyment of that which his efforts, carried on within these limits, obtain."[6]

I shall call this assemblage of views and its various corollaries, which I will not take time to detail, individualism.

Foremost among the criticisms of individualism is that it legitimizes a radically pluralistic conception of society. If society is nothing more than an association of atomistic individuals, each with his own conception of the good, and pursuing his own interests, there is no shared moral outlook by which disagreements can

---

[5] For a good bibliographic survey of the literature and issues on this topic, see Chandran Kukathas, "Liberalism and Its Critics," *Humane Studies Review* 4, no. 1 (Winter 1986-1987).

[6] Herbert Spencer, *The Principles of Ethics* (New York: D. Appleton and Company, 1910), 1: 223. John Rawls has more recently incorporated the first part of this in one of his two principles of justice, in *Theory of Justice* (Cambridge: Harvard University Press, 1971).

be resolved. In the absence of such an outlook, society cannot function smoothly and efficiently. And if it cannot do that, it cannot realize the greatest social good. Strife and contention over social, political, and moral issues will always stand in the way of its realization. Carried to its extreme politically, this view leads to anarchism; morally it leads to subjectivism or relativism. If there is no way to adjudicate disagreements, then each opinion counts for as much as any other. Coercion, manipulation, power, and ultimately force rather than reason become the arbiters of disagreements.

Implicit in this criticism is a strong communitarian orientation. It holds that the best society is achievable only if its members constitute a moral *community*. For only then will there exist the shared outlook that will enable them to resolve disagreements peacefully and decisively. And only then can individuals realize their true potential. In its weaker form it holds that in the absence of a moral community people will face overwhelming practical problems in rationally resolving their differences. In its stronger form it holds that in the absence of such a community the very conditions under which effective moral reasoning are possible fail to exist. The very ideas of good and bad moral reasons and of valid and invalid moral arguments cannot even be rendered intelligible except in the context of the institutions and social functions that a genuine community embodies. It is not simply that there must exist a political community in order to realize the greatest social good. No one but the anarchist denies that. And few but ascetics deny that the greatest individual good is achievable only in society with others. It is rather than we cannot even comprehend how the greatest social good *or* the greatest individual good is achievable so long as we think of persons as related only externally to others. Individuals are incomplete on their own. They are essentially connected with the broader social context that gives meaning to their lives. Relatedly, the individualistic outlook is criticized for neglecting the broader historical context from which society has emerged. It looks at society solely in terms of its present state, ignoring the historical forces that have given rise to its particular institutions, beliefs, and practices. Its understanding of society is therefore imperfect and its judgments about what makes for the good of society accordingly deficient.

I shall refer to the perspective underlying these criticisms as con-textualistic. Whereas individualism is pluralistic with regard to the nature of society and a-historical with regard to the nature and good of the individual, contextualism is monistic, historicist, and communitarian. It holds that that society is best which embodies a single moral perspective (where it is, of course, assumed this is the correct one), is viewed in its broader historical setting, and whose members constitute a moral community.

I want to suggest that the situation between the peoples of the United States and the Soviet Union replicates some of the issues just outlined between individualism and contextualism.

Marxism views social and international events as governed by historical laws. These explain the major transformations in socio-economic organization from primitive, to slave, to feudal, to capitalistic. It is not that one cannot *describe* these events a-historically. It is rather that one cannot fully understand them in that way. Nor can one understand the projected transformation of capitalist to socialist systems, and the expected eventual transition from socialism to communism, except in these terms. As a kernel of wheat can be fully understood only in the context of the processes of nature that produced it, and to which it will contribute as it matures and eventually produces new kernels of grain of its own, so the transformations of society can only be understood as part of the processes of history from which they emerge and to whose progressive evolution they contribute. The dialectical process runs throughout both the natural and social worlds.

The individual likewise must be understood as interconnected with others in a social context. The essence of man, Marx says, "is no abstraction inherent in each single individual. In its reality it is the ensemble of the social relations."[7] Only *as* a social animal can man be adequately understood. But this interconnectedness with others has a significance beyond simply the question of the nature of man. It points as well to the strong communitarian element in Marx and Engels. Writing in *The German Ideology*, they said: "Only within the community has each individual the means of cultivating his gifts in all directions; hence personal freedom becomes possible only within the community. In previous substitutes for the community, in the state, etc., personal freedom has existed only for the individuals who developed under the conditions of the ruling class, and only insofar as they were individuals of this class."[8] This says, in effect, that the *best* life for the individual is possible only

[7] Karl Marx and Frederick Engels, *Collected Works* (New York: International Publishers, 1976), 5: 7.
[8] Ibid, p. 78.

in community, and community of the sort possible only in a class-less society.

While this perspective does not entail criteria for resolving all disagreements within society no matter how specific the issue, it does provide criteria for assessing disagreements on broader social, political, and economic issues. And, depending upon how one interprets Marx, it provides criteria for resolving basic moral disagreements as well. That is, it provides a consistent and coherent framework within which disagreements can be understood and adjudicated. There is an objective truth about social issues, which can be brought into focus through the lens of Marxist-Leninist philosophy. And it can be fully embodied only in social institutions conforming to Marxist-Leninist principles.

This overall orientation is unmistakably contextualistic. A society founded on Marxist-Leninist principles will be monistic (it will in its broadest outline embody one conception of the truth, not many), historicist (society will be understood from the widest historical perspective), and communitarian (both the nature and good of individuals will be considered understandable only as they are part of a community). And it will have this orientation both towards its own society and towards the world at large.

The United States, on the other hand, is basically individualistic in its conception of its own society. Indeed, it is because America has had a predominantly individualistic orientation that the aforementioned issue over the character of classical liberalism arose. Whether it is still descriptively accurate is another question, though, as is the question whether individualism *should* be the predominant orientation of American or any other society. But toward the rest of the world its orientation is more ambiguous. Historically it was individualistic here as well, at least in the sense of looking upon the rest of the world as essentially pluralistic. Through much of its isolationist history it tacitly took the position that other societies could take whatever form they wanted but that the United States would steer its own course, staying free as nearly as possible (Latin American was an exception) from entanglements with them.

But more recently that has been changing. Since World War II the United States has been in transition from a pluralistic world outlook to an increasingly monistic one. While it does not have a clearly defined ideology in the manner of the Soviet Union, it has increasingly come to view itself as having a kind of mission in the world. What that is may not always be clear. But it has to do vaguely with promoting freedom and making the world safe for democracy. This was part of the rhetoric behind U.S. involvement in World War I. But it has been a particularly strong theme since the onset of the Cold War. "Democracy" and "freedom" have been the banners under which advocates of this approach have set their sails. In some of its forms it has strongly moralistic and religious overtones as well, representing America as contesting with "godless communism" for supremacy in the world. Ronald Reagan's 1983 branding of the Soviet Union as an evil empire was in this spirit and contrasts with the political realist strains we examined earlier. While much of this contains more emotive than cognitive content, and cannot in any event be said to constitute anything comparable to an ideology, it nonetheless serves some of the same functions. It contains the rudiments of a philosophy committed to the view that one particular type of socio-political-economic system is best for the world, not just for America.

Two more general philosophical claims are worth adding to this characterization of these competing perspectives. If true, they present even more serious obstacles to understanding between Soviet and American peoples.

The first maintains that the very standards of what is logical and illogical make sense only *within* a social context. This means that the principles of sound reasoning cannot be applied to those contexts themselves. Thus Peter Winch says that "criteria of logic are not a direct gift of God, but arise out of, and are only intelligible in the context of, ways of living or modes of social life. It follows that one cannot apply criteria of logic to modes of social life as such. . . . So within science or religion actions can be logical or illogical; . . . but we cannot sensibly say that either the practice of science or that of religion is either illogical or logical; both are nonlogical."[9]

To the extent that communism and capitalism represent different "modes of social life," containing, at least implicitly, their own standards of what is logical and illogical, rational discourse intended to resolve disagreements between them would, in this view, seem to be impossible. There is no point of view, or vantage point, outside of them from which to make such an assessment. In this spirit it has been maintained that validity and invalidity themselves can be understood only in the context of the functions of reasoning, and those presuppose a social setting, common en-

[9] Peter Winch, *The Idea of A Social Science and Its Relation to Philosophy* (New York: Humanities Press, 1958), p. 100.

deavors, and shared values. To the extent that these are absent cross-culturally, as when one compares communist and capitalist societies, the modes of reasoning that are functional within either of these contexts cannot be used to adjudicate differences extending across them.

The second claim goes even further. It holds that the very categories of language itself are context-bound in similar ways. As Winch again says, "there is no way of getting outside of the concepts in terms of which we think of the world. . . . The world *is* for us what is presented through these concepts."[10] If correct, this means that to the extent that peoples from communist and capitalist countries perceive the world through different concepts, the world is a different place for them.

For Marxism, for example, the very idea of war can only be fully understood within the perspective of a process philosophy. Wars are progressive or retrogressive depending on whether they hasten the overthrow of ossified, oppressive systems or perpetuate them. The moral categories of "just" and "unjust" as applied to wars have their significance within that historical context. Lenin wrote during World War I that "if tomorrow, Morocco were to declare war on France, India or England, Persia or China on Russia, and so forth, those would be 'just,' 'defensive' wars, *irrespective* of who attacked first; and every Socialist would sympathize with the victory of the oppressed, dependent, unequal states against the oppressing, slave-owning, predatory 'great' powers."[11] What is just is what promotes the interests of the oppressed peoples (or within capitalist societies, of proletarians); what is unjust is what perpetuates their oppression. Appeals to national defense, or defense of the fatherland, on the part of imperialist governments he denounced as "bourgeois deception."

For most Western thinkers, on the other hand, as we have seen in our examination of the just war theory, war can be understood and assessed in terms of the immediate issues giving rise to any particular war. Thus when just war theorists speak of the criteria for *jus ad bellum*, they cite such conditions as a just cause, legitimate authority, and a right intention. Just cause can normally be understood in terms of a violation of rights by a *particular state* on a *particular occasion*. It does not require that one look at the broader historical context. One does not need to determine whether the war is progressive or retrogressive. What is important is whether

---

[10] Ibid., p. 15.
[11] *Lenin on War and Peace* (Peking: Foreign Languages Press, 1966), p. 6.

285

a particular *state* is warranted in resorting to force. States are the principal actors for purposes of just war assessment, not classes, as in Marxism-Leninism.

This has serious consequences for the handling of disagreements. It means that a common model of how to deal with them is inadequate. According to that model, there are facts and there are values. To resolve disagreements all you need do *in principle* (not that it is maintained that it is always easy to do this in fact) is first get agreement on the facts and then apply your principles or values to them. If parties to a disagreement differ over values, at least one knows where to focus attention in trying to secure agreement. But on the view under consideration this will not work. And it will not work for deeply rooted reasons. For here what the facts are cannot even be agreed upon. And not because the two sides do not have enough information. They cannot be agreed upon because the very categories through which information is processed and understood differ for them. What the facts are perceived to be reflects from the first the value-orientations of the disputants.[12]

It might seem that this need be no problem, and that just as what is best for individuals may vary from person to person, so what is best in the way of social organization may vary from society to society. Life-styles vary among individuals. So why not socio-political-economic systems among countries?

But this would be simply to opt for a pluralistic view of the international world. Implicit in the opposing perspectives of the United States and the Soviet Union are claims to the effect that each is *superior* to the other. There may even be the further implicit claim that each *ought* to prevail over the other. It is these implicit claims that must be reckoned with when dealing with the issue of disagreements. Marxists believe that a classless society is best for people everywhere, not just in socialist countries; capitalists believe that democracy and free enterprise are best for people the world over, not merely in capitalist countries. Thus Marxists disparage capitalists for trying to create what they see as a system of world imperialism, exploiting and dominating people for profit;

---

[12] We have seen in Chapter Six another dimension of this problem, in the virtual impossibility of making a value-neutral determination of what constitutes consequences. I have here, it should be added, characterized these perspectives in somewhat purer form than they are found in either society. There is disagreement among experts, for example, over whether Soviet foreign policy decisions are really guided very much by Marxist-Leninist principles rather than by national interest, in much the same way as other nations.

capitalists condemn Marxists for what they see as totalitarianism domestically and the fomenting of world revolution internationally.

Where does this leave us? If the preceding is correct, the United States and the Soviet Union perceive the world more or less monistically, each interpreting events through categories that tend to support its particular values and orientation. Each is convinced that it alone has hold of the truth. The position of the other is dismissed as biased and designed only to further its own ends.

I do not know whether the more abstract of the preceding philosophical claims are correct. They are all controversial. But they *may* be correct. If they are, or even if there is a substantial amount of truth to them, as I suspect there is, they constitute formidable obstacles to effective communication. And that in turn is an obstacle to understanding and trust.

Yet, there is an approach that holds promise of promoting better understanding *even if* all of the preceding claims are correct. It does not compel either side to give up the essentials of its perspective, though it does require surrendering any claim to be sole possessor of the truth. Elements of it are found in the Gandhian method of Satyagraha. The central idea, as it bears upon the problems I have outlined, is to approach disagreements not in a spirit of conviction that you are right and your opponent wrong but rather with an openness to the possibility that each of you may have hold of a part of the truth, and that only by taking seriously that possibility are either of you likely to make progress toward a completer truth.

This becomes particularly important when we notice a feature of the defense of most social and political philosophies. There is tendency to represent them as though they were realized in a more or less idealized state, without the friction that typically attends their actualizations historically. Conviction of the superiority of one such philosophy over another often rests upon seeing it in this light. It enables one to abstract from the conditions that are likely to detract from it in the so-called "real world." These include opposition from those who disagree with it. Thus socialism and capitalism can be represented imaginatively to function superbly as economic systems. So can democracy or dictatorship as political systems. Make enough assumptions about the circumstances in which it is envisaged to exist and almost any system can look good. The problem is that in the absence of consensus about which system would be best, every attempt to actualize some such arrangement, or to maintain one already in existence, meets with

287

opposition from those who are convinced that some alternative would be better. That opposition is among the realities one must deal with when assessing the adequacy of one's own position. This makes it particularly important how one handles disagreement. For disagreement often contains within it signposts to the truth. Rather than being avoided or suppressed, its expression should be encouraged. It should be explored for the insights it may reveal. It may produce a synthesis unforeseen by either party to the disagreement. This takes the humility to acknowledge that our favorite theories may be deficient in ways we have not seen. And it takes the courage to acknowledge that the proposals of those we disagree with may ultimately prove more satisfactory. When both sides recognize this, they shift their disagreement to a new plane where avenues for creative solutions may begin to open up.

This makes it important to cultivate nonviolent means of conflict resolution. Violence is for the morally infallible. If you are convinced that you alone have the truth, there is little recourse but to threaten, intimidate, bribe, or coerce those who disagree with you if they do not come around to your view—or, ultimately, if these methods are unavailing, to use force. That, more or less, is what we see on the international scene today. These methods themselves make resolution of the issues more difficult. When national pride is at stake, it is seen as a sign of weakness to back down in the force of pressure. The risks of a conflict that both may want to avoid are thereby increased.

William James once said that the only way to change a position is to get inside of it, to move it from within. To do that requires understanding the position. That such understanding can be promoted by cooperative undertakings with a view to breaking down the stereotypes each cherishes and that reinforce the hardness of their respective positions. If there *is* a truth about the world and about social relations—and any scientific approach to understanding relations among peoples must start from the assumption there is—this is the only way it will ultimately be uncovered. I would like to think that this is at least part of what Mikhail Gorbachev had in mind when he maintained that the "unprecedented diversity" of the world has created a situation calling for new thinking. "Each people and country," he said, "has its own truth, its own national interests and its aspirations. At the same time, this world is full of deep contradictions which bear the ultimate danger." "Confidence," he said further, "needs to be built up through experience in cooperation, through knowing each other better, through solving common problems. . . . This is the rational way."[13]

Is there a moral basis for such a methodological orientation? I want to suggest one that represents something of a synthesis of the communitarian and individualistic outlooks. It can be seen as an expansion of the rudimentary moral personalism with which we began and is found in the writings of the American idealist, Josiah Royce. Royce wrote that:

> The moral insight . . . shows us that *whatever the highest human good may be, we can only attain it together, for it involves harmony.* The highest good then is not to be got by any one of us or by any clique of us separately. Either the highest good for humanity is unattainable, or the humanity of the future must get it *in common.* Therefore the sense of community, the power to work together, with clear insight into our reasons for so working, is the *first* need of humanity.[14]

The insight here, as I understand it, is that if there is a good beyond a mere social good, applying only to members of one's own society, that is, if the highest good is a *human good* that embraces all peoples everywhere, then, whatever it is, it can be found only in community, through common endeavor. The individualist, it seems to me, can accept much of this because it does not prejudge whether there is a human good, or at least whether it is attainable. And it certainly does not preclude, if there is one, that it consists of a summation of individual goods. It only holds open the possibility of such attainment, as something to be tested, so to speak. And the contextualist can accept it because it captures one of the principal strains in his thought, namely that it is only through *community* that the greatest good, if it exists, can ultimately be achieved.

Peoples of communist and capitalist societies need to cultivate an openness to the possibility that the truth about social, political, and international affairs, in the last analysis, will not turn out to be precisely what either of them antecedently thought. Perhaps it will be a synthesis of their socioeconomic systems. Perhaps it will be something radically different from either of them. But whatever it is, it will be achievable only as they come to view themselves as

[13] Quoted in *The Christian Science Monitor,* Mar. 18, 1987.
[14] Josiah Royce, *The Religious Aspect of Philosophy* (New York: Harper & Brothers, 1958), p. 175.

pursuing it altogether, in a mutual endeavor that accentuates the many things they share in common (like a mutual interest in survival and the preservation of the environment), rather than by stressing only their differences. In this way, and through the sort of cooperation of which Gorbachev speaks, they may gradually begin to create a broader community of shared values, shared meanings, and shared criteria for moral and logical evaluation. This should be possible even if the more skeptical of the preceding claims are true. For if they are true they are only relatively true. They are true because of deeply seated differences in philosophical and cultural perspectives. But those differences are not logically dictated. Nor are they immutable. They have evolved historically. And they can be replaced historically. It is within our power to bring it about that they cease to be true. If the two peoples do this, they may come increasingly to share the same perception of the world. And with that will begin to materialize the conditions under which disagreements can be resolved rationally and peacefully.

VI

The problem, in the last analysis, is not, as cocktail party wisdom would have it, with human nature. Human nature is not corrupt. But it can be tricked by the subtleties of complex social, political, and international systems. The problem is with the misdirection of loyalties, with too much rather than too little willingness to sacrifice at the behest of others. The peoples of both the United States and the Soviet Union exemplify this. Like men pulling oars from the hold of a ship from which they cannot see an approaching waterfall, good people can by their corporate effort, loyalty, and devotion to country sometimes ease themselves unwittingly toward catastrophe. All that is required is a few false beliefs about the motives and intentions of others and a willingness to follow political leaders unquestioningly.

From Nuremberg we should know that the key to understanding the horrors nations perpetuate is not the evil of the occasional Hitlers of this world. It is, rather, the dedication of functionaries who serve them and of the millions of ordinary persons like ourselves whose cooperation is essential to the success of their enterprises. Recognition of this fact is central to nonviolence. For unlike violence, which seeks to prevail over the physical manifestations of power—the weaponry and the warriors—nonviolence deals directly with the ultimate sources of governmental power, the people themselves. This is why it can be expected to be denounced by those who enjoy such power, whether to their personal advantage or in the service of ideological, religious, or moral causes.

What is needed is a new perspective that sees the people of the world as arrayed, not basically against one another, but against the deceit, ignorance, and arrogance of governments and the ways of thinking that have produced them. What is needed is a new respect for the preciousness and inviolability of the human person. This does not require changing human nature or transforming the world into a community of saints. It does require recognizing that if we do not cherish the human person, there is no point to the many other activities and strivings that consume our time; no point to saving the environment unless we value the beings that inhabit it; no virtue in self-sacrifice when it is at the expense of the lives and happiness of others. And it requires a massive commitment of time, energy, and moral and financial resources to exploring nonviolent ways of getting along in the world.

The aim should not be to end conflict. That would be utopian and might not even be desirable. The aim should be to develop nondestructive ways of dealing with conflict. Violence by its nature cannot do that. Nonviolence can.

As Gandhi demonstrated, rather than approaching conflict with a view to trying to prevail at any cost, it is possible to approach it with a view to trying to see that the truth prevail—trying to see that the best solution emerge, whether or not it be one to which you were predisposed at the outset. People can learn this. They can be trained in techniques to implement it. They can incorporate it in their institutions. It is a method that recognizes the fallibility of human judgments; that makes allowance for error in one's own thinking as well as that of others. It incorporates self-correcting mechanisms. Unlike violence, which is and has been the ultimate mode of conflict resolution for those who possess the truth with a capital 'T' and are determined to impose it upon others at whatever cost, it holds that the truth is to be found in the interactions among people; that it will emerge, given sufficient courage, determination, discipline, and hope. It is not just an alternative tactic to violence, designed to achieve power by different means. It does not seek to win power *over* people. It seeks rather to win power *with* them, through the liberation of understanding and insight. Even if one were convinced that theoretically war is justified, that is, that with perfect knowledge we could be confident that sometimes institutional violence is called for in response to certain offenses and that in those cases we would not be harming innocent persons, still practically speaking we do not have such knowledge and must make such decisions with varying degrees of uncertainty. Nonviolence is a way of life, and potentially a social and national way of life, that gives full recognition to that uncertainty and seeks to guide conduct in ways that do not presume a certainty we do not justifiably have.

Peace, in this view, is no longer understood as a static state to be achieved at some distant time in the future, as it is to Marxists who see eternal peace reigning once the classless society has been realized throughout the world. Much less is it understood as merely the absence of war, as Western leaders often understand it. It is to be understood rather as a process, a way of getting along in the world; a process that might be called peace making, so long as it it understood that the process is not a means to an end but is rather the end itself, a way of dealing with conflict that incorporates throughout the values of peace. Peace, in short, is peaceful conduct.

Marxists (like Augustine), however, rightly stress that peace as well as war may be just or unjust. And these categories do indeed have as much relevance to peace as they do to war and ought to become as common in discussions of the one as of the other. The mere existence of peace (in the sense of an absence of war) no more guarantees that injustice does not pervade that state of affairs than the mere presence of democracy (in the sense of regular elections) assures that injustice does not exist domestically. Thus when the United States brands as a threat to peace the efforts of revolutionaries to topple oppressive Third-World regimes, it is perfectly correct—insofar as peace is understood as merely the absence of war. But from the standpoint of the revolutionaries their efforts not only are no threat to peace (in the sense of a *just* peace, but because none existed there in the first place) but in fact are designed to bring about such a peace. Each then thinks of himself as the advocate of peace, and each is correct in the sense he has in mind. But they are at cross-purposes, not only in what they are doing, but in their way of viewing what they are doing. And so they resort to force and violence to realize their respective conceptions of peace, and it is the innocent people caught in the middle who suffer. Nonviolence can recognize what is sound in both of these outlooks and can provide a method of dealing with the conflict that minimizes harm to innocent persons and maximizes the possibility of each at least coming to understand the position of the other.

When reliance is solely upon methods of violence, and it is assumed that in the absence of war there is peace, it is easy to overlook the development of conditions that may eventually erupt into war. Germany was at peace for two decades between World War I and World War II; it had been militarily vanquished. Superior force had prevailed. But that superiority, because it achieved only the negative "peace" of the absence of war, allowed a period of incubation in which not only the worst sorts of injustice grew within German society but the way was prepared for an even more virulent outbreak of international violence. The only lasting peace can be a just peace, and the overwhelming weight of historical evidence shows that it cannot be produced by violence.

With the development of nonviolent means of defense a nation could unilaterally disarm without having to acquiesce in the depredations of possible aggressors.[15] It may indeed be only through a commitment to nonviolent defense that disarmament will ever come about. Mutual disarmament pursued while everything else remains the same (the suspicions, fears, deception), and while both sides seek to maximize their military and political advantage, holds little chance of success. Perhaps if civilization could count upon a few more centuries of existence, one could propose giving it a try; but one cannot do so on any realistic assessment of the future.

While to bring about disarmament requires the best in scientific and technical expertise, it requires first and foremost a moral decision that the effort is worth making. And faith that it can be made to succeed. William James once wrote that faith in certain facts may help to bring those facts into existence. So, we might say, with the power of nonviolence. We will never know whether there is a realistic moral alternative to violence unless we are willing to make an effort, comparable to the multibillion-dollar-a-year effort currently made to produce means of destruction and to train young people in their use, to explore the potential of nonviolent action; to explore the possibility of educating ourselves and others to a whole new way of getting along in the world—a way that people now hear of chiefly in the form of piously eloquent Sunday

---

[15] Gene Sharp has done extensive and invaluable work on this topic. See the Bibliography for his most important contributions.

morning ineffectualities that rarely filter down to the springs of conduct.

Why should such an effort be made? Here is where our moral thinking must be brought up to date with our thinking in science and technology. It may be that we have no choice. For we have reached the point at which mankind can no longer hope, as it may once have, to muddle interminably through war after war. The potential destructiveness of war has progressed too far for that. If the ends that we now desire (including peace and a future for our children) cannot conceivably be secured by the means we have traditionally relied upon, then it is at risk of forsaking our claim to rationality—not to mention our lives and well-being—that we fail to make a massive commitment of our moral, intellectual, and financial resources to devising new means. To wait until others do the same, or until that nonexistent future when nations are miraculously "ready" to lay down their arms, is visionary beyond anything proposed by those who today are called idealists.

[I]n spite of everything I still believe that people are really good at heart. I simply can't build up my hopes on a foundation consisting of confusion, misery, and death. I see the world gradually being turned into a wilderness, I hear the approaching thunder, which will destroy us too, I can feel the sufferings of millions and yet, if I look up into the heavens, I think that it will all come right, that this cruelty too will end, and that peace and tranquillity will return again.
—Anne Frank

I pictured to myself that instead of these national enmities which are instilled into us under the guise of love of one's country, and instead of those applauded slaughters called war, which from childhood are represented to us as the most heroic deeds—I imagined that we are imbued with horror at and contempt for all those activities, political, diplomatic, and military, which promote the separation of peoples; and that it was suggested to us that . . . to go to war—that is to say, to kill people, people personally unknown to us, without any grounds—is the most horrible villainy, to which only a lost and perverted man, degraded to the level of a beast, can descend. I pictured to myself that all men believed this, and I asked: What would be the result?
—Leo Tolstoy

SELECTED BIBLIOGRAPHY

Aldridge, Robert C. *The Counterforce Syndrome: A Guide to U.S. Nuclear Weapons and Strategic Doctrine.* Washington, D.C.: Institute for Policy Studies, 1978.

Aron, Raymond. *On War.* New York: W.W. Norton & Company, Inc., 1968.

————. *Peace and War: A Theory of International Relations.* New York: Praeger, 1967.

Augustine. *The City of God.* Translated by Marcus Dods. New York: Random House, 1950.

————. *De Libero Arbitrio.* Translated by Carroll Mason Sparrow. Charlottesville: Dietz Press, Inc., 1947.

————. *The Works of Aurelius Augustine.* Edited by Marcus Dods. Edinburgh: T. & T. Clark, 1871-1876.

Bainton, Roland H. *Christian Attitudes toward War and Peace: A Historical Survey and Critical Re-Evaluation.* New York: Abingdon Press, 1960.

Beau, Bryan, trans. *Problems of War and Peace: A Critical Analysis of Bourgeois Theories.* Moscow: Progress Publishers, 1972.

Best, Geoffrey. *Humanity in Warfare.* New York: Columbia University Press, 1980.

Betz, Joseph. "Violence: Garver's Definition and a Deweyan Correction." *Ethics* 87, no. 4 (July 1977): 339-351.

Bienen, H. *Violence and Social Change.* Chicago: University of Chicago Press, 1968.

Brodie, Bernard. *War and Politics.* New York: The Macmillan Company, 1973.

Bronowski, J. *The Face of Violence.* New York: The World Publishing Company, 1968.

Brown, Richard Maxwell, ed. *American Violence.* Englewood Cliffs, N.J.: Prentice-Hall, 1970.

Byers, R. B., ed. *Deterrence in the 1980s: Crisis and Dilemma.* London: Croom Helm, 1985.

Caldicott, Helen. *Missile Envy: The Arms Race and Nuclear War.* New York: William Morrow and Company, Inc., 1984.

Carnesale, Albert, Paul Doty, Stanley Hoffmann, Samuel P. Huntington, Joseph S. Nye, Jr., Scott Sagan. *Living with Nuclear Weapons.* New York: Bantam Books, 1983.

Clausewitz, Karl von. *On War.* Princeton, N.J.: Princeton University Press, 1976.

Cohen, A., and S. Lee, eds. *Nuclear Weapons and the Future of Humanity: The Fundamental Questions.* Totowa, N.J.: Rowman & Allanheld, 1986.

Cohen, Marshall. "Moral Skepticism and International Relations." In *International Ethics,* edited by C. Betiz, M. Cohen, T. Scanlon, and J. Simmons. Princeton, N.J.: Princeton University Press, 1985.

Cotta, Sergio. *Why Violence? A Philosophical Interpretation.* Gainesville: University of Florida Press, 1985.

Cox, Gray. *The Ways of Peace: A Philosophy of Peace as Action.* Mahwah, N.J.: Paulist Press, 1986.

Deane, Herbert A. *The Political and Social Ideas of St. Augustine.* New York: Columbia University Press, 1963.

De Beauvoir, Simone. *The Ethics of Ambiguity.* New York: Citadel Press, 1962.

De Vitoria, Francisco. *The Spanish Origins of International Law: Francisco De Vitoria and His Law of Nations,* pt. 1, app. B, *De Jure Belli.* In *The Classics of International Law,* edited by James Brown Scott. Oxford: Clarendon Press, 1934.

Engleman, S., ed. *Violence in the Streets.* Chicago: Quadrangle Books, 1968.

Eppstein, John. *The Catholic Tradition of the Law of Nations*. London: Burns, Oates and Washbourne, Ltd., 1935.

Erikson, Erik H. *Gandhi's Truth: On the Origins of Militant Nonviolence*. New York: Norton & Company, 1969.

Fagothy, Austin. *Right and Reason: Ethics in Theory and Practice*. St. Louis: The C.V. Mosby Company, 1953.

Falk, R., G. Kolko, and R. Lifton, eds. *Crimes of War*. New York: Vintage Books, 1971.

Ferguson, John. *The Politics of Love: The New Testament and Nonviolent Revolution*. Nyack, N.Y.: Fellowship Publications, 1979.

Fisher, David. *Morality and the Bomb: An Ethical Assessment of Nuclear Deterrence*. New York: St. Martin's Press, 1985.

Flanagan, P. "Wolff on Violence." *Australasian Journal of Philosophy* 50, no. 3 (Dec. 1972): 271-278.

Fox, M., and L. Groarke, eds. *Nuclear War: Philosophical Perspectives*. New York: Peter Lang, 1985.

Frank, Jerome. *Sanity and Survival: Psychological Aspects of War and Peace*. New York: Vintage Books, 1967.

Freedman, Lawrence. *The Evolution of Nuclear Strategy*. New York: St. Martin's Press, 1983.

Friedenberg, E. "Legitimate Violence." *The Nation*, June 24, 1968.

Gallie, W. B. *Philosophers of Peace and War: Kant, Clausewitz, Marx, Engels and Tolstoy*. Cambridge: At the University Press, 1978.

Gandhi, M. K. *Non-Violent Resistance*. New York: Schocken Books, 1961.

Garver, Newton. "What Violence Is." *The Nation*, June 24, 1968.

Gentili, Alberico. *De Jure Belli: Libri Tres*. In *The Classics of International Law*, edited by James Brown Scott, translated by John C. Rolfe. Oxford: Clarendon Press, 1933.

Gert, Bernard. "Justifying Violence." *Journal of Philosophy* 66 (Oct. 1969): 616-628.

Ginsberg, Robert, ed. *The Critique of War: Contemporary Philosophical Explorations*. Chicago: Henry Regnery Company, 1969.

Glossop, Ronald J. *Confronting War: An Examination of Humanity's Most Pressing Problem*. Jefferson & London: McFarland, 1983.

Gray, Colin S. *Strategic Studies: A Critical Assessment*. Westport, Conn.: Greenwood Press, 1982.

———. *Strategic Studies and Public Policy: The American Experience*. The University Press of Kentucky, 1982.

———, and Keith B. Payne. "Nuclear Policy and the Defensive Transition." *Foreign Affairs* 62, no. 4 (Spring 1984): 820-842.

Gray, Glen. *On Understanding Violence Philosophically*. New York: Harper and Row, 1970.

Green, Phillip. *Deadly Logic: The Theory of Nuclear Deterrence*. New York: Schocken Books, 1966.

Gregory, Donna Uthus, ed. *The Nuclear Predicament: A Sourcebook*. New York: St. Martin's Press, 1986.

Grotius, Hugo. *De Jure Belli ac Pacis Libri Tres*. In *The Classics of International Law*, edited by James Brown Scott, translated by Francis W. Kelsey. Oxford: Clarendon Press, 1925.

Hampshire, Stuart, ed. *Public and Private Morality*. Cambridge: At the University Press, 1978.

Hardin, R., J. J. Mearsheimer, G. Dworkin, and R. E. Goodin, eds. *Nuclear Deterrence: Ethics and Strategy*. Chicago: University of Chicago Press, 1985.

Hare, R. M. *Applications of Moral Philosophy*. Berkeley and Los Angeles: University of California Press, 1972.

Harnack, Adolf. *Militia Christi: The Christian Religion and the Military in the First Three Centuries*. Philadelphia: Fortress Press, 1981.

Hartogs, R., and E. Artzt, eds. *Violence: Causes and Solutions*. New York: Dell, 1970.

Held, V., S. Morgenbesser, and T. Nagel, eds. *Philosophy, Morality and International Affairs.* New York: Oxford University Press, 1974.

Iklé, Fred Charles. *Every War Must End.* New York: Columbia University Press, 1971.

Jervis, Robert, Richard Ned Lebow, and Janice Gross Stein. *Psychology and Deterrence.* Baltimore: The Johns Hopkins University Press, 1985.

Johnson, James Turner. *Can Modern War Be Just?* New Haven, Conn.: Yale University Press, 1984.

———. *Ideology, Reason, and the Limitation of War: Religious and Secular Concepts, 1200-1740.* Princeton, N.J.: Princeton University Press, 1975.

———. "Just War Theory: What's the Use?" *Worldview,* July-August 1976.

Kahn, Herman. *On Thermonuclear War.* New York: The Free Press, 1969.

Kennan, George. *American Diplomacy, 1900-1950.* Chicago: University of Chicago Press, 1951.

———. *Democracy and the Student Left.* New York: Bantam Books, 1968.

———. *Memoirs: 1925-1950.* Vol. 1. Boston: Little, Brown & Company, 1967.

———. *Memoirs: 1950-1963.* Vol. 2. Boston: Little, Brown & Company, 1972.

———. "Morality and Foreign Policy." *Foreign Affairs* 64, no. 3 (Winter 1985/86): 205-218.

———. *Realities of American Foreign Policy.* Princeton, N.J.: Princeton University Press, 1954.

Kipnis, Kenneth, and Diana T. Meyers, eds. *Political Realism and International Morality: Ethics in the Nuclear Age.* Boulder, Colo.: Westview Press, 1987.

Kissinger, Henry A. *Nuclear Weapons and Foreign Policy.* New York: Published for the Council on Foreign Relations by Harper and Brothers, 1957.

Knorr, Klaus. "Controlling Nuclear War." *International Security* 9, no. 4 (Spring 1985): 79-99.

Lackey, Douglas P. *Moral Principles and Nuclear Weapons.* Totowa, N.J.: Roman & Allanheld, 1984.

Lavere, George J. "The Political Realism of Saint Augustine." *Augustinian Studies* 11 (1980): 135-145.

Lefever, Earnest W., ed. *Ethics and World Politics: Four Perspectives.* Baltimore: The Johns Hopkins University Press, 1972.

Lenin on War and Peace. Peking: Foreign Languages Press, 1966.

Lider, Julian. *On the Nature of War.* Westmead, Eng.: Saxon House, 1977.

———. *The Political and Military Laws of War.* Westmead, Eng.: Saxon House, 1979.

Luban, David. "Just War and Human Rights." *Philosophy and Public Affairs* 9, no. 2 (Winter 1980): 160-181.

Luttwak, Edward. *Strategy and History: Collected Essays.* Vol. 2. New Brunswick, N.J.: Transaction Books, 1985.

Lynd, Staughton, ed. *Nonviolence in America: A Documentary History.* Indianapolis: Bobbs-Merrill, 1966.

McDougal, Meyers S., and Florentine P. Feliciano. *Law and Minimum World Public Order: The Legal Regulation of International Coercion.* New Haven, Conn.: Yale University Press, 1961.

Machiavelli, N. *The Prince.* Edited and translated by Robert M. Adams. New York: W.W. Norton & Company, Inc., 1977.

MacLean, Douglas, ed. *The Security Gamble: Deterrence and Dilemmas in the Nuclear Age.* Totowa, N.J.: Rowman & Allanheld, 1984.

Malcolmson, Robert W. *Nuclear Fallacies: How We Have Been Misguided since Hiroshima.* Kingston: McGill-Queen's University Press, 1985.

Martin, Laurence, ed. *Strategic Thought in the Nuclear Age.* Baltimore: The Johns Hopkins University Press, 1979.

Mearsheimer, John J. *Conventional Deterrence.* Ithaca, N.Y.: Cornell University Press, 1983.

Medvedev, Roy A., and Zhores A. Medvedev. "A Nuclear *Samizdat* on America's Arms Race." *The Nation,* Jan. 16, 1982.

Melzer, Yehuda. *Concepts of Just War*. Leyden: A. W. Sijthoff, 1975.

Miller, William Robert. *Nonviolence: A Christian Interpretation*. New York: Association Press, 1964.

Milne, A. A. *Peace with Honour*. New York: E. P. Dutton, 1934.

Morgan, Patrick M. *Deterrence: A Conceptual Analysis*. Beverly Hills, Calif.: Sage Publications, 1977.

Morgenthau, Hans. *Politics among Nations*. New York: Knopf, 1966.

Murphy, Jeffrie. "The Killing of the Innocent." *The Monist* 57, no. 4 (Oct. 1973): 527-551.

Naqvi, Ali Raza. "Laws of War in Islam." *Islamic Studies* 13, no. 1 (Mar. 1974): 25-43.

Narveson, Jan. "Violence and War." In *Matters of Life and Death: New Introductory Essays in Moral Philosophy*, edited by Tom Regan. New York: Random House, 1980.

Niebuhr, Reinhold. *The Children of Light and the Children of Darkness*. New York: Charles Scribner's Sons, 1944.

———. *An Interpretation of Christian Ethics*. New York: Meridian Books, 1956.

———. *Love and Justice: Selections from the Shorter Writings of Reinhold Niebuhr*. Edited by D. B. Robertson. Cleveland: World Publishing Company, 1967.

———. *Moral Man and Immoral Society*. New York: Charles Scribner's Sons, 1932.

Nye, Joseph S., Jr. *Nuclear Ethics*. New York: The Free Press, 1986.

O'Brien, William V. *The Conduct of a Just and Limited War*. New York: Praeger, 1981.

———. *Nuclear War, Deterrence, and Morality*. New York: Newman Press, 1967.

———, and John Langan, eds. *The Nuclear Dilemma and the Just War Tradition*. Lexington, Mass.: Lexington Books, 1986.

Office of Technology Assessment, Congress of the United States. *The Effects of Nuclear War*. Montclair, N.J.: Allanheld, Osmun, 1980.

Osgood, Robert E. *Ideals and Self-Interest in America's Foreign Relations*. Chicago: University of Chicago Press, 1953.

———. *Limited War: The Challenge to American Strategy*. Chicago: The University of Chicago Press, 1957.

Paskins, Barrie, and Michael Dockrill. *The Ethics of War*. Minneapolis: University of Minnesota Press, 1979.

The Pastoral Letter on War and Peace of the National Conference of Catholic Bishops. *The Challenge of Peace: God's Promise and Our Response*. Washington, D.C.: United States Catholic Conference, 1983.

Peace and Disarmament. Moscow: Progess Publishers, 1980.

Perry, Charner. "Violence—Visible and Invisible." *Ethics* 81 (Oct. 1970): 1-21.

Peterson, Jeannie, ed. *The Aftermath: The Human and Ecological Consequences of Nuclear War*. New York: Pantheon Books, 1983.

Proektor, Daniil. *The Choice Facing Europe*. Moscow: Novosti Press Agency Publishing House, 1981.

Ramsey, Paul. *The Just War: Force and Political Responsibility*. New York: Charles Scribner's Sons, 1968.

———. *War and the Christian Conscience: How Shall Modern War Be Conducted Justly?* Durham, N.C.: Duke University Press, 1961.

Roberts, Adam, ed. *Civilian Resistance As a National Defense*. Baltimore: Penguin Books, 1967.

Russell, Bertrand. *Common Sense and Nuclear Warfare*. New York: Simon and Schuster, 1959.

Russell, Frederick H. *The Just War in the Middle Ages*. Cambridge: At the University Press, 1975.

Sagan, Carl. "Nuclear War and Climatic Catastrophe: Some Policy Implications." *Foreign Affairs* 62, no. 2 (Winter 1983/84): 257-292.

Schell, Jonathan. *The Abolition*. New York: Knopf, 1984.

———. *The Fate of the Earth*. New York: Knopf, 1982.

Schelling, Thomas C. *Arms and Influence.* New Haven, Conn.: Yale University Press, 1966.

——. *The Strategy of Conflict.* Cambridge: Harvard University Press, 1960.

Schlesinger, Arthur M., Jr. *The Crisis of Confidence.* New York: Bantam Books, 1969.

——. "The Necessary Amorality of Foreign Affairs." *Harper's Magazine,* August 1971.

Shaffer, J., ed. *Violence.* New York: David McKay, 1971.

Sharp, Gene. *Exploring Nonviolent Alternatives.* Boston: Porter Sargent, 1970.

——. *Making Europe Unconquerable: The Potential of Civilian-Based Deterrence and Defense.* Cambridge: Ballinger Publishing Company, 1985.

——. *The Politics of Nonviolent Action.* Boston: Porter Sargent, 1973.

——. *Social Power and Political Freedom.* Boston: Porter Sargent, 1980.

Sterba, James, ed. *The Ethics of War and Nuclear Deterrence.* Belmont: Wadsworth Publishing Company, 1985.

Stockholm International Peace Research Institute. *Armaments and Disarmament in the Nuclear Age.* Atlantic Highlands, N.J.: Humanities Press, 1976.

Stone, Julius. *Conflict through Consensus: United Nations Approaches to Aggression.* Baltimore: The Johns Hopkins University Press, 1977.

Suárez, Francisco. *Selections from Three Works of Francisco Suárez,* specifically *On the Three Theological Virtues: On Charity* (disputation 13: On War). In *The Classics of International Law,* edited by James Brown Scott. Oxford: Clarendon Press, 1944.

Taylor, Telford. *Nuremberg and Vietnam: An American Tragedy.* Chicago: Quadrangle Books, 1970.

Teichman, Jenny. *Pacifism and the Just War.* Oxford: Basil Blackwell, 1986.

Thompson, Kenneth W. *Political Realism and the Crisis of World Politics.* New York: John Wiley & Sons, 1965.

Thompson, Starley L., and Stephen H. Schneider. "Nuclear Winter Reappraised." *Foreign Affairs* 64, no. 5 (Summer 1986): 981-1005.

Tolstoy, Leo. *A Confession, The Gospel in Brief, & What I Believe.* New York: Oxford University Press, 1961.

——. *The Kingdom of God is Within You.* New York: The Noonday Press, 1961.

Treitschke, Heinrich von. *Politics.* Edited by Hans Kohn. New York: Harcourt, Brace and World, 1963.

Tucker, Robert W. *The Just War: A Study in Contemporary American Doctrine.* Baltimore: The Johns Hopkins University Press, 1960.

Turco, Richard, O. Brian Toon, Thomas Ackerman, James Pollack, and Carl Sagan. "Nuclear Winter: Global Consequences of Multiple Nuclear Explosions." *Science,* Dec. 23, 1983, pp. 1283-1292.

Vattel, E. de, *The Law of Nations or the Principles of Natural Law: Applied to the Conduct and to the Affairs of Nations and of Sovereigns.* In *The Classics of International Law,* edited by James Brown Scott, translated by Charles G. Fenwick. Vol. 3. Washington: The Carnegie Institute of Washington, 1916.

Wade, Francis C. "On Violence." *Journal of Philosophy* 68 (June 1971): 369-377.

Walzer, Michael. *Just and Unjust Wars.* New York: Basic Books, 1977.

——. *Obligations: Essays on Disobedience, War and Citizenship.* Cambridge: Harvard University Press, 1970.

Wasserstrom, Richard, ed. *War and Morality.* Belmont, Calif.: Wadsworth Publishing Company, 1970.

Weil, Simone. *The Iliad, or The Poem of Force.* Translated by Mary McCarthy. Wallingford, Pa.: Pendle Hill, 1956.

Wells, Donald A. *The War Myth.* Indianapolis: The Bobbs-Merrill Company, Inc., 1967.

Wolff, Robert Paul. "On Violence." *Journal of Philosophy* 66 (Oct. 1969): 601-616.

Woolsey, R. James, ed. *Nuclear Arms: Ethics, Strategy, Politics.* San Francisco: Institute for Contemporary Studies, 1984.

INDEX

absolutism: regarding morality of killing innocents, 195
Acheson, Dean, 109, 110; on national survival, 99
acts: of omission, 203; of state, 90, 112
aggression: different senses of, 159–163; theory of, in Walzer, 168
Aldridge, Robert C., 254n
America: national interest and World War I, 62; perceived global role before World War I, 60
American Friends Service Committee: on draft, 47
anarchism, 88
Anscombe, Elizabeth, 160n, 195, 202; and absolute prohibition against intentional killing of innocents, 177; on double effect and Christianity, 194
Aquinas, Saint Thomas, 128n; on just war, 148–150; on natural law, 154; on right intention, 150
Arab-Israeli War of 1967, 161; Walzer's assessment of, 168
Ardrey, Robert, 66n
Arendt, Hannah, 266
Aron, Raymond, 69, 240n, 253
Artzt, E., 29n
atomic bomb: use considered in Korean War, 100; in World War II, 5
Audi, R., 29n, 34n, 43n
Augustine, Saint, 44, 58, 65; on Christian virtues, 129; on divine law, 126; and ethics of motivation, 144; on evil, 121–122, 134–135; evils in war, 128; on God's commands, 117–118, 128, 142; implications of view for World War II, 138–139; of innocents, no absolute prohibition against, 142–143; justice, true and temporal, 131–132, 137, 141, 173; just war theory in, 17; on killing, in self-defense, 122–127, 133; on legitimate authority, 130; and moral skepticism, 131; as political realist, 142; Ramsey and Johnson on interpreting, 118–121, 123, 137n; on reconciling war with loving one's enemies, 118–138; on state, as neces-

sary to society, 88; states, true and apparent, 130
Aurelius, Marcus, 42n

Bainton, Roland H., 116n
balance of power, 61, 70–72
balance of terror: necessary for deterrence to work, 251; in nuclear age, 27; and security, 238
Beitz, C., 51n
Beres, Louis Rene, 51n
Bernhardi, General F. von, 54n
Bernstein, Barton, 249
Best, Geoffrey, 108n
Betz, Joseph, 43n
Bienen, H., 36n
Bierman, A. K., 29n
Birks, John W., 228
brainwashing, 42
Brodie, Bernard, 240n, 243n
Bronowski, J., 47, 48n
Brunk, Conrad G., 56n
Burton, J. W., 56n
Bush, George, 239n

Caldicott, Helen, 214
Campbell, John Franklin, 70n
Camus, Albert, vii
capitalism and communism: different modes of social life, 284; shared outlook in willingness to wage wars, 114
Carnesale, Albert, 241n, 254n
Catholic Bishops, American: just war conditions stated in, 164; pastoral letter of, 150n, 160n, 164n, 181n
Chatterjee, Partha, 62n
Christian ethics: interiorization of by Augustine, 149
Christianity: conception of evil, 264; militarization of, as observed by Grotius, 153; thought to prohibit killing of innocents, 193
Christian virtues: Augustine's view of, 129
Churchill, Winston S., 70
Cicero: on natural law, 154

303

from ethics, 20; individual and collective, 54, 55; and international relations, 16, 22; misconceptions about nature of, 94; point of view of, 22, 49; public and private, 54, 55n, 57, 90, 91; and self-interest, 52; supremacy of, 23; versus having a morality, 98; of war, 14, 24
moral judgments: of persons and acts, 198
moral nihilism, 17, 21
moral personalism: as deontological, 213; and respect for persons, 43; starting point in discussing war, 24
moral philosophy: Western, 23
moral principles: for everyone alike, 87
moral responsibility: problems in determining, 203–205
moral rules, 23
moral skepticism: in Augustine, 131; regarding war, 21
moral theory: secondary to rightness in particular cases, 23
Morgan, Patrick M., 240n 243n, 244n
Morgenthau, Hans, 51, 66n, 81
motives and intentions, 136
Moynihan, Daniel P., 78
Murphy, Jeffrie G., 210
Mussolini, B., 47
My Lai: atrocities at, 16

Napoleonic War, 147, 152
Naroll, Raoul, 249n
Narveson, Jan, 120n
national defense: alternative means to, 270
national egoism: as having moral basis, 84, 87; and political realism, 57; and reason of state, 99
national interest: central to American realism, 99; Dulles's view of, 69; interpretations of, 90n; Liska's view of, 73; Osgood's view of, 61; if paramount, rationalizes any evil, 82; and reason of state, 58
national security: extension from international to domestic arenas, 108–112; revisions in conception of, by FDR, 77
NATO: threats against, 8
naturalistic fallacy, 53n
natural law: revival of, 156; as source of international law, 154
Nazism, 63, 169
neutrality, Wilsonian, 95n
Nicaragua: U.S. intervention in, 9

Niebuhr, Reinhold, 38, 51, 55, 58, 71, 73, 83, 85, 86, 91, 139; on collective egoism, 63; on divine judgment in history, 65; on paradox of patriotism, 66–67; political realism of, 64; on sinful human nature, 139, 265
Nietzsche, Friedrich, 53n
Nixon, Richard, 254
Nixon Doctrine, 253
Nobel, Alfred, 4
noncombatant immunity: and Augustine's views, 142
noncombatants and combatants: distinction not central to morality of war, 186
nonconsequentialism: in ethics, 96–97
noninnocent: the killing of the, 212
nonviolence: as alternative to war, 18; can harm, 40; concept of, allegedly confused, 29; as ideal, 270; minimizes harm to innocents, 292; and nondestructive ways of dealing with conflict, 291; as way of life, 274; whether effective versus violence, 274–279
nonviolent resistence: against Germans in World War II, 277
North Vietnamese: superior morale in Vietnam, 71
nuclear age: calls for new thinking, 25; changing character of war in, 148
nuclear weapons, 5–8, 24, 234, 235; deterrent uses of, 214; provocation values versus deterrent value of, 257; tactical versus strategic, 253; threat of, in Indochina War, 9
nuclear winter, 235; controversy over, 228–230
Nuremberg trials, 101, 155–156; extended international law to individuals as well as states, 152
Nye, Joseph A., Jr., 233n, 236n

Obligation and value, 23, 37
O'Brien, William V., 102n, 104n, 105n, 167, 171; on relevance of just war theory to nuclear age, 148; and Walzer, 173
Office of Technology Assessment: report on effects of nuclear war, 226
Osgood, Robert E., 51, 56n, 59n, 63, 64, 72, 74, 76, 77, 81, 83, 84, 85, 91, 93, 94n, 95; on individual happiness and identification with group, 86–90; on post-World War II period, 79–80; relationship of individual to state,

Osgood, Robert E. (*cont.*)
83–90; on U.S. entry into World War
I, 60–61, 93

pacifism: criticisms of, 38; of early
Christian Church, 116; and moral assessment of war, 49; and principle of
double effect, 202
Paley, William, 176
Payne, Keith B., 255n, 256n
peace: for Augustine, more than absence of war, 40; just or unjust, 292;
and justice, in Augustine, 136; as a
process, 292
Peloponnesian War, 52
Perry, Charner, 29n
Phillips, Robert L., 116n, 150n, 174n,
184n, 198n; on absolute prohibition
against killing innocents, 177; on
dirty hands, 202–203; on relevance of
just war theory to nuclear age, 148
Plato, 21, 43–44, 53, 57, 130, 264
pluralism: regarding American society,
280–281; versus monism, regarding
nature of society, 282; versus monism in world views, 283–284
political realism: and conduct of nations, 17; historical roots of, 52–55;
inadequacy of, 112–113; and national
egoism, 106; Neo, 68–75; normative,
historical, and theoretical, 57, 59–68,
91; positivistic, 56, 97–98; in post-
World War II period, 75–82
Powell, William: on internal threats to
security, 111
power, 271; nonviolent, 272
Presidential Directive Fifty-Nine, 254
pride: sin of, in Augustine, 141
prima facie rightness and wrongness,
193n
principle versus consequences in morality, 95; in ethics, 96–97
probability of sucess: just war condition, in pastoral letter of Catholic
Bishops, 164
proportionality: defined, in pastoral
letter of Catholic Bishops, 164

quantitative principle, 104–105
Quester, George, 240n

Ramsey, Paul, 116n, 118, 127n, 137n,
150n, 160n; on conditions of just
war, 165–167; on double effect in
Vietnam, 195; on interpreting Augustine, 119; on noncombatant im-

munity, 143; on responsibility for
killing innocents, 105
Rapoport, Anatol, 192
Rawls, John, 280n
Reagan, Ronald, 239n, 255, 284
realism, *see* political realism
Realpolitik, 50
reason of state, 57, 172; and military
necessity, 100, 106; and political realism, 17, 57–58; in relation to national
interest, 90n; and Walzer's just war
theory, 170
retaliation, nuclear: when irrational,
236
right intention: in Aquinas, 150; in just
war conditions, 150, 194; in pastoral
letter of Catholic Bishops, 164; in
Ramsey, 195–196. *See also* double effect, principle of
right and wrong, 23, 98, 154; by convention and by nature, 53; prima facie, actual and absolute, 193n; and
value, 23
rights, human: not to be harmed or
killed, 210; Walzer on, 170
Roosevelt, Franklin D., 106; and
national interest in World War II,
77; and national security, 109; a
Wilsonian, according to Schlesinger,
76
Root, Elihu, 101
Ross, W. D., 44n
Rothchild, John H., 220n
Rothstein, Robert L., 50n, 82n
Royal Swedish Academy of Sciences:
estimates of environmental damage
following nuclear war, 228
Royce, Josiah, 289
Russell, Bertrand, 3, 39, 246
Russell, Frederick H., 116n, 120n

Sagan, Carl, 232; on nuclear winter,
229
Santayana, George, 83
Satyagraha, 33, 287
Schell, Jonathan, 239n, 244
Schelling, Thomas C., 236n, 240n, 251n
Schlesinger, Arthur M., Jr., 51, 59, 71n,
72, 81; critique of early post-World
War II U.S. policy, 75–79; on Viet-
nam War, 79
Schneider, Stephen H., 229
Schroeder, Paul W., 95, 96n
security: absolute, quest for, 110; what
constitutes, 260
self-defense: Aquinas's justification of

killing in, 149; Augustine on, 120–127; of state, 261

self-interest: as point of view, 22

Seneca, 114

Shaffer, J., 29n

Sharma, I. C., 42n

Sharp, Gene, 293n

Social Darwinism, 54

society: essential to happiness of individuals, 88

Socrates, 21, 207

Soul Force: Martin Luther King, Jr.'s, philosophy of, 33

Soviet Union and United States: obstacles to understanding between, 279–290

Spanish-American War, 59

Spencer, Herbert, 280

spheres of influence versus universalism: Schlesinger's view of, 75

state, the, 260; and collective threat of violence, 26; instrument of God's agency, for Augustine, 130; Machiavelli and preservation of, 54; not a superperson, 85; its preservation, whether limits to, 107; and promotion of values, 57; sovereign, 53

state necessity: imperative of national security, 108

state of nature: threats in, 26

Stein, Janice Gross, 257n

Stockholm International Peace Research Institute, 250

Strategic Defense Initiative, 255

Súarez, Francisco, 176

supreme emergencies: the ethics of, according to O'Brien, 167; and Nazi threat, 200; Walzer's view of, 167

survival, national: criteria of, problematic, 231

Taylor, Telford, 101, 102n

Teichman, Jenny, 116n

Thompson, Kenneth W., 50n, 63n

Thompson, Starley L., 229

Thompson, W. Scott, 233n

Thoreau, Henry David, 206

Thrasymachus, 54

threats: irrational, 238; to national security, internal and external, 108, 110

Thucydides, 52

Tolstoy, 41, 42n, 71, 146, 192, 295

Tretischke, Heinrich von, 51n, 55

Tucker, Robert W., 176n, 214

United Nations Charter: on definition of aggression, 162

United States and Soviet Union, see Soviet Union and United States

universalism: Schlesinger's understanding of, 75–77

universalizability: and assessment of double effect, 196–200

utilitarian considerations: secondary to rights, in Walzer, 170

utilitarianism: inadequacy of, 213; and principles and consequences, 96–97

value: and consequences, 23; good and bad, 21; and obligation, 37

Vattel, E. de: on distinction between legality and morality in war, 151; on voluntary law, 157–159

Vietnam War, 16, 94, 206; conformed to realists' prescriptions, 75; and limitations of military power, 271; limited war, 80; Liska's view of, 74; and military necessity, 106; opposition to, 79; Schlesinger's analysis of policies leading to, 77–79; trauma of, 89; veterans of, 46; and violations of principle of innocence, 105

violence: acts of, 33–37; analysis of, 29–45; central to assessment of war, 37; doing, contrasted with physical violence, 42; effectiveness of, compared with nonviolence, 276–279; emotive use of term, 32; and force, 33; institutionalization of, 10, 16; and intention to harm, 37; and masculinity, 47; physical, defined, 32; primary and secondary, 30–37; psychological, 31–32; thought necessary to prevent violence, 27; whether concept of confused, 28–37

Vitoria, 150

von Moltke, Helmuth, 50

Wade, Francis C., 29n

Walzer, Michael, 83n, 148, 173, 176n; concept of aggression implicit in, 161; and killing of innocents, 189

war: all-out nuclear, irrationality of, 233; as commanded by God, 135; conventional, 4–7; defensive and aggressive, just and unjust, 159; and extinction of human life, 230; as human creation, 14; inevitability of, for some realists, 68; as institutionalized violence, 45; in Marxist philosophy, 285; nuclear, and just war theory,